touchofclassplants.com.au

facebook.com / touchofclassplants
vimeo.com / touchofclassplants

CONTENTS

Touch of Class® Plants.
Over thirty years of supplying quality plants for Australian gardens.

In 1981, Robert and Elizabeth Harrison commenced what is today one of Australia's biggest propagation nurseries, Greenhills Propagation Nursery.

Robert found his passion early in life; from the age of 10 he was working after school, on weekends and during school holidays in a local nursery. After completing his schooling Robert worked in this nursery for a further 14 ½ years and learnt from his mentors many valuable lessons, "Lessons I have never forgotten" say Robert.

Robert could see a gap in the market, which was for high quality products and the introduction of new plants to the Australian industry. In 1981 Robert built a glass house in the back yard of his father in laws property in Carrum Downs. He & Elizabeth worked long hours building their new business while raising two small children. The following year they rented land in Beaconsfield, Victoria, where they had two small igloos and no access to power.

Within a year their business had outgrown the Beaconsfield site. Robert and Elizabeth sold their family home in Narre Warren in 1983 and "took a punt," moving to its current location – a 67 acre property in Tynong, Victoria which now uses 18 acres for nursery purposes.

Greenhills employed its first apprentice in 1987 and by 1994 had surpassed six employees. After rapid growth, Greenhills now employs around 40 full time and casual staff members, including Robert and Elizabeth's children, Leah and Mark.

Greenhills operates as a tube stock propagation nursery which dispatches its products Australia wide. They are proud to introduce new release native and exotic plant lines from around the world into the Australian nursery industry. Greenhills Propagation supplies wholesale nurseries that grow their products to a larger size before finally being sold on to retailers.

In 2003, Touch of Class® Plants was introduced as the public brand for Greenhills Propagation Nursery. All plants produced by Greenhills bear the Touch of Class® Plants branding at a retail level through custom labelling.

All new plants are rigorously tested prior to their release onto the market to ensure they will tolerate Australia's vast climatic conditions. Plants in the Touch of Class range are exclusive, improved, and of the highest quality. Touch of Class® Plants aim is to continue introducing more exciting plant varieties to Australian gardeners.

Hebe Pretty & Pink®

ON A GRAND SCALE

Settled on a hillside down a quiet road near the charming New South Wales country town of Oberon is a garden of breathtaking proportions.

Mayfield is gardening on a grand scale. There is the 80-metre water cascade, the six-acre (two-and-a-half-hectare) water garden with a 16-metre-high obelisk, kilometres of hand-built stone walls, an almost equal length of box hedging and a natural amphitheatre that can seat 500, all spread across 300 acres (120 hectares) of carefully laid-out garden, itself sitting within a 5000-acre (2000-hectare) working farm.

Property owner Garrick Hawkins rarely speaks publicly about the motivation behind the garden except to acknowledge the original design was not intended to be so large. It seems he fell victim

Opposite: *The creek wanders through lush plantings of maples, ornamental pears and tulip trees to the lake, which evolved from a simple dam.* **Below:** *Water tumbles over the rock walls into the man-made lake.*

Words JAQUI CAMERON Photography JAQUI CAMERON & PETER GUMBERT

to the folly of many gardeners; his plans simply kept growing.

The inspiration came from family visits to the many impressive English country estates boasting centuries-old gardens, such as Chatsworth with its magnificent cascade water feature and Longstock Park on which the latest addition to Mayfield, the water garden, has been modelled. And so it is that the numbers tell only part of the Mayfield story.

It is extraordinary not only for its size, but also the fact it has emerged from what was a bare paddock less than 30 years ago. In comparison with those historic English gardens, Mayfield is still a mere babe but it is impressive nonetheless with mass plantings of mature deciduous trees including crabapples, ashes and oaks punctuating large swathes of soft green lawn.

Clockwise from below:
Hydrangeas lend their delicate charm to a seasonal parade of colour; even small plantings have been given thoughtful placement consideration; the lower ponds of the water garden during autumn.

The lake is bordered by a series of sunken garden rooms, which provides a more intimate space to sit beneath the English oaks and look across to the Chinese pagoda.

Like any garden, water plays an integral role in the practical design and delights at Mayfield. The large lake, nestled in a curve at the bottom of the garden, was originally built as a simple dam to capture run-off and rainfall to supply the irrigation system. However, demonstrating that practical can also be pretty, water now bubbles naturally over boulders and rocks as it makes its way down the hillside. The creek winds through an opulent grove of lush plantings of maples, ornamental pears and tulip trees with paths to guide visitors across charming stone bridges. The lake itself is bordered by a series of sunken garden rooms, which provides a more intimate space to sit beneath the English oaks and look across the water, perhaps to the Chinese pagoda sitting serenely on the lake and connected by a striking red bridge.

The entire garden opens to the public for selected weekends in spring and autumn, but in response to public demand, a 36-acre (15-hectare) area is now open year-round, including the water garden, fed from the lake by a small waterfall through an impressive stone bridge that took four stonemasons a year to construct. Those same dark stone walls line gravel pathways and terraced gardens that border the intricate collection of ponds filled with lilies and iris together with the dramatic splashes of red and contrasting green of Japanese maples.

Reaching out into the water around the lower ponds, the paths meander around groves of

Clockwise from below:
A Chinese pagoda sits at the lake's edge; boulders near the base of the creek gardens; a wooden bridge leading to the pagoda with a stone bridge that took stonemasons four years to build in the background.

stately birch trees underplanted with hellebores. A favourite spot of the owners, a lone liquidambar stands like a living sculpture reflected perfectly in the still water below.

Another more traditional sculpture perfectly positioned as a dramatic statement at the end of a path is the copper tree fountain. Found by the owners on a visit to the Chelsea Flower Show, it is mesmerising to stand and watch the water droplets fall like raindrops from each handcrafted leaf.

In a garden of such immense scale it is somewhat of a surprise to discover the delicate attention to detail where even the smallest plants have been considerately positioned, such as the Virginia creeper, which is starting to reach along the cracks of the stonework.

Within the grandeur there is a quiet simplicity throughout with the Mayfield logo etched into the side of a seat and echoed again in the arches of the Lamarque rose arbour that leads to the conservatory and potager. There again, the essence and beauty of practicality is the story of this garden. The kitchen garden is walled to

Opposite: Mayfield's water garden is modelled on the famous water garden at Longstock Park in Hampshire in the UK.
Below: The splendid cascade was modelled on the 300-year-old original at Chatsworth House in the English Peak District.

Many design elements are incorporated to create year-round interest. Little wonder Garrick Hawkins doesn't have to say much about this amazing garden. It speaks for itself.

protect it from the wind, with apples, figs and pears espaliered along the inner walls. The growing season is longer and usually more productive as a result.

Mayfield garden is a feast for the senses no matter the season. The deciduous trees mean it is particularly spectacular in spring and autumn but the maze, the aviary, the croquet lawn, the parterre, the chapel, the Islamic-inspired reflection pond and the Mayfield allée are among the many design elements incorporated to create year-round interest. Little wonder Garrick Hawkins doesn't have to say much about this amazing garden. It speaks for itself.

Opposite: The temple above the 80-metre cascade is one of many features in the 300-acre (120-hectare) garden. *Below:* Mayfield garden has been developed in the NSW Central Tablelands from what was a bare paddock only 30 years ago.

LANDSCAPE OF LEARNING

Making a tree change — literally — meant a steep learning curve for gardening novice Jaqui Cameron.

Above: The author and her husband bought Winter Hill Tree Farm with its six-acre garden in 2007.
Opposite: The garden had been designed in 1994 by landscape architect Michael Bligh.

When my husband and I moved to the New South Wales Southern Highlands eight years ago, our new home came with a five-acre garden classified as an arboretum. I didn't even know what an arboretum was. To me, it was simply a very large garden filled with amazing trees and plants that looked spectacular: the perfect place to play with our young boys. It was my dream come true.

My excitement was tempered a little by the first reaction of my mother, who is a garden expert. Following the meandering drive through the garden and parking under the rose-covered arches, Mum wasn't even out of the car before she announced there was no way I'd be able to maintain it on my own. Uh-oh.

The garden was designed by landscape architect Michael Bligh and its first trees were planted in what was a bare paddock in 1994. The garden was designed as a living showroom for Winter Hill Tree Farm, a 70-acre (28-hectare) nursery specialising in mature trees and hedging, which my husband and I bought in 2007.

The previous owners were keen and

knowledgeable gardeners with an eye for colour and an understanding of plants. They planted mature trees complemented by hundreds of bulbs, roses and shrubs to create a garden regularly showcased in the Open Garden Scheme.

Taking over the business and garden was a huge undertaking because neither my husband nor I are horticulturists. We took the concept of a tree change quite literally and so faced a very steep learning curve. The garden was my responsibility, but where to start and what to do?

I was given a lovingly prepared month-by-month garden to-do list by the previous owner but, unfortunately, it doesn't help to be told to prune and divide the *Penstemons* in June if you don't know what a *Penstemon* is.

So, for the first 12 months, I adopted what I call the Darwinian approach to gardening: survival of the fittest. I watched as the seasons passed, the colours changed and flowers came and went, too scared to cut, unsure whether or not to dig.

It was initially distressing to see the garden

Clockwise from opposite: Post-and-rail fences, masses of roses, avenues of agapanthus and a good measure of annuals balance mature trees, stone walls and formal hedging.

So, for the first 12 months, I adopted what I call the Darwinian approach to gardening: survival of the fittest. I watched as the seasons passed and flowers came and went.

change from meticulous to wild. I felt guilty and would apologise to guests, sorry it wasn't in pristine condition. But, slowly, I came to realise that nobody else noticed the little things.

The trees and hedges are the stars of our garden and, with little help from me, they continued to flourish. The avenue of linden trees, initially planted to be pleached (interwoven), is now left in all its woolly glory. The majestic expanse of Japanese and Chinese elms and the burst of colour of the golden robinia against the many shades of green in the grove of ornamental pears are all amazing just as they are.

Tucked beneath the trees, different types of hedging provide some structure to the garden layout and, like arrows on a map, help guide you from one space to the next. The soft cherry and Portuguese laurel hedges border the lawn while the more formal, structured lines of English box and *Berberis* feature along the gravel drive and stone paths. Clumps of silver germander sit like shimmering round boulders in surrounding gardens.

Clockwise from opposite: Stone walls lined with Berberis thunbergii 'Golden Glow' set the scene for a garden often showcased in the Open Gardens Scheme; trees are the stars of the garden, along with flowering plants.

I was lucky to inherit a good garden design, so I stopped sweating the small stuff and decided to own the informality of the garden rather than try to regain complete control. Don't get me wrong; it still takes a lot of work but I am constantly amazed at how forgiving a garden can be. Despite paying little attention to the clematis and endless variety of roses that climb the driveway arches and creep along the post-and-rail fence, I am rewarded each year with masses of delicate and often fragrant blooms.

I now value the vigour of the plants that survived my Darwinian garden phase. Swathes of purple and white violets carpet some of the garden beds and escape into the lawn. Thick clumps of shiny blue and white agapanthus line the driveway to the office and the floating wisps of beauty bush in blossom are like snow in early summer.

Best of all, I've come to be very proud of the garden. In a way, my mother was right when she said I would struggle to maintain the garden I inherited four years ago. I haven't maintained it. I've loved it, learnt from it and worked very hard in it but I have also changed it. It is now my garden.

Clockwise from opposite:
The garden, with its formal stone pathways, bursts of colour and quiet spots for contemplation, has grown with the author, who has learnt to accept its informal elements as integral to its broad-based appeal.

In a way, my mother was right when she said I would struggle to maintain the garden I inherited four years ago. I haven't maintained it. I've loved it, learnt from it and worked very hard in it but I have also changed it. It is now my garden.

Joss Chandler's garden has come a long way from the days when her sole ambition was to grow something higher than the fence. After 30-plus years of hard work, she has created a real outback oasis.

Words KIRSTY MCKENZIE Photography KEN BRASS

OUTBACK OASIS

When John and Joss Chandler arrived at Kyneton, the garden was bare except for two trees and a paddock full of burrs and buffel grass. These days, it's a verdant delight and a tribute to more than three decades of hard work.

Joss Chandler cheerfully confesses that in the 30-plus years she's been developing the garden at Kyneton station, she's shifted the fence so many times she has no idea what area her garden covers. She hazards an acre but a few days later, texts to let us know she has actually measured the park-like expanse that surrounds the homestead on the 43,000-acre (17,400-hectare) cattle station near Barcaldine in central-western Queensland. As it turns out, the garden is now a sizeable 2.5 acres (slightly more than a hectare), no mean feat in an environment where drought, flood and bushfire are ever-present threats, summer temperatures are routinely in the high 30s and low 40s and roos, rabbits and echidnas are constantly looking for opportunities to feast on the green fodder she has planted or dig up the soil she has so assiduously tended.

Joss and her husband, John, have been living at Kyneton since 1980. They met in the early '70s when Joss was studying occupational therapy and John economics at the University of Queensland. Joss had grown up on the Gold Coast and John on his family's property, North Delta, also in the Barcaldine district. They were married in 1976 and moved into the cottage on North Delta.

"I'd visited many times before so I knew what I was letting myself in for," Joss recalls. "But nothing could disguise the fact that a garden at North Delta was an impossible challenge. The homestead was on an ironstone ridge, which

meant gardening involved a mechanical digger and a crowbar, and the bore water was so poor deposits of soda stained the ground and killed everything. The only plants that thrived there were athel pines and cottonwoods, though I did have some success growing vegetables in cut-off tanks above the ground."

So, in spite of the fact that the homestead was uninhabitable and took two years of renovations before they could live in it, Joss was delighted to move to Kyneton, where the bore water was good quality and the soil was beautiful sandy loam on top of a clay base a metre below. Although the property's original owners, the Sealy family, had planted an extensive orchard, by the time John and Joss arrived, climate and neglect had exacted their toll. Joss had little more than a blank canvas to start with, with just one mango and one kurrajong tree standing in the otherwise bare block.

Bare, that is, except for the Mossman burr, which kept regenerating in the midst of the waist-high buffel grass. "It seemed indestructible," Joss says. "If you mow it off, it just seeds on the ground and comes back. I was constantly picking burrs from our clothes, and our second son, James, who was crawling at the time, had continual knee infections from the scratches. In the end, I tied a garbage bag around him to protect his legs. I must have picked up millions of seeds by dragging a weighted flannelette rag across the ground and, eventually, I started to win. Then we were able to plant buffalo grass runners and start the lawn."

With two more additions to the family in the following years, Joss describes early progress

This page: Bougainvillaea runs riot in the garden. *Above right:* The pond was added as an affordable alternative to a pool and the pontoon as a concession to daughter Meg's aversion to muddy feet as well as a good sunset-viewing spot.

in the garden as slow. Initially, her ambition was simply to grow something higher than the fence and she says plantings were fairly indiscriminate, based on what was available at the local nursery and which survived. *Melaleuca leucadendra* and *armillarus, Callistemon salignus, Eucalyptus, Casuarina cunninghamiana* and *Grevillea* were supplemented with exotics including *Tipuana tipu* 'rosewood', *Cassia fistula* 'golden shower tree', *Ficus hillii* 'weeping fig', duranta and bougainvillaea. Joss's mother, Margot Hogarth, a passionate gardener herself, would arrive from the Gold Coast with her car boot full of cuttings and seedlings. Mother and daughter worked side by side, weeding, carting leaf mould and soil and building beds for her offerings, which included *Hippeastrum* and ifafa lilies, hibiscus, Michaelmas and Shasta daisies, plumbago, salvias, evening primrose, chrysanthemums and geraniums.

"After that first decade of topsy-like growth, I started to introduce a bit more structure," Joss recalls. "With the kids all growing up, we added the pond as a cheap alternative to a swimming pool. It's very deep, about 12 feet, because we knew what the boys would get up to jumping into it." As a concession to daughter Meg's aversion to muddy feet, they added a pontoon, which is now a pleasant spot for enjoying the sunset and admiring the flock of gourd sculptures that adorn the water's edge.

A visit from Toowoomba landscape designer Mark Everingham prompted a major shift in the garden. "He suggested we should make more of a feature of the trunks of the *Melaleucas*. So we removed a lot of the trees and underlying shrubs

"*Summer is like a military operation just keeping everything alive. Pop-up sprinklers water the lawns and all the garden beds have manual sprinklers.*"

and we can now see through the trunks to the paddock outside. John likes to say I have probably pulled out more trees than most people have planted but, the fact is, the garden is better for it."

Mass plantings of roses are another evolution and Joss favours 'The Children's Rose' and 'Seduction' for their fragrance and 'Icebergs' for their prolific flowers. Creepers on fences, frames and tank stands include *Quisqualis*, *Antigonon*, honeysuckle and star jasmine, which add fragrance, while, as a concession to spring visitors, Joss adds a few pockets of flowering annuals. Although the garden remains a work in progress, she says the days of moving the fence are over.

"I think I have reached the size I can maintain and leave to someone else to handle when we are away," she says. "Summer is like a military operation just keeping everything alive. Pop-up sprinklers water the lawns and all the garden beds have manual sprinklers. Mulching is crucial and there is no such thing as too much. Fortunately, frosts are no longer a problem in the garden, though we still have them in winter. I'm not sure whether it's the protection from the trees or global warming, but now I can grow tomatoes and zucchinis right through winter without a worry."

While Joss says her favourite part of the garden used to be the big old mango tree, now her "best bits" change with the seasons. "When we first came here, the shade of that mango felt like a godsend," she says. "But now, my favourite part is usually a new bed or section I am developing or unusual plants given to me by friends. I guess that just means these days I can afford to be choosy."

Clockwise from above:
A flock of gourd sculptures patrols the pond and keeps watch over the paddocks beyond; on the advice of landscape designer Mark Everingham, Joss decided to remove trees and underplantings to make more of a feature of the Melaleuca trunks and allow glimpses of the expansive landscape; Joss has also planted hundreds of roses.

EASTERN INFLUENCE

A passion for peonies and all aspects of the cottage garden drives this Southern Highlands partnership to devote countless hours to turning their garden into a spring sensation.

Left: *Dominic Wong devotes at least 30 hours a week to his Southern Highlands cottage garden.* **Opposite:** *Poppies, wisteria and countless other cottage garden favourites lend their colours to the canvas of the garden.*

Above: *The tree peony is a spring sensation, the national flower of China and a symbol of feminine beauty and wealth.* **Right:** *Roses on climbing frames punctuate the one-and-a-half acre garden.*

European objects decorated with Chinese motifs is how Chris Styles and Dominic Wong describe Chinoiserie, and it is this beautiful decorating technique that they have incorporated into their home and B&B at Mittagong in the NSW Southern Highlands. Their home, a storybook-cottage design they had built on their vacant block of land in the late 1990s, has loads of old-world features including decorative bargeboards, dormer windows and a timeless veranda that allows it to blend in with the surroundings as if it has been there forever.

It sits on almost one-and-a-quarter acres with the B&B attached, allowing Chris and Dominic to cater easily for guests' needs — when Dominic is not hard at work in the extensive gardens, that is. Gardens include herbaceous borders, a pond and stream garden, a potager garden and an incredible collection of American, Chinese, Japanese and European tree peonies, which are stunning when at their peak in October and November. The astonishing thing about the gardens is that they were only planted at the end of 1998. Before that, the property was completely bare and it has been Dominic's hard work that has transformed the area into an Eden.

"Dominic spends more than 30 hours each week in the garden, tending to the plantings, weeding, dead-heading flowers, watering and potting up plants for sale," says Chris. "A flower garden does involve a fair amount of maintenance and Dominic does not have any help at all except for the mowing and edging.

"In Chinese culture, the peony is regarded as the regal flower that represents hierarchy, feminine beauty and wealth. It is also the national flower of China. Since not many gardeners choose to grow peonies, nor have the knowledge

Words DONNA MACPHERSON Photography KEN BRASS

of how to grow them, Dominic decided to specialise in growing them so that people can enjoy these flowers when they come to visit, especially on the garden open days we have.

"To have a garden like this, you need to have commitment and passion, a good eye for contrasts, textures and colour combinations as well as knowledge of what works in the local area, for example the soil type and quality, the amount of sun the garden receives and a good knowledge of where to put the plants, such as in sun or shade."

A favourite room from which to view the garden is the dining room as it's on a higher elevation and you can see the outline of all the garden beds, which suggests a parterre design. This was purposely created so the guests would have the best view of the garden while eating breakfast.

The Chinoiserie decorating style in the home has allowed Dominic and Chris to combine their love of European furniture pieces with Chinese influences such as the bedside tables in the B&B rooms. These are in the Chippendale style and have been decorated with Chinese fretwork. Dominic is always on the hunt for more items to continue this look throughout the home.

"Dominic chose this English-cottage style of decorating because it never dates and gives the interior a homely feel," says Chris. "He lived in England for two years and stayed in a lot of English homes and found that they have a certain decor about them that gives them a warm and cosy feel.

"In our home and B&B, we have used themes in the rooms. For example, the living room that overlooks the garden has a floral theme. We've

Clockwise from opposite: The garden is divided into sections including herbaceous borders, a pond and stream garden, a potager garden; daisies, tulips, irises, lavender and other annuals add colour and fragrance.

used roses and prints on sofas, curtains, paintings and lampshades; however, not in the same material or it would be overpowering. We then accessorised with objects that carry a rose motif. Most of our furniture is mahogany, which, as most people know, is a dark wood, so Dominic chose a warm, buttery colour for the walls to brighten up the room. A darker wall would be too gloomy."

As well as being a practising Buddhist, Dominic is hairdresser by trade, something he still does a little of each week and this may explain his flair for fashion, colour and decorating. He has had an interest in gardening since his youth and loves to collect items adorned with peonies. Chris is still working full-time and with retirement looming may soon have time to spend on one of his other passions: music. He presents a weekly program on community radio covering theatre and organ music and plays keyboard, as well as helping to care for local senior citizens.

"The Southern Highlands has four distinct seasons," says Chris. "In October, visitors come for the peonies; in November for the roses and perennials, which are at their peak at that time; and in autumn for the autumn foliage and late-summer perennials. I remember one visitor to our garden told Dominic one of his trees was badly diseased and pointed it out to him.

"Dominic had to tell her that it was not actually a disease but lichen growing on the tree. Lichen will only grow on trees if the air is clean and that's why you don't see it on trees in our polluted capital cities. The visitor was quite surprised on learning this as she did not know about lichen."

Running the B&B and caring for the gardens is hard work but rewarding, as Dominic and Chris admit to having delightful regular guests as well as new visitors to the area who come for a variety of reasons. These could include attending a wedding, to enjoy local events such as the jazz festival, polocrosse tournament, Tulip Time, A Day on the Green concert or to simply see the Southern Highlands in all its beauty.

There are few places more beautiful in the Southern Highlands than the Chinoiserie and its stunning gardens. If you are planning a weekend break or are travelling through Mittagong towards the end of the year, why not allow a few hours to stop and stroll through Chris and Dominic's wonderful gardens and maybe purchase a peony to plant to remind you of the experience?

For further information on the Chinoiserie, phone Chris or Dominic on (02) 4872 3003 or visit highlandsnsw.com.au/chinoiserie

Clockwise from opposite: It's hard to imagine that the block was bare when the couple bought it in the late '90s; Dominic is also a keen propagator; succulents also have their place in this stunning setting.

VISION SPLENDID

Pat and Bill Rhodin spend all year preparing their garden for opening for one short burst during spring. A recent visit confirms it's worth the wait.

This pic: Bill and Pat Rhodin tend more than 1000 blossom trees and half-a-million bulbs in their 10-acre garden, which they open in October each year. *Right: Layers of colour are provided by blossom and annual borders.*

Words KIRSTY MCKENZIE Photography KEN BRASS

Clockwise from above:
The Rhodins plant more than 500,000 bulbs at Tulip Top Gardens; apart from opening time, they maintain the garden on their own; visitors are welcome to picnic in the grounds; a colourful assault.

outhern Tablelands residents Pat and Bill Rhodin say their passion for gardening has taken them around the world. Twice, in fact, as on two occasions, their first home garden in Canberra won competitions with world trips as prizes. But 20 years ago, they moved out of the national capital in search of more space in which to build their dream garden. Now, for one month each year, the world comes to them to see their remarkable 10-acre (four-hectare) site at Sutton, north of Canberra on the Federal Highway.

"We bought the property in 1993 and, for the first few years, concentrated on developing around the house," Pat recalls. "We gradually spread out into the valley, planting conifers, willows, English elms and more than 1000 blossom trees. We added a waterfall, because the rocks were already there, and built up the beds for the bulbs and annuals."

While she makes it sound matter-of-fact, the spectacle that occurs each spring is testimony to the hard work that the Rhodins devote to their garden, which is called Tulip Top. There's a

staggering array of bulbs, more than 500,000 at last count, all arranged by colour and interspersed with annuals including pansies, primulas and *Bellis perennis* (English daisies), as well as flowering shrubs such as prolific forsythia.

But perhaps the most remarkable thing about the garden is that Pat and Bill manage the entire place on their own, except during the opening period from mid-September to mid-October, when they hire staff to run the ticket desk, catering facilities and gift stores that are set up in marquees around the property.

"Family members help out when they can on weekends but, for the rest of the time, Bill and I manage all the propagating, pruning, weeding, mowing, sewing and other maintenance," Pat says.

When the garden closes at the end of October, the first task is to dig up all those bulbs. They are graded and packed away in storage. The next project is to plan and design the beds for the following year's display. In autumn, all the bulbs go into cold storage for six weeks and in mid-June, the Rhodins are outdoors again, planting the bulbs during a two- to three-week period. As spring approaches, the pressure to be ready for opening mounts. Then, finally, the blossoms start ... countless

Below: Plants are thoughtfully labelled for garden enthusiasts. Opposite: The garden is a year-round project for the Rhodins, although they only open during October.

Clockwise from this page: The garden never feels crowded and family groups are encouraged with the lure of free sausage or egg sandwiches included in the admission price; layers of colour from blossom, tulips and flowering borders; blossom branch in full flower.

varieties of crabapple, peach, cherry, apricot, quince and plum with their understoreys of bulbs and annuals, all competing for visitors' attention.

Classical music is piped throughout the garden, which, thanks to its vast area, never feels crowded even on a fine Sunday morning when the promise of free poffertjes (Dutch pancakes) to complement all those tulips lures extra visitors. Free tea and coffee and a complimentary sausage or barbecued egg sandwich are included with the admission price, all part of the Rhodins' grand plan to make their garden as family friendly as possible. Visitors are welcome to bring picnics and their dogs, provided they are on a leash and cleaned up after.

Inevitably, comparisons are drawn with Canberra's other big spring attraction, Floriade. But it's not an apples with apples situation. Where Floriade is a brash and blowsy public event, Tulip Top is a testament to personal passion, to people who have devoted their lives to creating something so beautiful, it's a wonder it hasn't received any awards.

"Well not yet," Pat says. "But, then again, we haven't tried. We've been too busy to fill out the entry forms."

For more information on Tulip Top Gardens visit tuliptopgardens.com.au

TICKLE
YOUR FANCY

Tickle Tank, the enchanting water tank turned
home and garden, will do more than just tickle
your fancy. This house, and its talented owner,
are bound to capture your imagination.

Words: LAUREN MCKELLAR Photography: JOSS WILLIAMS Styling: BRONTE CAMILLERI

You only have to look at the photos in this article to fall in love with Tickle Tank. This property defines the term larger than life as its bright colours, exuberant garden and natural tones jump out off the page at you. However, in 1998 it was simply a rundown water tank. It was thanks to the vision of sculptor and artist Irene Pearce that it progressed to the beacon of beauty it is today.

"I had some life-changing situations happen, and I needed to find myself a new home on a very small budget," Irene says. "I didn't want to borrow money and have a mortgage tying me down in my mid-50s."

Irene went to the council to enquire about developing the land, curious to see if her housing idea would comply with engineering standards and health regulations. When she encountered no obstacles, she straightaway purchased the 450-square-metre Adelaide Hills block, and started her developments.

"I designed it myself," Irene says, adding that she then engaged the services of an architect to insert the correct terminology the plan needed to make it through council.

Still, this home is very much Irene's, with the initial plans developed by her, and the talented lady doing a lot of the work herself. Irene put in the doors and windows, and finished the frames and other internal fixtures. She also ordered three smaller tanks and had those lowered into the foundations via cranes, and then fitted them out on her own. One of the first projects Irene had to undertake, however, was some basic work in the garden; particularly since the original tank was partly underground.

"The winter of the year I bought it, 1998, I removed all the soil and cut the holes in the house," Irene says. "Then I had to think about [what would normally be considered] stage three, which was an urgent landscape to retain the walls, as otherwise I'd have all the dirt I'd removed from the tank wash back towards the house."

Due to the block's natural lines, Irene chose to optimise existing sunken areas and retain them, holding back the earth with stonework and other materials she salvaged from the building site, such as sandstone blocks and bricks. She then set about developing the garden in a fashion that would best suit the climate and her own lifestyle.

"I wanted it to be a hardy garden that worked for me. I didn't want to have to work for it too much," Irene says. "I don't want to spend my time nurturing it. I just trim it back now and then, when it gets a bit exuberant."

With all the sunken areas and these care considerations in mind, cool-climate plants such as ferns and ground covers that can go onto paths were the natural choice. They flourished, and soon Irene was the proud owner of a very well-developed garden that family and friends fell in love with.

Of course, they're not the only ones bewitched by the garden's beauty. Irene cites the curved seat outside her kitchen door as one of her favourite areas in the property for its ambience — and its convenience, too.

"I can open the kitchen door, take a cup of tea

Clockwise from this page: Irene opted to optimise sunken areas by creating sitting spaces and outdoor rooms. She has lent her skills as a mosaic artist to the decoration of the house and its garden.

woody tones and spots of bright colour and texture, all against the stark white backdrop of the building walls.

Irene also extended her artistic hand to the driveway and created an intricate stone design that really captures the creative, yet peaceful, vibe Tickle Tank gives off.

In fact, it's rare to walk a few metres on the property without seeing yet further proof of Irene's talent and vision, right down to an art retreat for some of her younger guests.

"Our water tank sprang a leak and I thought 'What a shame, I'll just have to make a bigger hole'," Irene says. She painted the interior, made two little chairs and purchased a board and some coloured pencils and chalks, and now this garden feature is a popular escape for the smaller visitors to the property. "There's usually a queue of people waiting to go in," Irene says.

When it comes to people lining up to spend some peaceful time at Tickle Tank, Irene is certainly accustomed to it. This property is a part of Open Gardens Australia, an achievement that certainly wasn't part of Irene's master plan for the property.

"I met a woman at a women's gathering and she said 'Oh my gosh, you need to put your garden in the Open Gardens Scheme!' Initially I wasn't interested, as it's a bit wild and quirky and recycled, and I don't have avenues of trees or professional gardeners.

"But she said to me, 'People relate to small gardens these days, and it's so different and gorgeous. Put it in once and see how you feel. I'll make sure you get the support'," Irene says. Despite her lack of confidence, she did end up opening the garden — and with absolutely overwhelming results.

"I had 750 people come through that weekend," Irene says. Three weeks prior, the house had been featured on *Burke's Backyard*, and the allure of Tickle Tank was too much for the general public to resist.

"It was so exciting to think this place that little old Irene built on a tiny budget had brought all these people in from everywhere," Irene says. These days, Tickle Tank is still open to visitors, allowing others to fall in love with the house during Open Gardens season exclusively (opengarden.org.au).

"It's a wonderful place to live, and I feel very happy here," she says. And, surrounded by this peaceful, self-sufficient and organic beauty, we have no doubt that this is indeed the case.

and a sandwich and just be surrounded by the garden while I eat," Irene says. "I can also add some mint or rosemary for the sandwich while I'm out there, or whiz out for some herbs while I'm cooking a meal. It connects me with nature and things that are living."

This connection with nature is evident inside the house, as well as out. Irene often brings clippings from the gardens inside, and has been known to find leaves trailing down her cupboards if the cuts happen to take root and grow. These cupboards were designed and created by Irene herself. So, as well as planning the transformation from water tank to house, Irene made a lot of the furniture herself, incorporating her love of natural

Clockwise from this page: While there are loads of spots for quiet contemplation, up to 750 visitors come through the gardens on open days; Irene's mosaics are everywhere; she appreciates being able to step outside for breaks; Irene says she only works in the garden when it becomes too exuberant and needs trimming and taming.

LADY OF THE LAKE

Whether she's at home in Auckland's inner suburbs or at her country bolthole overlooking Lake Wanaka, growing fresh produce and cooking it is in the DNA of New Zealand's first lady of the kitchen, Annabel Langbein.

Is it possible to have it all? Probably not, but New Zealand cook and publishing legend Annabel Langbein comes pretty close. As the author of 17 best-selling cookbooks and the star of her own TV show, *The Free Range Cook*, Annabel lives between her city home in the north and a remote cabin overlooking Lake Wanaka in the South Island's Central Otago district. She divides her working life and leisure between both addresses and growing her own fruit and vegies is central to the lifestyle she enjoys in each destination.

"By instinct I don't go to the fridge to decide what to have for dinner," she explains. "I go to the garden and see what's available. Or in the dead of winter, I might go to the pantry and see what I've preserved from more fruitful times."

In doing so, Annabel is preserving a tradition established by her parents as she was growing up in Wellington. Her father, a senior civil servant, unwound by tending a bountiful vegie garden. Her mother, a keen cook and consummate entertainer with a degree in home economics, was his willing cohort, turning the produce into splendid family meals and dinners.

"My mother knew I was a cook before I did," Annabel explains. "She gave me a copy of Julia Child's *Mastering the Art of French Cooking* when I was still a teenager. Although, at that stage, I was still raging against her decision to be a stay-at-home mum, she was subtly encouraging what would become my passion. I would make my own lobster pots and catch my own so I could cook Julia's lobster thermidor and I also used to shoot my own squab and make her roast squab with chicken liver canapés."

Fresh out of high school, Annabel did her obligatory "stint at self-sufficiency" as a '70s hippie and dabbled in adrenaline-fuelled occupations such as live deer recovery (by helicopter to catch breeding stock for farms) and possum trapping (for skins). In fact, the first time she saw her husband, Ted Hewetson, she was poaching on his family's farm and had to scarper up a tree to avoid being seen as he rode by on horseback.

"I had a short attention span and was looking for excitement," she recalls. "But the jobs paid well and I owned my first house by the time I was 20. Then I did a diploma in horticulture at Lincoln University and I guess my fate as a foodie was pretty much sealed."

A stint as the chef of a small Italian restaurant ("with Elizabeth David's *Italian Food* as my guide") funded a trip to South America, which marked a turning point in her life. "I became seriously ill

from food poisoning and ended up recuperating, courtesy of family friends, at the New Zealand embassy in Lima," she explains. "Then I went to Brazil and settled in a village called Búzios about an hour-and-a-half north of Rio de Janeiro."

Annabel found herself accommodation in a share house and true to her DNA, soon found herself cooking for the entire household. "It was at the time of the Falklands crisis so there were lots of Argentineans living in exile in Brazil," she recalls. "When people found out that I was keen to cook, some of the Argentineans came to me and asked me if I could make a savoury croissant that they missed from home. So I did a deal with a local pousada [small hotel] owner. I managed the hotel in the afternoons and, in exchange, I had free use of the kitchen to cook the croissants. That was when I fully realised food was something I could do to make a living."

When Annabel returned to New Zealand she worked variously as a vineyard manager, microwave oven demonstrator and film set caterer. "That's when you really learn to cook," she observes. "With minimal equipment and in

Clockwise from above:
Flowers and companion plants have an important place in Annabel's vegie garden; Annabel's garden is the crowning glory of her Wanaka holiday property; the garden that inspires.

Words KIRSTY MCKENZIE Photography KEN BRASS

"Once the children were born I wanted to spend more time with them and so we made the decision to scale back the marketing business and focus on publishing."

the most remote locations you have to produce everything from meat pies for the roadies to anorexic meals for the talent and learn to serve it all at once and somehow keep smiling."

By the mid-'80s she had started contributing to the NZ food media both on radio and in print and was working as the marketing director for a leading NZ cheese manufacturer. "But I knew I still hadn't found my niche," she says. "So I wrote to Julia Child telling her about what I had done so far and asking for her advice."

Amazingly, the woman who had taught an entire generation of Americans how to cook French food, wrote back. "She suggested I join the International Association of Culinary Professionals, which was then known as the American Association of Cooking Schools," Annabel continues. "I ended up going to Seattle for a conference where I met all these amazing people who worked in every aspect of food and the associated media."

In that serendipitous way life has of providing chance encounters at the very time they are most needed, Annabel also met Danièlle Delpeuch, one-time chef to former French President Mitterand, who assumed the role of mentor and offered her a "broom cupboard" in her apartment in New York.

"I used the time at her place to absorb everything I could," Annabel says. "I did a course in nutrition, which changed the way I cooked to using more wholegrains and a fresh, flavour-driven approach. Then I did a course about American regional cooking which was almost culinary anthropology in that it explored the way everything from climate and geography

to religion influences the way we cook. It kind of contextualised where I was heading in my approach to food."

Back in New Zealand, the '90s were a big decade for Annabel as she founded the Culinary Institute of New Zealand to market and promote her country's extraordinary range of produce, married Ted and had their children, Sean and Rose, who are now adults. During all of this she started producing and self-publishing an extraordinary library of cookbooks that celebrate her signature style of using the freshest local produce, treating it simply and preparing it with passion.

Along the way, her natural warmth, enthusiasm and exuberance have charmed a whole generation of Kiwis, who follow her every move, and her reputation has spread around the world. *The Free Range Cook*, published in 2010, sold an extraordinary 160,000 copies in New Zealand in its first 12 months on the stands and the accompanying TV series sold into 79 markets around the world.

"I was brought up believing that the good life is not about money," Annabel says. "It's about community service, engaging with people and taking time to appreciate the things that come your way. Once the children were born I wanted to spend more time with them and so we made the decision to scale back the marketing business and focus on publishing."

The cabin overlooking Lake Wanaka was a natural progression for Annabel and her family. Ted, who has stints as both a ski instructor and tennis coach on his CV, was a long-time visitor to the slopes of nearby Cardrona and Treble Cone and has a sheep farm near Wanaka. They bought the

23-acre block in 1997 and started planting almond and hazelnut orchards and an olive grove. Ted, who Annabel says missed his calling as an architect, designed the cabin, which was completed in 2001 and the family has enjoyed wonderful summer and winter holidays there ever since.

Of course, you'd expect Annabel to have a vegetable garden but nothing prepares you for the extraordinary plot she has developed. Spread over three terraces, which will eventually be shielded by cypress windbreaks, the garden is planted with every conceivable plant that can grow at latitude 45° south. From artichokes through to zucchinis, Annabel tends potatoes, onions, garlic, carrots, tomatoes, tomatillos, berries and all members of the squash family. Fruit trees and vegetables jostle for space alongside gladioli, sweet peas and dahlias. "I like to mix up the pretty with the productive," Annabel says. "I'm constantly experimenting with what I can grow and make. There are soy beans for edamame, buckwheat to make soba and maize, which will hopefully become polenta."

There's also a beneficial insect garden containing plants such as echinacea and coriander for their pest-controlling properties, and a remedy bed with herbs such as chamomile and various mints known for their curative powers. It's all part of a grand plan for the farm to be chemical-free, which Annabel has already achieved with the vegies, but has yet to completely roll out to the orchards.

As well as feeding the family, friends and neighbours, the garden is the inspiration for Annabel's recipes and the set for her TV series. When *Australian Country* visited, she was in the throes of preparing for another series. A whole terrace has been planted with corn and sunflowers to create a "garden room" which became the venue for one of the events in the show. Similarly, trout from the lake, local lamb, venison and game feature in the program, alongside some amazing Pinots and Chardonnays from Central Otago's wineries.

In spite of the flurry of activity taking place in the garden and in the cabin's modest kitchen, where Annabel tests most of her recipes and prepares food for shoots, she keeps feeding us all day long. "I always make scones," she says as she whips up a fetta and basil batch and serves them with freshly harvested tomatoes. "They take five minutes to make and everyone thinks you're so clever."

But that's just the beginning, and Annabel continues offering the food she has recipe-tested for our scrutiny: a poached chicken salad with a

spicy peanut sauce, barbecued venison, freshly dug potato salad, a new version of focaccia and apricot and ginger slice ... in the middle of all this creative energy, Annabel downs tools and declares it's time to "smell the roses". Or at least get out the boat so Ted can show us some of their favourite spots on Lake Wanaka, which is 58 kilometres long and a summer playground for many New Zealanders and tourists. In the utterly unlikely event that we will die of starvation during the outing, Annabel heads into picnic mode, packing stone fruit and nuts, drinks and an uber-moist figgy chocolate cake.

The lake sparkles in all its pristine glory and, apart from a few passing water skiers, we enjoy our afternoon tea in splendid waterfront isolation. "I truly believe I am the luckiest person on earth," Annabel says. "To be surrounded by family, friends and fine food is what it's all about as far as I'm concerned. I love being able to live between the city and the lake and to share all this with people through the books and TV. The American food writer M.F.K. Fisher put it most succinctly when she said, 'I cook for myself and others.' That surely is the art of living well."

Clockwise from above:
Annabel harvests potatoes;
the cabin nestles on the
shores of Lake Wanaka;
Ted, who missed his calling
as an architect, designed
the little cabin in the hills.

HARVEST HOME

For interior decorator, passionate gardener and keen cook Mickey Robertson, restoring Glenmore House has been a labour of love, — one that has delivered both a lifestyle change and a new career direction.

Mickey Robertson would probably hoot with laughter at being called a domestic goddess but, on hearing her philosophy on household duties, the phrase keeps coming to mind. Take laundry for example: "We all have to do it," she says in her pragmatic way. "So we might as well embrace it. I make doing the washing a joyous event. There are no plastic baskets or utilitarian pegs in my laundry. I have beautiful cane baskets and lovely wooden pegs. I keep in mind the unbeatable smell of sun-dried washing, which makes the chore worthwhile. And then I iron with lovely linen water so everything smells fresh and fragrant when you use it."

Always a glass-half-full kind of person, Mickey has applied this philosophy to the restoration of the home she shares with her leadership advisor husband, Larry, and their daughters Bonnie and Clementine. They came across the 28-acre (11-hectare) property in the foothills of the Razorback Range near Camden on Sydney's south-western perimeter in 1988, when they were looking for a potential site for English friends to develop a conference centre.

"Even the real estate person told Larry he didn't want to look at the place as it wouldn't be suitable," Mickey says. "But we inspected, fell in love with the 1840s' sandstone cottage and that was it. The beginning of the beginning. Or perhaps the beginning of the end, because we have been working on it ever since."

The land on which Glenmore House stands was part of an 1834 grant made to Hannibal

Words KIRSTY MCKENZIE Photography KEN BRASS

Macarthur, pastoralist, politician and nephew of Merino industry pioneers, John and Elizabeth Macarthur. The estate was later subdivided and sold to various members of the Moore family, who continue to have a presence in the district to the present day.

Glenmore House came with a collection of dilapidated early colonial outbuildings, so as well as restoring and extending the cottage, Mickey and Larry have progressively given new life to the former cowshed, dairy, stables, hay shed, barn and store room. Step by step during the past 25 years they have linked the buildings together with new fences, drystone walls, paths, steps, hedges and gardens.

"In the early days it was just mad," Mickey recalls. "I was still working in Sydney, so we'd come down on weekends and work on making the house habitable and clearing the grounds. After about a year, we could finally stay overnight. Then it became our weekender and finally 18 years ago, we moved down here permanently, though of course we both still go to the city for work."

The property now supports a small herd of red Angus cattle and ever resourceful, Mickey has set about making the buildings support themselves by turning them into a kitchen garden school. "Although I was raised between a flat in inner-Sydney and a boat on the harbour, as a child my imaginary home was something out of

"Predictably enough, I stuffed up my first attempt. It was then I realised you need to learn how to make a garden work."

Beatrix Potter," Mickey explains. "I've always loved gardens and garden plans, so was delighted at the opportunity to create a real vegie garden when we moved down here. Predictably enough, though, I stuffed up my first attempt. It was then that I realised you actually need to learn how to make a garden work. And then I set about finding someone to show me how to do it. I practically scoured the entire Sydney basin trying to find someone similar to Sarah Raven [the English writer, broadcaster and expert on all things to grow, cut and eat from the garden].

"Finally I met Linda Ross, who has qualifications in landscape architecture and horticulture and is passionate about growing her own organic vegies. So, five years ago, we started kitchen garden classes, which actually take people through what needs to happen in the garden month by month. So, this month, it might be all about harvesting this season's crops and preparing the soil and next month, it might be about planting the garden and showing them

Clockwise from above:
Produce informs Mickey's classes; wisteria in full spring glory; Mickey tames the Banksia rose; the vegie garden is an object lesson in sustainability; one of the colonial outbuildings.

how to build tunnels and wigwams and triangle trellises for tomatoes."

Along the way Mickey's own kitchen garden has become an object lesson in sustainability, with beds set out to demonstrate rotation cropping (to keep the soil healthy), companion planting (of complementary plants for shade or pest control purposes) and secession planting (which allows two crops which produce at different times to grow in the one row). In between there are various shelters housing chooks, which are "let out to do their job of scratching the soil" at appropriate times.

"I've got a bit of an obsession with rows," Mickey observes. "But I've had to let go of that to embrace guild planting, which basically aims to increase the productivity of a garden by integrating the components, be they plants, animals or structures. So I might plant spring onions, calendula and fennel together in a higgledy-piggledy fashion to confuse the pests, which generally are specific to one plant and move down the bed from one to the next. Amazingly enough it works."

As part of the kitchen garden experience Mickey started "spoiling the guests" by serving treats based on whatever was really new in the garden, whether it was peas fresh from the vine, new season's asparagus, or baby artichokes. "I'm

> "*When you have a productive garden, you'll often have a glut, so it's great to be able to make jams, preserves and chutneys.*"

just a home cook but having a kitchen garden teaches you to cook, because it forces you to use what you have to hand," she says. "The kitchen garden people started asking me how I'd made things, so I thought I might as well start cooking classes as well. Because when you have a productive garden, you'll often have a glut, so it's great to be able to make jams, preserves and chutneys to make the most of the surplus. We've had soup days, cake days, marmalade days."

Mickey also supplements the cooking class calendar with classes by visiting chefs, who demonstrate how to make the most of what's in the garden. She is also looking at expanding the curriculum with art and craft workshops.

"I've always loved domestic life," she says. "That's why I love decorating, cooking and beautiful gardens. I'm just incredibly lucky that Glenmore House has allowed me to bring all that together and turn it into a business and lifestyle."

For more information on the kitchen garden and cooking classes, visit glenmorehouse.com.au

Clockwise from above:
Chickens are part of the food cycle at Glenmore House; a spot for reflection; lavender-lined pathway; the property has many colonial outbuildings; a haven for horses.

PEACH SEASON

Peach Panfili has had a few careers in her time and there are traces of all of them in the house and garden she restored in Sydney.

You can usually trust your nearest and dearest to tell it like it is. So when artist and stylist Peach Panfili was told by her son the house she had just bought was a "complete dump", she knew there was an element of truth to his assessment. But through the pub carpet and worn lino, light bulbs hanging directly from the sockets, unlined ceilings and mission brown paint, Peach could see the low-slung timber cottage had potential. She has spent the past decade realising it.

"One end of the house was built in 1892, as the manager's cottage for an orchard," Peach says. "Then, in the 1970s, an owner got matching timbers and extended the house, reorienting it to face north in the process. When I came along it had been a rental property for 25 years so it needed lots of work."

"Onward, ever onward", Peach was just the right person to take on the task. The house had to be plumbed and rewired before it could be lived in. She spent a lot of time in timber yards "spitting on wood" to see what colour it would turn when polished before she chose the replacement floorboards. In the end, she settled on blue gum, because it's native to the area, and narrow boards because they can be secret nailed. For almost a year her kitchen consisted of a cast-iron, treadle-sewing-machine base with a door resting on it to form a bench, as well as a kettle, a microwave and a tiny benchtop oven with one ring burner on top.

Words KIRSTY MCKENZIE Photography MARK HERRIOT & SANDY DE BEYER

"It was basic, but I managed the catering for both my children's 21st birthday parties on it," Peach recalls. "Gradually it all came together, with lots of DIY and technical help from tradespeople when necessary. By the time I got to my en suite bathroom I let my hair down and splurged on a deep German cast-iron bath, Turkish stone, a waterfall spout and other Italian fittings. Then slowly, slowly I moved on to the garden. It was a huge challenge so I spent the first year concentrating on building up the soil with manure."

A self-proclaimed "Jack of all trades", Peach initially studied sculpture at art school, which she candidly admits is not all that helpful for earning a living. She started work as a set and costume designer for theatre and film, then for almost a decade ran Peach and Lavish, a hugely successful Sydney flower shop.

"It all started because I used to do bouquets

"Part of the house was built in 1892 ... when I came along it had been a rental property for 25 years so it needed work."

for friends' weddings," she says. "One day a well-meaning friend sent me one of those mock ikebana creations with tortured-looking flowers in a plastic bowl. She had probably spent a fortune on it, but I thought 'it's not hard to do better than this'. About the same time I saw a shop for lease in a great location and the next thing it was mine. It was very hard work with a young family and having to get up at 4am to go to the markets, but I loved it. I was also very fortunate in my timing in that I managed to get clients who allowed me to be creative."

Peach's sculpting background came to the

Clockwise from above:
With her background in sculpture and floristry Peach Panfili planted a garden that offered year-round interest and inspiration for her outsized floral studies on canvas; *she planted more than 100 rose bushes, most of them perfumed; part of the house was built in 1892 as an orchard manager's cottage and it was extended in the 1970s before Peach took over in the 1990s.*

fore as she experimented with arrangements containing fruit and vegies, such as pears and artichokes, nuts and berries, "at a time when most florists were still addicted to baby's breath".

"One bouquet I particularly remember was Julia roses with weeds and grass and another was kangaroo paw and chillies," she recalls. "I also became known for my white arrangements. Every week, I had to fill two huge urns in the Chanel shop with white flowers. I realise I was very lucky that people gave me free rein. I had a deal with a grower at the markets and he would sell me his entire output of white Mount Shasta roses. They became my signature flower. I still think there's nothing quite as gorgeous as a big bunch of perfumed, pastel, full-blown roses."

Her book, *Lavish Flowers*, followed and Peach ("only my bank manager calls me by my real name") was approached by various magazines

to do photographic styling and write articles. "All the time, I was doing landscaping on the side," she says. "The flower business kind of gave me a leg up into that world, as I knew what flowers suited climatically and grew well in particular areas. I still do styling work, wedding flowers and landscaping, so now it's kind of all rolled into one."

The house was called Roslyn when Peach bought it, so she says it was a no-brainer to plant roses. In fact, she's planted more than 100 bushes, most of them perfumed. "I like David Austin and other English roses," she explains. "Some of them do well and some don't. Then I came across Delbard, a French breed. They seem well suited to our conditions, which are more Mediterranean than English, and they do very well. I'm not a very interventionist gardener — I believe in good foundations. Plants are like children, you've got to train them properly. I feed and I mulch, but I

don't water much. I water heavily when I plant and then I let it be. If you water too often the roots grow close to the surface and the plant falls over at the first dry spell. If a plant doesn't thrive, I move it and if that doesn't work, I let nature take its course. I also don't like totally neat gardens. I think they're boring. And I feel much the same way about box hedges and iceberg roses."

Outstanding features of the garden now include the white section planted with white camellias, hydrangeas, lilies, blossom pear, dogwood, violets, fuchsias and hyacinths around the pond. A stunning old wisteria frames the garage that Peach has transformed into a studio, where she indulges her passion for painting ... currently oversized floral studies. There's an orchard as well, planted with all manner of citrus and low-chill stone fruit. It all adds up to a wonderful home for entertaining. "With verandas

"If a plant doesn't thrive, I move it and if that doesn't work, I let nature take its course. I don't like totally neat gardens."

on three sides, it doesn't matter if it rains," Peach says. "We always had open house on Boxing Day and we would drag the piano onto the veranda to keep everyone entertained."

Now that Peach's children are adults, it's time to move on. She's not sure what the future holds but, in the short term, she's off to Italy to refresh her connections (her family is from the north) and do some research for her next book.

"It's time to move on," she says. "I've invested a lot of myself in the house and garden, but now it's time for someone else to enjoy it. I'm not sure where I'll end up, but I'm sure I'll enjoy the journey."

Clockwise from above: As a florist, Peach was known for her white arrangments so her garden has a strong white element planted with roses, bulbs, lilies and annuals; Peach's whippets enjoy the garden their owner created; a magnificent old wisteria frames the house and the former garage Peach used as a studio to paint her outsized floral studies, many of which are inspired by the garden she has built.

COMING UP ROSES

Leonie and Terry Kearney have turned their garden in
the Samford Valley north of Brisbane into a celebration
of the cottage style, with a patchwork of roses,
perennials and tiny treasures propagated on-site.

On a rolling hilltop, 45 minutes north of Brisbane, an old chimney and single hoop pine pierced the landscape. Driving past, Leonie Kearney's attention was captured, as if beckoned for a makeover. She had no idea the property was for sale, when coincidence struck. "One day, the real estate agent drove us up a driveway and I kept hitting my husband Terry in the back seat of her car," she recalls. "I realised this was the same place and that I wanted it desperately, but it needed a lot of work." Up at the weather-beaten homestead, there were no gardens to speak of yet Leonie thought the two enormous Moreton Bay figs, two hoop pines, a big silky oak and a mango tree were indicators that establishing gardens would be relatively easy. Knowledge passed on from her grandmother

— "a proper English lady" — and gardening-savvy mother, plus many years of trial and error, compounded her profile as "The Rose Lady". If anyone could do it, Leonie could.

Using the outlook from every window of her near 90-year-old farmhouse as her pivotal point, Leonie began formulating garden layouts and designs. The windows framed her romantic visions, and she essentially built up a series of impressionist paintings in her head, each mirroring the informal style, the gentle flow, the focus on light, the watered-down hues and the thin brush strokes. "I like to look out on something beautiful wherever I am in the house, even if I'm making a bed," she says. "I love the old-fashioned species, not only the roses, and their wonderful perfumes. I have cupboards full of magazines for

Clockwise from this pic:
In designing the garden, Leonie created a series of impressionist paintings in her head and planted to mirror the informal style, the pale colours and thin brush strokes of the late-19th-century masters.

ideas but plant choices usually pop into my head when I'm working."

Husband Terry switches somewhere between Clark Kent and Superman. He digs holes, gathers rocks and logs with a bit of character and is chief lawnmower of the 15 acres (six hectares) of grass, which he claims is when he's his happiest. "I gaze around the property from the mower and I work out what else will keep my wife working," he jests. He mows one day, picks up the next, owns a butcher shop in town and is a regular country music DJ on a local FM radio station. Every six weeks he visits a friend to gather 40 to 50 bags of horse manure to spread on the garden, but reveals the real secret to Leonie's stunning success with plants is her conversations with them. "When you garden like us, you don't

have a life," he says. "Luckily most of the time our property looks like a rainbow."

Leonie admits they don't take holidays, but feels there's a sense she's living one. "I was a busy woman raising three boys," she says. "When they grew up I thought, 'how fortunate to wake up in the morning and be free to spend my day in the garden'." She doesn't like the heat, so prefers the cooler, southern side of the property where an incredibly long vista marked by a *Taxodium* cypress, stretches down to one of the dams. It's her top pick of all the views, her absolute favourite masterpiece in a garden that's full of them.

The Kearneys run some cattle to keep the grass down, but don't own a vegetable patch. "I grow food for the soul," Leonie says. "Wonderful farmers grow food for our bodies." With roughly

Clockwise from this pic: An existing hoop pine was a good indicator that the garden would thrive; Terry takes care of the hard yakka, mowing lawns, spreading manure and collecting interesting timbers for trellises and shade structures,

two acres of garden, the challenges are all "w" related — wind, water and weather. Water is pumped up from the dams on the property, for direct hosing. When Queensland's climate is cruel, particularly in the middle of the day, Leonie retreats indoors to her pots and focuses on propagating her roses. "I call my garden a country cottage garden, as it's flowery and pretty," she says. "I don't like clipping plants and I'm not a fan of hybridising, so I try to repeat patterns because I like a bit of order. I don't like the gardens looking too wild, but sometimes it's unavoidable because they're so big." Leonie runs a small nursery that is open every Saturday, where she sells old-fashioned roses, perennials and tiny treasures all propagated on site. Sometimes visitors contribute plants they think will suit her scheme.

Lizards tap on the door for food and families of blue wrens and finches flit about in hordes. In the early evening, the cricket chorus is deafening, and snakes hide near the quaint cottage on the dam, where the Kearneys' grandson often hangs out with friends. All manner of life is welcome. Yet, Leonie says her greatest achievement is all the lovely people she has the pleasure of sharing her garden with. "If I couldn't have a garden, I would fade away and become very despondent," she says. "I need to find a tiny patch of dirt to call my own, to keep my sanity."

A LABOUR OF LOVE

Beverley and Graham Thompson have devoted
three decades to transforming their Mount Wilson
garden from a back paddock to a parkland.

Clockwise from left:
Graham and Beverley Thompson have spent decades turning a paddock into a park with features including a waratah walk, crabapples and azalea, a lake from a dam and a fountain in the spruce alée.

W hen the Thompsons first visited the Mount Wilson property that was to become their home in the NSW Blue Mountains, their responses could not have been more opposite. Beverley saw a block that was bare except for marauding masses of blackberries, bracken, thornbush and native undergrowth. Graham saw only great potential to create the landscape of his dreams, a sentiment reminiscent of one of his garden heroes, 18th-century English landscape architect Lancelot "Capability" Brown.

Thirty years down the track, it's hard to imagine that the four-hectare showpiece garden inspired by the sweeping lawns and water features of English country parks was not always so. "Initially, Beverley thought I was out of my mind," Graham says. "At first, I probably was as it took us four years to clear the land and build the homestead. The only plants remaining were the towering gums and ferns, which are protected by conservation orders for being native to the surrounding Blue Mountains National Park."

During his long career in manufacturing, Graham had spent many weekends while travelling for work visiting both public and private

Words KIRSTY MCKENZIE Photography KEN BRASS

gardens in the UK, Europe and Asia. When he ventured into private consultancy, Beverley was able to accompany him and, together, they developed a clear vision of the type of garden they wanted to create. "From the outset, we knew we didn't want a fussy garden," Beverley says. "We are both fans of Gertrude Jekyll and Sir Edwin Lutyens, so we wanted to achieve expanses rather than vignettes."

The first of hundreds of rhododendrons and azaleas went in along the northern boundary in 1984. Feature trees including cherries, magnolias, dogwoods and maples were added to give filtered sunlight. The Thompsons then added an entry avenue of alternate plantings of tulip trees and *Liquidambars*. To soften the driveway, a curved garden bed of small to medium rhododendrons was established along with a canopy planting of spring flowering trees. Two natural rock gardens were created where the rocks were too numerous or large to move. In spring, masses of bulbs — mainly bluebells and daffodils — carpet the ground and add interest before the deciduous trees burst into leaf.

Each year brings new projects. On alternate years in the early 1990s, Beverley and Graham

Clockwise from left:
Spring is showtime at Bisley; the second lake is home to 13 carp; the Thompsons crowned the spruce allée with a fountain modelled on the one in the Raffles Hotel in Singapore; a quiet spot for enjoying the spring blossom display.

*The Thompsons also have a charming tradition
of celebrating significant anniversaries with additions
to the garden rather than conventional gifts.*

Clockwise from left:
Spring arrives in a blaze of colour; bronze by David Mackay Harrison against an azalea backdrop; a wisteria-covered way; a dam was turned into a lake; more spring profusion; rhododendron magic.

attended garden summer schools at Oxford University and came home fired with new enthusiasms and plans. A dam that was remnant of the days when the property supported cattle was turned into a lake, which was lined so it could become a haven for 200 rainbow trout. In the mid-'90s a second lake was constructed, now home to a family of 13 carp including the spectacular Red Riding Hood and 10-year-old Hoover, so named for his prodigious appetite.

The major project for 1995 was the planting of an Alberta spruce allée with a granite fountain — a replica of one in Singapore's Raffles Hotel — as its centrepiece. The entry to this section is via an Asian feature known as a moongate, which frames porthole vignettes of the garden. In spring, flowering cherries, wisteria and crabapples lend a profusion of pastels. In autumn, claret and golden ash, maples, golden elms and copper beech are ablaze with colour. Massed plantings of waratahs are thriving in their elevated position near the barn and in early spring they come alive with blooms ranging from creamy white to deep pink and scarlet.

The Thompsons also have a charming tradition of celebrating significant anniversaries with

additions to the garden rather than conventional gifts. Their ruby wedding anniversary was celebrated with a plantings of *Cornus rubra* dogwoods; the sundial was installed for Graham's 65th birthday; Blue Mountains' sculptor Tom Coley created *Motherhood* for a commanding position overlooking one of the expanses of lawn; and a bronze by David Mackay Harrison stands by the western side of the house.

Astonishingly, Beverley and Graham manage the garden with the help of a gardener for just four hours twice a week. They devote three days to its upkeep and Beverley says that mowing the lawns takes up two full days. Graham is in charge of the water supply, for which the property is entirely self-sufficient thanks to a combination of rainwater tanks and bore water.

"It will always be a work in progress," Beverley says. "There's always something that needs doing, but that's how we like it. The aim has been to create something that will continue to give pleasure long after we're gone."

The Thompsons open their garden twice a year — in spring and around Anzac Day — through the Open Gardens Scheme. For more information visit opengarden.org.au

Clockwise from left:
Tom Foley's Motherhood *was an anniversary purchase; a bridge over the creek leading to the lake; rhododendron splendour; azaleas lend a spash of colour; the garden is a haven for bird life; the splendid President Roosevelt rhododendron.*

A PHOENIX RISES

In the hot, dry summer of 2009, Penni Thompson nagged and nagged her husband, Tony, to move an irrigation pump down on to the river flats close to their home on the outskirts of Marysville. Eventually he complied and that pump probably saved their home and their lives when the devastating Black Saturday bushfires swept through.

For the people of Marysville in Victoria life will never be the same after the holocaust of Black Saturday, 2009. Penni and Tony Thompson count themselves lucky, however, as although most of their property was devastated by the inferno that raged across the district, they were able to save their home and none of their immediate family was injured or killed in the catastrophic event.

The road to recovery has not been without its challenges, but the people of Marysville are a determined lot. Penni and Tony are intent on restoring their property and its garden as a symbol of the indomitability of the human spirit and as a tribute to their friends and neighbours who lost loved ones and homes in the fires.

The Thompsons bought Maryton Park as a tree-change business in 2000. Trained as a baker and pastry chef, Tony decided after 17 years of 1am starts to look for a business that allowed him more sociable hours and hopefully a more balanced lifestyle. He and Penni found what they were looking for in Maryton Park, a 60-acre [24-hectare] farm with the picturesque Steavenson River on its boundary. The property was already established with six guest cottages dotted around the park-style garden that surrounds a water-lily-strewn lake. They served breakfast and dinner in a central restaurant, with a charming outdoor courtyard for the summer months, and gave the cottages and grounds a good spruce up. Gradually, word of the idyllic location spread and business grew as guests reported enthusiastically of the district's many outdoor attractions including bushwalks, cycling and cross-country skiing on nearby Lake Mountain. The Thompsons had just added three more self-catering cottages to their accommodation options when the Murrindindi

Mill fires ravaged through Marysville killing 34 locals and two tourists and destroying 90 per cent of the buildings.

"On the Friday before, it was hellishly hot, around 48 degrees, but there was no wind," Penni recalls. "I'd been hassling Tony to move the pump down to the river so we could start irrigating a crop. Eventually, my sister and brother-in-law and niece came to visit and, while we had the extra hands, they moved it down to the dam. On the Saturday afternoon, we could see the smoke coming from the north-west, but it wasn't until late in the afternoon that we realised the fire was coming from behind as well. By the time we realised what was happening, we were surrounded and there was no way we could leave."

Words KIRSTY MCKENZIE Photography DARYL HULL & KEN BRASS

While Penni, her sister, niece and four guests took refuge in the house, lining the doors and windows with wet towels, Tony, their chef, Stan, and brother-in-law Graham set up the pump and dropped the irrigation pipes in the lake so they could direct the water onto the house and restaurant. For four hours solid, they waged war against the devastating onslaught, putting out spot fire after spot fire. By the time they took their first breather, at around 11pm, they were surrounded by a scene of utter devastation. Through the smoke and embers, they could see that the garden was in cinders, a hayshed was smouldering, a row of blackwood trees that lined the driveway was gone and only one of 17 gums that encircled the lake was left standing.

"At that stage, I didn't even know that the town had gone," Tony says. "In the immediate aftermath, there was just shock, but gradually we pulled ourselves together and started on the recovery effort. We were a strong community before this happened, but I would say that we are an even stronger one now. Everyone looks out for everyone else."

With lives, homes and businesses destroyed, many Marysville residents had no option but to move away. The Thompsons threw themselves into the rebuilding program and Tony assumed the role of chairperson of the Community Recovery Committee, responsible for rebuilding, liaising with government agencies and charity relief funds, and keeping a weather eye on the mental health issues members of the community inevitably faced. Five years down the track, Marysville is once again open for business and the town's population, which at the time of the fire numbered somewhere between 430 and 450, is now around 250. Visitor beds, which once numbered around 2500, are gradually being restored and there are currently about 800 available. Business is coming back to town and there's a new school, new police station, general store and visitor centre, which contains a comprehensive display chronicling the fires, their aftermath and the rebuilding effort.

"We have received an astonishing amount of support," Tony says. "People from all over Australia opened their hearts and their wallets and contributed to the relief effort. The public bushfire appeal generated more than $390 million, which is an extraordinary figure, even when it was divided across all the affected areas."

The memory of Black Saturday is, however, omnipresent. There's undergrowth returning in the forests that were denuded by the fires, but the bare trunks still stand on the hillsides resembling

Clockwise from above:
Rhododendrons and roses frame an outdoor setting; irises beside the lake; visiting parrots give their seal of approval to the garden; resident chooks add to the garden's charm.

Daryl has lent his passion for gardening to Penni's effort. Now roses, blossoms, bulbs and rhododendrons add their colour to the sprawling grounds.

a northern-European winter scene, even in the height of spring. With the rebuilding programs, gardens are slowly being restored. Many are helped by a program called Plant Aid, which the Thompsons ran from their back paddock. "People from all over donated plants to help the community rebuild," Penni explains. "Individuals donated cuttings and seedlings in pots, nurseries sent truckloads of trees. One company from South Australia sent a trailer full of orchard trees. We stored them at our place and coordinated the redistribution. For the first 12 months after the fire, people just survived. But now a sense of normality is returning and people are rebuilding."

Penni adds that throwing themselves into the recovery program has been a good way of dealing with survivor guilt. "It's good to keep busy," she says. "At one stage. Tony was putting in about 60 volunteer hours a week. You have to keep moving. I couldn't wear jewellery for about two years after the fire because it just didn't seem right when so many others had lost everything."

In their "spare" time, the Thompsons have gradually rebuilt their garden to the showpiece it once was. Given the devastation, they had little choice but to cut the garden back to nothing and start again. In this endeavour, they have been helped by another Marysville fire survivor, Daryl Hull, whose own story of surviving the fire by taking refuge in the town's lake went viral when he posted video footage of the aftermath on the internet. Daryl has been living in one of the Thompsons' cabins and has lent his passion for gardening to Penni's effort. Now roses, blossoms, bulbs and rhododendrons add their colour to the sprawling grounds, and locals once more come to Maryton Park to enjoy beer and platter afternoons and evenings in the courtyard on weekends.

"We tried reopening the restaurant, but it was just too early," Tony says. "So we've opted for a more low-key alternative and it seems to be working. Gradually, events are returning to town. We have the Marysville Really Long Lunch in March, Australia's only sparkling wine festival in October, the Marysville Marathon in November and lots of cycling events come through town during the year. We have to constantly keep working to make sure that when people do visit, they have a reason to want to return. It's not an easy task, but I'm confident that having survived this far, we will eventually get there."

For more information on Maryton Park accommodation, visit marytonpark.com.au

Clockwise from above:
Penni says she always wanted a picket fence, but the fires were an extreme way to go about getting one; blossom trees are a spring highlight; the lake saved Maryton Park as well as the Thompsons' and their guests' lives.

VALLEY GIRL

Cherie Hausler divides her time between her South
Australian base, her Sydney apartment and her business
interests in Bangkok. But the Barossa Valley is her
home and it's there that she lives the bucolic dream and
recharges her apparently inexhaustible batteries.

Words KIRSTY McKENZIE Photography SUE STUBBS

I n Cherie Hausler's early-childhood recollections, her father always drove looking out the side window with occasional glances at the road. As a Barossa Valley vineyard manager he always had one eye on the vines as they progressed through the seasons. "Grapes were our life," she says. "I still love that sensation of driving between the rows of vines. It's like driving through a sea of green, a truly amazing experience and one that doubtless influenced my awareness of our natural environment."

Although not aware of the significance of the wine industry at the time, Cherie developed an appreciation of the processes almost by osmosis, as her mother also worked in wine sales. She recalls practising her gymnastic skills by "walking the plank" on big, open concrete fermenters, the buzz of the winery at vintage time and growing up surrounded by families with iconic Barossa surnames. Little wonder then that her life has always been loosely involved with the food and wine industry and that, once again, Cherie and her husband, Damien Feuerherdt, who is also

> ## "I still love that sensation of driving between the rows of vines. It's like driving through a sea of green, a truly amazing experience."

Barossa born and bred, find themselves living in a farmhouse on 10 acres (four hectares) on Koonunga Hill. "We drifted away for a while," she says. "But it was very easy to come back."

Cherie and Damien met as students at Nuriootpa High, at the age of 14, and have been together ever since. They went to Melbourne and Sydney basically to work hard to raise money to travel, then headed off for London as soon as they could and spent two years working and travelling all over the UK and Europe. On the way home, they met up with Cherie's brother, Darren, in Bangkok and in the way life has of taking unpredictable turns, Cherie and Darren ended up as co-owners of Eat Me, a restaurant just off Convent Road. While Darren is now a Bangkok resident, Cherie is a regular visitor. She consults

"We were surrounded by bare paddock with cattle pretty much grazing up to the windows. The first job was to put a fence around it, get rid of decades of junk and make a garden."

on the menu and spends several weeks at a time in the kitchen as the new dishes are introduced.

In her other lives, Cherie has worked as a lifestyle- and music-TV presenter, as a nanny, swimming teacher and in restaurants. Since returning to the Valley seven years ago, she has been a consulting PR to Barossa food identity Maggie Beer, and she has a sideline as a food and travel stylist and writer. She's also established the Scullery Made label, which blends fine-quality leaf tea with Barossa fruits and herbs and sells to specialty food stores, online and at the Barossa Farmers Markets, held in Vintners Sheds in Angaston, every Saturday morning. Horticulturalist turned musician Damien is also a budding sourdough baker and turns out breads, muffins and gluten-free, organic-baked goodies for sale at the markets.

Cherie adds that she and Damien are not the "kind of people who have proper jobs". "If you want to live in inner-city Sydney or Melbourne you have to have a proper job to service the

mortgage," she says. "So, because we couldn't be that committed to a mortgage, we decided to buy in the Barossa and rent a bolthole in Surry Hills [Sydney] for the occasional city fix. But the Valley is very definitely home."

The original four-room bluestone cottage was built in 1840 as the residence of Father Michael Ryan, priest of the parish of St John's. A shearing shed, which is now an art space and music room, and extensions that included the large room, which is now the master bedroom, were later additions. By the time Cherie and Damien arrived, however, the house was in serious disrepair and known locally as "the ruin".

"We were surrounded by bare paddock with cattle pretty much grazing up to the windows," Cherie recalls. "The first job was to put a fence around it, get rid of decades of junk and make a garden. Then we fixed up the chook shed and planted some vegies."

Meanwhile, the house itself required serious attention and Cherie and Damien rolled up

Clockwise from above: *Cherie and Damien started the renovation of their property with the garden; chooks were an early priority; the original four-* *room bluestone cottage was built as a parish priest's residence in 1840; Cherie harvests lavender in the garden, which is now the farmhouse's crowning glory.*

"Season by season we've built up the beds with compost, stable manure and mulch. It probably takes about half an hour a day now that it's established, but I see that as good respite from the computer."

their sleeves to do most of the "deconstruction" work before builders, plumbers and electricians could come in to replace the tongue-and-groove matchboard, install new recycled cabinetry and ceilings and reconnect the services.

"We pulled up the carpet to discover colonies of earwigs and millipedes," Cherie says. "We sandblasted off layers and layers of paint to reveal the stunning bluestone underneath. Even the repointers commented on the quality of the stonework. We repainted throughout but we didn't want anything to be too fancy. Ours is a 'boots-on' house; it's meant to be lived in. The original cement floor is polished by people walking on it for more than 170 years and we like it that way. You want to be able to see the house's story and now it's our story as well."

Meanwhile, Cherie and Damien are well on the way to producing much of their own food with hours in the garden rewarding them with sweet corn, tomatoes, cucumber, zucchini, eggplant, herbs, squash, strawberries, lettuce, beetroot and pumpkin at the time of *Australian Country*'s visit. Everything is run on organic

principles with no chemicals and lots of mulch taking care of weeds.

"There was no arable soil when we arrived seven years ago," Cherie recalls. "So season by season, we've built up the beds with compost, stable manure and mulch. It probably takes about half an hour a day now that it's established, but I see that as good respite from the computer."

Their chickens keep them in eggs, they have a flock of Indian runner ducks to keep the snails and earwigs at bay and there have been no snakes near the house since they added geese.

"They are fantastic guard dogs," Cherie says. "They always let us know when someone is coming. They also look great on the landscape. Our objective is to live as well and sustainably as possible. On any given day being able to grow our own food, collect eggs and honey, watch sunsets, see the seasons change, ride horses, stargaze or tidy up another bit of the property is what makes it home. Animals die of old age at our place — and that's what I call success."

For more information on Scullery Made teas, visit scullerymade.org.

Clockwise from above: There was no arable soil when Cherie and Damien bought their Barossa Valley property; lavender thrives both in pots and in the ground; the farmhouse and garden sits on 10 acres (four hectares) on top of Koonunga Hill and enjoys sweeping views of the surrounding pastoral land.

MAD ABOUT
FLOWERS

An urban existence came to an abrupt halt when Bede and Mary Gibson moved to, and later purchased, their daughter's property, in Victoria's Castlemaine district.

Words MERYL HANCOCK Photography KIM SELBY

Just over an hour north of Melbourne, near Sutton Grange, there's a ridge overlooking the valley all the way to the Great Dividing Range. It's an area marked by meteorite-like granite boulders, a combination of hilly and rocky country, perfect for grazing and perfect for growing "just about anything", according to Mary Gibson. When the Gibsons' daughter bought Mica Grange more than nine years ago, it came with a 14-year-old house and a 150-year-old yellow box gum. The rest was a blank canvas. The family toiled together to establish the garden, utilising the trees showered on their daughter as wedding presents. Planting limitations were few, given vegetables and citrus fruits thrive in the frost-free climate, and the property's spring-fed dams also assist with its self-sufficiency.

Clockwise from above:
Mary has always been mad about flowers; she and Bede moved from Queensland to take over the property; brides love the settings.

There's no doubting her design background and impeccable style, her subtle choice of palette and attention to detail. Even the vegie patch is immaculately boxed.

When their daughter moved to Melbourne, Bede happily shelved his Sydney office job and Mary farewelled her fashion design business to take on the 40 hectares of paradise with no regrets. Mary admits she has always been mad about flowers, working in floristry when she was younger, and creating many wedding bouquets over the years. She relished the opportunity to expand on the gardens they initially created with their daughter. There's no doubting her design background and impeccable style, her subtle choice of palette and attention to detail. Even the vegetable patch is immaculately boxed up and recycled tubs and quaint containers burst with healthy produce. Her planting schemes are based on the right balance between colour and perfume, all formed in her head — that's a lot of templates for the 360-degree loop of gardens around the house.

"My flowers are mainly English as I don't believe you get the beautiful flowers unless you specialise in those varieties," she says. However, it still is an Australian garden. With more than 220 different types of roses dotted around, there's a sense of

Clockwise from this pic:
Even the vegie garden is immaculately boxed; Mary prefers English flowers; vegetables are Bede's domain; stunning blooms are a feature in the garden.

Behind every amazing gardener is a supportive mower and hole digger, an area in which Bede excels.

nostalgia and old-fashioned whimsy. The long and winding driveway lined with elms adds a hint of drama, and the wreaths Mary makes from poppy heads and vines make for eye-catching artworks.

"The sensational weather and the changing views are such a highlight," she says. "Every day is a new day. The back room is designed as a picture-book room — it has 15 windows that all look onto a different view." Recently a studio mimicking this design has been added, with the purpose of hosting artist workshops on a monthly basis. "It's a lovely atmosphere in there and people enjoy being able to paint, walk out and sit on the garden benches to enjoy the view," Mary adds. "We're also home to fantastic lizards, which people are fascinated with. They live in the boulders and you can spot five to 10 at a time."

Naturally, behind every amazing gardener is a supportive mower and hole digger, an area in which Bede excels. "I love the physicality," he says. "I worked in an office all my life and I feel so lucky to be out in the open in such a lovely spot, away from the corporate world. I like the peace and tranquillity and I don't miss the social intensity. We've got a great social group here but we can enjoy our surroundings without the hassle of feeling we have to catch up with people all the time."

Bede's favourite garden is the Australian

Clockwise from above:
As a former florist, Mary loves roses; a corrugated-iron cow grazes in the garden; meteorite-like granite boulders punctuate the rolling landscape of Victoria's Goldfields region.

shrubbery and he admits loving waking up to beautiful sunrises. There is protection from the wintry winds, due to the house facing north. For him, the best time of day is the evening, when he can relax with a glass of wine, and autumn is his pick of the seasons. "The weather is so perfect and the colours are glorious," he says. "The major work is in the spring time, then there's constant watering in summer, but in autumn, I enjoy not having to mow the lawn so often."

Last year, Mica Grange was invited to feature in the Australian Open Garden Scheme, as a result of participating in the Castlemaine Garden Festival ... an awestruck visitor dobbed them in. On open days, Bede and Mary serve morning and afternoon teas, incorporating freshly plucked produce into home-made cakes and preserves. "I feel very content and very privileged and I think the visitors feel the same," Mary says. "We've hosted a few weddings and banquets, which have been very successful as there's a huge shortage of smaller venues."

After such a mammoth investment of time and energy, the future looks bright. The Gibsons are now intent on sharing their slice of heaven with the public. Organised garden tours and garden openings are regular calendar entries, and each autumn, they run a sculpture exhibition that provides local artists with an opportunity to display their artworks in the most breathtaking surroundings. **Visit micagrange.com**

LESS IS MORE

A passion for plants and a belief in the supremacy of simplicity are the guiding forces behind this Southern Highlands garden.

For a garden with such a defined elegance, it seems a little incongruous to learn that Yarrawa, in the New South Wales Southern Highlands, was designed on the back of a lawnmower. But that is exactly how Bruce Rosenberg explains the evolution of his garden on the edge of the village of Burrawang, included in Holly Kerr Forsyth's 2009 book, *Gardens of Eden*.

"There was no grand plan," Bruce says. "I wanted it to be easy to mow and I wanted it to flow, to take advantage of the gentle slopes and the borrowed landscape of the neighbouring rolling hills and dairy farms."

Those ambitions have certainly been achieved in this lush five-acre (two-hectare) garden, which was a bare paddock when Bruce purchased the block in the early 1990s. His first job was an ambitious planting of 900 tubestocks along the western boundary of the property, with a view to recreating the dense rainforest that once covered the area and for the plants to act as a windbreak.

"I was thrilled to have them all planted but, unfortunately, despite a traditional annual rainfall of 1500mm, the area fell into terrible drought and I lost the lot," Bruce says matter of factly. "I had to start again but, the second time, I also planted native trees to provide some initial protection for the small tubestocks.

It is through that thick, rough canopy that visitors enter the property down a gravel drive

Words JAQUI CAMERON Photography SUE STUBBS

Above: *A pyramid made from rocks excavated for the pond adds a focal point.*
Opposite: *The house is low-profile to allow maximum appreciation of the Edna Walling-style garden.*

that holds no hint of the glorious views beyond. "I love the principles of Edna Walling garden design and that, in turn, strongly influenced the design of my home," Bruce says. "It sits low in the landscape but still provides a lovely outlook over the garden, which embraces the Walling concept of masses and voids."

Serpentine hedges of *Escallonia bifida*, *Escallonia iveyi* and *Viburnum odoratissimum* boundary distinct areas of the garden that are too subtle to be classified as formal rooms. These, together with large sweeping garden beds strategically spread around the garden, unconsciously draw visitors along undefined pathways, leaving dewy footprints in the lawn.

"It is quite a simple design really because it actually contains quite a limited variety of plants," Bruce says. "I prefer to use bulk plantings of single species and completely cover every inch of the garden beds. My belief is that less is more."

The impact of that design is showcased with simple elegance along one side of the house where a mass of *Teucrium, Cotoneaster* (*horizontalis* and *dammeri*), *Buxus* (English box) and *Erigeron* (an Edna Walling favourite) is softly pruned to echo the line of the rolling hills of the Southern Highlands in the distance.

Another view from the house is guided up a gently sloping hill by parallel rows of western red cedars (*Thuja plicata*), standing like burly

Clockwise from opposite: Subtle pruning mimics the rolling hills beyond; Bruce has planted more varieties of hydrangea than he can remember; simplicity is the ultimate sophistication in the garden.

"I prefer to use bulk plantings of single species and completely cover every inch of the garden beds. My belief is that less is more."

soldiers in formation, with each pair clipped to appear slightly smaller as they march away from the house and up the slope, thus exaggerating the perspective. This strikingly formal avenue is punctuated at its end by a stone pyramid, made from rocks excavated to create the large pond that sits neatly below the house. Often shrouded in mist, the pond serves as a glistening mirror reflecting the ever-changing cloud formations that so regularly fill the sky and a quirky pair of shearwaters made from old hand shears.

"I like to think of this as a 'stroll garden'," Bruce says, "It entices you to wander so I have railway sleeper benches tucked away where I can sit, protected from the sun or wind under the shade

of a Chinese or Japanese elm, and enjoy the space."

Also tucked in among the shrubs is a wonderful selection of understated sculptures, each with a story to tell. A favourite is an evocative stainless-steel sculpture of Lysistrata, a mythical figure who is said to have led Athenian women on a sex strike to force their husbands to vote for peace. She stands delicately beneath the silvery white branches of a paper birch tree.

"I did quite honestly consider and design much of this garden while I was sitting on the lawnmower," Bruce says. "I wanted it to be easy to mow and relatively low maintenance, which is why many of my trees are planted within the garden beds."

Clockwise from opposite: Bruce likes to think of his creation as a stroll garden to be appreciated from benches made from railway sleepers dotted throughout and with lawns urging exploration of the many flowering plants.

"I did quite honestly consider and design much of this garden while I was sitting on the lawnmower. I wanted it to be easy to mow and relatively low maintenance."

"Those trees not planted in beds, including the ornamental pears (*Pyrus*), Trident and Norway maples (*Acer buergerianum* and *Acer platanoides*) and Japanese elm (*Zelkova serrata*), are planted in copses and I mow beneath them only sporadically and roughly," Bruce says. "I work often in the garden and am lucky to have some help, but I never wanted to become a slave to it. I agree with Edna Walling when she said, 'don't feel you have to do something every day. There will always be leaves on the ground and masses and voids.'"

When showing visitors around his garden, Bruce usually saves his most favoured area until last. Beneath a canopy of deciduous cherry trees (*Prunus* 'Mt Fuji') is a walkway almost hidden by the rich foliage of a large collection of hydrangeas. "I think the hydrangea is a very rewarding plant because it gives colour and interest from late spring through to late summer," Bruce says. His collection is extensive with more varieties than even he can now remember, but the result is a dense grove with a delicate fragrance that envelopes you as you weave along the path.

Bruce describes his approach to the garden as relaxed. A master of understatement, Yarrawa has been created as a result of a grand passion rather than a grand vision but it is a living testament to the Leonardo da Vinci quote: "simplicity is the ultimate sophistication".

Clockwise from opposite: A large pond sits neatly below the house; sculptures, including these shearwaters made from hand shears are a feature of the garden; Jeremy says he designed the garden while riding on the lawnmower.

"I agree with Edna Walling when she said, 'don't feel you have to do something every day. There will always be leaves on the ground and masses and voids.'"

GIVERNY IMPRESSIONS

A water-lily-studded pond and a Monet-inspired bridge are just the beginnings of an expansive garden in central Victoria.

The village of Toolangi is named for an Aboriginal word meaning tall trees, and there are both natives and exotics in abundance at Giverny Estate, a restful cool-climate garden on the outskirts of town.

When Lorraine Hunter and Fred Swainston bought the property in 2003, they inherited a five-acre (two-hectare) kiwi fruit orchard and a two-and-a-half acre garden with sweeping lawns framed by the towering mountain ashes that originally attracted timber-getters to the district, as well as Norwegian and Douglas firs, numerous spruces and a massive American redwood.

"I was accustomed to gardening in Templestowe, which was real mattock and pick territory," Lorraine explains. "By comparison, this garden is just a dream. Everything grows so well, there's good soil and lots of rain. It's just a joy to work in."

Lorraine has spent countless hours refining and rearranging the garden, which, in spring, is ablaze with colour with weeping maples, rhododendrons, azaleas, clematis, crabapples, flag irises, roses and tulips, all competing for attention. Lorraine is fond of garden rooms themed around colours

Below: Giverny's spring-fed pond drains into the nearby Yea River and serves as bushfire protection as well as a permanent supply of water for the garden.
Opposite: It wouldn't be Giverny without a bridge.

Words KIRSTY MCKENZIE Photography KEN BRASS

and has a yellow room with Toolangi Gold mollis azaleas, yellow daphnes and pansies, a blue room with azaleas, bluebells, flag irises and four different penstemons. Red and white, and blue and pink sections are in developmental stages. The vegetable garden is a constant as is the chicken run, home to a family of Faverolles.

Although Lorraine knew little about growing kiwi fruit when she bought the property, she assumed her extensive gardening experience would see her through. Her instincts were right and the entire 10- to 12-tonne crop is now made into wine and cider, which is sold at farmers' markets in Kinglake and the Yarra Valley. "The only secret is the quality of the fruit," she explains. "Supermarket kiwis would typically have a baumé [sugar] count of six to seven. But we don't harvest until they are at 10, which means our fruit is full of flavour."

Giverny's spring-fed lily pond drains into the nearby Yea River and is covered in blooms

from early November until Christmas. For the rest of the year it's a magnet for birdlife, swamp wallabies, water rats and the odd platypus and has a resident population of Australian bass. It's also home to the *Pomaderris vacciniifolia*, which is endemic to the region. Ironically, the increased proliferation of this rare plant is one of the few good news stories to come out of the Black Saturday bushfires of 2009.

"There was great consternation that the fires might have destroyed a number of rare plants," Lorraine says. "But, in fact, the opposite was the case as some plants have sprung back stronger than ever."

Miraculously, the village of Toolangi and Giverny Estate escaped the wrath of the fires, which claimed two lives and destroyed 18 homes in the locality as well as razing significant sections of the Toolangi State Forest.

"We were surrounded by fire for weeks,"

Lorraine recalls. "At the end, we were like a little green hole in a doughnut of blackened devastation. Fred's been in the County Fire Authority for a long time and, with the pond, we were in a good position to fight the fires. For most of the year, I use the fire pump to water the garden, but it's very comforting to know we are well protected if and when we have to face a similar ordeal."

With the vegie garden, flower beds and extensive lawns on top of the kiwi orchard to maintain, it's hardly surprising Lorraine says she sometimes goes out in the morning to feed the chooks and doesn't get back inside until sundown. "It's an all-consuming passion," she admits. "But it gives such pleasure that I never for a moment wonder if it's worth the effort."

Giverny Estate garden is open through Open Gardens Australia in October. For more information visit opengarden.org.au

Clockwise from this pic:
The property is open to the public in October; tulips are part of the spring display; Lorraine surveys a decade's hard work from the lily pond; azaleas in front of the kiwi fruit orchard; the garden is planted according to colour.

· OSERIAN ·

A BROAD CANVAS

Artist Jeremy Goodman's detailed watercolours capture a moment in time as a lasting record for passionate gardeners.

A beautiful garden can be described as a work of art and Crookwell artist Jeremy Goodman has taken that concept quite literally, creating incredibly detailed watercolour paintings of garden designs that are themselves works of art.

"My paintings reflect the grand visions of garden owners," Jeremy explains. "I showcase the overall layout together with a scale and colour palette that gives a sense of depth to the artwork. It's a very honest interpretation of the garden."

While candidly admitting he is himself not an avid gardener, Jeremy has always been inspired by the careful thought, consideration and attention people lavish on their gardens. "I think you can really see the love that goes into a beautiful garden," he says. Jeremy discovered his talent almost by chance. Leaning against the gardening section

Words JAQUI CAMERON Photography LOUISE JENSEN

Above: Jeremy Goodman captures a moment in time in a garden as a record of the owners' hard work.
Opposite: It took Jeremy several days to step out and record the layout of the garden at Southdown in the NSW Southern Highlands.

in the Goulburn public library he started flicking
through a book on Edna Walling garden design
while waiting to use the photocopier.

"It was full of amazingly evocative watercolour
pictures of her gardens," he recalls. "It was long
before computers so the paintings were Edna's
way of transferring her garden vision onto paper
for clients." Having originally trained as a graphic
artist, Jeremy was inspired to try his own hand at
this traditional approach to capturing landscape
designs, which nowadays are generated using
computer programs and high-spec printers.

"I am as low-tech as you can get," Jeremy
says with a hint of pride. "The length of my pace
is exactly one metre so I visit a garden with
my board, pencil and a piece of graph paper
and simply step out the distances between
trees, garden beds and features. I do look a bit
funny striding around the garden but, while I'm
measuring, I'm also sketching."

For a six-acre (two-and-a-half-hectare) garden,
such as Southdown in the NSW Southern
Highlands, the process of stepping out the layout
took a couple of days with hundreds of trees each
marked out on the plan.

"It was a fantastic challenge because of the
sheer size of the garden," Jeremy says. "Within the
space there are large garden beds as well as nine
smaller garden rooms with very individual design
stories and a huge variety of trees and hedging."

The final watercolour is awash with a soft
palette of green together with delicate pencil
sketches of the steps, water features and the

winding pathways leading to numerous garden
cottages; all drawn freehand without the use
of even a ruler. For garden owner Margaret
Chadwick the finished artwork was the perfect
way to showcase her 16 years of hard work.

"Jeremy's painting illustrates the evolution of
the garden with the traditional 1850s' layout of the
homestead garden and the more formal design
inspirations I have laid out over the past 13 years
in what was originally a bare pony paddock,"
Margaret says. "It tells the very personal story of
our garden and not only is it beautiful, it has also
proved very practical as a garden map for visitors
staying in our guest accommodation cottages."

Indeed, Jeremy meticulously replicates the
ridgeline of homesteads and outbuildings in
his designs and for Southdown, he included a
sketch of the front entrance and sign, all with the

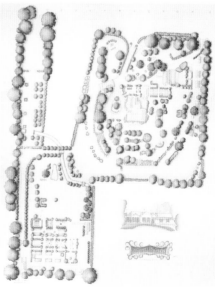

shadows carefully falling true to the northerly
aspect. His efforts have seen him commissioned
to travel across the country to create original
artworks of gardens large and small.

"I did a smaller Italian-inspired garden recently
with spectacular stonework and a water feature
so I included a series of smaller illustrations as well
as the overall layout," Jeremy says. "The owner also
wanted all the plants to be shown in flowers at
the one time. I can almost defy the seasons in my
illustrations if that is what the client wants."

Quirky requests are common with Jeremy
often asked to include a pet, a swing or some
other specific feature in the painting which has
significance for the family.

"A wonderful garden is much more than a
collection of plants and trees," he says. "It will
also hold very special and personal memories
of family and friends. The detail may be tiny and
appear insignificant in the overall painting but it's
those little things which bring the artwork to life
and give it soul."

The illustrations also reflect a moment in time
as Jeremy says that many of his clients guiltily
admit to making changes in their garden even
before his work is completed, a process that
usually takes several weeks.

"Gardeners talk of the joy of working with their
hands to create something beautiful and that's
how I feel about my paintings," he says. "I feel
honoured to be invited into the gardens and
entrusted to bring them to life on paper."
jeremysgardenportraits.com

Clockwise from above:
Jeremy includes details
such as sculpture in his
illustrations; he recorded
hundreds of trees and
their placement in the
Southdown work; the house
is also included in Jeremy's
detailed watercolours.

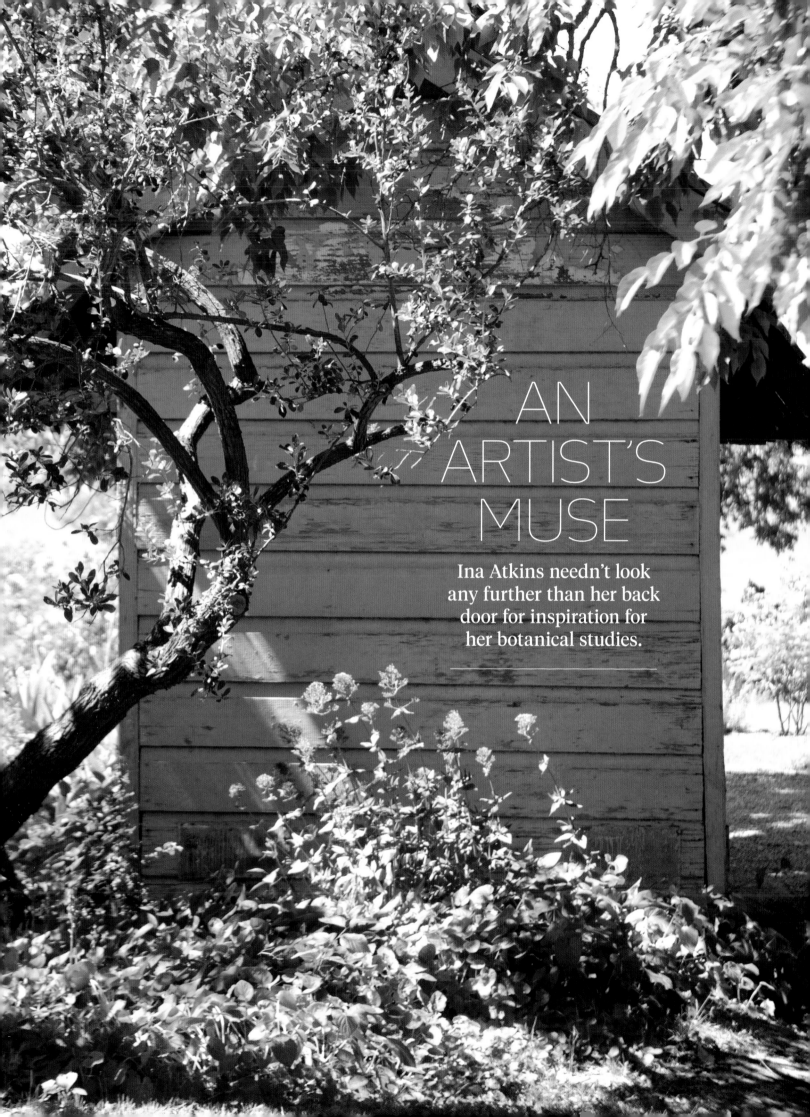

AN ARTIST'S MUSE

Ina Atkins needn't look any further than her back door for inspiration for her botanical studies.

Solitude affects people in various ways. Some retreat and become more insular, while others utilise such an environment to tap into previously unexplored passions. The latter is what Ina Atkins did.

She made the move from the hustle and bustle of Sydney to a remote, sprawling property located in the New South Wales Southern Tablelands. The contrast could not have been sharper.

"When I first moved here, I was blinded by the romance of living on this beautiful property with the man I loved," Ina says. "I had always adored the garden, but I'd come from the city where people don't really have much space for a proper garden. I embraced the chance to tend enormous trees and grow my own vegetables and now all I do is work!"

But Ina's obvious love of the garden is not just limited to her green thumbs. She is an accomplished botanical artist with many prizes under her belt. "When I lived in Sydney, I taught folk art," Ina recalls. "But when I moved to the country, there wasn't the same demand for it, so I turned to painting more traditional landscapes in watercolour."

Ina's studio is nestled in her garden, by the vegie patch. It's an old shed that is separate from the main house and it is full of complete and incomplete paintings. The dusty windows are lined with tubes, pots and brushes, while the benches are strewn with pencils, sketches and books. It's the place where Ina goes whenever she is not weeding her beloved garden, cooking

Words SIOBHAN O'BRIEN Photography SUE STUBBS

Clockwise from opposite: The main homestead dates from 1846; Ina's studio is in a garden shed; a rose against one of the outbuildings.

in her kitchen or decorating her house with exotic botanical finds that she collects from the land around her.

But the house that Ina shares with her husband, Harry, is nothing run-of-the-mill. Pomeroy station, as it has long been known, was established as a vast country estate by Thomas Woore in 1839. Woore was both an engineer and a naval officer, and was prominent in early colonial society. Among other accomplishments, he was instrumental in the development of the Warragamba Dam and Sydney's water supply. In 1846, he also privately funded a survey for the location of the southern railway line to Goulburn in an effort to encourage its eventual construction.

The main house, where Ina and Harry now live, was constructed by Woore in the early 1840s. It's a substantial Gothic-style stone homestead with lofty ceilings, six bedrooms and three living areas. It features a large entry hall with self-contained servants' quarters to the right, and ample guest bedrooms upstairs. The kitchen and main living

zones are towards the left and rear of the property.

"We ran it as a guest house for a while, but the work got too much for us," Ina says. "Now, we just enjoy having our family and friends come and stay. The house is always full of people. We're always busy and entertaining."

The original property also features other buildings constructed around the same time as the main house: stone cottage farm buildings, a large shearing shed, a stone flour mill and water wheel on the river. The mill ruins still stand today. When Woore died in 1898, the property was sold to the Dalglish family, before it was later divided among extended family members in the 1960s. When the portion that features the main house became available about 30 years ago, Harry Atkins snapped it up.

By the time Ina arrived some years later, the landscape was in desperate need of attention. She set to work and has now transformed it into an impressive garden that enjoys four seasons. As a result of her hard work, the garden now

features a mixture of trees and plants that are both old and new.

"I'd like to think I've transformed the grounds," Ina says. "I tackled the rose garden at the front of the house first and brought it back to life. Then I worked on the beds around the house and next to the vegie patch. The large celtis tree at the front of the house is always a talking point. It is a very old tree and I have been told it is the mother to all other such trees in Australia."

Ina's garden also features an assortment of golden elms, poplars and wisterias. In spring the grounds are dotted with tulips, daffodils, snowbells and other bulbs. The vegetable garden produces a variety of vegetables, berries and herbs — strawberries, raspberries and rhubarb are often on Ina's menu and fresh snowpeas, sugarsnaps and tomatoes often fill the larder.

"One of the best things that I grow in the garden is Russian garlic," Ina says. "It's so sweet and not easy to buy. Once my guests try it, they always want more! It's the same with how they feel when they've been here. They always want to come back."

Clockwise from above:
Ina doesn't have to look beyond her front door for floral inspiration for her watercolours; a blue note for the studio; Harry takes a break; the garden features both old and new plants.

BY A BILLABONG

In Phillip Johnson's ideal world, all gardens and landscapes would be designed, if not actually built, before work starts on the house.

Words KIRSTY McKENZIE Photography KEN BRASS

Well, as a multi-award-winning landscape designer, he would say the garden should be designed first, wouldn't he? But, take a stroll around Phillip's own garden in Victoria's Dandenong Ranges and you can't help but see his point of view. As the recipient of many accolades from Melbourne International Flower & Garden Shows (MIFGS), and winner of the 2013 Best in Show award at the Chelsea Flower Show, Phillip says it's time we stopped thinking of landscape as the "green lipstick" applied as an afterthought to pretty up a property.

In fact, the contemporary sustainable garden has many more important roles to play, as it can shade or protect a house from the elements, expose it when sunshine and natural light are required, capture and store rainwater for the household's needs and even save the dwelling from the bushfires that are a constant threat in the area.

Phillip has been refining his notion of a sustainable Australian landscape since he planted his first vegie patch in his parents' Glen Waverly backyard as a child. He never contemplated any other career than landscaping, has been running his business for more than 20 years and has built more than 300 gardens, all but a handful of them with a billabong as its central feature.

Unfortunately, when Phillip came to build his own home in the bush at Olinda 10 years ago, a combination of available resources and timing meant the house had to come first. Given his passion for the natural environment, its orientation and passive solar design were of paramount importance. Double glazing and top-grade insulation were used throughout and materials were chosen for durability and low maintenance. Timbers were "reclaimed" from building demolition sites or, in the case of one massive mountain ash, milled after the tree had to be felled in the course of clearing the building site.

While Phillip acknowledges the input of many family members and friends in the design and construction of the house, he nominates a former teacher and furniture designer Brendan Stamp as the inspired creator of many of the house's internal features, including a display unit on the wall and a table with a splendid spiral base. Phil's brother, Miles, a renowned glass artist, has coloured in the details with numerous pieces displayed around the house. Miles also made a fabulous fibre-optic light sculpture that dominates the open-plan living area, a prototype for a feature installation that drew much attention at one of Phillip's MIFGS display gardens.

A wood-fired heater is central to the heating of the house as it powers a hydronic system, which is piped through the whole house and includes underfloor heating. The circulation pump runs off solar and batteries, meaning it will function in the event of a power blackout. Two SmartBurn block inserts improve the efficiency of the stove, reduce the amount of fuel needed to run it, cut down on smoke emissions and reduce soot and sap on the roof, ensuring cleaner water entering the rainwater tanks.

The house is independent of mains water, with two 6000-gallon tanks (about 60,000 litres) as well as a 13,000-litre back-up tank for the County Fire Authority. Then there's more than 100,000 litres stored in the two billabongs, which are central to Phillip's garden design and fire management strategy. "I knew when I bought the property that this was a high bushfire-risk zone" he says. "Part of the problem is that the native vegetation has evolved over centuries to be regularly burnt and we've stopped that happening. So, when fire does come, it hits with even greater ferocity."

In preparation for what Phillip describes as "the inevitability of a fire", the house is equipped with a sprinkler system. He credits electrical contractors True Solar Time for technological

"If the pump is the heart of the system, solar power is the brains because in a fire, mains electricity will be the first thing to go."

advice on installing the solar energy to power the pump and an infrared sensor that activates the system even when the house is not occupied. "In theory, I could be at the beach or somewhere miles away and the sensors will kick in and set the sprinklers off," he explains. "If the pump is the heart of the whole system, the solar panels and the batteries are the brains because in the event of a fire, mains electricity will be the first thing to go. I just wish there were more funds available to test these systems, because they are crucial to any bushfire survival strategy."

Cross-ventilation achieved by strategically positioned windows and sliding glass doors doubles duty in cooling the house and connecting it with the surrounding remnant eucalyptus forest. Electricity needs not provided by the solar panels are taken care of by green power. Energy-efficient globes are used throughout and all green waste is composited on site and fed to the vegie patch or the surrounding garden, which covers about one-fifth of the five-acre (two-hectare) site.

Clockwise from above:
Sculpture in the garden is symbolic of its restful nature; the house was located for minimal site disturbance; Phillip takes a dip in one of the billabongs.

The garden, which Phil describes as his "research laboratory", has evolved during the past seven years but has been his whole lifetime in planning. And, as is the nature of most experimental work, it will probably always be a work in progress. Plants are trialed, vertical gardens perfected and water-management strategies effected. Grey and black water are treated on-site and used to water the plants and recycled into the waterways that run through the property.

"I knew where every rock was going before it was craned into place," he explains. "This site is a high-risk landslip area, so storm water drainage and retaining walls were critical to the design." The billabong concept is central to Phillip's water-sensitive ethos as it captures and stores all available storm water and excess roof water once the tanks are full. In this garden, the two billabongs and 11 waterfalls replicate nature as they are designed to dry out during drought periods. Indigenous drought-tolerant plants ensure the vegetation will survive until the next rains replenish the waterways.

"There's no lawn," Phillip says. "In fact, my company doesn't own a lawnmower, because we don't use water-thirsty lawn. Nor do we irrigate. We'll water a plant through its first summer, but after that it's on its own. It adds up to a very low-maintenance garden. In fact, the most work is in keeping the leaves off the roof, which is another essential in a bushfire-prone area."

"Kids love this garden. They can run wild and lose themselves in relative safety. There are also a million places to hide."

Apart from providing a cool setting for the house, the billabongs are great swimming pools and provide sanctuary for all manner of frogs, insects, wallabies, echidnas, lizards, birds and other wildlife. Phillip has introduced silver perch to the lower billabong and relishes the opportunity to be able to catch his dinner and cook it on the barbie.

"Kids love this garden," Phillip observes. "They can run wild and lose themselves in relative safety. There are a million places to hide and as many opportunities to connect with nature. In an increasingly urban world, that need to get back to nature is a pressing one. I like to think we're not creating gardens — we're building habitats that will last for hundreds of years. The billabongs are the soul of the habitat. They create an Australian identity that works with our weather extremes. They just make sense in this environment."

Clockwise from above:
The garden attracts all manner of bird life; ferns screen an outdoor shower; Phillip enjoys his tree house seclusion; two billabongs, 11 waterfalls and solar power are central to the garden's carefully planned design.

THE BIG PICTURE

Patricia Copes has lent her artist's eye
to the design of her park-like garden
in the NSW Southern Highlands.

Words JAQUI CAMERON Photography SUE STUBBS

Above: *The land behind he ha-ha is built up so the wall can't be seen from the house.* **Opposite:** *The delicate dogwood tree blossom.*

t is slightly ironic that as a botanical artist Patricia Copes focuses on the fine detail of nature while the defining feature of her elegant garden in the New South Wales Southern Highlands is the expansive views. Since Tim and Patricia bought their block in 1989, the seven-acre (three-hectare) Prittlewell garden has evolved from neglected farmland covered in hundreds of dead wattles into a majestic private park.

"We initially had a garden plan drawn up by landscape architect Michael Bligh, which really helped focus our ideas," Patricia explains. "It made the prospect of turning the ramshackle block into a garden much less daunting. The garden has grown far beyond the original design intention but Michael's principles have always guided its development."

Claiming no technical horticultural knowledge, Patricia says she adopts a "less is more" approach to gardening, favouring the simple rather than the busy, and flowing rather than formal. However, she also admits to regularly succumbing to the allure of achieving instant impact.

> *"I can't wait for things to grow, so I tend to over plant. Three years later, it's all overgrown, so I have to dig much of it up."*

"I'm always collecting ideas and will come back from a trip full of enthusiasm, but I'm also a bit impatient," she says. "I can't wait for things to grow, so I tend to over plant. Three years later, it's all overgrown, so I have to dig much of it up, which means I then have to find somewhere to replant it all. And so the cycle begins again."

Strolling around the garden, the visitor is struck by the balance and beauty of Prittlewell, named after the English village that was home to Patricia's mother. It is amazing to learn this balance and beauty has evolved from practical necessity rather than artistic design. For example, Michael suggested a ha-ha across the front of the house, so the soil excavated for the lake was used to fill and level the land behind the wall. And what exactly is a ha-ha? Patricia points to the low stone

wall that runs along the front of the house but is deliberately tucked into the slope so it is visible only from the lake.

"The concept dates back to the grand estates in England and was designed to prevent animals entering the formal gardens without interrupting the views from the manor house," she explains. "The actual name is thought to come from the exclamations of surprise by those who unexpectedly encountered the hidden walls."

It certainly makes a great conversation topic when guests gather for lunch under the clematis-covered pergola and look down to the lake under the high branches of a massive claret ash. The story of how the luxuriant bog garden and rill came to life is equally practical, emerging as a way to deal with the recycled water from the environmental septic system.

"Tim is in charge of keeping the lawns in order and he hated having to move all the sprinklers whenever he was mowing," Patricia says. "So we decided to incorporate them into a garden feature

> *"The name ha-ha is thought to come from the exclamations of surprise by those who unexpectedly encountered the hidden walls."*

making it possible to use that water more effectively."

The bog garden is watered by the purified water and supplemented by recirculating water from the lake, creating a lush environment for a riot of plants, from feathery *Miscanthus* to sculptural *Gunnera*. The practical also extends to the paper-birch grove underplanted with *Vinca* to camouflage the water tank. Then there is the herb and rose garden, entered through a gate with cumquat trees on each side and filled with raised garden beds radiating out from a central bay tree. Even the little blue rowing boat on the lake has a story to tell.

"Our 10-year-old grandson [James] longed for a boat, so Tim suggested they build one together," Patricia says. "James found the plans on the

internet and the finished product now sits proudly tied up to the wharf."

A garden visit to Japan was the inspiration for the Japanese garden and pavilion, which is neatly tucked under a raised canopy of conifer trees. A sandstone path leading from the house to Patricia's studio, in the glass-fronted pavilion, is bordered by meticulously clipped balls of small-leafed box hedging softened by the umbrellas of weeping Japanese maples.

"It is quite a formal space but I think it sits well within the rest of the garden because it is so tranquil," Patricia says. "From the studio you still have a view down to the lake but it is also wonderful to have the sound of the waterfall in the background while I paint."

And, of course, there is no end of colour, form and flowers for Patricia to paint. Prittlewell is a garden that has grown out of a love of plants, an artistic eye, lots of hard work and a good dose of practical reality.

"I walk around the garden each day and always see jobs that need to be done but I also appreciate the beauty of the garden we have created," Patricia adds. "Every season brings its own delights. The mist on the lake on a winter's morning, the dogwood blossom in spring or the colours of the Manchurian pear tree in autumn ... every day there is something different to see. It is very rewarding but I think it might be big enough now."

Clockwise from above:
Calla lilies thrive in the bog garden; there are no end of flowers for Patricia to paint; the garden has evolved from neglected farmland to a private park; natives and exotics frame the entrance.

Words KIRSTY MCKENZIE Photography KEN BRASS

A LIFE'S WORK

John and Lyn Colquhoun have devoted most of their adult lives to transforming a house and garden perched on a rural NSW hilltop.

When neighbours started telling Lyn and John Colquhoun that their five sons were causing traffic disruptions with their street cricket games, the couple realised that they needed more space. As an Albury property developer, John was well positioned to locate a home that could accommodate the family and all their friends, who often numbered in cricket teams. He found just what they were looking for in Mulberry Hill, at that stage, a 38-acre (15-hectare) block on the outskirts of the town on the NSW/Victorian border.

Forty years on, the boys are all grown up and

long since left home and it's time for Lyn and John to downsize. But in the meantime, they've built the most extraordinary home and garden for some other young family to grow and prosper in. "The block was bare except for the lemon-scented gum and a big *Cedrus deodara* (Himalayan cedar) at the front of the house," Lyn recalls. "So, gradually, we went to work, extending the house and planting the garden."

Inspired by various trips to the Mediterranean, Lyn and John have created an Australian version of a Tuscan or Provençal villa, with massive wrought-iron doors framing the entrance and vast expanses of windows framing every conceivable view of the garden.

"I take influences from everywhere," Lyn explains. "But the common denominator has been that the garden had to be low maintenance and the plants drought tolerant. We experience all the climatic extremes this wide brown land can offer, so everything had to be hardy."

Clockwise from opposite: The garden was developed to be low maintenance and use drought-tolerant plants; flowers add splashes of colour in beds and in pots; geraniums guard the gate.

The property was reduced in recent years when the Colquhouns subdivided. "I only agreed on the grounds that I got a decent enclosure out of it," Lyn says. "As we ended up with a brushwood fence, I could hardly complain. I did have to sacrifice a wonderful old mulberry tree, which gave the property its name, as it couldn't be transplanted. But we replaced it with a weeping mulberry at the front and an avenue of glossy-leafed white mulberries lining the driveway. It looks wonderful year-round and gives us and our neighbours fruit for more jam than we could ever eat."

Access to the property is via a winding road that leads the visitor to the front of the house, framed by two *Pyrus salicifolia* (ornamental pears) and announced by a towering urn water feature. On one side is the "wild garden", which pretty much looks after itself, on the other is a formal section of clipped hedges and the tennis court. The rear of the house looks over the swimming pool with views to the ranges beyond

and an olive grove planted with Barouni and Sevillano, both table varieties. Lavender, roses and lilies add colour and fragrance, and expanses of lawn are kept in shape by John, who is "the king of the tractor mower".

"The olives were inspired by a wonderful southern European family holiday in 1997," Lyn explains. "At other times, I have been influenced by landscape architects, including Spain's Fernando Caruncho, and writers, including Mariella Sgaravatti, who celebrates the Tuscan environment. From them, I've learned the beauty of the minimalist contemporary style and that geometry is fundamental to a successful garden."

Inside the house, the broad expanses outdoors are mirrored with large-scale rooms, high ceilings and loads of natural light. "It's been a great place to bring up a family," Lyn says. "But, unfortunately, it's now time to hand it on to someone who can do this kind of space justice. I'm sure the right family will come along."

Clockwise from opposite: With an olive grove and profuse lavender, the garden pays homage to Tuscany; the lemon-scented gum towers above a water feature; the olive grove was planted after a holiday in southern Europe.

A PASSION FOR PLANTS

Plantsmen Wayne and Sue Tapping
have spent the past 30 years refining
their sprawling garden in the
NSW Blue Mountains.

There's a feast for every sense in Wayne and Sue Tapping's garden in the heart of apple and stone fruit farms at Bilpin. Called Wildwood for the fact that it's surrounded by native eucalypt forest, the garden is an amazing amalgam of the couple's long careers in the nursery business. The sight of spring blossom and autumn colour clamours for attention against the heady scent of roses, daphne and weeping cherry and the sound of water tumbling through the cascades and chiming bellbirds. There's touch in the cool calm of the shade and the many seats dotted throughout the grounds and taste in the delicious meals served up in the tea rooms the Tappings run in conjunction with a gift store at the entrance.

The Tappings bought the 10-hectare Wildwood in 1980. In the years between the wars, the property was part of the Powell Estates, where timber cutters logged the native trees and many of them ring the property to the present day. By "starting at the front and working down the hill", Wayne and Sue have gradually filled in the garden, though leaving a parkland expanse that rolls down to the dam at the bottom of the property. They now have about two hectares of the entire property devoted to formal plantings.

"The volcanic soil is so black and so rich and the rainfall usually high enough that we can grow just about anything," Sue explains. "The dam is filled by the rain and we've bore water to see us through dry times. In all the years of running nurseries in Richmond, Kurrajong and Windsor, we've used Wildwood as a kind of plant hospital. Anything that was not saleable, because it had

Clockwise from above:
Water-lily in full glory;
wisteria climbing on an
old gate; massed lilies on
the rain-filled dam at the
bottom of the garden.

Words KIRSTY MCKENZIE Photography KEN BRASS & NICK WOOD

been in the pot too long or wasn't really thriving, we've brought home and stuck in the ground. Nine times out of 10, it's done well."

Sue adds that their plan for the garden was loose, but they always wanted to create a formal garden without losing the wildness of the native surrounds. Their daughter's wedding in the garden lead to a flurry of activity in the late '90s, during which Sue fulfilled her long-time ambition for installing a waterfall with ponds. She was married on the bridge that spans the lower level of this feature. Nearby, there's a fairy dell, more accurately a goblin garden, while the rainforest walk below is a cool haven on a hot summer's day.

In late winter, magnolias, hellebores, daphnes and bulbs put on a show, while spring arrives with a parade of azaleas, dogwoods and wisteria. Wayne jokes that the only trees he's ever been allowed to plant are the nine weeping trees (*Prunus subhirtella* 'Rosea'), which are underplanted with hellebores for a knock-out walk in spring. By summer, Wildwood is a shady retreat with banks of blue hydrangeas lining the green. In autumn, it's hard to know where to look with deciduous trees all competing with their hues of red, gold and orange.

In 2010, the Tappings closed their last nursery and fulfilled their long-time ambition of opening the property as a garden with tearooms and a gift shop. They open Wildwood during spring and

Clockwise from above:
The garden is designed for year-round colour with roses, clivias and water-lilies lending their interest; the ponds and cascades were added in time for a family wedding held there.

autumn and use the closure periods to develop
new beds and work on the constant maintenance
such a large area involves. "Wayne does most of
the heavy work and mows the steepest sections,"
Sue explains. "I do the rest of the mowing. It
takes me two 10-hour days to get round the entire
garden. In summer, when it's warm and wet, I
have to do it every week but in winter, that drops
back to once every four to six weeks."

While this sounds like a bit of a Clayton's
retirement, Sue points out that compared with
running a nursery seven days a week, life at Bilpin
is considerably more relaxed than when they were
commuting down the Mountains and squeezing
work in the garden around their day jobs.

"People are so appreciative of our efforts,"
she says. "They can bring a picnic and sit in the
garden or have lunch or morning or afternoon
tea in the tea room. They tend to make a day of
it and visit other local attractions, which include
the Blue Mountains Botanic Gardens at Mount
Tomah, other open gardens at Mount Wilson or
the pick-your-own fruit orchards. It's more like
having a procession of friends come to visit than
customers who want everything yesterday."
**Wildwood is open during spring and autumn
from Friday to Monday, 10am to 4pm. Groups are
welcome by appointment. For more information,
visit wildwoodgarden.com.au**

Words MEREDITH KIRTON Photography SUE STUBBS

BARREN TO BOUNTIFUL

Creating a garden in a prolonged period of drought has been a labour of love for this NSW couple.

Named for the red-browed firetail finches that inhabit the garden, Redbrow is beautiful in all seasons thanks not only to the surrounds, but also to the abundant wildlife. While many gardens can look a little drab in winter, here there is the stark beauty of a white frost on the grass and fog laying thick in the gullies and rising above the lake. In autumn, the many deciduous trees add their showy array of reds and yellows and spring is always pretty with the cherry blossom and crabapples.

David and Elisabeth Judge set out to develop a continually evolving, innovative tourist and local-visitor attraction, but they also had an environmental agenda in mind. The result, despite eight years of drought during the planting

stage, is a multi-award-winning farmstay and a comfortable country life for the family. There are free-ranging chickens there too, so eggs for breakfast are a must.

The Judges are an interesting couple, with joint experiences in nursing, teaching, farming, hospitality and adventure-travel operations. Chatting to them is like going on an around-the-world-conversation tour, as they tell of tales from Asia, Europe, Africa, Papua New Guinea and even a stint volunteering on a kibbutz in Israel in the '70s.

Situated near the suburb of Hall, Redbrow is on the Poachers Trail, the cuisine tourist trail of the Canberra region, which features foodie hotspots including the Poachers Pantry and many cool-climate vineyards. It's only 20 minutes

Above: David and Elisabeth Judge's garden at Redbrow on an early morning in spring.
Opposite: An arbour frames views of the stables.

to the national capital and a world away, making it popular with everyone from international guests to travellers with their horses, who can also stay the night and house their four-legged companions in on-site stables.

Located near the Murrumbateman Region, which is renowned for its food crops, this critical piece of wetland is home to many birds. Thanks to the planting of more than 50,000 trees, it's an oasis for creatures, both travelling and wild. The centrepiece is a large lake, which is home to many feathered friends including ducks and two black swans, who wander right up to visitors. The results from the revegetation are most obvious in terms of bird life. When they first started there were only 10 species, while now there are more than 120, including beautiful satin bowerbirds.

David and Elisabeth have worked tirelessly on this property and each season brings a beautiful treasure in the garden. The subtle winter flowers of the hellebores and the dainty cloud of crabapples in spring build to a crescendo when all the natives start flowering in summer and diminishes finally with the autumn's last hurrah of leaf colour. As with many gardeners, the couple's favourite time of the day is at "down tools", when they can sit outside and enjoy the company of friends and a well-earned drink under the shade of a tree. At Redbrow, they have the added bonus of their own lake lapping in the background.

Clockwise from opposite: Raised vegie garden beds feed family and friends; a bird feeder entices the many visiting species; Dutch iris and blossom lend splashes of colour; the lake is a haven for bird life; old garden equipment enjoys a new lease on life in the garden.

The Judges are also a treasure trove of local knowledge and revegetation insights, which they are happy to share with guests. They have learnt the hard way that its best to deep-rip virgin soil before planting, and recommend mostly planting native species or, at the very least, plants that thrive on neglect.

Recently, the couple has decided to take things a little easier. Although still staying on to look after their precious garden, they are selling the hospitality business side of things. They rate their greatest successes in the garden as the 95 per cent survival rate of all those seedlings, which, now the drought is over, are flourishing and have transformed the property from barren to bountiful.

Redbrow Garden Guesthouse
redbrowgarden@bigpond.com
Phone: 02 6226 8166

Clockwise from opposite: Every lake needs a boat; bountiful bulbs; spring abundance with blossom and Dutch iris; cherry blossom and crabapple are highlights in the garden in spring.

LIVING HISTORY

Markdale station in the NSW Southern Tablelands has evolved under the benevolent hands of three generations of the polo-loving Ashton family.

Think about it. The context of the present is the result of what is past. This is why towns, properties and houses that offer us a glimpse of history are so important. They're our guideposts on the linear road of time and when they're knocked down, renovated insensitively or squeezed out by modern monstrosities, we lose not only something from yesteryear but a bit of our present day.

Many places in Australia rekindle a sense of history, but a real standout is Markdale, a sprawling sheep and cattle property located on the outskirts of Crookwell, New South Wales. It's considered a treasure by heritage and horticultural groups and has been well tended by the same polo-loving family for three generations.

"Our family has been living and working on this 8000-acre (3200-hectare) property since the 1920s," explains the current owner, Mary Ashton. "The original homestead was built from local timber and concrete blocks, all hand-cut, hewn and sawn on-site, but it's been through some fairly dramatic changes and improvements since then. Now we even offer Markdale as a place for people to come to stay, which means we are able to share it with others."

It was in the late 1940s and early 1950s that Markdale metamorphosised. This was when two of Australia's most revered designers, architect Professor Leslie Wilkinson and English-born, Victorian landscape designer Edna Walling, joined

Clockwise from this page: Markdale has one of only two Edna Walling designed homestead gardens in NSW; a picturesque footbridge; a cottage garden display.

Words SIOBHAN O'BRIEN Photography SUE STUBBS

forces to create the magical haven that it is today.

"The garden is one of only two homestead gardens designed by Edna Walling in New South Wales," Mary says. "It's part of a dwindling legacy of her work. It is widely acknowledged as one of the great country gardens of Australia."

The verdant oasis that enjoys four seasons was first planted in the 1920s but, around 30 years later, Walling removed many of the existing hedges and shifted the focus of the garden toward the natural scenery of the surrounding paddocks, hills and fields. Today, golden elms, silver birch, aspens and native eucalypts frame the garden without obscuring the view.

At various times of the year, expect to see a flower in bloom, a crop of greenery or a canopy of trees. Mature roses, wisterias, magnolias, weeping elms and claret ash are just a part of the backdrop. But a real constant is the sweeping lawn that meanders down to a small central lake and curved granite walls that provide an elegant yet robust boundary. "It's a truly wonderful garden that takes a lot of hard work," Mary says. "But it has continued to improve with each passing year. It never ceases to delight me."

The main homestead and nearby stone cottages that date back to the 1850s are equally compelling. The latter were renovated and refurnished with a period flourish around 14 years ago and now provide self-contained accommodation for paying guests. The cottages include spacious living areas that feature open fireplaces, bedrooms with ensuites and all mod cons. Additionally, the nearby shearers' quarters offer more basic accommodation for larger families or small conference groups.

Clockwise from this picture: Roses climb over a rustic arbour; ramble over the fences; lend profuse colour and fragrance to every corner of the garden.

Clockwise from this picture: Large trees provide ample shade and a beautiful canopy; leaf detail; roses are a feature in this landmark garden.

"The shearers' quarters were traditionally used to accommodate the shearing teams when they came to Markdale," Mary explains. "Now we use them as a quintessentially Australian retreat. The good thing about the different styles of accommodation is that we can cater for small or large groups and also groups with different budgets."

The main homestead, which Mary and husband Geoff call home, is a grand and supremely elegant abode that features characteristic Wilkinson touches, including pale blue-grey shutters and a copper-roofed cupola on the exterior. Inside, it features high ceilings and sizeable sitting rooms filled with antiques, books, art and ample places to sit. Each room is decorated with original, individual pieces of antique furniture and generous windows that offer views out into the garden. A startling feature is the bold use of colour in the interiors: emerald green and red in the dining room; pale pink and lambent green in the bedroom. Remnants of this family's pioneering polo past are still in existence on the property. There's a wooden horse in the polo practice pit and books on the subject are scattered throughout the main homestead. It's a sport that's been in the family since the 1920s, but it wasn't until 1930 that they made history when four Ashton brothers sailed from Australia to compete in the English polo season. The men travelled more than 21,000 kilometres to compete against elite sportsmen from the United States, United Kingdom and India. To the amazement of all, the Ashtons won most of their matches, including England's Hurlingham Championship and the Indian Empire Shield. They returned home as heroes and remained unbeaten until they retired in 1938.

Wherever you look, there is a real sense of history at this property. It's the way it should remain, so that others can enjoy it in the future.
For accommodation info, visit markdale.com

The 74th
Art Directors
Annual and
Ninth Annual
International
Exhibition

The 74th
Art Directors
Annual and
Ninth Annual
International
Exhibition

Editor
Myrna Davis

Art Director/Graphic Design
Cara Galowitz

Associate Editors
Antje Lenthe Arcia
Mary Fichter

Copy Editors
Laura Morris
Jennifer Knox White

Production Liaison
Fiona L'Estrange

Jacket Design
Woody Pirtle, Pentagram

Exhibition Director
Luis De Jesus

Published in 1995 by
RotoVision SA
Route de Suisse 9,
CH-1295 Mies/VD,
Switzerland

The Art Directors Club, Inc.
250 Park Avenue South,
New York, New York 10003-1402,
U.S.A.

ISSN: 0735-2026
RotoVision SA ISBN: 2-88046-244-4
Watson Guptill ISBN: 0-8230-6402-6

Distribution in the United States and Canada by
Watson Guptill Publications
1515 Broadway,
New York, New York 10036,
U.S.A.

International distribution by
RotoVision SA
Route de Suisse 9,
CH-1295 Mies/VD,
Switzerland

Production and color separation in Singapore by
Provision Pte Ltd
Tel: (65) 334-7720
Fax: (65) 334-7721

Printed in Singapore

TABLE OF CONTENTS

I once picked a dye-transfer print of Irving Penn's elegant New York Still Life, 1947 *out of the art department trash bin. That's how it is with commerce: once art has served its purpose, it can be lost forever. Most of the work you will see in this book is ephemeral. That is why the Annual, published continuously for three-quarters of a century, has become so useful to professionals and students of the graphic arts.*

The first exhibition of advertising art was hung in 1908 by the National Arts Club in New York. One review said the work "would surprise a good many people who had not realized that there was so much good designing in advertising." It was not until 1920, when the Art Directors Club established its annual exhibition, that such work would be preserved.

W. H. Beatty wrote in the sixth Annual, "Who knows, perhaps when a future historian of this American scene has relegated such things as business profits, quotas, and earnings to footnotes . . . it will be bits of pageantry like this that will appeal to him as saying, 'I guess they were just about like that on December 5th, 1927.'"

This, then, is just about the way we were in 1994.

—Carl Fischer
President, The Art Directors Club

1972
M. F. Agha
Lester Beall
Alexey Brodovitch
A. M. Cassandre
René Clark
Robert Gage
William Golden
Paul Rand

1973
Charles Coiner
Paul Smith
Jack Tinker

1974
Will Burtin
Leo Lionni

1975
Gordon Aymar
Herbert Bayer
Cipes Pineles Burtin
Heyworth Campbell
Alexander Liberman
L. Moholy-Nagy

1976
E. McKnight Kauffer
Herbert Matter

1977
Saul Bass
Herb Lubalin
Bradbury Thompson

1978
Thomas M. Cleland
Lou Dorfsman
Allen Hurlburt
George Lois

1979
W. A. Dwiggins
George Giusti
Milton Glaser
Helmut Krone
Willem Sandberg
Ladislav Sutnar
Jan Tschichold

1980
Gene Federico
Otto Storch
Henry Wolf

1981
Lucian Bernhard
Ivan Chermayeff
Gyorgy Kepes
George Krikorian
William Taubin

1982
Richard Avedon
Amil Gargano
Jerome Snyder
Massimo Vignelli

1983
Aaron Burns
Seymour Chwast
Steve Frankfurt

1984
Charles Eames
Wallace Elton
Sam Scali
Louis Silverstein

1985
Art Kane
Len Sirowitz
Charles Tudor

1986
Walt Disney
Roy Grace
Alvin Lustig
Arthur Paul

1987
Willy Fleckhaus
Shigeo Fukuda
Steve Horn
Tony Palladino

1988
Ben Shahn
Bert Steinhauser
Mike Tesch

1989
Rudolph de Harak
Raymond Loewy

1990
Lee Clow
Reba Sochis
Frank Zachary

1991
Bea Feitler
Bob Gill
Bob Giraldi
Richard Hess

1992
Eiko Ishioka
Rick Levine
Onofrio Paccione
Gordon Parks

1993
Leo Burnett
Yusaku Kamekura
Robert Wilvers
Howard Zieff

1994
Alan Fletcher
Norman Rockwell
Ikko Tanaka
Rochelle Udell
Andy Warhol

1995
Robert Brownjohn
Paul Davis
Roy Kuhlman
Jay Maisel

Our industry, which is promotional by nature, has often neglected to promote itself. The Art Directors Hall of Fame takes a leadership position in recognizing and chronicling the contributions of those exceptional talents who have shaped the visual language of our culture.

Nomination for this honor is acknowledgement of lifetime achievement in the field of visual communications. Each of these laureates has demonstrated the ability to discern the difference between the ordinary and the excellent, a strong sense of ethical responsibility, and an aesthetic that has served to define and describe our times and raise the accepted standards of excellence.

—Richard Wilde
Selection Chairperson, Hall of Fame Committee

Throughout his career, Robert Brownjohn maintained a fast-paced life-style, which was integral to his art, his theory of graphic design, and his method of working. He ate, drank, and spoke extravagantly, demanded the highest wages, and socialized with rock stars and glamorous fashion designers, models, and actors.

All who knew Brownjohn speak of there having been an aura of brilliance about him. Architectural Forum *noted that he "may have been the most talented student ever to have graduated from Chicago's Institute of Design." He personified the ideal his teacher László Moholy-Nagy expressed in* Vision in Motion, *that art and life can be integrated: "The true artist is the grindstone of the sense; he sharpens his eyes, mind and feeling; he interprets ideas and concepts through his own media."*

In his short but intense working life, Brownjohn helped to redefine graphic design, to move it from a formal to a conceptual art. His projects exemplified every aspect of his relationship to design, including his emphasis on content over form and his preference for ordinary and personal images. His spirit of invention and designs for living in the machine age were balanced with references to the aesthetic models that Moholy-Nagy admired.

"Bj," as he signed his name and was familiarly called, arrived at the Institute of Design in 1944. He worked with Moholy-Nagy on advertising and exhibitions, and was appointed as a special student in architecture by Serge Chermayeff. After leaving the Institute in 1947, he remained in Chicago and free-lanced for several advertising and architectural offices until Chermayeff invited him to return in 1949 to teach full time. A professor without a degree at the age of 24, Bj stayed for barely a year before leaving for New York.

To support himself in New York, Brownjohn free-lanced in graphic design. He worked for brief periods with The Herman Miller Furniture Company, George Nelson, and Ed Bartolucci at Bob Cato Associates. His clients included Columbia Records, the American Crafts Museum, and Pepsi Cola. In 1957, Brownjohn joined forces with Ivan Chermayeff and Tom Geismar. As ringleader of Brownjohn Chermayeff & Geismar, he always insisted on new ideas, fresh imagery, and the best conceptual solution to the problem at hand. His goal was not to make things pretty but to arrive at a design that would solve a problem both conceptually and formally.

Bj looked to the physical world around him for inspiration and fresh ideas. Tony Palladino describes a trip he took to Coney Island with Brownjohn, Chermayeff, Geismar, Bob Gill, and George Tscherny: "We were looking for graphic turn-ons that later we could apply to jobs . . . the fresher the essence, the better the job was." Brownjohn believed that if an idea couldn't be described over the telephone, it wasn't simple, clear, and direct enough to work.

Brownjohn Chermayeff & Geismar did well in its first year. The partners celebrated the first anniversary with their families. Sara Chermayeff, Ivan's wife at the time, recalls that Bj made the dessert, "which was a big bowl of Jell-O full of nickels and dimes. He was the original Pop artist for sure."

Two years later, the partnership ended amicably. With his wife, Donna, and daughter, Eliza, Brownjohn moved to England, where he worked for J. Walter Thompson as creative director. His style was a new experience for the JWT staff. He was interested in found objects and typographic "junk" collected in the street, kept odd hours, was often absent, and spoke his mind. The fact that he was paid so much more than everyone else earned him a good deal of resentment at first, but soon he was accepted, respected, and loved.

Wooed away by McCann-Erickson, Brownjohn's first important

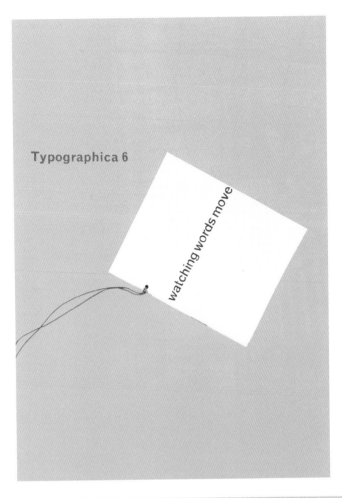

Typographica 6

watching words move

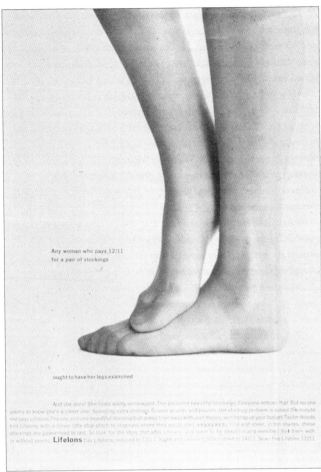

Any woman who pays 12/11
for a pair of stockings

ought to have her legs examined

And she does! She looks wildly extravagant. The girl in the beautiful stockings. Everyone notices that. But no one seems to know she's a clever one. Spending extra shillings to save pounds and pounds. Her stocking problem is solved this minute. she says Lifelons. The one and only beautiful stocking that doesn't run away with your money, won't snag up your budget. Taylor Woods knit Lifelons with a clever little stop-stitch to stop runs where they would start. Lifelons fine and sheer, in six shades. these stockings are guaranteed to last. So look for the store that sells Lifelons and learn to be beautiful and sensible! Buy them with or without seams. **Lifelons** Day Lifelons reduced to 12/11. Night and Leisure Lifelons down to 14/11. Seam-free Lifelons 12/11

commission there was for Taylor-Woods's Lifelon stockings. To convince exhausted women with bad legs to buy expensive hosiery, Bj used a black-and-white photograph of glamorous legs, cropped to a sensuous abstraction—a simple, sculptural form reminiscent of Constantin Brancusi's sculptures. The advertisement read, "A girl who would spend 12/11 on a pair of stockings ought to have her legs examined," and won every award possible in England and abroad. "The words and the design came together," McCann-Erickson's David Burnstein said, referring to the fact that Brownjohn often wrote his own copy. "He was a great synthesizer, that's better than simplifier . . . he loved accidents, making accidents, he was a walking accident."

At the same time Brownjohn was working at McCann-Erickson, he was commissioned on a free-lance basis to design titles for the first James Bond film, From Russia with Love. Alan Fletcher describes Brownjohn's original presentation of the concept to the film's producers: "Bj set up the projector, everyone filed in and sat down. Bj turned off the lights, took off his jacket and shirt, and wiggled in front of the titles from the lit projector. 'It'll be just like this, only we'll use a pretty girl.'"

Largely on the strength of these titles, Brownjohn joined a film-production company, Cammell Hudson (which later became Cammell Hudson & Brownjohn), in 1964. Carrying out, in his own style, the teachings and aspirations of Moholy-Nagy, he used architecture as comparison and model. "Architecture is the greatest catalyst in design," he said. "It provides a structural sense and discipline to your composition. I like working with film because it is a very architectonic medium. Making a movie is building in space." Brownjohn took the simplest technical capabilities of the camera and used them to enlarge the conceptual limits of filmmaking. In David Cammell's words, "He was so experimental and restless that he gave the impression of being an amateur."

Brownjohn continued to design for print as well as film. When Michael Cooper, the well-known photographer of the Beatles, insisted that Bj design his business stationery, the result was both funny and indicative of Bj's own reputation at the time, featuring Bj's name in gigantic type, as large as Cooper's own name.

Brownjohn's last completed project was for Dick Davidson, a longtime friend from New York, who commissioned designs for a series of peace posters from well-known artists in New York and abroad. Brownjohn's design utilized his own handwriting and is signed, as if to his friends, "Love, Bj." The death card, the question, the lack of color, and the emptiness of the poster imply the nature of the peace Brownjohn foresaw for the world around him, and for himself. He died at the age of 44.

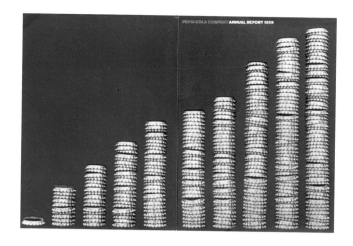

Robert Brownjohn
designed this Business Card
for Michael Cooper of
4 Chelsea Manor Studios
Flood Street London SW3
FLAxman 9762

Paul Davis's restless nature—which reveals itself in the variety of visual approaches and problems he has chosen to explore in his career as an artist, graphic designer, and art director—may trace its origins to his pioneer ancestors. The son of a Methodist preacher from Texas and grandson of a Kansas newspaper man, Davis grew up in various small towns in the West and Southwest before attending Will Rogers High School in Tulsa. His art teacher there, Hortense Bateholts, was the first person to tell the young Davis he might be able to make a living as an artist. More encouragement came at the age of 17, when he won a full scholarship to the School of Visual Arts and moved to New York. His work was noticed by Art Paul, art director of Playboy, and merited him some assignments even before graduation. In 1959, six months out of art school, Davis joined the very influential Push Pin Studios, spending three years there before leaving to begin his free-lance career.

Davis's discoveries and enthusiasms of those years included early American painting, the works of René Magritte and the Surrealists, artists of the early Italian Renaissance, and Jasper Johns's stunning target paintings, which coalesced into a style distinctively his own in a seminal series of paintings and portraits on wood completed in the early 1960s. Employing the vocabulary and techniques of his influences, Davis borrowed from popular media such as old postcards and etchings. Jerome Snyder of Graphis observed, "One of the persistent strengths of Davis's art is its independence of any prevailing faddishness or stylistic trends . . . The durability of {his} prodigious output rests on more permanent pillars."

Soon after Davis opened his own studio in 1963, his work began to be published in most major magazines of the period, including Audience, Esquire, Horizon, Life, Look, McCall's, Monocle, Ramparts, Redbook, Show, Sports Illustrated, and Time. Davis's style was a marked departure in the field, and paved the way for an entire generation of illustrators. In 1972, a young artist from Texas told him it was hard to get work from regional magazines "unless your work looked like Paul Davis." One art director, after being told that Davis would not execute a painting to his specific instructions, argued, "But I want your style."

"A lot of people can do my style," Davis replied.

"You mean you want to do the thinking?" Davis was told. "You should have been an art director!"

In 1974, Giorgio Soavi, author and creative director of Olivetti, commissioned twelve paintings for Olivetti's yearly desk calendar. Davis produced a series of pastoral images based on his recollections and fantasies of the past. The edition was enormously successful, but did not contain any information about the artist. One Italian critic praised the paintings and determined that they were by an obscure 19th-century American painter, whose work had gone unpublished but obviously was endowed with strictly pictorial qualities. He wrote: "None other could indulge in similar descriptions, just like in the old days. He created a 'trompe l'oeil' so dear to our forefathers."

Davis's paintings were included in gallery and museum shows in New York, Paris, and Rome. After seeing Davis's portraits of animals at Galleria Il Gabbiano in Rome, Soavi noted: "With their dignified eyes gazing into our own eyes, as if staring at the eyes of their first photograph, these whimsical animals watch us, impatient to come to life."

Davis's human portraits, too, captured attention because they seemed to reflect their subjects' inner reality. His paintings of the famous and not-so-famous include many political, literary, and entertainment figures—Joan Baez, Ingrid Bergman, Jimmy Carter,

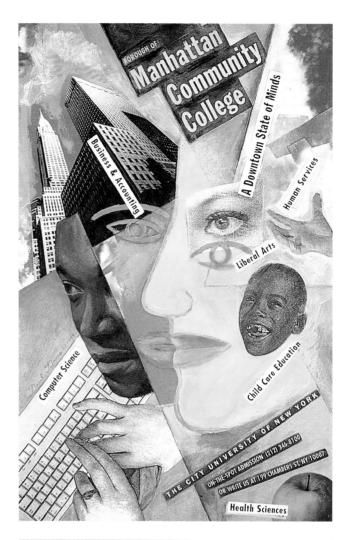

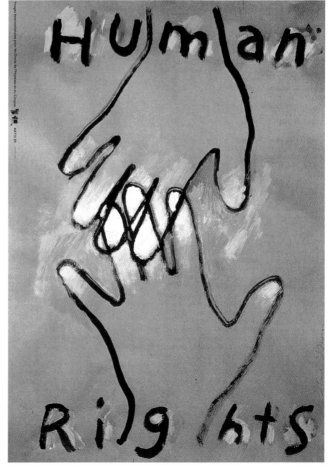

Lyndon Johnson, numerous members of the Kennedy family, Timothy Leary, Jack Nicholson, George Orwell, Ronald Reagan, and Meryl Streep, among them. His first famous poster, a romantic portrait of Che Guevera for Evergreen Review, aroused such a strong reaction when it appeared around New York City in 1967 that many copies were defaced and the magazine's offices were bombed by Cuban dissidents. By the same token, the piece became an enduring icon of the period.

Throughout the 1970s and 1980s, Davis's work became familiar to New Yorkers through entertainment posters on buses, subway platforms, and city walls. Kurt Vonnegut once wrote, "{Davis's} work is the face of the city at its best to an amazing degree." In 1987, a special Drama Desk Award was created to honor him for his theater posters.

Davis served as art director for Joseph Papp's New York Shakespeare Festival from 1985 until the producer's death, and was founding art director for the American Museum of the Moving Image in Queens and for the magazines Normal and Wigwag. Many public and private collections around the world house his paintings and posters; his 1976 Three Penny Opera poster, for instance, is in the permanent collection of the Museum of Modern Art, New York.

In the mid-1970s, the first of three major retrospectives of Davis's paintings was presented in Kamakura, Kyoto, and Gunma, Japan, and at the opening of the Centre Georges Pompidou in Paris. A 1987 retrospective included more than 180 paintings, drawings, and posters, and another in 1989, of 85 posters, toured throughout Japan. In 1990, Davis received an honorary Doctor of Fine Arts degree from his alma mater, the School of Visual Arts, where he also teaches; the coveted Medal from the American Institute of Graphic Arts, upon whose board he later served; and the Lifetime Achievement Medal in Visual Arts from the American Academy of Arts of Guild Hall, East Hampton.

Ever interested by the chance to experiment, Davis acquired his first computer in 1988 and eventually taught workshops at Kodak's short-lived Center for Creative Imaging in Camden, Maine. He still refuses to confine himself to a single style. "Sometimes a stick figure can express the human form more eloquently than a skillfully modeled drawing or a photo-realistic painting," he once said. "I don't believe that one is inherently more truthful than another."

Pursuing his childhood dream to become the next Rembrandt, Roy Kuhlman studied at the Chouinard Art Institute in Los Angeles and, after moving to New York in 1946, the Art Students League; but after a number of years he realized he was looking for something else. This he found when he ran into Arnie Copeland, a friend from California who had just become art director at Lockwood Studios. Copeland introduced Kuhlman to Lockwood's bull pen as a troubleshooter and pasteup expert. Knowing practically nothing, "except on which side to smear the rubber cement," Kuhlman proved a quick study and soon lived up to his presumed reputation. At night, he taught a basic design course at the School of Advertising and Editorial Art, alongside such professionals as Eugene Carlin and Jerome Snyder.

Another big break came for Kuhlman when he was offered a job at Sudler & Hennessy, where he worked with Carl Fischer, Art Ludwig, and Ernie Smith, as well as the consummate designer and teacher Herb Lubalin. In 1954, Neil Fujita asked him to take over his position at Columbia Records. There, he gradually pooled a staff of young designers such as Ivan Chermayeff and Al Zalon, producing some of the period's most innovative work.

One year later, Kuhlman was hired by Ruder and Finn to establish an in-house art department. The budget was low and the graphic pieces sent out were small in number. Kuhlman worked with Ed Brodsky, and together they began to gain recognition until Kuhlman felt it was time to move on and try his hand at something new.

Having decided to go out on his own, Kuhlman rented a studio above Fischer's, on East 54th Street. Influenced by his friend's photographic skills, Kuhlman began solving design challenges with photography. This led to an introduction to Bill Buckley at Benton & Bowles, who gave Kuhlman the most challenging assignment of his career up to that time—the famous IBM series "Mathematics Serving Man," which won the AIGA Best Ads of the Year Award in 1958.

Although Kuhlman cites Alvin Lustig and Paul Rand as influences, it was the Abstract Expressionists, particularly the "strong, simple" style of Franz Kline, that truly inspired him. Kuhlman was one of the first to apply Abstract Expressionist ideas to design. His approach was loose, spontaneous, and serendipitous, and he worked quickly and instinctively. Because he felt there was a loss of quality if art was resized, he prepared comps in the same size as the final mechanical. Kuhlman developed a graphic language of his own, and anything within reach became part of the developing visual pastiche: old engravings, the insides of bank envelopes, his own photography, photograms, Zipatone sheets and collages, and odd pieces of letterpress type left over from other jobs.

In 1962, Kuhlman entered the movie industry. His film colleagues at Elektra Films, Jack Goodford and Lee Savage, described him as "the first film primitive." After two years, he returned to "motionless" graphics, as creative director in charge of corporate literature and sales promotion at U.S. Plywood, where he remained for almost five years. Then, on a recommendation from Kuhlman's friend Henry Wolf, IBM invited Kuhlman to create an educational seminar on the concepts and technologies behind the development and the future of the computer. In three years, he produced 700 slides and 52 live-action and animated 35-mm shorts. After this challenge, Kuhlman decided to concentrate on special effects for film animation. Just as he completed his sample reel, video special-effects generators made his newly acquired skills redundant, and he chose to retire. "In this business, if you have a ten-year life span, you're lucky—mine lasted

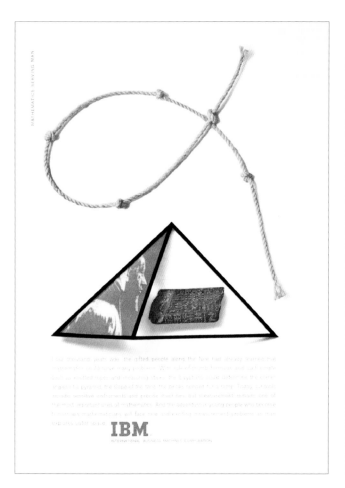

IBM
INTERNATIONAL BUSINESS MACHINES CORPORATION

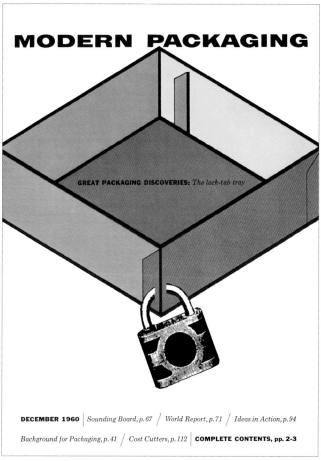

MODERN PACKAGING

GREAT PACKAGING DISCOVERIES: *The lock-tab tray*

The Spanish Inn
a novel by Jean Louis Bergonzo

Krapp's Last Tape
and other dramatic pieces
by Samuel Beckett

EVERGREEN ORIGINAL E-226 $1.95

KRAPP'S
LAST
TAPE

35 years."

One of Kuhlman's fondest memories of his career took place in *1951,* in a small Greenwich Village office of Grove Press, the fledgling publishing company that eventually brought to national prominence the writers, art, and artists of the avant-garde. He showed his portfolio of illustrations and comps, "mostly bad black-and-white photos, clumsy type, mostly sans-serif," to publisher Barney Rosset, who was not impressed. Just as Kuhlman was about to close the portfolio, Rosset caught a glimpse of doodles Kuhlman had been planning to show to record companies. When Rosset, who numbered among his friends Willem de Kooning, Kline, and Jackson Pollock, saw them, he said emphatically, "This is what I want."

For the next twenty years, Kuhlman produced some of his most brilliant work for Grove Press. His designs were the perfect counterpoint to the texts Rosset was publishing. Story of O, *the erotic novel by Henry Miller, for example, was packaged in a plain white jacket to camouflage what was inside. After Grove — the first to publish third-world titles in the United States — began publishing foreign titles in 1966, Kuhlman produced such covers as* The Brave African Huntress *by Amos Tutuola and* The No Plays of Japan *by Arthur Waley, which demonstrate his ability to reach both conceptual and abstract solutions. Rosset rejected only a few cover ideas. "I usually had five seconds to get a yes or no from Rosset. So, I walked slowly across the office toward Rosset's desk, holding the comp up so he'd have some {extra} time to look at it," Kuhlman says, adding, "Barney was the greatest client I ever had. He gave me the freedom to explore, to fail, and to win."*

*Jay Maisel finds beauty in a thousand places—some whose
association with beauty is incongruous, all where there was beauty to
begin with. The distinctive light and gesture in Maisel's vibrant
photographs, which set them apart from the work of other
photographers, have earned their creator a reputation of excellence.
By the time Maisel was 24 years old, he was given a solo show at
Photographers Gallery in New York. Yet it took at least five years
more before Maisel would admit to being a photographer.*

*Maisel became interested in the visual arts at an early age. He
concentrated on graphic design in high school, and after graduation
studied privately with painter Joseph Hirsch. He spent the next three
years at Cooper Union in New York, where he studied painting,
drawing, architectural design, and calligraphy. Maisel's interest in
painting and graphics then led him to Yale University and, there, to
Bauhaus master Josef Albers. Although Maisel was at the top of
Albers's class in color perception, his restless personality was
incompatible with the pace of painting. Morris Kantor, a teacher,
concurred, describing Maisel's paintings as "emotional outbursts."*

*At Yale, working with a group of student artists and architects
and philosopher/engineer Buckminster Fuller, Maisel chanced to use
a camera seriously for the first time. While his only formal
photography instruction was a class with Herbert Matter, he
absorbed Andreas Feininger's* Introduction to Photography *and
found himself sneaking off to take pictures when he was supposed to be
painting and drawing. It is not surprising that his photographs have
been described as "painterly" and compared to the work of J. M. W.
Turner and Andrew Wyeth.*

*Before becoming a free-lance photographer for major advertising
agencies and corporations in the United States and abroad, Maisel
photographed extensively on his own. At the age of 25, he decided to
see every art director at BBDO and sat in their offices every day for
weeks. With no luck there, he moved on to J. Walter Thompson.
Finally, after a month, his patience paid off and he received his first
assignment. Once home, he looked at his portfolio, reread the
requisition, then looked at his portfolio again. The agency wanted
him to shoot a woman lifting a curtain in a studio, yet his entire
portfolio consisted of outdoor shots using available light. He had no
idea how to use lighting. Approaching crisis point, he recalled a
lesson Alexey Brodovitch had taught him: "Do the assignment for
yourself even if you're doing it for them; do it for yourself as well as
for them." With that in mind, Maisel made the client wait a week
and a half until the available light was right.*

*Choice and selection, rather than imposition and manipulation,
are the hallmarks of Maisel's philosophy. He does not believe in
manipulating the image either before or after he releases the shutter.
When asked by Pete Turner—famous for his imaginative use of
filters—how he achieved such fantastic lighting effects without
polarizers or filtration, Maisel replied, "I wait."*

*Maisel takes many of his personal photos while on assignment for
corporations, and sells dye transfers to private collections. A Maisel
photograph seen in a gallery may also show up in a commercial
work. "He doesn't make a distinction between art and commercial
work," says friend and artist Joel Meyerowitz, "and probably
Rubens didn't make a distinction, either, when he made things for
himself and when he made things on commission. Jay's biggest
following and celebrity is in the world of commercial photography,
and he is revered there as a real heavyweight professional with a
great appetite and an engaging eye."*

John Morrison, an art director for Campbell-Mithun in

Minneapolis, once accompanied Maisel to photograph Winnebago motor homes in North Dakota and was "a little concerned because of the photographer's 'superstar status.' I thought, 'Does he really want to go to North Dakota and shoot motor homes? Will I be getting the back of his hand?'" Not only did Maisel shoot from 4 a.m. to 11 p.m. for six days straight, but Morrison insists that Maisel must have influenced the very weather. "That week we had glorious sunrises, sunsets, a thunderstorm. I told him, 'I've never seen this kind of light before,' and Jay said, 'It's always around. You just don't see it.'"

Maisel has taught at the School of Visual Arts, and at Cooper Union from 1969 to 1974. His work has been recognized with awards from, among others, Cooper Union, The Art Directors Club, The American Society of Media Photographers, Syracuse, and the International Center of Photography, New York, and with solo exhibitions at Cooper Union, the International Center of Photography, The Silver Image Gallery, the Alternative Center for International Arts, and the Space Gallery, which he co-founded with Ernst Haas and Turner in 1977 in New York when none of the city's galleries were showing color photography.

Maisel continues to teach young photographers at workshops, seminars, and lectures around the world and in his studio, a six-story former bank building on the Bowery in New York. Visitors are ushered onto an indoor basketball court, entrance to the domain of a self-described "pack-rat collector" who readily admits to having "the soul of a janitor." The Bank is filled with his photographs and "esoteric aesthetica."

For over 30 years, Maisel's unique images have made people stop and look—a horizontal shot of the Eiffel Tower for United Technologies Corporation; a scorching sun in a brilliant red sky for Carrier air conditioners; a stunningly red car hood for Inmont paint. In each, copy is minimal, the advertisement relying on the photograph to make its point. Maisel has used a surreal image of helicopters, shot for a Sikorsky spread, as his own promotional piece. He gives the same meticulous attention to both his commercial and his personal work. Maisel tells his students, "If you're really lucky, you can structure your work, on rare occasions, to where you're doing exactly what you would like to do. Which is to wander around, blindly looking for things, without any preconceived notion. That's the way I like to do it."

THE 74TH ANNUAL EXHIBITION

Advertising

Judging Chairperson

Parry Merkley
Merkley Newman Harty,
New York

Judges

Jeff Atlas
San Francisco

Tom Carnase
Carnase Inc.,
New York

Roy Carruthers
New York

Skip D'Amico
New York

Lynn Dangel
Evanston, Illinois

Kwang-Kyu Kim
Seoul

Koji Mizutani
Mizutani Studio,
Tokyo

Sharon Occhipinti
Wilton, Connecticut

Mylene Pollock
Ogilvy & Mather,
New York

Christian Reuilly
Ogilvy & Mather,
Paris

Tom Rost
FCB Leber Katz,
New York

Donna Weinheim
BBDO,
New York

Graphic Design

Judging Chairperson

Dana Arnett
VSA Partners, Inc.,
Chicago

Judges

Neal Ashby
Recording Industries of America,
Washington, D.C.

Eric Baker
Eric Baker Design Associates,
New York

bill butt
Paris

Andreas Combüchen
Frankfurt Balkind Partners,
New York

Michael Cronan
Michael Cronan Design,
San Francisco

Gail Rigelhaupt
Westpoint Stevens,
New York

Lana Rigsby
Rigsby Design, Inc.,
Houston

I think you'll agree that this is the best Art Directors Annual yet and mirrors the new energy of the organization.

The chairpersons for this year's Advertising and Graphic Design juries were my first choices.

Parry Merkley began his stellar career in Salt Lake City, then moved to New York to work at Ogilvy & Mather on the multiple-award-winning American Express campaign. Two years ago, he opened his own agency, Merkley Newman Harty.

Dana Arnett of VSA Partners, Chicago, has distinguished himself as a designer of vision and style with his work for Harley-Davidson, Potlatch, and the Chicago Board of Trade.

Both of these talented individuals are young enough to appreciate the tremendous diversity of current work and old enough to be tempered a little by tradition. They brought together appropriately wide-ranging panels of jurors, who, with great diligence, reviewed more than 10,000 pieces of work and made the final selection of the 700 pieces represented in this book.

I applaud the Art Directors Club for this exceptional exhibition, and thank Parry and Dana, the jurors, and the support staff under the direction of Luis De Jesus, who all worked so hard to make it happen.

—B. Martin Pedersen
Exhibition Chairperson

This was the 74th time in the history of the industry's oldest creative awards that a distinguished group of judges sifted through a large body of work looking for silver and gold.

Gold was rare, but easy to find. The work was self-evident, readily apparent, and shone brightly. Silver, though more plentiful, took digging and generated debate. The Distinctive Merit awards elicited noisy and often heated disputes.

But one thing is clear: this year's winners are based on solid ideas, rather than execution alone. Entries that relied on fads or trends or intended to shock were quickly passed over.

The classic and the timeless seem to have enjoyed a renaissance this year. Once, I found the judges lingering over a beautifully illustrated color spread as if it were an oasis amid the busy clutter of frenetic computer-generated work. Had the illustration been matched with a headline or an idea worthy of it, the piece would have risen to the top. Instead, it was discarded among thousands of others that failed to withstand thoughtful scrutiny.

In our world, where high technology has now made the surreal, the impossible, and the fantastic the norm, what seems to stand out most is still a simple truth, produced with integrity.

—Parry Merkley
Judging Chairperson,
National and International Advertising

In writing this statement, I am reminded of a line from a Johnny Cash song: "Lies have to be covered up. Truth can run around naked."

Through the milky veneer of Photoshop and eight colors of printed inks on premium paper, can we truly distinguish any virtues in today's work? Is there a great idea here? Does it make sense? Am I actually getting goose bumps or is it just cold? Below the surface of all masterpieces lies the bare essential we define as "truth." My fellow judges and I used it as our standard for evaluating this year's entries.

I am quite sure that many of us "creatives" have, on more than one occasion, pictured the judging process as a glorified clipping shed manned by tourist trimmers. I am happy to smite this canard. Judges are, in fact, a bunch of easy marks, eager to find truth and meaning in the work laid before them.

The individual works may appear to differ, but as a whole you will note in this year's choices a consistent character — the great execution of great ideas. There are still no magic formulas in the big creative laboratory, just a bunch of mad scientists, the next Frankensteins, hard at work. In light of all those steel-gray robots running around out there, maybe we can use a few more monsters. Igor, bring me the idea.

—Dana Arnett
Judging Chairperson,
National and International Graphic Design

GOLD AND SILVER MEDALISTS

GOLD AND SILVER MEDALISTS

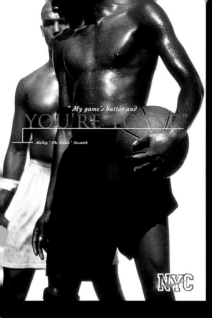

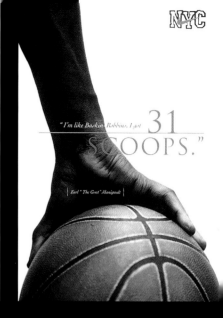

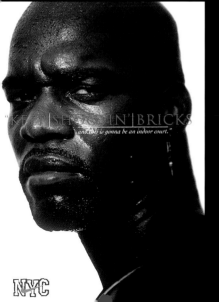

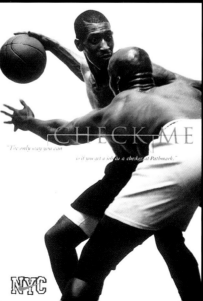

Silver Medalist/National

TRANSIT, CAMPAIGN
Nike NYC "Graffiti"
ART DIRECTOR *John C. Jay*
CREATIVE DIRECTOR *Dan Wieden*
DESIGNER *Petra Langhammer*
PHOTOGRAPHER *Stanley Bach*
AGENCY *Wieden & Kennedy*
CLIENT *Nike*

got milk?

got milk?

Gold Medalist/International

GENERAL, SINGLE
The 200th Anniversary of Sharaku
ART DIRECTOR *Mitsuo Katsui*
DESIGNER *Mitsuo Katsui*
AGENCY *PARCO*
CLIENT *The Mainichi Newspapers*

Gold Medalist/International

GENERAL, SINGLE
PREXCEED "HFX"
ART DIRECTOR *Koji Mizutani*
CREATIVE DIRECTOR *Tamotsu Kawashima*
DESIGNERS *Masashi Yamashita, Hiroshi Ohmizo*
COPYWRITER *Kazushi Shimoda*
PHOTOGRAPHER *Sachiko Kuru*
AGENCY *Dentsu, Inc.*
STUDIO *Mizutani Studio*
CLIENT *Yanagiya Co., Ltd.*

注意、要ス。

注意、要ス。

YOU MAY HAVE HEARD THAT THERE ARE STARVING CHILDREN IN CHINA. MAYBE IT'S BECAUSE WE HIRED AWAY THEIR BEST CHEF.

HUNAN GARDEN 湖南園

11532 PAGE SERVICE RD. 314.432.7015

WHICH WOULD YOU RATHER HAVE AT OUR RESTAURANT, GOOD ENGLISH OR GOOD CHINESE?

HUNAN GARDEN 湖南園

11532 PAGE SERVICE RD. 314.432.7015

SAVE A ROT AT ONE OF ST. ROUIS' MOST DERICIOUS RESTAURANTS.

HUNAN GARDEN 湖南園

11532 PAGE SERVICE RD. 314.432.7015

Silver Medalist/National

GENERAL, CAMPAIGN
Rots and Rots
ART DIRECTOR *David Nien-Li Yang*
COPYWRITERS *Eric Weltner, Rich Wolchock,*
David Nien-Li Yang
AGENCY *The Puckett Group*
CLIENT *Hunan Garden Restaurant*

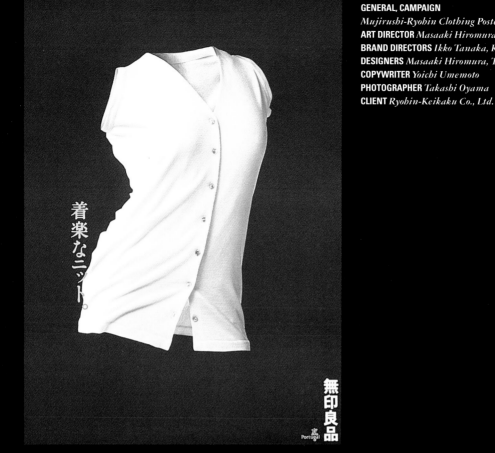

着楽なニット。

無印良品

GENERAL, CAMPAIGN
Mujirushi-Ryohin Clothing Posters
ART DIRECTOR *Masaaki Hiromura*
BRAND DIRECTORS *Ikko Tanaka, Kazuko Koike*
DESIGNERS *Masaaki Hiromura, Toshiyuki Kojima*
COPYWRITER *Yoichi Umemoto*
PHOTOGRAPHER *Takashi Oyama*
CLIENT *Ryohin-Keikaku Co., Ltd.*

ポルトガルは着心地の国。

無印良品

Silver Medalist/International

GENERAL, CAMPAIGN
In the Course of Nature
ART DIRECTOR *Andrei Shelutto*
CREATIVE DIRECTORS *Andrei Shelutto,*
Igor Gurovich
DESIGNERS *Andrei Shelutto, Igor Gurovich*
COPYWRITER *Roman Frolov*
PHOTOGRAPHER *Eduard Basilija*
AGENCY *IMA Press Publishers*
CLIENT *IMA-Press Association*

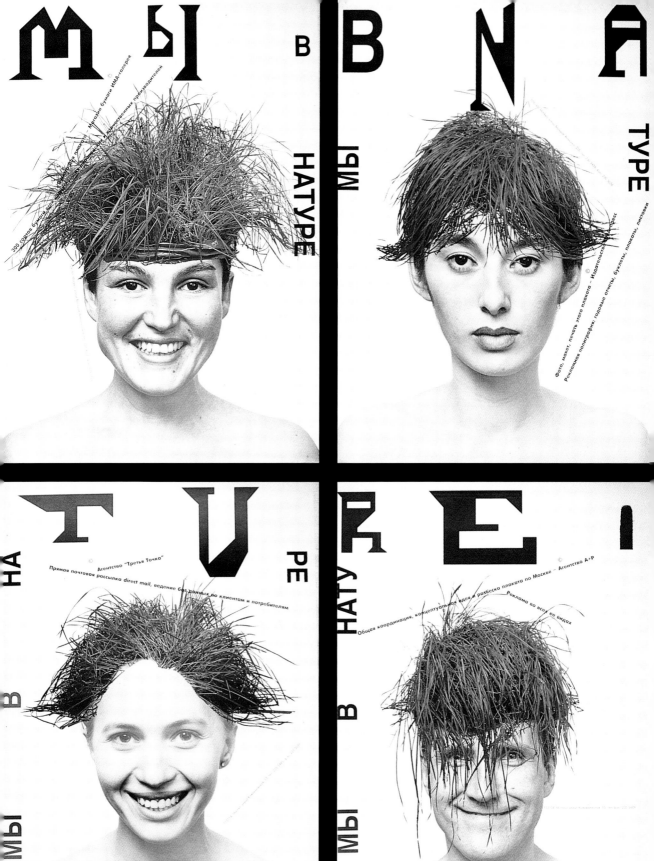

Silver Medalist/National

COMMERCIAL, 30 SECONDS OR LESS
Sound Toner
ART DIRECTOR *Jerry Gentile*
CREATIVE DIRECTOR *Steve Rabosky*
COPYWRITER *Scott Vincent*
PRODUCER *Michelle Burke*
DIRECTOR *Jeff Gorman*
AGENCY *Chiat/Day Inc. Advertising*
CLIENT *Sunkist California Pistachios*

VISUAL: *Open on August Priest doing various sweeping arm motions around a man with his back to Priest.*
INTERVIEWER: *So what does sound toning do?*
VISUAL: *Close-up of man, August Priest.*
PRIEST: *It opens your heart chakra, so you feel unconditional love just vibrating throughout all of you. Comfortably and easily. You can feel your guardian angel surrounding you. Creating balance and harmony.*
SUPER: *August Priest, Sound Toner.*
VISUAL: *Cut to Priest and Dan McLoughlin standing. Priest sound toning into Dan's back.*
SFX: *Sound-toning noises.*
FADE TO SUPER: *Everybody knows the best nuts come from California.*
VISUAL: *Cut to product shot of pistachio bag crashing.*
ANNCR. VO: *Sunkist California Pistachios. Now that's a nut.*
SUPER: *California Pistachios.*

EVERYBODY KNOWS THE BEST NUTS COME FROM CALIFORNIA.

CALIFORNIA PISTACHIOS

Gold Medalist/National

COMMERCIAL, 30 SECONDS OR LESS, CAMPAIGN
Soul, Fighting Fruit, 30 Seconds
ART DIRECTORS *Mike Rosen, Ducan Milner*
CREATIVE DIRECTOR *Marty Cooke*
COPYWRITER *Marty Cooke*
PRODUCERS *Peter Cline, Andrew Chinich*
DIRECTOR *Greg Ramsey*
MUSIC *Kate Bush*
AGENCY *Chiat/Day, New York*
CLIENT *Fruitopia*

ADDITIONAL AWARD

Silver Medalist
COMMERCIAL, 30 SECONDS OR LESS
30 Seconds

Soul
SUPER: *This is what Citrus Consciousness* ™
do to your tongue. Imagine what it can do fo
your soul. Fruitopia ™ *from Minute Maid* ®.
the (mind/icon, body/icon, planet/icon).

Silver Medalist/National

COMMERCIAL, OVER 30 SECONDS
Faces
ART DIRECTOR *Dean Stefanides*
CREATIVE DIRECTORS *Dean Stefanides,*
Larry Hampel
DESIGNERS *Jakob Trollbeck, R/Greenberg*
Associates
COPYWRITER *Larry Hampel*
PRODUCTION COMPANY *Sandbank, Kamen &*
Partners with R/Greenberg Associates
PRODUCER *Jean Muchmore*
DIRECTOR/CINEMATOGRAPHER *Henry Sandbank*
AGENCY *Houston Effler Hampel & Stefanides*
CLIENT *NEC Technologies*

ANNCR. VO: *Multimedia is here. And NEC is making it more powerful than ever. With sharper monitors. Faster* CD-ROM *readers. And advanced networking capabilities. NEC. See, hear, and feel the difference.*

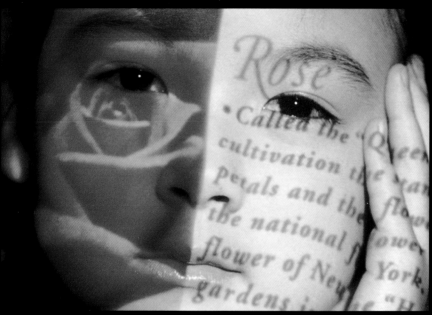

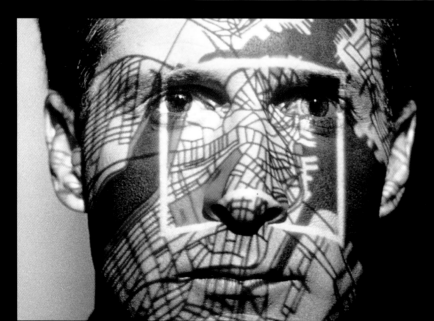

Gold Medalist/National

COMMERCIAL, OVER 30 SECONDS, CAMPAIGN
*Press Conference, Why So Tough, I Had a Dream
Playground/Mother, Street Dribbler*
ART DIRECTORS *Jason Peterson, Paul Hirsch,
Izzy DeBellis*
CREATIVE DIRECTOR *Andy Berlin*
COPYWRITERS *Izzy DeBellis, Paul Hirsch,
Jason Peterson*
PRODUCER *Deborah Sullivan*
DIRECTOR *Jeff Priess*
AGENCY *Berlin Cameron Doyle*
CLIENT *NBA*

ADDITIONAL AWARD

Silver Medalist
COMMERCIAL, OVER 30 SECONDS
Press Conference

Street Dribbler
VISUAL: *Bill Murray dribbling basketball on city
street at night.*
MUSIC: *Dominican monk "chantlike" music.*
MURRAY: *It's like a religion with me. I believe in
myself. I'm there for me. I believe in the ball.
The ball is there for me. I believe in the court.
But I just can't find the court. I have a ball and
I'm here...I just can't find my court. I know it's
out there...somewhere.*
VISUAL: *Fade to black.*

Silver Medalist/National

COMMERCIAL, OVER 30 SECONDS, CAMPAIGN
Grandma's Hero, Dorm Room, Child Reads
ART DIRECTOR *Brian Fandetti*
CREATIVE DIRECTOR *Fred Bertino*
COPYWRITER *Al Lowe*
PRODUCER *Deb Martin*
DIRECTOR *Paul Dektor*
AGENCY *Hill, Holliday, Connors, Cosmopulos*
STUDIO *Dektor Higgins & Associates*
CLIENT *John Hancock Insurance Co.*

Grandma's Hero
SUPER: *Need: To save for a secure retirement.*
WIFE: *I've been thinking about having my mother
move in here...She's old, she needs help, she needs
somebody to, to take care of her, you know—*
SUPER: *Answer: John Hancock's retirement
savings products, including annuities.*
HUSBAND: *Here?*
WIFE: *Yeah...*
SUPER: *Real life, real answers logo.*
HUSBAND: *With us?*
WIFE: *Yeah...*
SUPER: *John Hancock Worldwide Olympic Sponsor
logo. John Hancock Life Insurance Company and
Affiliated Companies, Boston, MA 02117.*
HUSBAND: *Honey, I love your mother, you know I
do, and I would love to have your mother come
live with us. But where?*
WIFE: *Well, um...*
HUSBAND: *There's no room.*
WIFE: *Well, I was thinking maybe we could
add on.*
HUSBAND: *Oh honey, the money. We can't afford
that right now. We got the kids, the cars,
uh...their education.*
WIFE: *What if, what if...*
HUSBAND: *And on top of that, we've got to look at
our retirement. We've got to start looking at that
very seriously.*
WIFE: *But honey, she's my—*
HUSBAND: *We're not getting any younger.*
WIFE: *She's my mother.*
HUSBAND: *I just don't see what we can do.*
CHILD: *Dad? (pause) Grandma could have my
room. OK?*

Michael Conrad.

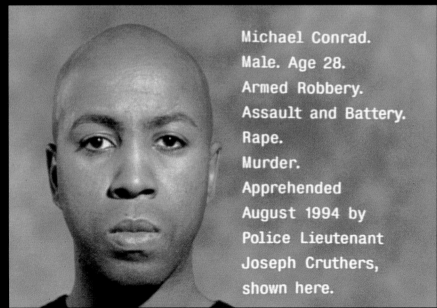

Michael Conrad.
Male. Age 28.
Armed Robbery.
Assault and Battery.
Rape.
Murder.
Apprehended
August 1994 by
Police Lieutenant
Joseph Cruthers,
shown here.

Silver Medalist/International

COMMERCIAL, PUBLIC SERVICE
Policeman
ART DIRECTOR *Benjamin Vendramin*
CREATIVE DIRECTOR *Paul Hains*
COPYWRITER *Robert McDougall*
PRODUCER *Joan Bell-Acosta*
DIRECTOR *Drew Jarvis*
MUSIC *Rick Shurman*
AGENCY *Bozell Palmer Bonner*
STUDIO *Stripes*
CLIENT *Urban Alliance on Race Relations*

VISUAL: *Open on the face of a black man. A series of supers appears through to the end of the spot a we linger on the face.*
MUSIC: *Dramatic notes punctuate supers throughout.*
SUPERS: *Michael Conrad. Male. Age 28. Armed robbery. Assault and battery. Rape. Murder. Apprehended August 1994 by Police Lieutenant Joseph Cruthers, shown here.*
FADE TO LAST SUPER: *Urban Alliance on Race Relations.*

Alex Bishop.
Killed by a drunk driver
on November 8, 1992
on Kent-Kangley Road
in Kent, Washington.

Gold Medalist/National

COMMERCIAL, PUBLIC SERVICE, CAMPAIGN
Bishop, Standiford, Chambers
ART DIRECTOR *Carol DeMelio*
CREATIVE DIRECTORS *Steven Landsberg,*
Carol DeMelio
COPYWRITER *Steven Landsberg*
PRODUCERS *Sally Hotchkiss, Neal Bergman*
AGENCY *Wells Rich Greene BDDP*
CLIENT *The Ad Council/Department of*
Transportation

ADDITIONAL AWARDS

Gold Medalist
COMMERCIAL, PUBLIC SERVICE
Bishop

Silver Medalist
COMMERCIAL, PUBLIC SERVICE
Standiford

Merit
COMMERCIAL, PUBLIC SERVICE
Chambers

Bishop
VISUAL: *Alex swimming in large pool.*
MOM (OFF CAMERA): *Who is that swimming?*
Get your legs up!
ALEX: *Like this?*
MOM: *That's the way.*
FRIEND (OFF CAMERA): *What are you doing? Now*
you're kicking Al!
ALEX: *I'm almost there.*
DISSOLVE TO SUPER: *Alex Bishop. Killed by a*
drunk driver on November 8, 1992 on Kent-
Kangley Road in Kent, Washington.
MOM: *Whoa, you made it all the way.*
ANNCR.: *If you don't stop your friend from driving*
drunk, who will?
MOM: *Good job!*
VISUAL: *Dissolve to Alex reaching the edge of*
the pool.
ANNCR.: *Do whatever it takes.*
MOM: *Are you having a good time?*
ALEX: *Yeah.*
SUPER: *Friends don't let friends drive drunk logo.*

Silver Medalist/National

COMMERCIAL, PUBLIC SERVICE, CAMPAIGN
Truth: Sackman, Crawford, Reynolds
ART DIRECTOR *Dave Gardiner*
CREATIVE DIRECTORS *Rich Herstek, Peter Favat*
ASSOCIATE CREATIVE DIRECTOR *Stu Cooperrider*
COPYWRITERS *Ken Lewis, Stu Cooperrider*
PRODUCERS *Harry McCoy, John Bick*
DIRECTOR *Neil Abramson*
AGENCY *Houston Effler Herstek Favat*
STUDIO *Palomar/Picture Park*
CLIENT *Massachusetts Department of
Public Health*

ADDITIONAL AWARD

Silver Medalist
COMMERCIAL, PUBLIC SERVICE
Truth: Sackman

Truth: Crawford
VICTOR CRAWFORD: *Maybe they'll get to your little
brother or sister. Or maybe the kid down the
block. But one thing is perfectly clear to me,
tobacco companies are after children. Why?
Because tobacco companies know that 90% of
smokers start as children before they know any
better. Of course, marketing to kids is unethical,
so they just deny it. I'm Victor Crawford. I was a
tobacco lobbyist for five years so I know how
tobacco companies work. I lied. And I'm sorry.*

Silver Medalist/National

COMMERCIAL, LOW BUDGET
Nike NYC Series #2, Five Spots
ART DIRECTOR *John C. Jay*
CREATIVE DIRECTORS *Dan Wieden, Jamie Barrett,*
Jim Riswold
COPYWRITER *Jimmy Smith*
PRODUCERS *Renee Raab, Radical-Media*
DIRECTOR *Robert Leacock*
AGENCY *Wieden & Kennedy*
CLIENT *Nike*

Trash Talk
*Then I bring it back out cause I wanna
embarrass him. I wanna shake him and fake
him, and I'm lookin' at his face sayin' whatcha
want me to do, make a lay-up, make a jump
shot? Make up your mind whatcha want me to
do. Bam bam bam, I'm goin' through my legs
twice, then I'm gonna reverse, hesitate, stop. I
freeze, then I pull up on him, then I back up on
him. "Yeah, c'mon nah nah nah uh oh, you ain't
guardin' me, oh here I'm back again, oh I thought
you was guardin' me." An' I'm sayin', "Now let's
go, push up, push up, push up now." Up, he's in
the air, I done faked him, but I goin' back and
fake him again, and I goin' to the basket, layin'
it up, behind my back double reverse fake head
fake, I'm lookin' at him sayin', "Hey you can't
guard me man, I got so many moves last game I
shook myself."*

Silver Medalist/National

FULL PAGE OR SPREAD
Absolut Brooklyn Bridge
ART DIRECTORS *Dan Braun, Bart Slomkowski*
CREATIVE DIRECTORS *Arnie Arlow, Peter Lubalin*
COPYWRITERS *Dan Braun, Bart Slomkowski*
PHOTOGRAPHER *Steve Bronstein*
AGENCY *TBWA Advertising, Inc.*
CLIENT *Absolut*

ABSOLUT BRO

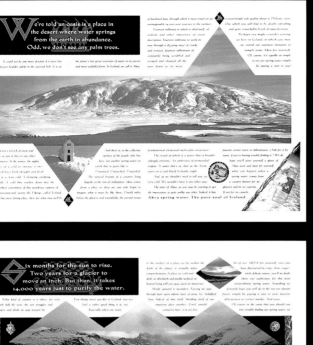

We're told an oasis is a place in the desert where water springs from the earth in abundance. Odd, we don't see any palm trees.

Akva spring water. The pure soul of Iceland.

Six months for the sun to rise. Two years for a glacier to move an inch. But then, it takes 14,000 years just to purify the water.

Akva spring water. The pure soul of Iceland.

Just thinking about how pure our water is sends chills down our spines. (Granted, being within a whisper of the Arctic Circle might have something to do with it.)

Akva spring water. The pure soul of Iceland.

Ponce de Leon went to his grave believing the fountain of youth lay hidden in some snake infested swamp in Florida. If only he'd tried a bit further north.

Akva spring water. The pure soul of Iceland.

Silver Medalist/National

CAMPAIGN

Oasis, Arctic Circle, Ponce de Leon, 14,0

ART DIRECTOR *John Doyle*

CREATIVE DIRECTOR *John Doyle*

COPYWRITER *Ernie Schenck*

PHOTOGRAPHERS *Sigugeir Sigurjonsson, Jamey Stillings, Pall Steffansson*

ILLUSTRATOR *Peter Hall*

PRODUCER *Michelle Caraccia*

STUDIO *Berlin Cameron Doyle*

CLIENT *AKVA Spring Water*

ADDITIONAL AWARD

Distinctive Merit

FULL PAGE OR SPREAD

14,000 Years

Silver Medalist/International

SERIES
Zanders "Z" with Design
DESIGNERS *Alain LeQuernec, Shigeo Fukuda,*
Alan Fletcher, Uwe Loesch, Dan Reisinger,
Milton Glaser

Silver Medalist/National

COMMERCIAL, OVER 30 SECONDS, CAMPAIGN
Paulo, Francesca, Carlo and Maria
CREATIVE DIRECTOR *Bob Hoffman*
COPYWRITER *Sam Pond*
PRODUCER *Patti Dudgeon*
AGENCY *Hoffman/Lewis*
CLIENT *Spectrum Foods, Inc.*

MUSIC: *Theme from* A Man and a Woman

AVO: *Paulo has just enjoyed his fabulous meal of Capellini al Pomodoro at Prego, the restaurant. He pays the bill and makes his way toward the bar. Everyone admires him. Or so it seems to Paulo. He is on the prowl. He is a cat. A panther. He is...Paulo. Does he care that his fly is down? No, he doesn't care. He doesn't know! So why should he care? He waves to the Prego staff and calls them by name. Giancarlo! Giuseppe! Roberto! They do not answer. These are not their names. But Paulo is pleased. He believes he has made an impression on the leggy brunette perched at the end of the bar. She is kittenish, thinks Paulo. But I am a* bigger *cat. A lion, thinks Paulo. She looks up. What is it that she sees? Is it the blueness of his eyes? The strength of his chin? No, it is the spinach caught between his teeth. It has been there for hours. Prego. Union Street, San Francisco. See. Be seen. Be seen eating.*

Silver Medalist/National

COMMERCIAL, PUBLIC SERVICE
Jen, Lonnie/Gene, Michael/Sandy
CREATIVE DIRECTORS *Steve St. Clair, Andrew Payton*
COPYWRITERS *Steve St. Clair, Andrew Payton*
PRODUCER *Phil Lee*
AGENCY *Lord, Dentsu & Partners*
STUDIO *Full House Productions*
CLIENT *Partnership for a Drug-Free America*

Michael/Sandy

SFX: *Crackle of answering machine.*

SFX: *Beep.*

SANDY: *This is to Michael. I love you more than anything in the world. And you destroyed your life...you destroyed our lives...you took away everything that we had and we loved...and you're going to kill yourself and you won't listen to nobody and I don't want to see that happen to you. So please wake up and go for help before something goes wrong and you'll never be able to take that...to make that step to go. I love you. Sandy.*

SFX: *Phone hangs up.*

ANNCR.: *If someone you know is using drugs, you better talk to them. And if they won't listen, talk to us. Call 212-727-8502. Leave a recording, and we'll get it on the air. 212-727-8502. Millions will hear it. Maybe one person out there will get the message. A message from The Partnership for a Drug-Free America.*

DISTINCTIVE MERIT AWARDS

Distinctive Merit/International

OUTDOOR, CAMPAIGN
Dog Bone, Dog Collar, Dog Face
ART DIRECTOR *Michael McLaughlin*
CREATIVE DIRECTORS *Larry Tolpin,*
Michael McLaughlin, Stephen Creet
COPYWRITER *Stephen Creet*
ILLUSTRATORS *Various*
AGENCY *BBDO Canada*
CLIENT *Molson Breweries*

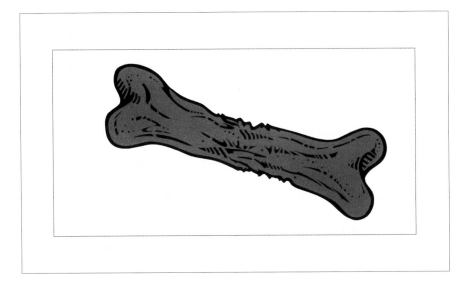

Distinctive Merit/International

OUTDOOR, CAMPAIGN
Kodak Gold D.I.A.R. Film: Yellow, Red, Blue
ART DIRECTOR *Jean-Michel Alirol*
CREATIVE DIRECTOR *Jean-Paul Bacquer*
COPYWRITER *Dominique Marchand*
PHOTOGRAPHER *Richard Croft*
ART BUYER *Elaine Harris*
AGENCY *Young & Rubicam France*
CLIENT *Kodak Pathe, Philippe Veron*

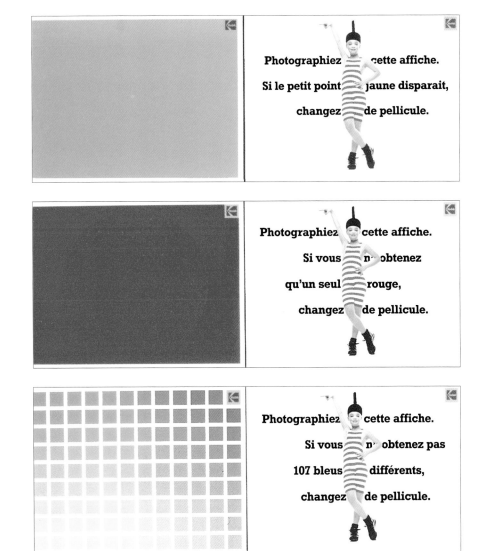

THE LOS ANGELES COUNTY CORONER'S OFFICE GIFT SHOP

1104 North Mission Road, Room 216 (213) 343-0786. Proceeds benefit the Youthful Drunk Driving Visitation Program.

To claim that only tough guys wear Everlast is probably a generalization.
However, it's doubtful many start the day with a croissant and a cup of cappuccino.

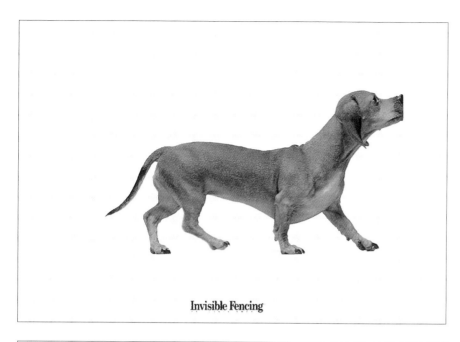

Invisible Fencing

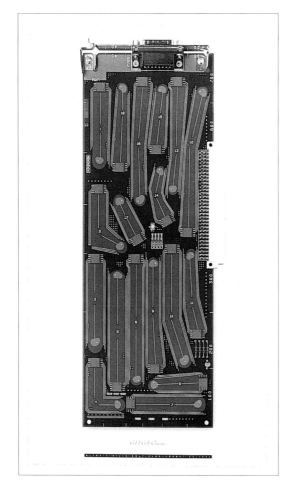

Distinctive Merit/National

GENERAL, SINGLE
Golf Outing
ART DIRECTOR *Jeff Jahn*
CREATIVE DIRECTOR *Lyle Wedemeyer*
COPYWRITER *Pete Smith*
PHOTOGRAPHER *Scott McCulley*
ILLUSTRATOR *Scott McCulley*
AGENCY *Martin/Williams, Pete Smith Advertising*
STUDIO *Parallel Productions*
CLIENT *GTI*

Distinctive Merit/International

GENERAL, SINGLE
Frankfurter Büchernacht
ART DIRECTOR *Gunter Rambow*
CREATIVE DIRECTOR *Gunter Rambow*
DESIGNER *Gunter Rambow*
ILLUSTRATOR *Gunter Rambow*
AGENCY *Rambow + van de Sand*
STUDIO *Rambow + van de Sand*
CLIENT *Frankfurter Buchhändler und Verleger*

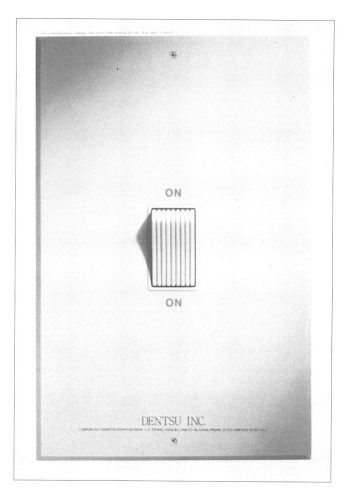

Distinctive Merit/International

GENERAL, SINGLE
A Total Communications Company That Never Stops Working
ART DIRECTOR *Takashi Fukui*
CREATIVE DIRECTOR *Masaharu Nakano*
DESIGNER *Takashi Fukui*
COPYWRITER *Marc X. Grigoroff*
PHOTOGRAPHER *Takashi Seo*
AGENCY *Dentsu, Inc.*
STUDIO *Dentsu Cotec Inc.*
CLIENT *Dentsu, Inc.*

Distinctive Merit/International

GENERAL, SINGLE
Wedding Ceremony
ART DIRECTORS *Motoya Sugisaki, Fuhmihiko Enokido*
CREATIVE DIRECTOR *Motoya Sugisaki*
DESIGNER *Motoya Sugisaki*
PHOTOGRAPHER *Toru Kinoshita*
ILLUSTRATOR *Motoya Sugisaki*
AGENCY *Motoya Sugisaki Design Office*
CLIENT *St. Sonea Chapel*

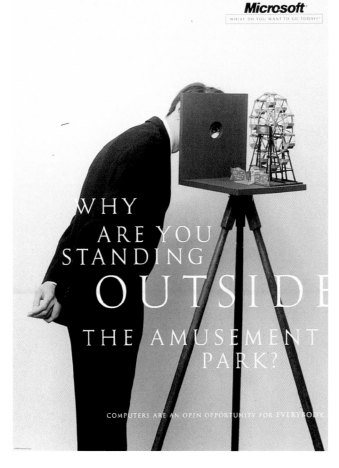

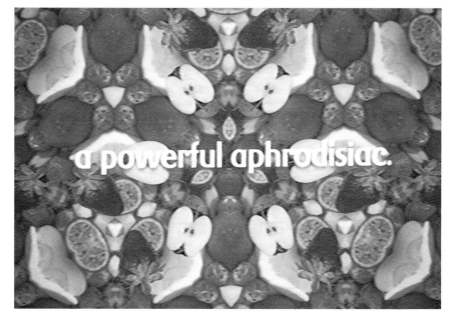

(facing page)
Distinctive Merit/National

POSTERS, GENERAL, CAMPAIGN
Where Do You Want to Go Today? P.O.S.
ART DIRECTORS *John Jay, Steve Sandstrom*
CREATIVE DIRECTOR *John Jay*
DESIGNER *Steve Sandstrom*
COPYWRITER *Jim Riswold*
PHOTOGRAPHER *Geoff Kern*
AGENCY *Wieden & Kennedy*
STUDIO *Sandstrom Design*
CLIENT *Microsoft*

(right)
Distinctive Merit/National

COMMERCIAL, 30 SECONDS OR LESS
Aphrodisiac
ART DIRECTORS *Mike Rosen, Ducan Milner*
CREATIVE DIRECTOR *Marty Cooke*
COPYWRITER *Marty Cooke*
PRODUCERS *Peter Cline, Andrew Chinich*
DIRECTOR *Greg Ramsey*
MUSIC *Kate Bush*
AGENCY *Chiat/Day, New York*
CLIENT *Fruitopia*

SUPER: *The ancient Maori believed passion fruit was a powerful aphrodisiac. Hey, it couldn't hurt. Try Strawberry Passion Awareness™, Fruitopia™ from Minute Maid®. For the (mind/icon, body/icon, planet/icon).*

Distinctive Merit/National

COMMERCIAL, 30 SECONDS OR LESS
Ping Pong Lady
ART DIRECTOR *Jerry Gentile*
CREATIVE DIRECTOR *Steve Rabosky*
COPYWRITER *Scott Vincent*
PRODUCER *Michelle Burke*
DIRECTOR *Jeff Gorman*
AGENCY *Chiat/Day Inc. Advertising*
CLIENT *Sunkist California Pistachios*

VISUAL: *Open on close-up of a woman in front of a bike path.*
SFX: *Bike bell rings.*
VISUAL: *Cut to Ruth playing solo with ping pong balls, catching them in her mouth. Ruth catches ping pong balls with hand and bows. Ruth plays "Three Blind Mice" on the xylophone using the ping pong balls shooting from her mouth.*
MUSIC: *From the song "Three Blind Mice."*
FADE INTO SUPER: *Everybody knows the best nuts come from California.*
VISUAL: *Cut to product shot of pistachio bag crashing.*
ANNCR. VO: *Sunkist California Pistachios. Now that's a nut.*
SUPER: *California Pistachios.*

EVERYBODY KNOWS
THE BEST NUTS COME
FROM CALIFORNIA.

CALIFORNIA PISTACHIOS

Distinctive Merit/National

COMMERCIAL, 30 SECONDS OR LESS
Orangutan
ART DIRECTOR *Bruce Hurwit*
CREATIVE DIRECTOR *Arthur Bijur*
COPYWRITER *Arthur Bijur*
PRODUCER *MaryEllen Duggan*
DIRECTOR *Bruce Hurwit*
AGENCY *Cliff Freeman & Partners*
STUDIO *Crossroads Films*
CLIENT *Little Caesars*

VISUAL: *Open on orangutan in testing lab. In front of him on counter is one button with a sign that reads "1" and another big button that reads "2." A mechanical hand enters and shows the orangutan a single banana.*
VOICE THROUGH SPEAKER: *One banana?...(another hand presents two bananas)...Or two bananas?*
VISUAL: *Ape ponders, scratches head and then pushes button marked "2." "2" lights up.*
SFX: *Buzzz.*
VISUAL: *Cut to an orangutan wearing a nighty in a come-hither pose.*
ANNCR.: *One female orangutan?...*
VISUAL: *Pan to reveal two orangs blowing kisses.*
ANNCR.: *...Or two female orangutans?*
VISUAL: *Immediately cut back to male hitting "2" buzzer almost before sentence is completed.*
SFX: *Buzzzzzzzzz!*
VISUAL: *Cut to pizza graphic on an easel of one pizza and two pizzas.*
ANNCR.: *One pizza for $9.98...Or two for $9.98?*
VISUAL: *Cut back to orangutan now flanked by the two females who are kissing him, stroking his hair, etc. He smiles a huge smile.*
ANNCR.: *He seems to prefer two.*
VISUAL: *Cut to food.*
ANNCR.: *Two is better than one, so why settle for one supreme pizza when you can get* two *at Little Caesars for just $9.98!*
LITTLE CAESAR: *Pizza, pizza!*

Distinctive Merit/National

COMMERCIAL, 30 SECONDS OR LESS
Workaholic
ART DIRECTORS *Bruce Hurwit, Matt Vescovo*
CREATIVE DIRECTOR *Arthur Bijur*
COPYWRITER *Arthur Bijur*
PRODUCER *Anne Kurtzman*
DIRECTOR *Henry Holzman*
AGENCY *Cliff Freeman & Partners*
STUDIO *Industrial Artists*
CLIENT *Staples*

VISUAL: *Open on a man sitting behind his desk in his home office talking to camera.*
MAN: *(sincere) I came to the realization that I'm a workaholic. I was putting my work before my family. I was missing my kid's childhood. So I quit my job and now I'm working out of my home. And I'll tell you something, I wouldn't miss these years for anything in the world…(suddenly very professional) How ya comin' with those copies, hon?*
VISUAL: *Quick pan to three-year-old girl at copier.*
GIRL: *OK, Daddy.*
VISUAL: *Cut to wide shot of the scene. Prices pop on over supplies. Little girl still working away.*
ANNCR.: *Staples has everything you need to set up a home office. Over 5000 office supplies all at the guaranteed low price.*
VISUAL: *Little girl walks over to her father with a really big pile of papers.*
MAN: *Can you collate those for Daddy?*
VISUAL: *Cut to logo.*
ANNCR.: *Staples. Yeah, we've got that.*

Distinctive Merit/International

COMMERCIAL, 30 SECONDS OR LESS
NEC Parabola
ART DIRECTORS *Mario Sanasi, Paul Rauch*
CREATIVE DIRECTOR *Guy Winston*
COPYWRITERS *Paul Rauch, Mario Sanasi*
PRODUCERS *Denise McKeon, Phillip Dagg*
DIRECTOR *Paul Middleditch*
AGENCY *Lintas Sydney*
CLIENT *NEC HEA*

VISUAL: *We open on two men facing the camera. They are both somewhat dull-looking characters. The man behind is talking enthusiastically about the NEC Parabola and its features. The man in front is politely trying to interrupt to talk about the Parabola also.*
MAN 1: *Bob and I are here to tell you about something that's got us very excited. NEC's Parabola range of televisions. They've got a three-year warranty, which we think is fantastic. They're from the people who've sold over a million Australian-made color TVs. Superb sound comes from the surround-sound speaker system, but the best feature of the NEC Parabola is its...*
VISUAL: *After repeatedly trying to say his part, the man in front picks up a remote control, points it toward the man behind and switches him off. The camera pulls back to reveal him standing in front of the NEC Parabola. The man behind was only a lifelike image on the TV screen.*
MAN 2: *...lifelike picture.*
SUPER: *NEC logo, Parabola logo.*

Distinctive Merit/International

COMMERCIAL, 30 SECONDS OR LESS, CAMPAIGN
Child, Small Creature, An Old Mercedes
ART DIRECTORS *Kazuo Tsutsumi, Tomoko Kanezaki*
CREATIVE DIRECTOR *Takehiko Miura*
COPYWRITER *Makoto Tsunoda*
PHOTOGRAPHER *Tamotsu Fujii*
PRODUCER *Shuji Kamimoto*
DIRECTOR *Shiego Yuki*
MUSIC *Kayoko Higashi*
AGENCY *Dentsu, Inc.*
STUDIO *TYO Production Inc.*
CLIENT *Mercedes-Benz Japan Co., Ltd.*

Child
ANNCR.: *Everyone makes mistakes. This is our basic premise for safety.*

Distinctive Merit/National

COMMERCIAL, OVER 30 SECONDS
Microphone
ART DIRECTOR *Emily Oberman*
CREATIVE DIRECTOR *Andy Berlin*
DESIGNER *Number 17*
COPYWRITER *Scott Burns*
PRODUCER *Deborah Sullivan*
DIRECTOR *Mark Coppos*
MUSIC *Machine Head*
AGENCY *Berlin Cameron Doyle*
CLIENT *Condé Nast*

VO 1: *It's the 500-channel man. He's got all the satellites winking at each other. He's got ones and zeros for everyone. He's here today with tomorrow for you. He's got a strand of magic running below the street, worming its way into your living room and your living room. He wants to whisper in your ear about the future. He's come for your attention span. But, now that everyone's listening, does anyone have anything to say?*
VO 2: *From the Gutenberg press to the information superhighway, the importance of technology will never be greater than the ideas it is meant to convey. Content comes first. Condé Nast.*

Distinctive Merit/National

COMMERCIAL, OVER 30 SECONDS
Peaceable Kingdom
ART DIRECTOR *Brian Fandetti*
CREATIVE DIRECTOR *Fred Bertino*
COPYWRITER *Al Lowe*
PRODUCER *Deb Martin*
DIRECTOR *Henry Sandbank*
AGENCY *Hill, Holliday, Connors, Cosmopulos*
STUDIO *Sandbank Films*
CLIENT *John Hancock Financial Services*

VISUAL: *Animals walk into screen and assemble in a woodland setting one by one as spot progresses, as in the Granville Hicks painting* Peaceable Kingdom.
ANNCR.: *Once every few years, we get a glimpse of what life on earth could be — a life in which we can all live together, despite all our differences, in harmony and peace. This is the spirit of the Olympic Games. And at John Hancock, it's our hope that someday this is what real life will be.*
SUPER: *John Hancock/USA five-rings, Official Life Insurance, Sponsor 1994/1996 U.S. Olympic teams* logo.
LEGAL SUPER: *John Hancock Mutual Life Insurance Company and Affiliated Companies, Boston, MA 02117.*

Distinctive Merit/National

COMMERCIAL, OVER 30 SECONDS
Memories
ART DIRECTORS *Jerry Andelin, James Dalthorp*
CREATIVE DIRECTOR *Joe O'Neal*
COPYWRITERS *Paul Mimiaga, Joe O'Neal*
PRODUCER *Victoria Waldock*
DIRECTOR *Leslie Dektor*
AGENCY *Hal Riney & Partners, San Francisco*
STUDIO *Dektor Higgins & Associates*
CLIENT *Buena Vista*

Series of different kids, 3 to 9, telling in their own words the story of "Snow White and the Seven Dwarfs."
BOY, 7: *Well, there was a girl and she was a princess and she was as white as snow so they called her Snow White...*
GIRL, 6: *...and the mirror said she's the prettiest of all and the Wicked Queen was very angry...*
TITLE: *The Story of Snow White and the Seven Dwarfs.*
GIRL, 8: *...and the hunter was going to kill her, but she was so beautiful he couldn't...*
BOY, 3: *...and then she sees a big, bad wolf...*
TITLE: *More or less.*
GIRL, 5: *...and she runs away to a cottage and her and the animals clean it up and then the seven dwarfs find Snow White in their bed and she has to live with them for a little while...*
TITLE: *As told by the first generation of children...*
GIRL, 9: *...and the Queen, she keeps trying to kill her, then finally she does with a poisonous apple, and she dies...*
TITLE: *...who are finally able to own it.*
BOY, 6: *...and the seven dwarfs try to help her no matter what, but they can't...*
TITLE: *Snow White and the Seven Dwarfs.*
GIRL, 7: *...then one day a prince kisses her and she wakes up...*
TITLE: *Available on video October 28.*
GIRL, 4: *...and the prince and the Snow White live happily ever after. The end.*
VISUAL: *Clips of the movie.*
TITLE: *Someday has finally come.*

Distinctive Merit/National

COMMERCIAL, OVER 30 SECONDS, CAMPAIGN
Magic Fingers, Singing Baby, Focus Group
ART DIRECTORS *Greg Bell, John Leu,*
Donna Weinheim
CREATIVE DIRECTORS *Cliff Freeman, Arthur Bijur,*
Donna Weinheim
COPYWRITERS *Greg Bell, John Leu, Cliff Freeman,*
Arthur Bijur, Michelle Roufa
PRODUCERS *Anne Kurtzman, MaryEllen Duggan*
DIRECTORS *Bruce Hurwit, Mark Story,*
Charles Wittenmaier
MUSIC *Michael Carroll Music*
AGENCY *Cliff Freeman & Partners*
STUDIO *Crossroads Films, Harmony Pictures*
CLIENT *Little Caesars*

ADDITIONAL AWARDS

Merit
COMMERCIAL, 30 SECONDS OR LESS
Magic Fingers

Distinctive Merit
COMMERCIAL, OVER 30 SECONDS
Focus Group

Singing Baby
VISUAL: *Open on a dad and a grandmother at dining*
table admiring two Little Caesars Pizzas.
GRANNY: *Have you ever seen anything more amazing*
than Little Caesars Italian Sausage pizza?
VISUAL: *Father looks up. Cut to reveal a baby sitting in*
a high chair spinning plates on sticks. On baby's head is
a cat doing a handstand while balancing a full goldfish
bowl on its foot. Baby sings "Give My Regards to
Broadway." Cut back to father.
FATHER: *No.*
VISUAL: *Cut to food section.*
ANNCR.: *Italian Sausage pizza! Loaded with sausage,*
peppers, and onions. The newest from a whole menu of
Little Caesars Pleasers. Any two for $9.98!
LITTLE CAESARS: *Pizza, pizza!*
ANNCR.: *Or get one for $5.99!*
LITTLE CAESAR: *Pizza!*

Distinctive Merit/National

COMMERCIAL, PUBLIC SERVICE
Celebrity Endorsement
ART DIRECTOR *Matthew Schwartz*
CREATIVE DIRECTOR *Stan Becker*
DESIGNER *Matthew Schwartz*
COPYWRITER *David George*
PRODUCER *Jerry Boyle*
AGENCY *Saatchi & Saatchi DFS/Pacific*
STUDIO *Saatchi & Saatchi DFS/Pacific*
CLIENT *Partnership for a Drug-Free America*

Audio only
ANNCR.: *In advertising they say one of the surest ways to get your message across is to put celebrities in your commercial. We hope they're right.*

Distinctive Merit/National

COMMERCIAL, PUBLIC SERVICE
Eastern Veterinary Blood Bank
ART DIRECTOR *Ty Harper*
CREATIVE DIRECTOR *Rob Shapiro*
COPYWRITER *Rob Shapiro*
PRODUCER *Frank Soukup*
DIRECTOR *Gary Johns*
AGENCY *Earle Palmer Brown, Richmond*
CLIENT *Eastern Veterinary Blood Bank*

ONE DAY NATURE
IS GOING TO LOSE RESPECT
FOR HUMAN BEINGS.

Distinctive Merit/International

COMMERCIAL, PUBLIC SERVICE
Birds
ART DIRECTORS *Luiz Claudio de Carvalho,*
Roberto Esteves
CREATIVE DIRECTOR *Clovis Calia*
COPYWRITERS *Fábio Victória, Paulo Leite*
PHOTOGRAPHER *Klaus Meewes*
PRODUCER *José Augusto Machado*
DIRECTOR *Vinicius Galcliardi*
MUSIC *MCR*
AGENCY *Standard, Ogilvy & Mathers*
CLIENT *Gazeta Television*

Distinctive Merit/National

COMMERCIAL, LOW BUDGET
Accountant
ART DIRECTOR *Robert Shaw West*
CREATIVE DIRECTOR *Mike Drazen*
COPYWRITER *Ken Cills*
PRODUCER *Joe Mosca*
AGENCY *Earle Palmer Brown, Philadelphia*
STUDIO *Earle Palmer Brown, Philadelphia*
CLIENT *WMMR 93.3 FM*

VO: *Doctors have this theory that if you play classical music to infants they'll grow up with a better understanding of complex relationships like math. They don't know what effect rock and roll will have, but I play this stuff for him anyway. I figure the world can live with one less accountant.*
SUPER: *Logo.*

Distinctive Merit/National

COMMERCIAL, LOW BUDGET
Litter
ART DIRECTOR *Peter Cohen*
COPYWRITER *Jay Taub*
PRODUCERS *Peter Cohen, Jay Taub*
DIRECTOR *Daniel Fisher*
AGENCY *StreetSmart Advertising*
CLIENT *Coalition for the Homeless*

ADDITIONAL AWARD

Merit
COMMERCIAL, PUBLIC SERVICE

SFX: *City-street sounds throughout.*
VISUAL: *Open on a busy New York City sidewalk strewn with garbage, litter, and debris. Camera dollies down sidewalk as people walk by. More litter blows through frame.*
SUPER: *Please don't litter.*
VISUAL: *Camera still dollying. We pass more debris and litter until we come across a homeless man lying on the sidewalk.*
SUPER: *People have to sleep here.*
VISUAL: *Dissolve to black.*
SUPER: *Coalition for the Homeless. 212-964-5900.*

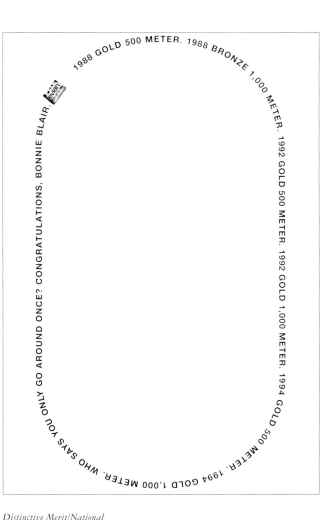

Distinctive Merit/National

FULL PAGE OR SPREAD
Absolut D.C.
ART DIRECTOR *Maria Kostyk-Petro*
CREATIVE DIRECTORS *Arnie Arlow, Peter Lubalin*
COPYWRITERS *Lisa Retting-Falcone, Alan Levine*
PHOTOGRAPHER *Steve Bronstein*
AGENCY *TBWA Advertising, Inc.*
CLIENT *Absolut*

Distinctive Merit/National

FULL PAGE OR SPREAD
Bonnie Blair
ART DIRECTORS *Maria Kostyk-Petro, Lisa Lipkin*
CREATIVE DIRECTORS *Arnie Arlow, Peter Lubalin*
DESIGNERS *Maria Kostyk-Petro, Lisa Lipkin*
COPYWRITERS *Lisa Lipkin, Maria Kostyk-Petro*
AGENCY *TBWA Advertising, Inc.*
CLIENT *Evian*

TO YOU IT LOOKS LIKE A
HALF-EATEN RED APPLE.

TO SOMEONE WHO'S BEEN
THROUGH OUR EXHIBIT, IT
LOOKS LIKE IT WAS EATEN
BETWEEN 6 AND 12 P.M. BY
A MALE WITH A CHIPPED
UPPER-RIGHT BICUSPID,
AN EXTREME OVERBITE,
AND A MISSING LOWER
LEFT FIRST MOLAR THAT
POSITIVELY CONFIRMS THE
IDENTITY OF THE VICTIM IN
YOUR FIRST MURDER CASE.

A robbery in a diner. A dead body in the alley. Whodunit?
It's the new interactive exhibit where you hear the eye
witnesses, gather the evidence, and use the science of
forensics to crack the case. Investigation is now underway.

WHODUNIT?
MUSEUM OF SCIENCE
It's Alive!™

TO YOU IT LOOKS LIKE AN
ORDINARY BLACK COMB.

TO SOMEONE WHO'S BEEN
THROUGH OUR EXHIBIT IT
LOOKS LIKE IT BELONGED
TO A RIGHT-HANDED, CURLY
GRAY-HAIRED, MIDDLE-AGED
CAUCASIAN MALE, WHO
PARTS HIS HAIR ON THE LEFT
SIDE, IS A HEAVY SMOKER
OF BOTH CIGARETTES AND
MARIJUANA, MOST LIKELY
HAS A JOB THAT INVOLVES
WORKING WITH INDUSTRIAL
INSECTICIDES AND COULD BE
AN EXTREMLY IMPORTANT
KEY TO SOLVING YOUR
VERY FIRST MURDER CASE.

A robbery in a diner. A dead body in the alley. Whodunit?
It's the new interactive exhibit where you hear the eye
witnesses, gather the evidence, and use the science of
forensics to crack the case. Investigation is now underway.

WHODUNIT?
MUSEUM OF SCIENCE
It's Alive!™

Distinctive Merit/National

CAMPAIGN
Whodunit
ART DIRECTOR *Ron Rosen*
CREATIVE DIRECTORS *Rich Herstek, Peter Favat*
COPYWRITER *Pete Nichols*
PHOTOGRAPHER *Bruce Peterson*
AGENCY *Houston Effler Herstek Favat*
CLIENT *Museum of Science, Boston*

TO YOU IT LOOKS LIKE
A TUBE OF LIPSTICK.

TO SOMEONE WHO'S BEEN
TO OUR EXHIBIT IT LOOKS
LIKE IT BELONGED TO
A HEAVY, LEFT-HANDED,
5'10", BROWN-HAIRED
WOMAN WHO'S WANTED
IN CONNECTION WITH
TWO ROBBERIES IN
ST. PETERSBURG, FLORIDA
AND FLED TO BOSTON
FOUR MONTHS AGO AND
IS NOW ONE OF THE
PRIME SUSPECTS IN YOUR
FIRST MURDER CASE.

A robbery in a diner. A dead body in the alley. Whodunit?
It's the new interactive exhibit where you hear the eye
witnesses, gather the evidence, and use the science of
forensics to crack the case. Investigation is now underway.

WHODUNIT?
MUSEUM OF SCIENCE
It's Alive!™

Distinctive Merit/National

CAMPAIGN
EDS Management Consulting Services
ART DIRECTORS *Dick Mitchell, Leslie Davis*
CREATIVE DIRECTOR *Dick Mitchell*
DESIGNER *Dick Mitchell*
COPYWRITERS *Leslie Davis, Dick Mitchell*
PHOTOGRAPHER *Brian Fewell*
AGENCY *The Richards Group*
STUDIO *RBMM*
CLIENT *EDS*

(facing page)
Distinctive Merit/National

NEWSPAPER, PUBLIC SERVICE, FULL PAGE OR SPREAD
She Couldn't Vote
ART DIRECTOR *Marc Galucci*
CREATIVE DIRECTOR *Michael Sheehan*
COPYWRITER *Michael Sheehan*
ILLUSTRATORS *Kent Barton, Leslie Bistrowitz*
AGENCY *Clarke Goward*
CLIENT *Abigail Adams Historical Society*

She married a President.
She gave birth to a President.
Pity she couldn't vote for one.

John Adams,
2nd U.S. President

John Quincy Adams,
6th U.S. President

Abigail Smith Adams was, most certainly, one of America's more eminent women. In 1764, she wed John Adams, the second president of the United States. In 1767, she gave birth to John Quincy Adams, the sixth President of the United States. What's even more remarkable about her life is that she was, like every other American woman of the time, forbidden by law to vote for either of them. While her voice was silenced at the polls, her influence on both domestic and international matters was, in no way, subdued. To her husband and son, she was a valued counselor. Her letters touched on any number of timeless issues, including the poor financial state of the nation, the equality of women, and even the injustice of slavery. In one letter to her husband, she questioned the "passion of Liberty" among Virginians since they "have been accustomed to deprive their fellow Creatures of theirs." Her opinions on racial and sexual discrimination were, for the time, radical. Today, they are law. For a closer look at her life and times, visit the Abigail Adams Birthplace at North and Norton Streets in Weymouth. And pay tribute to America's most influential daughter. Not to mention wife and mother.

Abigail Adams Historical Society

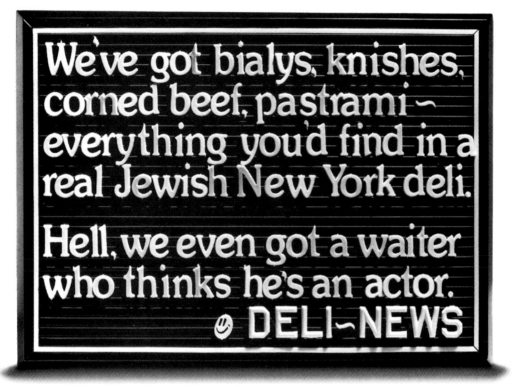

Two locations in Dallas: 15775 Hillcrest (392-3354) and 500 The Crescent Court (922-3354)

Distinctive Merit/National

LESS THAN A FULL PAGE
Waiter
ART DIRECTOR *Grant Richards*
CREATIVE DIRECTOR *Grant Richards*
COPYWRITER *Vinnie Chieco*
PRODUCER *Rebecca Brady*
AGENCY *The Richards Group*
CLIENT *Deli-News*

HE SAID ALL HE WANTS THIS YEAR ARE

SOCKS AND UNDERWEAR.

LIAR

Galleria

Shops of distinction at 69th & France

IF YOU HAVE TO RELY

ON MISTLETOE FOR A KISS,

YOU'VE BEEN SHOPPING AT THE WRONG PLACES.

Galleria

Shops of distinction at 69th & France

Distinctive Merit/National

CAMPAIGN
Shoplifters, Mistletoe, Liar
ART DIRECTOR *Chris Lange*
CREATIVE DIRECTOR *John Cevette*
COPYWRITER *Michael Hart*
PHOTOGRAPHER *Curtis Johnson*
AGENCY *Cevette and Company*
CLIENT *Galleria*

ADDITIONAL AWARDS

Merit

FULL PAGE OR SPREAD
Shoplifters

Merit
FULL PAGE OR SPREAD
Mistletoe

Merit
FULL PAGE OR SPREAD
Liar

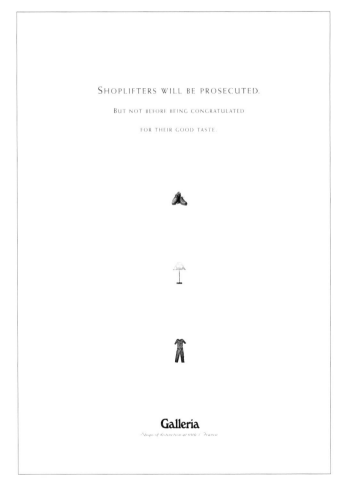

SHOPLIFTERS WILL BE PROSECUTED.

BUT NOT BEFORE BEING CONGRATULATED

FOR THEIR GOOD TASTE.

Galleria

Shops of distinction at 69th & France

IT'S LIKE A LANDSCAPE PAINTING
BY MONET OR CÉZANNE.
ONLY YOU CAN WALK AROUND IN IT.

NORTH CAROLINA

SHOW YOUR CHILDREN THAT
NOT ALL ENCHANTED FORESTS
EXIST IN FAIRY TALES.

NORTH CAROLINA

Distinctive Merit/National

CAMPAIGN
Monet, Enchanted Forest, Hula Hoops
ART DIRECTOR *Andy Azula*
CREATIVE DIRECTOR *Jim Mountjoy*
COPYWRITER *Ed Jones*
PHOTOGRAPHER *Harry DeZitter*
AGENCY *Loeffler Ketchum Mountjoy*
CLIENT *North Carolina Travel and Tourism*

ADDITIONAL AWARDS

Merit
FULL PAGE OR SPREAD
Monet

Distinctive Merit
LESS THAN A FULL PAGE
Enchanted Forest

Distinctive Merit
FULL PAGE OR SPREAD
Enchanted Forest

Merit
FULL PAGE OR SPREAD
Hula Hoops

THINGS MOVE SO SLOWLY OUT
HERE, TV DIDN'T ARRIVE UNTIL 1985.
CAN HULA HOOPS BE FAR BEHIND?

NORTH CAROLINA

Distinctive Merit/International

CAMPAIGN
O-Zone
ART DIRECTOR *Oswaldo Miranda*
DESIGNER *Oswaldo Miranda*
COPYWRITER *Cibele Machado*
ILLUSTRATORS *Brad Holland, Greg Couch, and others*
STUDIO *Miran Design Inc.*
CLIENT *Casa de Idéias*

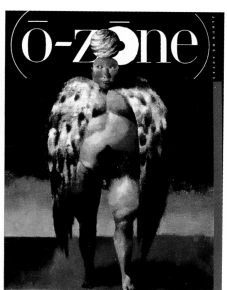

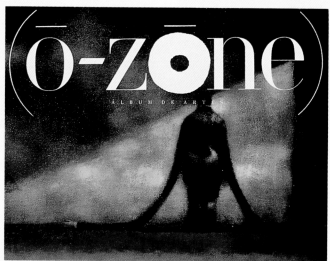

Nine/Brad Holland/Mieczyslaw Górowski/Michel Enricot/
Stasys Eidrigericius/Kent Williams/Victor Sadowski, etc.

Álbum de arte de ilustração publicado pela revista Gráfica/Casa de Idéias

Distinctive Merit/International

CAMPAIGN
*Everyone Makes Mistakes, We Don't Consider the
Well-Being of People Alone, Don't Be in a Rush to
Grow Old*
ART DIRECTOR *Kazumi Murata*
CREATIVE DIRECTOR *Takehiko Miura*
DESIGNERS *Koichi Sugimoto, Eiji Nakazawa*
COPYWRITER *Makoto Tsunoda*
PHOTOGRAPHER *Tamotsu Fujii*
AGENCY *Dentsu, Inc.*
CLIENT *Mercedes-Benz Japan Co., Ltd.*

(facing page, top)
Distinctive Merit/National

MAGAZINE, TRADE, FULL PAGE OR SPREAD
Beauty Contest
ART DIRECTOR *Cabell Harris*
CREATIVE DIRECTOR *Cabell Harris*
COPYWRITER *Steve Skibba*
AGENCY *WORK*
CLIENT *Smith & Nelson*

(facing page, bottom)
Distinctive Merit/National

MAGAZINE, TRADE, FULL PAGE OR SPREAD
Proud Parents
ART DIRECTOR *Cabell Harris*
CREATIVE DIRECTOR *Cabell Harris*
COPYWRITER *Steve Skibba*
AGENCY *WORK*
CLIENT *Smith & Nelson*

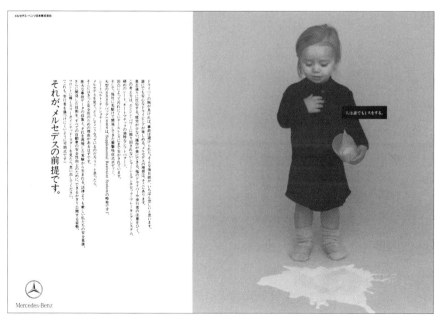

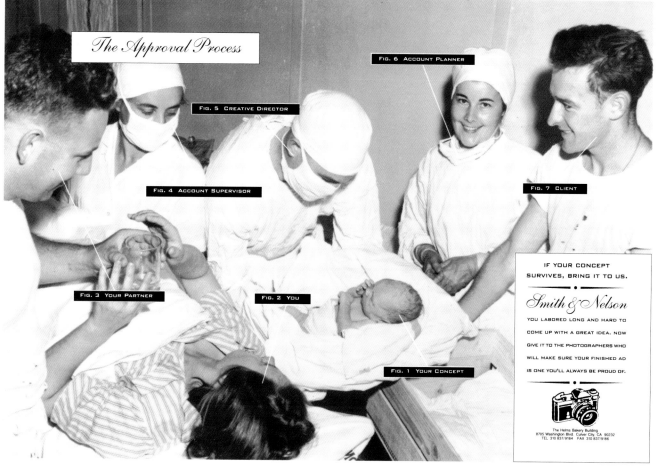

Distinctive Merit/National

DIRECT MAIL
Rhymes and Reasons
ART DIRECTOR *Steve Ditko*
CREATIVE DIRECTOR *Steve Ditko*
DESIGNER *Steve Ditko*
COPYWRITER *Jill Spear*
PHOTOGRAPHER *Rick Rusing*
AGENCY *CFD Design*
CLIENT *UH, OH Clothing Boutique*

Distinctive Merit/National

DIRECT MAIL
Spring Training
ART DIRECTOR *Marion English*
CREATIVE DIRECTOR *Terry Slaughter*
DESIGNER *Marion English*
COPYWRITERS *Marion English, Laura Holmes*
PHOTOGRAPHERS *Underwood Archives, FPG,*
Bettmann Archives
ILLUSTRATOR *Maya Metz*
AGENCY *Slaughter-Hanson*
CLIENT *Plainclothes*

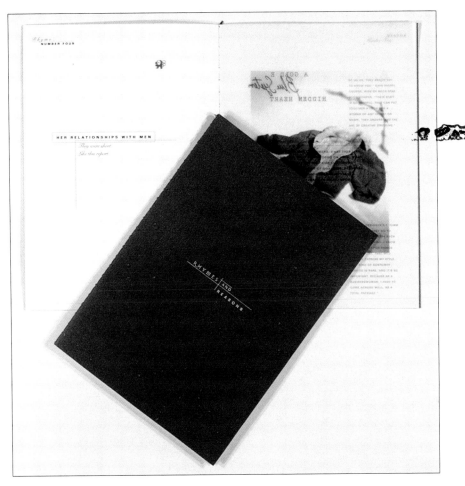

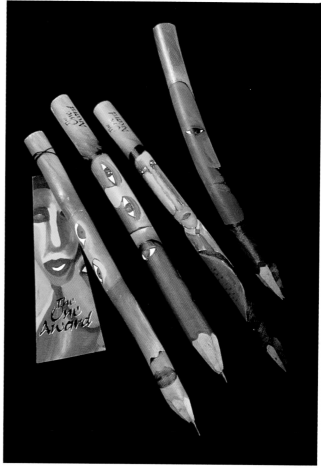

Distinctive Merit/International

DIRECT MAIL, CAMPAIGN
One Award Pencil Package
ART DIRECTOR *Red Nail*
CREATIVE DIRECTOR *Red Nail*
DESIGNER *Red Nail*
COPYWRITER *Red Nail*
ILLUSTRATOR *Thulani Dube*
AGENCY *Red Nail*
STUDIO *Red Nail*
CLIENT *TV1*

Distinctive Merit/National

COMMERCIAL, OVER 30 SECONDS
Rapunzel
CREATIVE DIRECTOR *Ron Henderson*
COPYWRITER *Ron Henderson*
PRODUCER *Jessica Coats*
STUDIO *Real to Reel*
CLIENT *G. Heileman*

ANNCR.: *And now the story of Rapunzel and Her Golden Beer, as told by a paid spokesman for Rainier.*

MAN: *OK so once upon a time in Seattle there was this really big-haired Chi Omega Kega or Kappa Krappa Flappa or Ate-a Plate-a Ziti, anyway, some bowhead named Nancy Rapunzel III who supplied all the sorority parties with second-rate funk bands and this golden beer called Rainier, made with Yakima Valley hops and pure Cascade Mountain water from right here in the Northwest. So one night while Rapunzel was polishing her pearls, these really witchy girls from Delta Felta Shmelta kidnap her and the beer and lock 'em up in the Space Needle. So while Nancy's up in the tower crying "Why me, why me" the jealous Delta Feltas are throwing a party with some wimpy, trucked-in beer from St. Louis and even though the band was fresh the beer wasn't, so everyone from Alpha to Zeta heads over to the Space Needle where this guy named Moose screams "Rapunzel, Rapunzel, let down your beer." So Rapunzel undoes her big velvet bow, ties a case of Rainier to her long bleach-blonde hair and lowers it down to the thirsty crowd. So everybody's cheering and Rapunzel's feeling really good about herself until some Beta Theta Geeka yells out that 20 feet of her dark roots are showing. The end.*

ANNCR.: *Rainier. The beer from here. Rainier Brewing Company, Seattle, Washington.*

MERIT AWARDS

Merit/National

OUTDOOR, SINGLE
Sign from God
ART DIRECTOR *Mike Gustafson*
COPYWRITER *Eric Sorensen*
AGENCY *Chuck Ruhr Advertising*
CLIENT *St. Philip the Deacon*

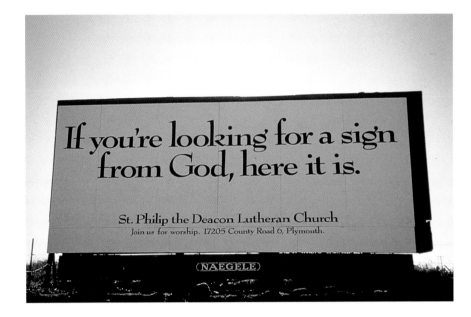

Merit/International

OUTDOOR, SINGLE
Pathfinder—Swiss Army
ART DIRECTOR *Carl van Wijk*
CREATIVE DIRECTORS *Carl van Wijk, Mark D'Arcy*
DESIGNER *Carl van Wijk*
COPYWRITER *Mark D'Arcy*
PHOTOGRAPHER *Chriss Lewis*
RETOUCHING *Grame Smallfield*
AGENCY *D'Arcy Masius Benton & Bowles,
New Zealand*
CLIENT *Nissan*

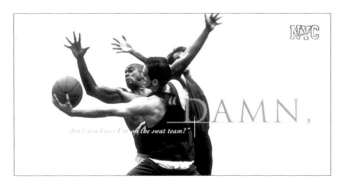

Merit/National

OUTDOOR, CAMPAIGN
Nike NYC "Trash Talk" 2nd series
ART DIRECTOR *John C. Jay*
CREATIVE DIRECTORS *Dan Wieden, Jamie Barrett,*
Jim Riswold
DESIGNER *Pao*
COPYWRITER *Jimmy Smith*
PHOTOGRAPHER *John Huet*
AGENCY *Wieden & Kennedy*
CLIENT *Nike*

Merit/National

OUTDOOR, CAMPAIGN
Nike NYC "Trash Talk" 1st series
ART DIRECTOR *John C. Jay*
CREATIVE DIRECTORS *Dan Wieden, Jamie Barrett,*
Jim Riswold
DESIGNER *Pao*
COPYWRITER *Jimmy Smith*
PHOTOGRAPHER *John Huet*
AGENCY *Wieden & Kennedy*
CLIENT *Nike*

OUTDOOR, CAMPAIGN
Nike NYC "Trash Talk" 1st series

Merit/International

TRANSIT, SINGLE
Loose Fit Dog
ART DIRECTOR *John Iredale*
CREATIVE DIRECTOR *Trevor Purvis*
COPYWRITERS *Jon Iredale, Matt McGrath*
ILLUSTRATOR *Jon Iredale*
AGENCY *McCann-Erickson, Sydney*
CLIENT *Levi Strauss Aust Pty Ltd*

Merit/National

TRANSIT, CAMPAIGN
Nike NYC "Graffiti" Wild Posting
ART DIRECTOR *John C. Jay*
CREATIVE DIRECTOR *John C. Jay*
DESIGNER *Chris Shipman*
PHOTOGRAPHER *Stanley Bach*
ILLUSTRATOR *Petra Langhammer*
AGENCY *Wieden & Kennedy*
CLIENT *Nike*

Merit/National

TRANSIT, CAMPAIGN
Steak, Commuter, Flyswatter
ART DIRECTORS *Tony Angotti, Max Jerome*
CREATIVE DIRECTORS *Tony Angotti, Dion Hughes*
COPYWRITERS *Dion Hughes, Steve Biegel*
PHOTOGRAPHERS *Jeff Divine, Jerry Cailor*
CLIENT *Molson Breweries USA, Inc.*

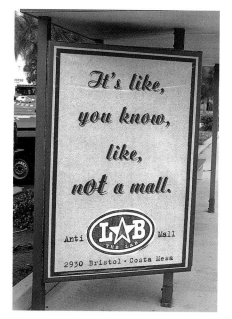

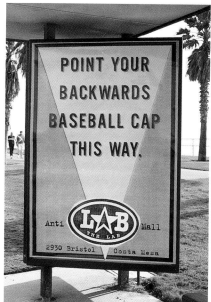

Merit/National

TRANSIT, CAMPAIGN
*Not a Mall, Backwards Baseball Cap, Mom's Friends,
HS Cool, Let the Majority Pick Your President*
ART DIRECTOR *Pat Zimmerman*
CREATIVE DIRECTORS *Pat Zimmerman, Max Godsil*
DESIGNER *Pat Zimmerman*
COPYWRITER *Max Godsil*
PRODUCER *Patrick Media*
AGENCY *Pat Advertising*
CLIENT *The Lab*

Merit/International

TRANSIT, CAMPAIGN
Sumo Wrestler, Baby Elephants, Grandmother
ART DIRECTOR *David Adams*
CREATIVE DIRECTORS *David Adams, Neil McOstrich*
DESIGNERS *David Adams, Neil McOstrich*
COPYWRITER *Neil McOstrich*
PRODUCER *Laurie-Ann Collin*
AGENCY *MacLaren Lintas Inc.*
STUDIO *McGill Productions*
CLIENT *CN Tower – Mindwarp*

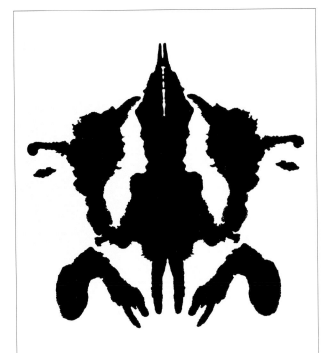

IF YOU DON'T SEE A SUMO WRESTLER WITH BIG HAIR
EATING CRUNCHY GHERKIN PICKLES,
YOU HAVEN'T BEEN TO MINDWARP THEATRE
NOW AT THE CN TOWER.

IF YOU DON'T SEE FOUR BABY ELEPHANTS
PLAYING BACKGAMMON IN A BOBSLED,
YOU HAVEN'T BEEN TO MINDWARP THEATRE
NOW AT THE CN TOWER.

IF YOU DON'T SEE A GRANDMOTHER EXECUTING
THE HEIMLICH MANOEUVRE ON A FRENCH POODLE,
YOU HAVEN'T BEEN TO MINDWARP THEATRE
NOW AT THE CN TOWER.

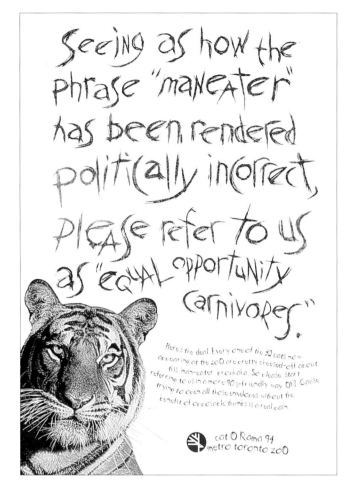

Merit/International

TRANSIT, CAMPAIGN
Equal Opportunity, Organ Donor, Here, Human Human
ART DIRECTOR *Richard Mirabelli*
CREATIVE DIRECTOR *Peter McHugh*
COPYWRITER *Peter McHugh*
PRODUCER *Gina Shank*
AGENCY *Chiat/Day Inc. Advertising*
STUDIO *Chiat/Day*
CLIENT *Metropolitan Toronto Zoo*

Merit/International

PUBLIC SERVICE, SINGLE
The 200th Anniversary of Sharaku
ART DIRECTOR *Takashi Akiyama*
DESIGNER *Takashi Akiyama*
ILLUSTRATOR *Takashi Akiyama*
CLIENT *The Mainichi Newspapers*

Merit/International

PUBLIC SERVICE, SINGLE
Poster Collection from Ekkehard Vaubel
ART DIRECTOR *Lex Drewinski*
CREATIVE DIRECTOR *Lex Drewinski*
DESIGNER *Lex Drewinski*
ILLUSTRATOR *Lex Drewinski*
PRODUCER *Lex Drewinski*
CLIENT *FH Potsdam*

Merit/National

PUBLIC SERVICE, CAMPAIGN
Sit. Stay. See., You See a Puppy, Four Eyes
ART DIRECTOR *Kevin McCarthy*
CREATIVE DIRECTORS *Steve Beaumont, Bill Stenton*
COPYWRITER *Peter Brown*
PHOTOGRAPHER *Pete Bleyer*
PRODUCER *Jill Mathews*
AGENCY *Ketchum Advertising, Los Angeles*
CLIENT *Guide Dog Foundation*

Merit/National

GENERAL, SINGLE
Taxi Driver Licenses
ART DIRECTOR *Henriette Lienke*
CREATIVE DIRECTOR *Gary Goldsmith*
COPYWRITER *Tom Miller*
PHOTOGRAPHER *Henriette Lienke*
AGENCY *Goldsmith/Jeffrey*
CLIENT *Crain's New York Business*

Merit/National

GENERAL, SINGLE
Noise Is Relative
ART DIRECTOR *Greg Cerny*
COPYWRITER *Greg Cerny*
PHOTOGRAPHER *Greg Cerny*
AGENCY *Capitalist Conspiracy Advertising*
CLIENT *Reconstruction Records*

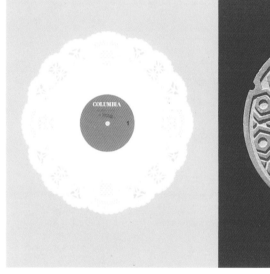

Merit/National

GENERAL, SINGLE
Shoes
ART DIRECTOR *Randy Tatum*
COPYWRITER *Mark Wegwerth*
PHOTOGRAPHER *Marvy!*
AGENCY *Chuck Ruhr Advertising*
CLIENT *Weber's Supper Club*

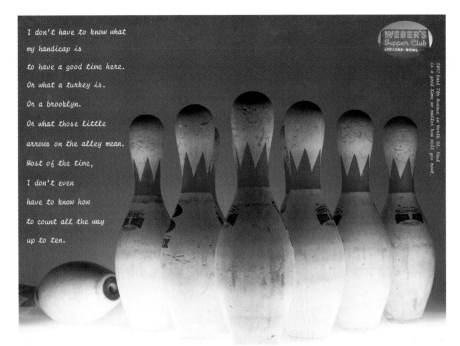

Merit/National

GENERAL, SINGLE
Pins
ART DIRECTOR *Randy Tatum*
COPYWRITER *Mark Wegwerth*
PHOTOGRAPHER *Marvy!*
AGENCY *Chuck Ruhr Advertising*
CLIENT *Weber's Supper Club*

Merit/National

GENERAL, SINGLE
Cucumber
ART DIRECTOR *J. Kent Pepper*
CREATIVE DIRECTOR *David Kasabian*
COPYWRITER *Daniel Swanson*
PHOTOGRAPHY *Henderson/Cartledge*
AGENCY *DRK Inc.*
CLIENT *Zoo Doo Compost Company*

Merit/National

GENERAL, SINGLE
Shar-Pei
ART DIRECTOR *Marta Ibarrondo*
COPYWRITER *Tom Givone*
AGENCY *Mezzina Brown*
CLIENT *Applied Graphics –Printbox*

Merit/National

GENERAL, SINGLE
Confessions of a Short-Order Artist
ART DIRECTOR *Brad Holland*
CREATIVE DIRECTOR *Jim McLune*
DESIGNER *Jim McLune*
ILLUSTRATOR *Brad Holland*
CLIENT *L.S.C.A.*

Merit/National

GENERAL, SINGLE
Necktie
ART DIRECTOR *Patrick Murray*
CREATIVE DIRECTOR *Todd Tilford*
COPYWRITER *Todd Tilford*
PHOTOGRAPHER *Richard Reens*
AGENCY *The Richards Group*
CLIENT *Harley-Davidson of North Texas*

Merit/International

GENERAL, SINGLE
Oh Cet Echo
ART DIRECTOR *Andréas Netthoevel*
CREATIVE DIRECTOR *Andréas Netthoevel*
DESIGNER *Andréas Netthoevel*
COPYWRITER *André Thomkins*
STUDIO *second floor south*
CLIENT *Centre Pasquart*

(facing page, top)
Merit/International

GENERAL, SINGLE
Mouth
ART DIRECTOR *Ramón Roda*
CREATIVE DIRECTOR *Xavi García, Ramón Roda*
PHOTOGRAPHERS *Ramón Eguiguren,*
Antón Eguiguren
AGENCY *Casadevall Pedreño & PRG*
CLIENTS *Dr. Arturo Costa, Dr. Marcos Costa*

(facing page, bottom)
Merit/National

GENERAL, CAMPAIGN
Beer Can
ART DIRECTOR *Gary Goldsmith*
CREATIVE DIRECTOR *Gary Goldsmith*
COPYWRITER *Gary Goldsmith*
PHOTOGRAPHER *Steve Hellerstein*
AGENCY *Goldsmith/Jeffrey*

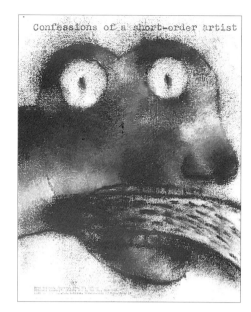

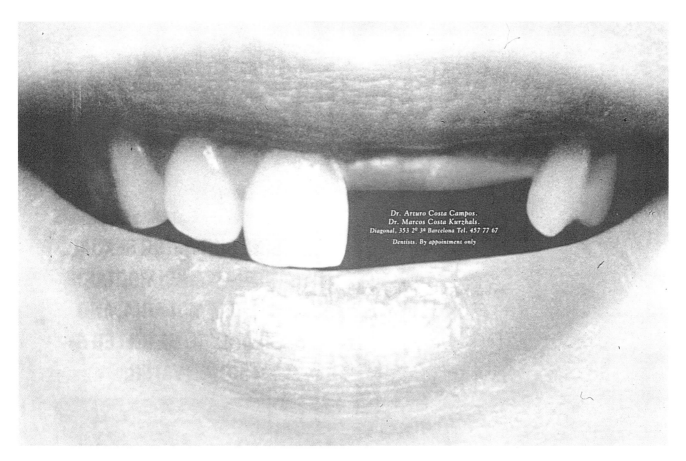

YOUR BABY
SHOULD
GO
HERE.

IMAGINE SURVIVING SEXUAL ASSAULT, GUNFIRE, MORTARS, MACHETES, MALARIA, AND POISON ONLY TO BE KILLED BY A SIP OF WATER.

The Rwandan refugees face new obstacles every hour. Please, give today. With your funds, fresh water, food, medicine and shelter will be supplied to help combat the many enemies in this struggle.

✚ AMERICAN RED CROSS RWANDAN RELIEF. 1-800-842-2200.

Merit/National

GENERAL, SINGLE
Earth General Diaper Poster
ART DIRECTOR *Debbie Klonk*
DESIGNER *Debbie Klonk*
COPYWRITER *Debbie Klonk*
AGENCY *Corn Fed Advertising*
CLIENT *Earth General*

Merit/National

GENERAL, SINGLE
Imagine Surviving Sexual Assault
ART DIRECTOR *Cliff Sorah*
CREATIVE DIRECTOR *Mike Hughes*
COPYWRITER *Joe Alexander*
PHOTOGRAPHERS *Martin Adler, Frank Fournier*
PRODUCER *Tom Maher*
AGENCY *The Martin Agency*
CLIENT *American Red Cross*

GENERAL, SINGLE
GAM, Graphic Arts Message, '94
ART DIRECTOR *Katsumi Asaba*
CREATIVE DIRECTOR *Naomi Enami*
DESIGNER *Daikoku Hisaya, Propeller Art Works Co., Ltd.*
PHOTOGRAPHER *Hajime Sawatari*
CLIENT *Too Corporation*

Merit/International

GENERAL, SINGLE
Diva
ART DIRECTOR *Katsumi Asaba*
DESIGNER *Keiko Mineishi*
PHOTOGRAPHER *Naruyasu Nabeshima*
CLIENT *Gaga Communications Inc.*

Merit/International

GENERAL, SINGLE
The 13th ISHII Award Typeface Contest Call for Entry
ART DIRECTOR *Katsumi Asaba*
DESIGNER *Keiko Mineishi*
COPYWRITER *Takako Terunuma*
ARTWORK *Hiroshi Tomura*
CLIENT *Shaken Co., Ltd.*

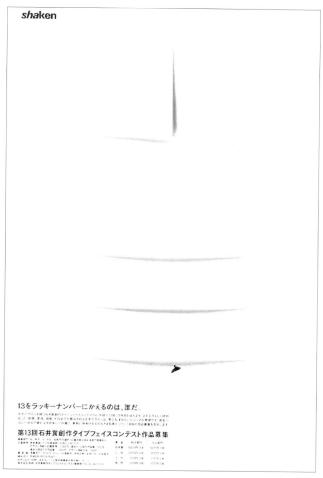

Merit/International

GENERAL, SINGLE
Basho Graphic Images
ART DIRECTOR *Masakazu Tanabe*
DESIGNER *Masakazu Tanabe*
ILLUSTRATORS *Masakazu Tanabe, Masahiko Hirano*
AGENCY *Media Co., Ltd.*
CLIENT *Chubu Creators Club*

Merit/International

GENERAL, SINGLE
The 200th Anniversary of Sharaku
ART DIRECTOR *Masakazu Tanabe*
DESIGNER *Masakazu Tanabe*
ILLUSTRATOR *Masakazu Tanabe*
AGENCY *Media Co., Ltd.*
CLIENT *The Mainichi Newspapers*

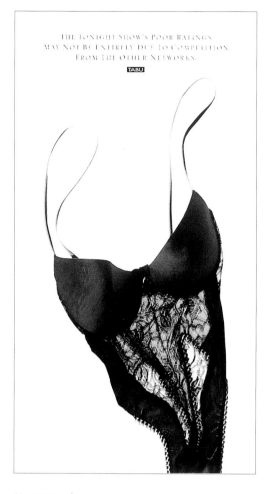

Merit/National

GENERAL, SINGLE
Poor Ratings
ART DIRECTOR *Grant Richards*
CREATIVE DIRECTORS *Todd Tilford, Grant Richards*
COPYWRITER *Todd Tilford*
PHOTOGRAPHER *Robb Debenport*
AGENCY *The Richards Group*
CLIENT *Tabu Lingerie*

Merit/International

GENERAL, SINGLE
Dictionary
ART DIRECTOR *Kins Lee*
DESIGNER *Kins Lee*
COPYWRITER *Janet Lee*
PHOTOGRAPHER *Stills Studio*
ILLUSTRATORS *Hau Theng Hui, Patrick Fong*
AGENCY *Spider Malaysia*
CLIENT *Cadbury Confectionary (M) SDN BHD*

Merit/International

GENERAL, SINGLE
Quality and Humanity
ART DIRECTOR *Kan Akita*
DESIGNERS *Kan Akita, Masayoshi Kodaira*
COPYWRITER *Shinzo Higurashi*
CLIENT *TOTO Ltd.*

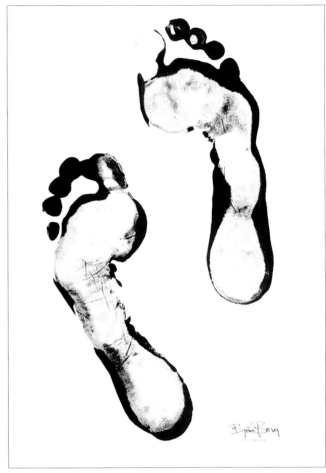

Merit/International

GENERAL, SINGLE
I Prefer Being Here to in the Sea
ART DIRECTOR *Masaharu Higashizawa*
CREATIVE DIRECTORS *Katsunori Tsuyama, Shuji Muya*
DESIGNERS *Shinji Kita, Takeshi Ishikawa,*
Yuko Onishi
COPYWRITER *Keisuke Yamashita*
PHOTOGRAPHER *Kanmei Matsumoto*
AGENCY *Daiko Advertising, Inc.*
CLIENT *Matsushita Electric Industrial Co.*

Merit/International

GENERAL, SINGLE
Bjorn Borg Footwear
ART DIRECTOR *Pelle Korberg*
CREATIVE DIRECTOR *Pelle Korberg*
COPYWRITER *Johan Brink*
PHOTOGRAPHER *Henrik Halvarsson*
AGENCY *Korberg & Co. Annonsbyra*
CLIENT *Scandinavian Footwear*

Merit/International

GENERAL, SINGLE
The 200th Anniversary of Sharaku
ART DIRECTOR *Masato Ohki*
DESIGNER *Masato Ohki*
PHOTOGRAPHER *Masato Ohki*
SCULPTOR *Masato Ohki*
CLIENT *The Mainichi Newspapers*

Merit/International

GENERAL, SINGLE
Eating This
ART DIRECTOR *Bradley Wood*
CREATIVE DIRECTOR *Peter McHugh*
DESIGNERS *Bob Rickert, Bradley Wood*
COPYWRITER *Bob Rickert*
PHOTOGRAPHER *Joe Jacobs*
AGENCY *Chiat/Day Inc. Advertising*
CLIENT *Ontario Ministry of Transportation*

GENERAL, CAMPAIGN
What You Can Do with Frozen Beef Trayliner
ART DIRECTOR *Steve Sandstrom*
CREATIVE DIRECTOR *Steve Sandoz*
DESIGNER *Steve Sandstrom*
COPYWRITER *Steve Sandoz*
ILLUSTRATOR *Eric Larsen*
AGENCIES *Sandstrom Design, Artsy Fartsy Productions*
CLIENT *Burgerville USA*

GENERAL, CAMPAIGN
Burger Hockey Trayliner
ART DIRECTOR *Steve Sandstrom*
CREATIVE DIRECTOR *Steve Sandoz*
DESIGNER *Steve Sandstrom*
COPYWRITER *Steve Sandoz*
AGENCIES *Sandstrom Design, Artsy Fartsy Productions*
CLIENT *Burgerville USA*

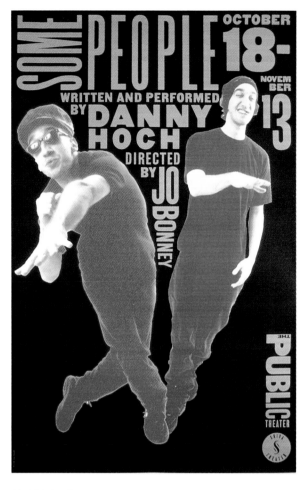

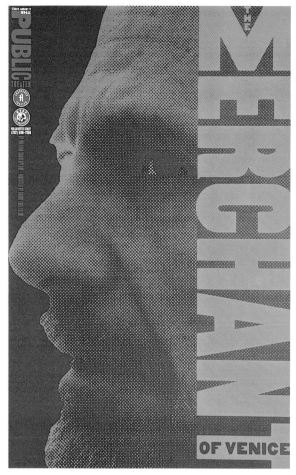

Merit/National

GENERAL, CAMPAIGN
Public Theater Poster Campaign
ART DIRECTOR *Paula Scher*
DESIGNERS *Ron Louie, Lisa Mazur, Paula Scher*
STUDIO *Pentagram Design*
CLIENT *The Public Theater*

Merit/National

GENERAL, CAMPAIGN
Wrinkle Resistant Pants and Shirts, Fade Resistant,
Earthtones
ART DIRECTOR *Bob Meagher*
CREATIVE DIRECTOR *Mike Hughes*
COPYWRITERS *Joe Alexander, Steve Dolbinski*
PHOTOGRAPHERS *Mark Scott, Panoramic Images,*
Tony Sylvestro
PRODUCER *Jenny Schoenherr*
AGENCY *The Martin Agency*
CLIENT *Wrangler Company*

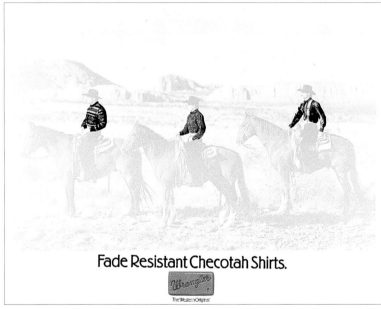

IN AMERICA, THE BOY SCOUTS HELP PEOPLE ACROSS THE STREET. IN ZAIRE, THEY HELP PEOPLE INTO THEIR GRAVES.

IF ONLY COMPASSION WERE SPREADING AS FAST AS THE CHOLERA.

There are so many dead Rwandans that the Boy Scouts of nearby
Zaire have been asked to help bury the deceased. Please, give today.
Your funds will help relieve the misery this entire region faces.

✚ AMERICAN RED CROSS RWANDAN RELIEF. 1-800-842-2200.

The response to the Rwandan situation has been incredible.
But more help is desperately needed. Please, give. With your funds,
we'll be able to supply even more fresh water, food and medicine.

✚ AMERICAN RED CROSS RWANDAN RELIEF. 1-800-842-2200.

Merit/National

GENERAL, CAMPAIGN
Boy Scouts, Imagine Surviving Sexual Assault,
Cholera
ART DIRECTOR *Cliff Sorah*
CREATIVE DIRECTOR *Mike Hughes*
COPYWRITER *Joe Alexander*
PHOTOGRAPHERS *Martin Adler, Frank Fournier*
PRODUCER *Tom Maher*
AGENCY *The Martin Agency*
CLIENT *American Red Cross*

Merit/National

GENERAL, CAMPAIGN
Handsome, Mother, Free Call
ART DIRECTOR *Chris Lange*
CREATIVE DIRECTORS *John Cevette, Michael Hart*
COPYWRITER *Michael Hart*
AGENCY *Cevette and Company*
CLIENT *Jewish Dating Service*

ADDITIONAL AWARDS

Merit
GENERAL, SINGLE
Handsome

Merit
GENERAL, SINGLE
Mother

Merit
GENERAL, SINGLE
Free Call

Looking for tall, dark and handsome?

Willing to skip the tall part?

✡ Jewish Dating Service
542-9790

*If you don't call us
your mother will.*

✡ Jewish Dating Service
542-9790

It's a free call.

✡ Jewish Dating Service
542-9790

Merit/International

GENERAL, CAMPAIGN
Lenny, Otto, Duke
ART DIRECTOR *Wayne Thompson*
CREATIVE DIRECTOR *Lyle Wedemeyer*
COPYWRITER *Christopher Wilson*
PHOTOGRAPHER *Joe Lampi, Dublin Productions*
ILLUSTRATOR *Brad Palm*
AGENCY *Martin/Williams*
CLIENT *Grand Groomers*

Merit/International

GENERAL, CAMPAIGN
On People's Minds Since 1898
ART DIRECTOR *Mats Fredriksson*
CREATIVE DIRECTOR *Martin Graap*
COPYWRITER *Stefan Lindholm*
PHOTOGRAPHER *Eva-Marie Rundquist*
AGENCY *Arnek Advertising Agency*
CLIENT *Barlach Frisor/Schwarzkopf*

ADDITIONAL AWARD

Merit
OUTDOOR, SINGLE

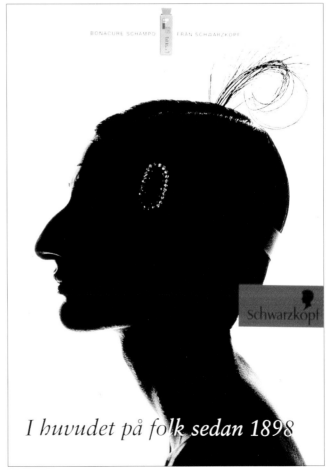

Merit/International

GENERAL, CAMPAIGN
HIT
ART DIRECTORS *Zempaku Suzuki, Jun Ueno*
DESIGNERS *Zempaku Suzuki, Masahiro Naito*
COPYWRITER *Mariko Hayashi*
ILLUSTRATOR *Hanna-Barbera*
AGENCY *Dentsu, Inc.*
STUDIO *B-BI Studio Inc.*
CLIENT *The Toyo Trust & Banking Co., Ltd.*

Merit/International

GENERAL, CAMPAIGN
King Printing
ART DIRECTOR *Koji Mizutani*
CREATIVE DIRECTOR *Koji Mizutani*
DESIGNER *Hiroshi Ohmizo*
ILLUSTRATOR *Hiroshi Ohmizo*
AGENCY *Mizutani Studio*
STUDIO *Mizutani Studio*
CLIENT *King Printing Co., Ltd.*

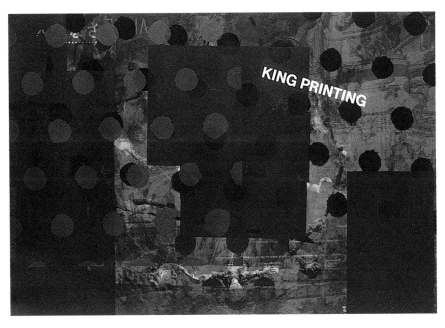

Merit/International

GENERAL, CAMPAIGN
Push – In Order to Make Life Fun
ART DIRECTOR *Koichi Sawada*
CREATIVE DIRECTOR *Hiroshi Sasaki*
DESIGNERS *Yuji Tokuda, Kazuaki Aikawa,*
Takahiro Kurashima
COPYWRITERS *Naoto Ohdate, Tetsuya Watanabe*
PHOTOGRAPHER *Eiichiro Sakata*
ILLUSTRATOR *Koichi Sawada*
ART *Yasuhide Kobayashi*
AGENCY *Dentsu, Inc.*
STUDIO *Dentsu Cotec & Common Design*
CLIENT *Fuji Television Network*

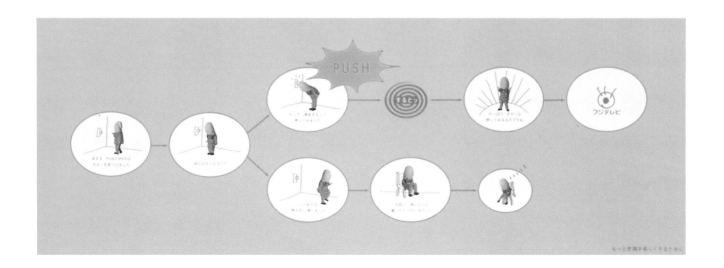

Merit/International

GENERAL, CAMPAIGN
A Light Bulb, A Disciple, The Queen's Husband
ART DIRECTOR *Carl van Wijk*
CREATIVE DIRECTOR *Raj Marwah*
DESIGNER *Carl van Wijk*
COPYWRITER *Mark D'Arcy*
PRODUCER *John Hutchinson*
AGENCY *D'Arcy Masius Benton & Bowles,
New Zealand*
CLIENT *Phillips Fox*

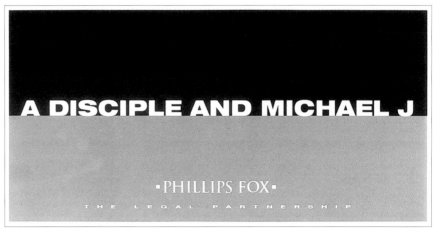

Merit/National

COMMERCIAL, 30 SECONDS OR LESS
Buddy
ART DIRECTOR *Jerry Gentile*
CREATIVE DIRECTOR *Steve Rabosky*
COPYWRITER *Scott Vincent*
PRODUCERS *Michelle Burke, Jeff Gorman*
AGENCY *Chiat/Day Inc. Advertising*
CLIENT *Sunkist California Pistachios*

Merit/National

COMMERCIAL, 30 SECONDS OR LESS
Piniella
ART DIRECTOR *Kristy Willson*
CREATIVE DIRECTOR *Jim Walker*
COPYWRITERS *John Schofield, Jim Copacino*
PRODUCER *Michelle Woodruff*
AGENCY *McCann-Erickson Seattle*
CLIENT *Mariners Baseball*

Merit/National

COMMERCIAL, 30 SECONDS OR LESS
Buhner
ART DIRECTOR *Kristy Willson*
CREATIVE DIRECTOR *Jim Walker*
COPYWRITERS *John Schofield, Jim Copacino*
PRODUCER *Michelle Woodruff*
AGENCY *McCann-Erickson Seattle*
CLIENT *Mariners Baseball*

Merit/National

COMMERCIAL, 30 SECONDS OR LESS
Universal Excuses
ART DIRECTOR *Mark Oakley*
CREATIVE DIRECTORS *Todd Seisser, Jay Taub*
COPYWRITER *David Bernstein*
PRODUCER *Susan Shipman*
DIRECTOR *Jeff Stark*
AGENCY *Ammirati & Puris, Lintas*
CLIENT *United Parcel Service*

Merit/National

COMMERCIAL, 30 SECONDS OR LESS
Choir
ART DIRECTOR *Rick Rabe*
CREATIVE DIRECTOR *Parry Merkley*
COPYWRITER *David Leite*
PRODUCER *Will McDonald*
DIRECTOR *Graham Henman*
AGENCY *Merkley Newman Harty, Inc.*
CLIENT *Casio, Inc.*

Merit/National

COMMERCIAL, 30 SECONDS OR LESS
You'll Love the Way It Wears – Rug
ART DIRECTOR *Bob Ranew*
COPYWRITER *Liz Paradise*
AGENCY *McKinney and Silver*
CLIENT *Karastan-Bigelow*

Merit/National

COMMERCIAL, 30 SECONDS OR LESS
It's All Fuel
ART DIRECTOR *Jeanne Byers*
CREATIVE DIRECTOR *Rochelle Klein*
COPYWRITER *Rochelle Klein*
PRODUCER *Pam Ferman*
DIRECTOR *Osbert Parker*
MUSIC *Bruce Wooley*
AGENCY *Angotti, Thomas, Hedge, Inc.*
CLIENT *Sun Company, Inc.*

Merit/National

COMMERCIAL, 30 SECONDS OR LESS
Chihuahua
ART DIRECTOR *Kent Johnson*
CREATIVE DIRECTORS *Glenn Dady, Mike Malone*
COPYWRITERS *David Coats, Kevin Sutton*
PRODUCER *Carol Leftwich*
DIRECTOR *Robert Hannant*
AGENCY *The Richards Group*
CLIENT *EyeMasters*

Merit/National

COMMERCIAL, 30 SECONDS OR LESS
The State "More Miserable Crap"
ART DIRECTOR *Kenan Moran*
CREATIVE DIRECTOR *Angie Li*
PRODUCER *Kenan Moran*
DIRECTOR *Kenan Moran*
AGENCY *MTV Networks*
CLIENT *MTV*

Merit/National	*Merit/National*	*Merit/International*

COMMERCIAL, 30 SECONDS OR LESS
Dumplings
ART DIRECTOR *Doug Hill*
CREATIVE DIRECTOR *Mike Drazen*
COPYWRITER *Kelly Simmons*
PRODUCER *Pat Cannon*
DIRECTOR *Mark Tiedemann*
MUSIC *Tomandandy*
AGENCY *Earle Palmer Brown, Philadelphia*
STUDIO *Crossroads Films*
CLIENT *The Philadelphia Inquirer*

COMMERCIAL, 30 SECONDS OR LESS
Dreyer's Cop
ART DIRECTOR *Joey LaCascia*
CREATIVE DIRECTORS *Brian O'Neil, Paul Carek*
PHOTOGRAPHER *D. P. Kirk Bachman*
PRODUCERS *Michael King, Debra Trotz*
DIRECTOR *Brenton Thomas*
MUSIC *Ad Music, Los Angeles*
AGENCY *Goldberg, Moser, O'Neil*
CLIENT *Dreyer's Grand Ice Cream*

COMMERCIAL, 30 SECONDS OR LESS
Spur
ART DIRECTOR *Jordi Almuni*
CREATIVE DIRECTORS *Paco Segarra,*
Manolo Portabella
COPYWRITER *Juan Finger*
DIRECTOR *João Daniel Thikomiroff*
MUSIC *Red Back*
AGENCY *Vinizius/Young & Rubicam*
CLIENT *Textil Zedesa*

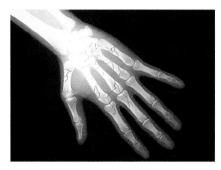

Merit/International

COMMERCIAL, 30 SECONDS OR LESS
Head into the Mouth
CREATIVE DIRECTORS *Alexandre Gama,*
Marcello Serpa
COPYWRITER *Alexandre Gama*
PRODUCER *Luiza Jatobá*
DIRECTOR *João Daniel Thikomiroff*
MUSIC *MCR*
AGENCY *ALMAP BBDO*
STUDIO *Jodaf*
CLIENT *Playboy Magazine*

Merit/International

COMMERCIAL, 30 SECONDS OR LESS
The Board
ART DIRECTOR *Yoshimitsu Sawamoto*
CREATIVE DIRECTOR *Toshiaki Nozue*
DESIGNER *Hiroshi Yoda*
COPYWRITERS *Yoshimitsu Sawamoto, Hiroshi Yoda*
PHOTOGRAPHER *Etsuo Itoyama*
PRODUCER *Hideki Murakami*
DIRECTOR *Akihiro Iijima*
MUSIC *M Network*
AGENCY *Dentsu, Inc.*
STUDIO *Taiyo Kikaku Co., Ltd.*
CLIENT *The Japan Dairy Council*

Merit/International

COMMERCIAL, 30 SECONDS OR LESS
Wedding
CREATIVE DIRECTOR *Nizao Guanaes*
COPYWRITER *Eugênio Mohallem*
PHOTOGRAPHER *Abraão Metri*
PRODUCER *Maurício Guimarães*
DIRECTOR *Nando Olival*
MUSIC *Dr. D. D.*
AGENCY *DM9 Publicidade*
CLIENT *Sharp*

Merit/International

COMMERCIAL, 30 SECONDS OR LESS
Antiseptic
CREATIVE DIRECTOR *Nizao Guanaes*
COPYWRITER *Eugênio Mohallem*
PHOTOGRAPHER *Cesar Charlone*
PRODUCER *Maurício Guimarães*
DIRECTOR *Antonio Melo*
MUSIC *Voices*
AGENCY *DM 9 Publicidade*
CLIENT *Baruel*

Merit/National

COMMERCIAL, 30 SECONDS OR LESS, CAMPAIGN
Surveillance Campaign 9 Failure, Robbery, Hold-up
ART DIRECTOR *Jeff Martin*
CREATIVE DIRECTOR *Jeff Martin*
COPYWRITERS *Jack Becker, Kevin Sutton*
PRODUCER *Keith Browne*
DIRECTOR *Eric McClellan*
AGENCY *Lawler Ballard Van Durand*
STUDIO *Truth Inc.*
CLIENT *First Commerce Corporation*

Merit/National

COMMERCIAL, 30 SECONDS OR LESS, CAMPAIGN
Mailbox, Learning, Business at Home
ART DIRECTOR *Gavin Milner*
CREATIVE DIRECTOR *David Lubars*
COPYWRITER *Maggie Powers*
PRODUCER *Jackie Vidor*
DIRECTOR *Joe Pytka*
MUSIC *Ear to Ear Music*
AGENCY *BBDO*
STUDIO *Pytka Productions*
CLIENT *Apple Computers*

Merit/National

COMMERCIAL, 30 SECONDS OR LESS, CAMPAIGN
Most Wonderful Time, Mailman, No Surprises
ART DIRECTORS *Greg Bell, Matt Vescovo, John Leu*
CREATIVE DIRECTOR *Arthur Bijur*
COPYWRITER *Steve Dildarian*
PRODUCERS *Anne Kurtzman, MaryEllen Duggan*
DIRECTORS *Henry Holzman, Mark Tiedemann*
MUSIC *Michael Carroll*
AGENCY *Cliff Freeman & Partners*
STUDIO *Industrial Artists, Crossroads Films*
CLIENT *Staples*

ADDITIONAL AWARD

Merit
COMMERCIAL, 30 SECONDS OR LESS
Mailman

Merit/National

COMMERCIAL, 30 SECONDS OR LESS, CAMPAIGN
Nightmare before Christmas...,
Nightmare after Christmas..., The Visitor
ART DIRECTOR *Denise Crandall*
CREATIVE DIRECTOR *David Lubars*
COPYWRITER *Greg Ketchum*
PRODUCERS *Chris Anthony, Shelly Eisener*
DIRECTOR *Joe Pytka*
MUSIC *Chris Bell Music*
AGENCY *BBDO*
STUDIO *Pytka Productions*
CLIENT *Apple Computers*

ADDITIONAL AWARD

Merit
COMMERCIAL, 30 SECONDS OR LESS
Nightmare after Christmas

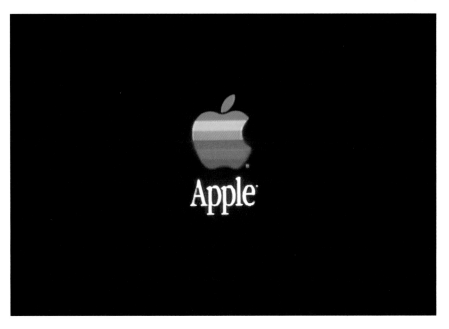

 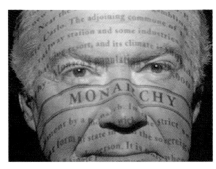 

Merit/National

COMMERCIAL, 30 SECONDS OR LESS, CAMPAIGN
French Guys, Moroccan Guys, Nuns
ART DIRECTOR *Bruce Bousman*
CREATIVE DIRECTOR *Bill Hamilton*
COPYWRITER *Charlie Tereck*
PRODUCER *Bruce Davidson*
DIRECTOR *Leslie Dektor*
AGENCY *Ogilvy & Mather, New York*
STUDIO *Dektor Higgins & Associates*
CLIENT *IBM*

Merit/National

COMMERCIAL, OVER 30 SECONDS
Faces
ART DIRECTOR *Dean Stefanides*
CREATIVE DIRECTORS *Dean Stefanides, Larry Hampel*
COPYWRITER *Larry Hampel*
PRODUCER *Jean Muchmore*
DIRECTOR *Henry Sandbank*
MUSIC *Jim Kremins*
AGENCY *Houston Effler Hampel & Stefanides*
STUDIO *Sandbank*
CLIENT *NEC Technologies*

Merit/National

COMMERCIAL, OVER 30 SECONDS
Pool Hall
ART DIRECTOR *Andy Hirsch*
CREATIVE DIRECTOR *Lee Garfinkel*
COPYWRITER *Barbara Siegel*
PRODUCER *Bob Nelson*
DIRECTOR *Tony Scott*
AGENCY *Lowe & Partners/SMS*
CLIENT *Coca-Cola Global Marketing – Diet Coke*

Merit/National

COMMERCIAL, OVER 30 SECONDS
Particles
ART DIRECTOR *Heidi Flora*
CREATIVE DIRECTOR *Robert Brihn*
COPYWRITER *Kevin Jones*
PRODUCER *Sam Walsh*
EDITOR *Johnna Turiano*
AUDIO *Jason Brown at McDonald Recording*
AGENCY *Cole & Weber*
CLIENT *Seattle International Film Festival*

Merit/International

COMMERCIAL, OVER 30 SECONDS
Light and Shadow
ART DIRECTOR *Junichiro Akiyoshi*
CREATIVE DIRECTORS *Toshiaki Nozue, Akira Kagami*
COPYWRITERS *Izuru Toi, Yoshimitsu Sawamoto,*
Hanako Suzuki
PHOTOGRAPHER *Toshio Tateishi*
PRODUCER *Hiroshi Yoshida*
DIRECTOR *Masatake Satomi*
MUSIC *Hiroaki Kondo*
AGENCY *Dentsu, Inc.*
CLIENT *Matsushita Electric Industrial Co., Ltd.*

Merit/National

COMMERCIAL, OVER 30 SECONDS, CAMPAIGN
Chimps, Summer of Love, A Day in the Life (Shaq)
ART DIRECTOR *Don Schneider*
CREATIVE DIRECTORS *Ted Sann, Michael Patti,*
Don Schneider
COPYWRITERS *Ted Sann, Michael Patti*
PRODUCERS *Regina Ebel, Rani Vaz*
DIRECTORS *James Gartner, Joe Pytka*
MUSIC *Sicurella & Associates*
AGENCY *BBDO*
STUDIO *Gartner-Grasso, Pytka Productions*
CLIENT *Pepsi Cola Co.*

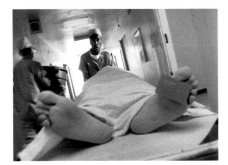

Merit/National

COMMERCIAL, PUBLIC SERVICE
Gurney
ART DIRECTOR *Ian Barry*
CREATIVE DIRECTOR *Matt Smith*
COPYWRITER *Steve Dolbinski*
CINEMATOGRAPHER *Tom Olgierson*
PRODUCER *Sylvia Kahn*
DIRECTOR *Jeff Gorman*
PRODUCTION *Johns & Gorman Films*
AGENCY *Richard Clark with Rye Films (editor)*
CLIENT *Los Angeles County Coroner*

Merit/National

COMMERCIAL, LOW BUDGET
Subtitles
ART DIRECTORS *Rich Wakefield, Marne Brobeck*
CREATIVE DIRECTOR *Jim Noble*
COPYWRITERS *Jim Noble, Lisa Farris*
AGENCY *Fahlgren*
CLIENT *Atlanta Film and Video Festival–IMAGE*

Merit/National

COMMERCIAL, LOW BUDGET
Let It Snow
ART DIRECTOR *Shari Hindman*
CREATIVE DIRECTOR *Mike Hughes*
COPYWRITER *Ron Huey*
PRODUCER *Pam Campagnoli*
AGENCY *The Martin Agency*
STUDIO *In Your Ear*
CLIENT *Richmond Symphony*

Merit/International

COMMERCIAL, LOW BUDGET
Mask
ART DIRECTORS *Stephan Pfeiffer, Reinhold Rahm*
CREATIVE DIRECTOR *Hermann Vaske*
COPYWRITER *Hermann Vaske*
PRODUCER *Charles V. Bender*
DIRECTOR *Hermann Vaske*
MUSIC *Einstürzende Neubauten*
FILM PRODUCTION *Laszlo Kadar Films*
AGENCY *FCB Hamburg*
CLIENT *Erotic Art Museum*

Merit/National

COMMERCIAL, PROMOTION VIDEO
Concept 1
CREATIVE DIRECTOR *Dennis Merritt*
COPYWRITER *Steve Hutchison*
DIRECTOR/CAMERAMAN *Dennis Merritt*
PRODUCER *Joe Callahan*
MUSIC *Brian Neumeister*
AGENCY *SHR Perceptual Management*
STUDIO *Callahan & Associates*
CLIENT *Volkswagen of America*

Merit/National

COMMERCIAL, ART DIRECTION
Burro
ART DIRECTOR *Rick Hanson*
CREATIVE DIRECTORS *Charlie Miesmer, Jimmy Siegel*
COPYWRITER *Jimmy Siegel*
PRODUCER *David Frankel*
DIRECTOR *James Gartner*
AGENCY *BBDO*
STUDIO *Gartner-Grasso*
CLIENT *Visa*

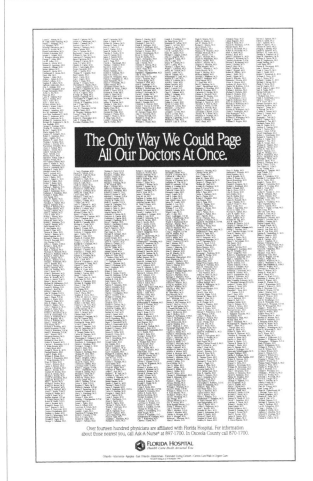

Merit/National

FULL PAGE OR SPREAD
Herend
ART DIRECTOR *John Doyle*
CREATIVE DIRECTOR *John Doyle*
COPYWRITER *Ernie Schenck*
PHOTOGRAPHER *Geoffrey Stein*
PRODUCER *Michelle Caraccia*
AGENCY *Berlin Cameron Doyle*
CLIENT *Shreve, Crump & Low*

Merit/National

FULL PAGE OR SPREAD
Bridge to New York
ART DIRECTORS *Everett Wilder, Greg Gerhard*
CREATIVE DIRECTORS *Carl Warner, Mark Cacciatore*
COPYWRITER *David Parson*
AGENCY *DDB Needham Worldwide Dallas*
CLIENT *American Airlines*

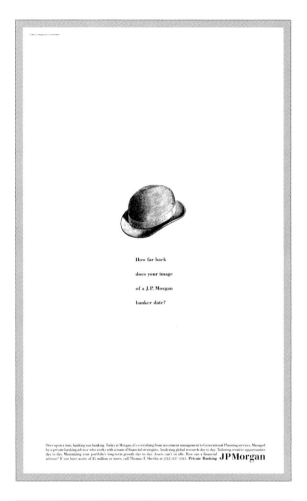

Merit/National

FULL PAGE OR SPREAD
Derby
ART DIRECTOR *Gary Goldsmith*
CREATIVE DIRECTOR *Gary Goldsmith*
COPYWRITER *Dean Hacohen*
ILLUSTRATOR *Christopher Wormell*
AGENCY *Goldsmith/Jeffrey*
CLIENT *J. P. Morgan Private Banking*

Merit/International

FULL PAGE OR SPREAD
Corn Kernel
ART DIRECTOR *Terry Iles*
CREATIVE DIRECTOR *Michael Fromowitz*
COPYWRITER *John Kewley*
ILLUSTRATOR *Rod Grigor*
AGENCY *McCann-Erickson/Toronto*
STUDIO *Lakefront Studio*
CLIENT *Nabisco Brands Ltd (Del Monte)*

Merit/International

FULL PAGE OR SPREAD
Wallet
ART DIRECTOR *Steven Ang*
CREATIVE DIRECTOR *Rick Lane*
COPYWRITERS *Rick Lane, Steven Ang*
PHOTOGRAPHER *Hock of Studio Pashe*
AGENCY *Dentsu, Young & Rubicam*
CLIENT *Overseas Chinese Banking Corporation*

WE'D LIKE TO REPORT
A MISSING TOMATO.
APPARENTLY ONE OF OUR
COMPETITORS VISITED
OUR FIELDS AFTER DARK
AND BORROWED IT.
THEY'RE TRYING TO
FIGURE OUT WHY OUR
DEL MONTE TOMATOES TASTE
SO GOOD, WHY THEY'RE
SO RED, SO FIRM.
WE WISH THEM THE
BEST OF LUCK.
TO US, THE ANSWER
IS SIMPLE. QUALITY IS IN
EVERYTHING WE DO.

When you have to go, we don't have to stop.

Isn't it strange how on long trips you need to go when there's no loo for fifty kms? It can't happen on a train. Because trains have toilets, and showers to keep you fresh. You also get all the space you need for comfort and 50 kg of luggage free, not to mention hearty meals. Plus children under 7 go free, and from 7 - 11 travel half-price. And only on a train can you choose to have a good night's sleep in a real bed. Of course, they're reliable too, so you can feel sure of arriving safely. (When did you ever hear of a train with a flat?) So, next time you need to go ... go by train.

SPOORNET BRIDGE THE DISTANCE. TAKE THE TRAIN.

Merit/International

FULL PAGE OR SPREAD
Tomato Sprig
ART DIRECTOR *Terry Iles*
CREATIVE DIRECTOR *Michael Fromowitz*
COPYWRITER *John Kewley*
ILLUSTRATOR *Rod Grigor*
AGENCY *McCann-Erickson/Toronto*
STUDIO *Lakefront Studio*
CLIENT *Nabisco Brands Ltd (Del Monte)*

Merit/International

FULL PAGE OR SPREAD
When You Have to Go
ART DIRECTOR *Mike Rossi*
CREATIVE DIRECTORS *Gaby Bush, Graham de Lacy*
COPYWRITER *Athalie Russell*
ILLUSTRATOR *Mike Rossi*
AGENCY *Lindsay Smithers-FCB*
CLIENT *Spoornet*

Merit/International

FULL PAGE OR SPREAD
Raffles Hotel Opens a Singles Bar
ART DIRECTOR *Grover Tham*
CREATIVE DIRECTOR *Tim Evill*
COPYWRITERS *Jim Aitchison, Kash Sree,*
Tham Khai Meng
AGENCY *Batey Ads Singapore*
CLIENT *Raffles Hotel, Singapore*

BOWING TO PUBLIC PRESSURE, RAFFLES HOTEL OPENS A SINGLES BAR.

Which immediately presents us with two problems.
The first problem first: Young men, eager to cohabit with lithe members of the opposite sex are not encouraged to invade the Bar & Billiard Room.

(Well, having said that, let us hasten to add they are most welcome to attempt enjoyment of the prime purpose of this advertisement.)

Which raises the second problem. We are offering you tonight an unbridled opportunity to explore some of Scotland's finest achievements.

The most noble array of single malt Scotch Whisky, this side of Skye.

However, there is a prevailing view that a single malt whisky is but another manifestation of the Scottish national trait: reluctance to part with things of value.

Like money.

Or whisky.

Sadly, many a novice Scotch drinker is convinced that a single malt whisky will not deliver his money's worth, whereas a bottle containing several malt whiskies will.

Ah, clever people the Scots. For nothing could be further from the truth.

THE TRUTH IS, a blend is merely a blend. Read our lips. A 12-year old blended whisky

means that one of the whiskies has been aged for 12 years, whilst its companions are anyone's guess, laddie.

Whereas a 12-year old single malt whisky is purely and precisely that: one grand old whisky in all its majestic and undiluted glory.

HAVING GRASPED THAT inescapable fact, you may think the rest is easy. Not so, for the Scots are full of contradictions.

As if foreseeing the day when our Bar & Billiard Room would voraciously pry sizeable quantities of their precious single malt whiskies from their homeland, the Scots set about giving them virtually unpronounceable names.

Glenfiddich, Glenmorangie, Dalwhinnie, Auchentoshan, Bladnoch and Laphroaig. A fiendish deterrent, indeed, but one which can be simply overcome by the use of our single malt whisky guide and an index finger.

One final hurdle remains.

Unravelling the mysteries of classic single and rare malt whiskies is as daunting as the

distiller's art itself. The subtle aromas and flavours have never been quite fully explored, possibly because no one is sufficiently sober afterwards.

THE FACT THAT a proud single malt calls to mind the misty glens, heather-blanketed hillocks, crystal streams teeming with trout, skirling pipes, etcetera, should also call to mind one other minuscule detail: the price.

Rest assured, with all their true canny, the Scots will endeavour to extract as much money from your pocket as they can in exchange for their best single malts. And who's to blame them?

OF COURSE, OUR Bar & Billiard Room offers many other aristocratic distractions.

A Krug, the Grande Cuvée predictable. Or La Grande Dame 1985, secured at no little expense from the Home of Veuve Clicquot.

Or an amber Belle Vue Gueuze from Belgium's master brewers.

Not forgetting the most fastidious array of fine armagnacs, cognacs, ports, coffees and Valrhona chocolates ever to be savoured over a lazy game of billiards.

SUCH IS THE Bar & Billiard Room. If not a singles bar, by every means a singular bar. And a haven which awaits you after work, after dinner or after the theatre, tonight and every night.

BAR
& BILLIARD
ESTABLISHED 1915

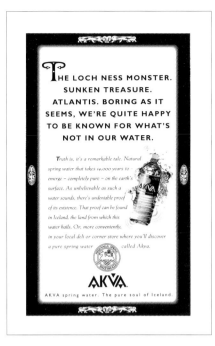

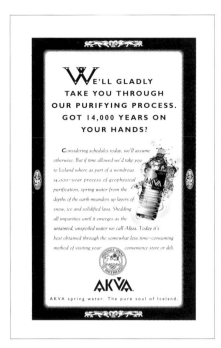

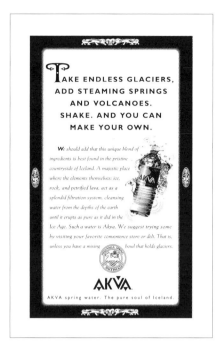

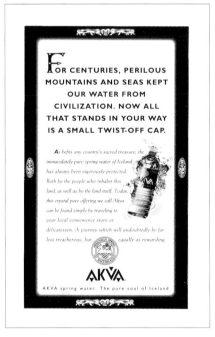

Merit/National

CAMPAIGN
*Loch Ness, 14,000 Years, Glaciers, Twist-off Cap,
Vikings*
ART DIRECTOR *John Doyle*
CREATIVE DIRECTOR *John Doyle*
COPYWRITERS *Jim Garaventi, Ed Crayton*
PHOTOGRAPHER *Hashi*
PRODUCER *Michelle Caraccia*
AGENCY *Berlin Cameron Doyle*
CLIENT *AKVA Spring Water*

Merit/National

CAMPAIGN
*This Tiny Bit of Peace and Quiet..., If You Can't
Remember the Last Time..., Please Arrive Exhausted*
ART DIRECTOR *Lara Gilmore*
CREATIVE DIRECTORS *Dennis Stevens,
Joanna Templeton, Mike Rogers*
COPYWRITER *Lori McNulty*
AGENCY *DDB Needham Worldwide/New York*
CLIENT *Bermuda Tourism*

PLEASE

ARRIVE

EXHAUSTED.

B E R M U D A
CALL YOUR TRAVEL AGENT OR CALL 1-800-BERMUDA.

THIS TINY BIT OF PEACE AND QUIET
HAS BEEN BROUGHT TO YOU BY
B E R M U D A
CALL YOUR TRAVEL AGENT OR CALL 1-800-BERMUDA.

YOU PACKED IN THE DARK.
UNFORTUNATELY, YOUR MEETING'S IN BROAD DAYLIGHT.

THE REST WILL BE EASY.   SHONEY'S INN
1-800-222-2222

3 CUPS OF COFFEE FOR BREAKFAST. BIG GULP FOR LUNCH.
NEXT BATHROOM 57 MILES.

THE REST WILL BE EASY.   SHONEY'S INN
1-800-222-2222

THE BOWL OF CHILI. THE BROKEN WINDOW HANDLE.
THE SILENCE.

THE REST WILL BE EASY.   SHONEY'S INN
1-800-222-2222

Merit/National

CAMPAIGN
Socks, Long Road, Skunk, Chili
ART DIRECTOR *Jeff Jahn*
CREATIVE DIRECTOR *Lyle Wedemeyer*
DESIGNER *Jeff Jahn*
COPYWRITER *Greg Beaupre*
PHOTOGRAPHER *Craig Perman*
AGENCY *Martin/Williams*
CLIENT *Shoney's Inns*

Merit/National

CAMPAIGN
August 18, 1895, June 18, 1896, July 6, 1901
ART DIRECTOR *Michelle Manasseri*
CREATIVE DIRECTOR *Paul Silverman*
COPYWRITER *Walt Burns*
PHOTOGRAPHY *Boston Floating Hospital Archives*
AGENCY *Mullen*
CLIENT *The Boston Floating Hospital*

(facing page)
Merit/National

CAMPAIGN
Micro, Good Look, Hard to Find
ART DIRECTOR *Jim Baldwin*
CREATIVE DIRECTOR *Jim Baldwin*
COPYWRITERS *Ron Henderson, Jim Baldwin*
AGENCY *The Richards Group*
CLIENT *G. Heileman Brewing Co.*

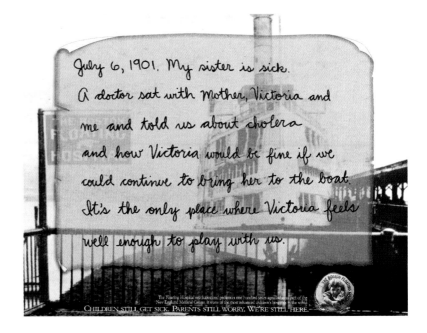

A micro ad. What else would you
expect from a small brewery in Oregon?
Try Weinhard's Boar's Head Red Lager.

For a good look at our beer, see
your bartender. Or your optometrist.
Try Henry Weinhard's Private Reserve.

Henry Weinhard's Private Reserve
is here. Unfortunately, right now, it's as
hard to find as our ads.

Merit/International

CAMPAIGN
Remember Qatar, No More Yellow Cards
ART DIRECTOR *Hiroaki Shuto*
CREATIVE DIRECTOR *Shinsuke Kasahara*
DESIGNERS *Koji Yamada, Gen Ishii*
COPYWRITER *Tomomi Maeda*
PHOTOGRAPHER *Kazumi Kurigami*
AGENCY *Hakuhodo, Inc.*
CLIENT *SONY Creative Products Inc.*

Merit/International

CAMPAIGN
Liberty, Building, Apple
ART DIRECTOR *John Finn*
CREATIVE DIRECTOR *John Finn*
COPYWRITER *Tim Evill*
AGENCY *Batey Ads Singapore*
CLIENT *Singapore Airlines*

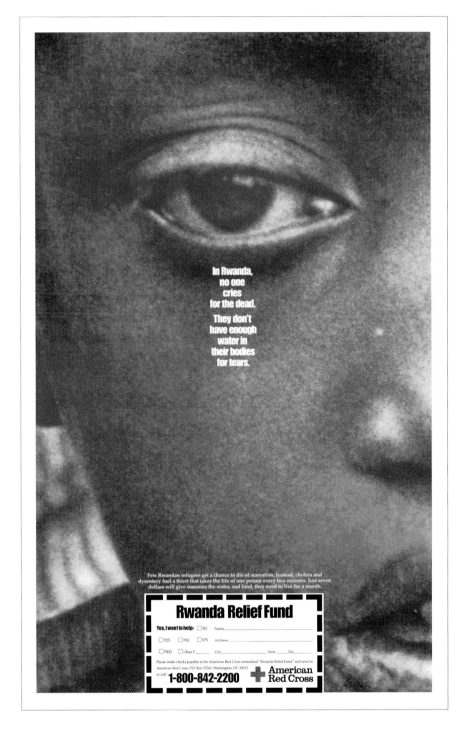

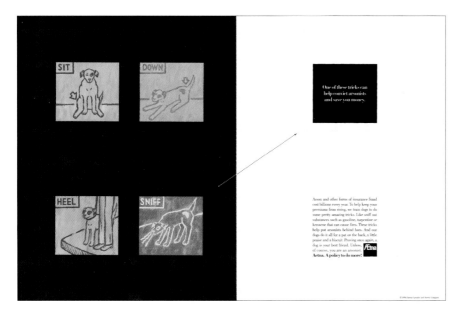

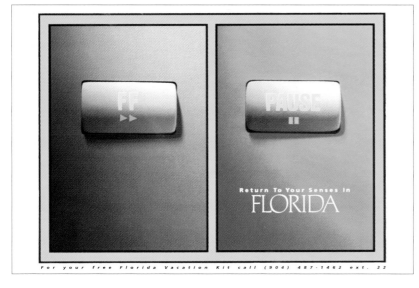

Merit/National

FULL PAGE OR SPREAD
All-Terrain Vehicle
ART DIRECTOR *Jamie Mahoney*
CREATIVE DIRECTOR *Mike Hughes*
COPYWRITER *Raymond McKinney*
PHOTOGRAPHY *Dublin Productions*
PRODUCER *Kay Franz*
AGENCY *The Martin Agency*
CLIENT *Healthtex, Inc.*

Merit/National

FULL PAGE OR SPREAD
The Subtle Things
ART DIRECTORS *John Carter, Ronda Hagen Dunn*
CREATIVE DIRECTOR *Rod Kilpatrick*
COPYWRITERS *Eric Brown, Roger Richards*
PRODUCER *Lillian Lisa*
AGENCY *BBDO West*
CLIENT *Benziger Family Winery*

Merit/National

FULL PAGE OR SPREAD
Long Legs
ART DIRECTOR *Andre Cohen*
CREATIVE DIRECTOR *David Nobay*
COPYWRITER *David Nobay*
AGENCY *Cohn & Wells, San Francisco*
CLIENT *Neographics*

Merit/National

FULL PAGE OR SPREAD
George Smith
ART DIRECTOR *Andy Shemeta*
CREATIVE DIRECTOR *Dick Scott*
DESIGNER *Andy Shemeta*
COPYWRITERS *Cedric Giese, Dan Steenburgh*
PHOTOGRAPHER *Stephen LaVere*
AGENCY *Edelmann Scott, Inc.*
CLIENT *Hohner*

SOMEWHERE BETWEEN HOME AND WORK IS A VACATION.

RALEIGH

Merit/National

FULL PAGE OR SPREAD
Somewhere between Home and Work
ART DIRECTOR *Fred Hammerquist*
CREATIVE DIRECTORS *Fred Hammerquist, Hugh Saffel*
COPYWRITER *Hugh Saffel*
PHOTOGRAPHER *Richard Hamilton Smith*
AGENCY *Hammerquist and Saffel Creative Services*
CLIENT *Raleigh USA*

EXERCISE YOUR RIGHT TO LEAVE YOUR CAR AT HOME.

RALEIGH

Merit/National

FULL PAGE OR SPREAD
Exercise Your Right
ART DIRECTOR *Fred Hammerquist*
CREATIVE DIRECTORS *Fred Hammerquist, Hugh Saffel*
COPYWRITER *Hugh Saffel*
PHOTOGRAPHER *Steve Bonini*
AGENCY *Hammerquist and Saffel Creative Services*
CLIENT *Raleigh USA*

Merit/National

FULL PAGE OR SPREAD
Naked
ART DIRECTOR *Jeff Hopfer*
CREATIVE DIRECTORS *Jeff Hopfer, Ron Henderson*
DESIGNER *Jeff Hopfer*
COPYWRITER *Ron Henderson*
PHOTOGRAPHER *Nadav Kander*
AGENCY *The Richards Group*
CLIENT *Oxxford Clothing, Inc.*

Merit/National

FULL PAGE OR SPREAD
War
ART DIRECTOR *Jeff Hopfer*
CREATIVE DIRECTORS *Jeff Hopfer, Ron Henderson*
DESIGNER *Jeff Hopfer*
COPYWRITER *Ron Henderson*
PHOTOGRAPHER *Nadav Kander*
AGENCY *The Richards Group*
CLIENT *Oxxford Clothing, Inc.*

Merit/National

FULL PAGE OR SPREAD
Woodstock
ART DIRECTOR *Margaret Johnson*
CREATIVE DIRECTOR *Todd Tilford*
COPYWRITER *Vinnie Chieco*
ILLUSTRATOR *Mike Schroder*
PRODUCER *Rebecca Brady*
AGENCY *The Richards Group*
STUDIO *Laser Tech Color*
CLIENT *Continental Airlines*

FULL PAGE OR SPREAD
"Win" Ad
ART DIRECTOR *John Vitro*
CREATIVE DIRECTION *VITROROBERTSON*
COPYWRITER *John Robertson*
PHOTOGRAPHER *Marshall Harrington*
AGENCY *VITROROBERTSON*
CLIENT *Odyssey Golf*

FULL PAGE OR SPREAD
Reaper
ART DIRECTOR *Tracy Wong*
CREATIVE DIRECTOR *Tracy Wong*
DESIGNERS *Tracy Wong, Michael Boychuck*
COPYWRITER *Craig Hoit*
PHOTOGRAPHER *Steve Bonini*
PRODUCER *Kathy Blakley*
AGENCY *Wongdoody*
CLIENT *Pro-Flex Mountain Bikes*

Merit/International

FULL PAGE OR SPREAD
Lips
ART DIRECTOR *Huw Williams*
CREATIVE DIRECTOR *Guy Winston*
COPYWRITER *Laurie Geddes*
PHOTOGRAPHER *Julian Watt*
AGENCY *Lintas Sydney*
CLIENT *Nestle Confectionery*

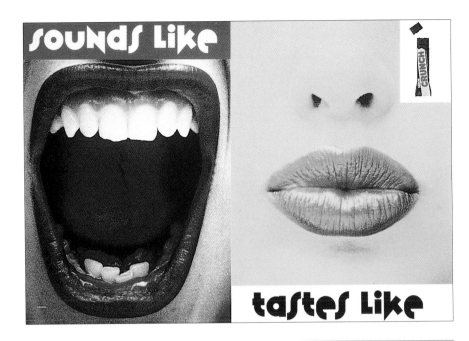

Merit/International

FULL PAGE OR SPREAD
Dog
ART DIRECTOR *Huw Williams*
CREATIVE DIRECTOR *Guy Winston*
COPYWRITER *Laurie Geddes*
PHOTOGRAPHER *Julian Watt*
AGENCY *Lintas Sydney*
CLIENT *Nestle Confectionery*

Merit/International

FULL PAGE OR SPREAD
Barbie
ART DIRECTOR *Huw Williams*
CREATIVE DIRECTOR *Guy Winston*
COPYWRITER *Laurie Geddes*
PHOTOGRAPHER *Julian Watt*
AGENCY *Lintas Sydney*
CLIENT *Nestle Confectionery*

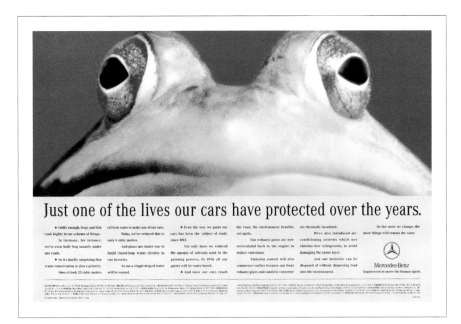

Merit/International

FULL PAGE OR SPREAD
Just One of the Lives
ART DIRECTOR *Lye Kok Hong*
CREATIVE DIRECTORS *Jim Aitchison, Tim Evill*
COPYWRITERS *Daniel Lim, Jim Aitchison, Tim Evill*
PHOTOGRAPHY *Procolor*
AGENCY *Batey Ads Singapore*
CLIENT *Mercedes-Benz Asia*

Merit/International

FULL PAGE OR SPREAD
Better Buy a Honda Motorcycle
ART DIRECTOR *Carlos Garcia*
CREATIVE DIRECTOR *Nizao Guanaes*
COPYWRITER *Carlos Domingos*
PHOTOGRAPHY *Agencia Estado*
PRODUCER *Anelito Nobrega*
AGENCY *DM9 Publicidade*
CLIENT *Moto Honda da Amazonia*

Merit/National

CAMPAIGN
Aromas, Ingredients, Beauty
ART DIRECTOR *Amy Watt*
CREATIVE DIRECTORS *Edward Boches, Amy Watt*
COPYWRITER *Edward Boches*
AGENCY *Mullen*
CLIENT *Aveda Corporation*

Truly natural aromas are found in
flowers, leaves, roots and barks.

Not glued to the pages of this magazine.

If you can peel the corner of this page and detect an aroma, chances are that aroma is anything but natural. Instead it was probably formulated from petro-chemicals. Undoubtedly conceived in a laboratory rather than harvested from a mountainside.

At Aveda we believe that not only are such ingredients bad for your body, they're equally bad for the planet. Which is why you'll never find any of the synthetic or petro-chemical based ingredients common to other manufacturers' perfumes and scents in any aroma or fragrance with the Aveda name on it.

In fact, you'll find quite the contrary. Nothing but pure flower and plant essences. Ingredients whose natural aromas possess such power to arouse your senses and stimulate your spirit you'll begin to wonder why any company would bother to manufacture synthetic, artificial scents.

Better yet, with a visit to one of the Aveda Esthetiques or Concept Salons you can experience hundreds of Aveda aromas. You can sample single notes that run from anise to ylang ylang. Try one of our unique Chakras, compounds of pure plant essences, with the ability to soothe or stimulate, to calm or seduce. Or choose from an entire line of Aveda Pure-fumes. Every one of them far too natural to adhere to the pages of a magazine.

AVEDA
THE ART AND SCIENCE OF PURE FLOWER AND PLANT ESSENCES

The ingredients in our products aren't purchased,
procured or acquired. They're borrowed.

From the earth.

For centuries, across the continents, the world's indigenous peoples have sensed instinctively that the body is an eco-system.

They've understood that what we put onto our skin or absorb through our pores is reflected in our appearance and well-being. And they've known that the true secrets to both a beautiful appearance and a state of good health are often to farther away than the trees, plants and flowers that surround them.

Today, such wisdom is alive and well in Aveda's skin care products and the philosophy behind them. For in an entire collection of cleansers, toners and hydrating lotions, we have captured the molecular energy of pure flower and plant essences, and with it nature's unsurpassed power to restore and maintain the natural beauty of your skin.

Perhaps just as importantly, these remarkable products were created with ingredients grown organically, free of fertilizers, pesticides and herbicides. They were formulated without any petro-chemical by-products. And, not surprisingly they were tested without the use of animals.

Which means when you use Aveda skin care products, you're not just preserving your skin, you're sustaining the planet. A full line of Aveda products is available at your salon as well as at any Aveda Esthetique.

AVEDA
THE ART AND SCIENCE OF PURE FLOWER AND PLANT ESSENCES

Most cosmetic companies go to New York,
Paris and Milan to learn about beauty.

We go to the Rain Forest.

Almost every company in the beauty business goes to a factory to find its colors, emollients and aromas. At Aveda, we go somewhere else. To the rain forests of the Amazon. The mountain ranges of the Himalayas. The remote Indian villages of the Far East. There we harvest some of the earth's purest flowers and plants, botanical wonders whose natural ingredients provide the tone, textures, flavors and scents that define Aveda's cosmetics.

The results? Natural Colour Cosmetics that not only complement your features, but actually revitalize your skin and stimulate your senses.

There are Fresh Essence Lip-Colours whose long-lasting satin finish not only coats your lips but tantalizes them with flower essences and then protects them with a natural base of rosewax and beeswax enriched with hydrating emollients.

Our Definitive Eye Pencils will both accent your natural beauty and rewrite the book on how cosmetics should be made in the first place. For they were formulated with natural waxes derived from plants and made without the use of any artificial preservatives.

The same holds true for an entire collection of concealers, foundations, powders and blushes. All rich in plant essences. Free from animal testing. And created with as much concern for your health as for your beauty.

You'll find Aveda cosmetics at all of our Esthetiques in New York and Los Angeles as well as at any one of our many Aveda Concept Salons.

AVEDA
THE ART AND SCIENCE OF PURE FLOWER AND PLANT ESSENCES

The game of golf was created in Scotland in 1744. But that doesn't mean the meal afterwards should taste that way.

IS THERE SOME OBSCURE GOLF RULE SOMEWHERE THAT SAYS GREAT GOLF AND GREAT FOOD MUST BE MUTUALLY EXCLUSIVE? IF SO, WE THOUGHT OF 108 HOLES OF GOLF WHET YOUR APPETITE? THEN COME ENJOY UNLIMITED GOLF ON FIVE COURSES. FLAT COURSES, ROLLING COURSES, LET'S **$166*** JUST SAY YOU'LL NEVER BE BORED. OUR "GOLF HOLIDAY" ALSO INCLUDES BREAKFAST AND DINNER IN YOUR CHOICE OF RESTAURANTS, INCLUDING THE MEMORABLE EL BIZCOCHO (TOP-RATED IN SAN DIEGO). ALL INCLUDED FOR ONE PRICE. CALL US AT 1-800-542-6096. CHALLENGE IT EVERY DAY AT THE RANCHO BERNARDO INN. AND SPEAKING OF CHALLENGES, DOES THE

RANCHO BERNARDO INN
The way the world is supposed to be

The holidays are a perfect time to spend with loved ones. (Do a masseuse and a room service waiter qualify as loved ones?)

WE'VE ALWAYS BEEN. UNPRETENTIOUS AND GENUINE. **$166*** SO WHY NOT TAKE A BREAK AND JOIN US? YOU CAN PLAY UNLIMITED GOLF ON FIVE COURSES, 108 HOLES IN ALL. THERE'S TENNIS AND A SPA. BREAKFAST AND DINNER

IN THE MIDDLE OF ALL THE HOLIDAY RUSH-RUSH-RUSH, DON'T FORGET TO STOP, RELAX AND ENJOY. WE'RE ALL DRESSED UP FOR THE OCCASION. THE LIGHTS ARE IN THE TREES— AND THERE ARE A LOT OF TREES. WINE GLASSES ARE SPARKLING. THE FIREPLACE IS WARMED UP. AND SO ARE THE CAROLERS. BUT WE'RE STILL THE SAME PLACE ARE INCLUDED EACH DAY—AND IT WILL BE A DINNER YOU WISH WOULD NEVER END. ISN'T THIS HOW TRADITIONS GET STARTED? 1-800-542-6096.

RANCHO BERNARDO INN
The way the world is supposed to be

Most golf pros advise you to spend plenty of time warming up before a round. So, how does 72 degrees sound?

LIKE TOMORROW (SAME AS TODAY). THE RANCHO BERNARDO INN, NORTH OF SAN DIEGO. **$166*** THAW OUT YOUR SWING ON FIVE DIFFERENT COURSES, 108 HOLES IN ALL. THERE'S A HEALTH SPA AND TENNIS, AS YOU'D EXPECT. BUT, AS YOU WOULDN'T EXPECT, BREAKFAST AND DINNER ARE INCLUDED EACH DAY. AND THE FOOD HAS BEEN RATED AMONG THE BEST IN ALL OF SAN DIEGO. (GREAT GOLF AND GREAT FOOD IN ONE LOCATION? YES, THIS IS PARADISE.) 1-800-542-6096.

IF THE THOUGHT OF A FRESHLY MOWED FAIRWAY SEEMS MORE APPEALING THAN FRESHLY PLOWED SNOW, ESCAPE TO A PLACE WHERE THE MOOD IS WARM, THE PEOPLE ARE WARMER AND YOU DON'T HAVE TO WASTE ANY TIME WONDERING WHAT THE WEATHER IS GOING TO BE

RANCHO BERNARDO INN
The way the world is supposed to be

Merit/National

CAMPAIGN
RBI Magazine Campaign: The Game of Golf, Loved Ones, Warming Up
ART DIRECTOR *John Vitro*
CREATIVE DIRECTION *VITROROBERTSON*
COPYWRITER *John Robertson*
ILLUSTRATOR *Tracy Sabin*
AGENCY *VITROROBERTSON*
CLIENT *JC Resorts*

When you consider the strength
of Minnesota's forests, maybe the
Land of 10,000 Lakes should be called
the Land of 10,000,000,000 Trees.

That might be a little too long to fit on our license plates, but it pretty much sums up Minnesota's forests.

As you can imagine, ten billion trees in a state of our size make for some vast forest lands. In fact, forests cover a full third of our state. They support 24 different kinds of trees and are home to countless species of wildlife.

Of course, it's not just the size of our forests that's important. It's also their health and vitality. (Research indicates that a managed forest is more resistant to diseases and catastrophic fires.)

As it is, 28 trees die of natural causes for every one tree harvested.

Yet every year thirty-one new trees spring up in their places. Ultimately that leads not only to more trees, but also healthier trees, in a state where our forests are as much a part of our quality of life as, well...our lakes.

According to a recent environmental study, planned timber harvesting will not negatively impact lake sedimentation, streamflow patterns, or fish populations.

M i n n e s o t a   F o r e s t   I n d u s t r i e s

© 1994 Minnesota Forest Industries

Statistics show that if you
grow up in Minnesota you'll be stronger,
healthier and better looking.
(Particularly if you're a tree.)

It's only natural that a state's forests should reflect the values of the people who take care of them.

Which may be why Minnesota forests are in good shape.

This according to the most comprehensive environmental impact study ever conducted on timber harvesting.

Forests cover a third

of our state. Recent U.S. Forest Service inventories show 20 million trees have diameters greater than 19 inches. That's six million more large trees than existed just fifteen years ago.

The tightrope walk between our economic growth and forest management is difficult. But our state

does it well—better, in fact, than other states.

We can all share the credit. Conservation interests, private landowners, governmental bodies and our forest industries are all working together to make a difference.

After all, isn't that the Minnesota way?

Since 1980, more than 243 million trees have been planted in Minnesota by public and private groups.

M i n n e s o t a   F o r e s t   I n d u s t r i e s

© 1994 Minnesota Forest Industries

Merit/National

CAMPAIGN
Forest Campaign
ART DIRECTOR *Bill Winchester*
CREATIVE DIRECTOR *Bill Winchester*
COPYWRITER *Tom Evans*
PHOTOGRAPHER *Craig Perman*
AGENCY *Colle & McVoy Marketing Communications*
CLIENT *Minnesota Forest Industries*

Ironically, the state that's
home to the world's most famous
logger has some of the best
forests in the country.

You wouldn't think a society that honored a larger-than-life mythical figure like Paul Bunyan would have any forests left to speak of.

Yet the truth is, according to the largest environmental impact study ever to assess timber harvesting anywhere in the world, Minnesota's forests are in good shape.

And along with the state and local governments, forest industries themselves have done much to manage our forests effectively.

The result? Over 10 billion trees are growing in Minnesota today. Statewide, the latest U.S. Forest Service Inventory shows tree

volume has increased 28% since 1977. And there will be more trees in the 1990s than in any decade since official records have been kept.

We're proud of how forestry has kept evolving for the better.

We think Minnesota should be, too.

Every year in Minnesota, more trees grow than are harvested. In fact, only 1% of our 16.6 million acres of woodlands is annually harvested.

M i n n e s o t a   F o r e s t   I n d u s t r i e s

© 1994 Minnesota Forest Industries

Caspa não cai do céu.

Pode reparar: durante o inverno, pessoas do Brasil inteiro carregam pequenas partículas brancas nos ombros. E você já deve ter reparado: não é neve. O fato é que, quando a temperatura cai, o número de pessoas com caspa sobe. O causador desse problema é um fungo: o *Pityrosporum ovale*. Só após anos de pesquisas a comunidade científica pôde chegar a esta conclusão. Esse fungo vive inofensivamente em nossa pele e couro cabeludo. Porém, o frio é um dos fatores que provocam a sua proliferação. E aí começam os problemas: inflamação da raiz do cabelo, coceira, descamação, a visível e desagradável caspa. Uma vez descoberta a causa, foi possível desenvolver um tratamento: TRIATOP®. Um shampoo anticaspa que contém um derivado imidazólico, o mais eficaz agente ativo contra o *Pityrosporum ovale*. Alguns shampoos anticaspa podem apresentar um resultado superficial ou temporário, mas TRIATOP® ataca diretamente a causa do problema, controlando os seus efeitos. Além disso, TRIATOP® não prejudica a beleza dos cabelos, porque sua fórmula exclusiva contém colágeno, uma proteína nutriente e umectante que deixa os cabelos macios e sedosos. TRIATOP® é dermatologicamente testado e pode ser usado em todo tipo de cabelo. Nas primeiras 3 semanas de tratamento, o uso deve ser diário. Depois, 2 vezes por semana, de forma preventiva. Se você quiser mais informações sobre TRIATOP®, ligue grátis: 0800-11-8514.

P. ovale, o fungo causador da caspa.

Caspa nunca mais. Cabelos bonitos sempre.

Merit/International

CAMPAIGN
Dandruff Does Not Fall from the Sky...
ART DIRECTOR *Diego Zaragoza*
CREATIVE DIRECTOR *Luiz Toledo*
COPYWRITERS *Luiz Toledo, Fabio Saboya*
PHOTOGRAPHER *Paulo Vainer*
AGENCY *DDB Needham Brazil*
CLIENT *Janssen—The Pharmaceutical Division of J&J*

Merit/International

CAMPAIGN
Nature Is Wise, Only the Stick Was Missing
ART DIRECTOR *Marcello Serpa*
CREATIVE DIRECTORS *Alexandre Gama,*
Marcello Serpa
COPYWRITER *Alexandre Gama*
PHOTOGRAPHER *Freitas*
AGENCY *ALMAP/BBDO*
CLIENT *Kibon*

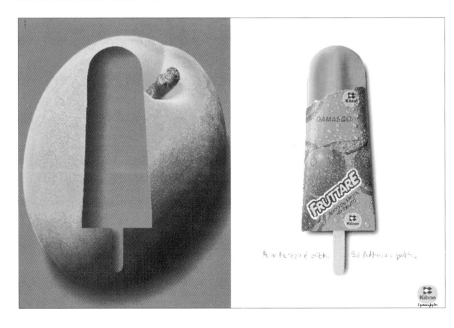

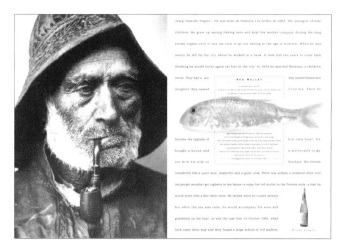

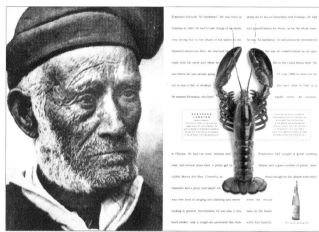

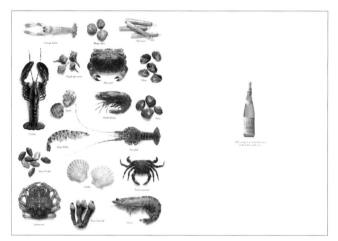

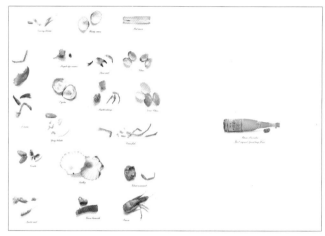

Merit/International

CAMPAIGN
Fisherman and Fish, Seafood Special, Hooks
ART DIRECTOR *Ramón Roda*
CREATIVE DIRECTORS *Xavi García, Ramón Roda,*
Angel Sanchez
COPYWRITERS *Sebastian Mendez, Xavi García,*
Angel Sanchez
PHOTOGRAPHER *Sisco Soler*
AGENCY *Casadevall Pedreño & PRG*
CLIENT *Cavas Del Ampurda, S.A.—Blanc Pescador*

Merit/International

CAMPAIGN
Porsche
ART DIRECTORS *John Buchner, Carlos Ferreira*
CREATIVE DIRECTOR *Klaus Erich Kuster*
DESIGNER *Carlos Ferreira*
COPYWRITERS *Klaus Erich Kuster, Sven Niemeyer*
PHOTOGRAPHER *Jerry Oke, London*
COPYWRITER *Sven Niemeyer*
AGENCY *Klaus E. Kuster Werbeagentur GmbH*
CLIENT *Dr. Ing.h.c.F. Porsche AG, Ludwigsburg*

Merit/International

CAMPAIGN
Faithful
ART DIRECTOR *Ramón Roda*
CREATIVE DIRECTORS *Xavi García, Angel Sanchez*
COPYWRITERS *Xavi García, Angel Sanchez*
PHOTOGRAPHER *David Levin*
AGENCY *Casadevall Pedreño & PRG*
CLIENT *Diario el País, S.A.*

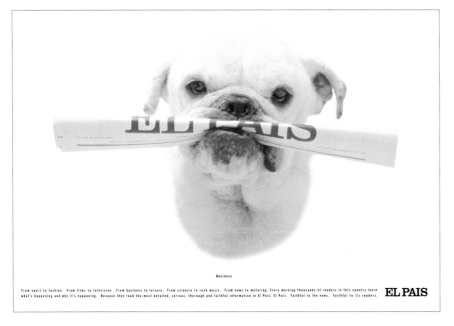

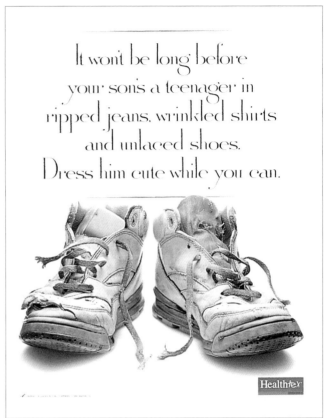

Merit/National

LESS THAN A FULL PAGE
Renoir
ART DIRECTOR *Jamie Mahoney*
CREATIVE DIRECTOR *Mike Hughes*
COPYWRITER *Joe Alexander*
PHOTOGRAPHY *Dublin Productions*
PRODUCER *Kay Franz*
AGENCY *The Martin Agency*
CLIENT *Healthtex, Inc.*

Merit/National

LESS THAN A FULL PAGE
Teenager
ART DIRECTOR *Jamie Mahoney*
CREATIVE DIRECTOR *Mike Hughes*
COPYWRITER *Raymond McKinney*
PHOTOGRAPHY *Dublin Productions*
PRODUCER *Kay Franz*
AGENCY *The Martin Agency*
CLIENT *Healthtex, Inc.*

Merit/National

LESS THAN A FULL PAGE
Someone Feeds You
ART DIRECTOR *Jamie Mahoney*
CREATIVE DIRECTOR *Mike Hughes*
COPYWRITER *Joe Alexander*
PHOTOGRAPHY *Dublin Productions*
PRODUCER *Kay Franz*
AGENCY *The Martin Agency*
CLIENT *Healthtex, Inc.*

Merit/National

FULL PAGE OR SPREAD
Raising Home Theatre
ART DIRECTOR *Darrell Credeur*
CREATIVE DIRECTORS *Tony Gomes, Bill Schwab*
COPYWRITER *David Smith*
PHOTOGRAPHERS *Craig Cutler, R. Greenberg,*
Dennis Blachut
AGENCY *Ammirati & Puris, Lintas*
CLIENT *Thomson Consumer Electronics, RCA*

Merit/National

FULL PAGE OR SPREAD
Idea Ribbon
ART DIRECTOR *Joe Ivey*
CREATIVE DIRECTOR *Gary H. Knutson*
DESIGNER *Joe Ivey*
COPYWRITER *Adam Cohen*
PHOTOGRAPHER *Alex Bee*
ILLUSTRATOR *Roy Carruthers*
AGENCY *Howard, Merrell & Partners*
CLIENT *Ciba Geigy Turf & Ornamental Products*

FULL PAGE OR SPREAD
Paris, Texas
ART DIRECTOR *Margaret McGovern*
CREATIVE DIRECTORS *Paul Silverman,*
Margaret McGovern
COPYWRITER *Paul Silverman*
PHOTOGRAPHER *John Holt Studio*
AGENCY *Mullen*
CLIENT *The Timberland Company*

FULL PAGE OR SPREAD
Laughing Bugs
ART DIRECTOR *Hal Tench*
CREATIVE DIRECTOR *Hal Tench*
COPYWRITER *Raymond McKinney*
ILLUSTRATOR *Hal Mayfordth*
PRODUCER *Karen Smith*
AGENCY *The Martin Agency*
CLIENT *FMC Corporation*

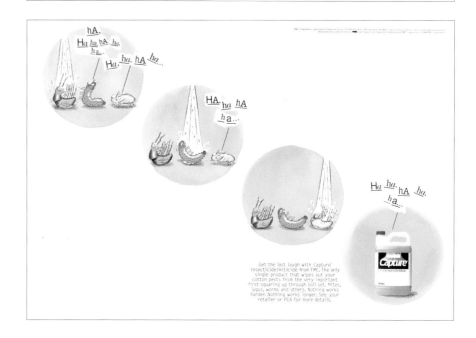

Merit/National

CAMPAIGN
Bats, Fireworks, Pterodactyl
ART DIRECTORS *Jim Mountjoy, Andy Azula*
CREATIVE DIRECTOR *Jim Mountjoy*
DESIGNER *Jim Mountjoy*
COPYWRITERS *Ed Jones, Bill Milkereit*
PHOTOGRAPHER *Jim Arndt*
AGENCY *Loeffler Ketchum Mountjoy*
CLIENT *Verbatim*

(left)
Merit/International

CAMPAIGN
EPSON: Prison, Tatouage, Dalmatien, Le Nu,
Parchemin
ART DIRECTOR *Robin de Lestrade*
CREATIVE DIRECTOR *Jean-Claude Jouis*
COPYWRITER *Olivier Altman*
PHOTOGRAPHER *Robin de Lestrade*
AGENCY *BDDP*
CLIENT *EPSON*

(facing page)
Merit/International

CAMPAIGN
Spots, 30 Seconds
ART DIRECTOR *Gary Marshall*
CREATIVE DIRECTORS *Paul Marshall, Gary Marshall*
DESIGNER *Gary Marshall*
COPYWRITER *Paul Marshall*
PHOTOGRAPHER *Dean Steadman*
AGENCY *Bean MC*
CLIENT *Laser Sales*

SPOTS

GIVING YOU CAUSE FOR CONCERN?
MAYBE YOU'RE USING THE WRONG SOAP.

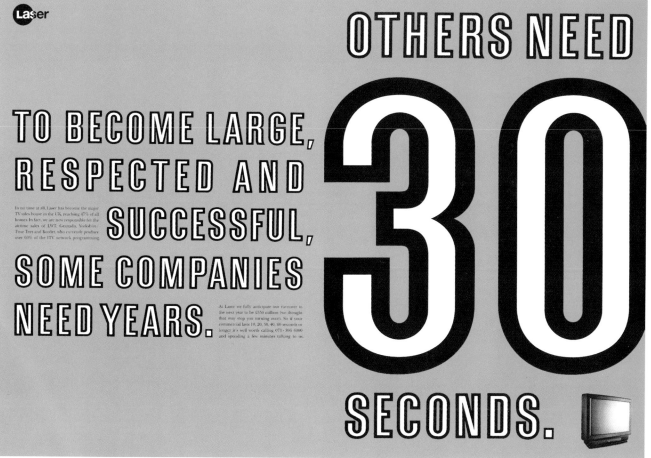

TO BECOME LARGE, RESPECTED AND SUCCESSFUL, SOME COMPANIES NEED YEARS.

OTHERS NEED **30** SECONDS.

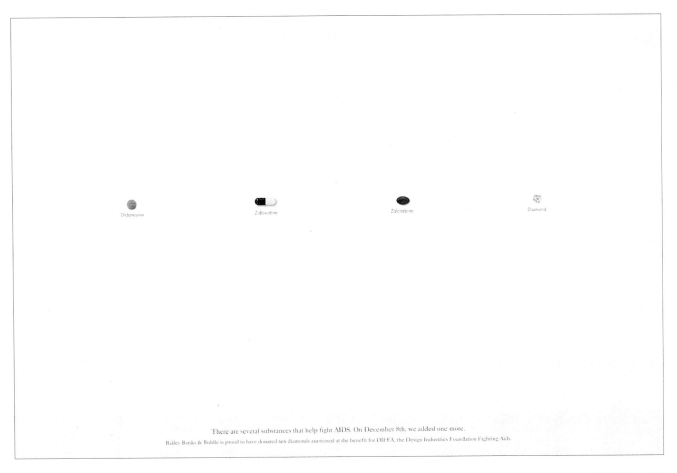

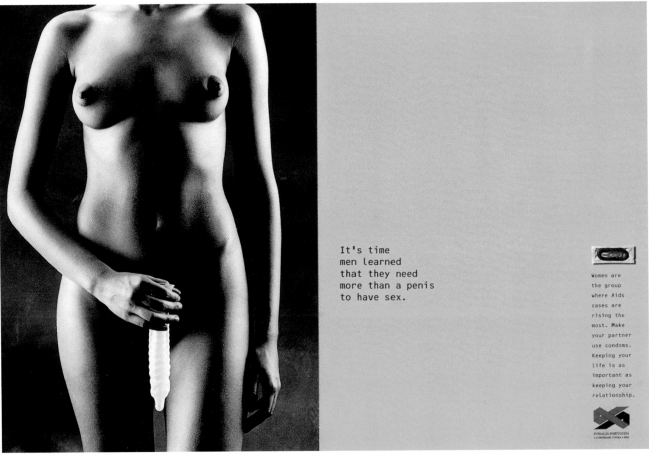

(facing page, top)
Merit/National

CAMPAIGN
AIDS
ART DIRECTOR *Jason Gaboriau*
CREATIVE DIRECTOR *Gary Goldsmith*
COPYWRITER *Justin Rohrlich*
AGENCY *Goldsmith/Jeffrey*
CLIENT *Fine Jewelers Guild*

(facing page, bottom)
Merit/International

FULL PAGE OR SPREAD
Condom
ART DIRECTOR *Paulo Diehl*
CREATIVE DIRECTOR *Edson Athayde*
COPYWRITERS *Edson Athayde, Frederico Saldanha*
PHOTOGRAPHER *Mario Cabrita Gil*
AGENCY *Young & Rubicam Portugal*
CLIENT *Fundação Portuguesa a Comunidade Contra a SIDA*

(right)
Merit/National

CAMPAIGN
Catboy, Catgirl, Dogboy,
ART DIRECTOR *Sally Wagner*
CREATIVE DIRECTOR *Lyle Wedemeyer*
COPYWRITER *Christopher Wilson*
PHOTOGRAPHER *Joe Lampe*
RETOUCHING *Brad Palm*
AGENCY *Martin/Williams*
CLIENT *American Humane Association*

Merit/National

SINGLE
Shopping Tips for the Most Difficult Cases
CREATIVE DIRECTOR *Ronnie Cooke*
DESIGNERS *Barbara Sullivan, Donald S. Montgomery*
COPYWRITER *Glenn O'Brien*
AGENCY *Barneys New York*
CLIENT *Barneys New York*

Merit/National

SINGLE
Alambré Eye Wear, Male D. M.
ART DIRECTOR *Daniel Miyahara*
CREATIVE DIRECTORS *Daniel Miyahara, Ward Parker*
DESIGNER *Daniel Miyahara*
COPYWRITER *Ward Parker*
PHOTOGRAPHER *Duane Dyck*
AGENCY *Reign Advertising and Design*
CLIENT *Alambré*

Merit/National

SINGLE
{T-26} Font Kit
ART DIRECTOR *Carlos Segura*
CREATIVE DIRECTOR *Carlos Segura*
DESIGNERS *Carlos Segura, Scott Smith*
POETRY *Dan X'Oneil*
AGENCY *Segura Inc.*
CLIENT *{T-26} A new digital type foundry*

(facing page, top)
Merit/National

SINGLE
Tailgate/Fall 1994
ART DIRECTOR *Marion English*
CREATIVE DIRECTOR *Terry Slaughter*
DESIGNERS *Marion English, Rebecca Fulmer*
COPYWRITER *Laura Holmes*
PHOTOGRAPHER *Liz Vonhoene*
AGENCY *Slaughter-Hanson*
CLIENT *Plainclothes*

(facing page, bottom)
Merit/National

SINGLE
Regal
ART DIRECTOR *Bob Dennard*
CREATIVE DIRECTOR *Bob Dennard*
DESIGNERS *Chris Wood, Wayne Geyer*
COPYWRITER *Wayne Geyer*
ILLUSTRATOR *Chris Wood*
STUDIO *Dennard Creative, Inc.*
CLIENT *Regal Printing*

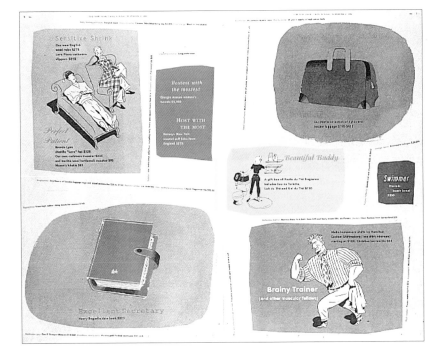

THE BEST PLACE

TO HANG

GLASSES

(since the nose).

ALAMBRÉ
EYE WEAR HOLDER

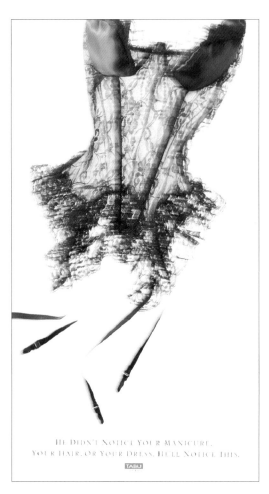

Merit/National

SINGLE
You Take
ART DIRECTOR *Michael Kadin*
COPYWRITERS *Renee Miller, David Stolberg*
PHOTOGRAPHER *Markku*
AGENCY *The Miller Group*
CLIENT *Wolf Range Co.*

Merit/National

SINGLE
Notice
ART DIRECTOR *Grant Richards*
CREATIVE DIRECTORS *Todd Tilford, Grant Richards*
COPYWRITER *Todd Tilford*
PHOTOGRAPHER *Robb Debenport*
PRODUCER *Gail Beckman*
AGENCY *The Richards Group*
STUDIO *Laser Tech Color*
CLIENT *Tabu Lingerie*

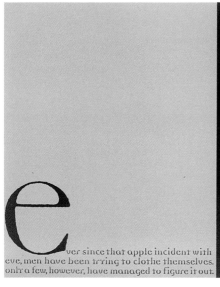

ver since that apple incident with
eve, men have been trying to clothe themselves.
only a few, however, have managed to figure it out.

ccording to article 7, #183, it is illegal
to go without clothing in public. in our opinion, wearing a
tie with a short-sleeve shirt is a far more serious offense.

o attract a female, all a male grasshopper has
to do is rub his legs together. man doesn't have it so easy.

Merit/National

CAMPAIGN
Apple Incident, Serious Offense, Grasshopper
ART DIRECTOR *Eric Tilford*
CREATIVE DIRECTOR *Todd Tilford*
COPYWRITER *Todd Tilford*
PHOTOGRAPHER *Richard Reens*
PRODUCER *Gail Beckman*
AGENCY *The Richards Group*
STUDIO *Laser Tech Color*
CLIENT *Lombardo Custom Apparel*

Merit/National

Merit/International

CAMPAIGN
Mandela Cup Cricket Package
ART DIRECTOR *Red Nail*
CREATIVE DIRECTOR *Red Nail*
DESIGNER *Red Nail*
COPYWRITER *Red Nail*
PHOTOGRAPHER *Michael Meyersfeld*
AGENCY *Red Nail*
STUDIO *Red Nail*
CLIENT *TV1*

Merit/International

CAMPAIGN
Hiroko Koshino Collection
ART DIRECTOR *Koji Mizutani*
CREATIVE DIRECTOR *Koji Mizutani*
DESIGNERS *Hiroshi Ohmizo, Junko Horiuchi*
PHOTOGRAPHER *Hiroshi Murakami*
AGENCY *Mizutani Studio*
STUDIO *Mizutani Studio*
CLIENT *Hiroko Koshino Design Office, Inc.*

Merit/National

COMMERCIAL, OVER 30 SECONDS
Cyber Lany
CREATIVE DIRECTOR *Kathy Kiely*
COPYWRITERS *Leticia Martin, Kathy Kiely*
PRODUCER *Matt Pedone*
AGENCY *Pedone & Partners*
STUDIO *Bob Pomann Sound*
CLIENT *Genesee Brewing Company*

HE: *It's the usual Wednesday night in cyberspace. The usual names come up on the computer screen. Fifi. Miss G. Zany Lany? That's unusual.*
HE: *(Clicking) What makes you so zany, Lany?*
SHE: *I'll try anything once.*
HE: *Ooooh. Wow. (Clicking) Ever let a St. Bernard lick your toes while listening to Bolero? (No response.)*
HE: *I lost her.*
HE: *(Clicking) I bet you haven't tried JW Dundee's Honey Brown Lager. (No response.) C'mon, Zany.*
HE: *(Clicking) It's brewed with honey for a real smooth taste. How about I buy you one to make up for the St. Bernard.*
SHE: *OK, since I can't slap your face in cyberspace.*
HE: *(Clicking) FYI, I'm cute. But I'm bald.*
SHE: *That's OK. I am too.*
AVO: *JW Dundee's Honey Brown Lager. Anything but the usual. Dundee's Brewery, Rochester, New York.*

Merit/National

COMMERCIAL, OVER 30 SECONDS
Lies
CREATIVE DIRECTOR *Rob Ingalls*
COPYWRITER *Adam Lau*
PRODUCER *Tamara Remington*
AGENCY *Saatchi & Saatchi Advertising, San Francisco*
STUDIO *Chicago Recording Company*
CLIENT *Hewlett-Packard*

FRED: *Um...is this normal for a job interview?*
BOB: *I'm afraid lie detector tests are standard procedure. Now, are you comfortable?*
FRED: *Yes.*
SFX: *BZZZ.*
BOB: *Excellent. If hired by this company, would you do all you could to enhance productivity?*
FRED: *Yes.*
SFX: *BZZZ.*
FRED: *Well, I wouldn't leave early or anything.*
SFX: *BZZZ.*
FRED: *I mean, only when I had to.*
SFX: *BZZZ.*
FRED: *Or if I had an HP ScanJet IIp flatbed scanner. It helps me be more efficient. Get the job done.*
BOB: *Hm. And do you expect the company to purchase this HP ScanJet IIp for you?*
FRED: *Of course not.*
SFX: *BZZZ.*
FRED: *I mean, yes. It's not expensive. Their prices have just been cut to under $599 and that includes free OCR software for text scans and built-in software to make scanning easier.*
BOB: *Hm. Efficiency. Price drop. I like your thinking. When would you like to start?*
FRED: *Immediately.*
SFX: *BZZZ.*
FRED: *Well, tomorrow.*
SFX: *BZZZ.*
ANNCR.: *Get an HP ScanJet IIp for the new low price of $599.*
FRED: *Next week would be better for me.*
SFX: *BZZZ.*
FRED: *How about in a month or two?*
ANNCR.: *See your Yellow Pages for the Hewlett-Packard dealer nearest you or call 1-800-SCANJET for a free video.*
SFX: *BZZZ.*
FRED: *Look. I'll start whenever you like.*
SFX: *BZZZ.*

Merit/National

COMMERCIAL, OVER 30 SECONDS
Coach
COPYWRITERS *David Corr (Chiat/Day), David Shane (Are These My Shoes? Productions)*
PRODUCERS *Lee Ann Daly (Are These My Shoes? Productions), Roxanne Karsch (Chiat/Day)*
DIRECTOR *David Shane*
AGENCY *Chiat/Day*
STUDIO *Superdupe*
CLIENT *Nick at Nite*

SFX: *Telephone ringing*
NICK AT NITE MAN: *Hello, Nick at Nite Hotline. May I help you?*
COACH: *What's all this I hear about y'all not showin' any football games New Year's Day?*
NICK AT NITE MAN: *That's right, we'll be televising the Nick at Nite Classic TV Countdown, hosted by Casey Kasem.*
COACH: *Son, it is an American tradition to watch football on New Year's Day. Goes back...thousands of years.*
NICK AT NITE MAN: *More or less, yes. But you know this is a special countdown, Sir, of the year's 25 best episodes from Mary Tyler Moore, Dragnet, Dick Van Dyke.*
COACH: *So you're tellin' me no football.*
NICK AT NITE MAN: *Pretty much, yeah. We start at noon and end with the best episode of 1993.*
COACH: *Where are you from, boy?*
NICK AT NITE MAN: *Excuse me?*
COACH: *Parlez-vous français, boy?*
NICK AT NITE MAN: *Sir, maybe I could interest you in something special for the kids?*
COACH: *Is it football?*
NICK AT NITE MAN: *No. Nickelodeon's got a special New Year's lineup—Roundhouse, Pete and Pete, Ren & Stimpy...*
COACH: *Son, why are ya doin' this?*
NICK AT NITE MAN: *Just wanted to give the kids something fun to do while they stay up New Year's Eve. It starts at eight.*
COACH: *Ya know what I think? I think you're some kind of soccer boy.*
NICK AT NITE MAN: *I am not.*
COACH: *That's what I think.*
NICK AT NITE MAN: *I'm not a soccer boy.*
COACH: *I think ya are.*
NICK AT NITE MAN: *Stop it.*
AVO: *Watch Nickelodeon's New Year's Weekend. To get cable call 1-800-CABLE-ME.*

Merit/National

COMMERCIAL, OVER 30 SECONDS
Boxing Barney
CREATIVE DIRECTOR *Ron Sackett*
COPYWRITER *Ruth E. Harvey*
PRODUCER *Wendy Johnson-Ness*
AGENCY *Case Foley*
STUDIO *Voiceworks*
CLIENT *Title Wave Music and Video*

ANNCR.: *Ladies and Gentlemen!!! Tonight's scheduled event is a championship heavyweight bout. In this corner, wearing purple and green trunks is the reigning world champion, Barney. In this corner, the challenger, facing his first title bout—Vinny the Velociraptor. Your referee tonight is Bobby Tuchavinio.*
REFEREE: *OK. Let's keep it a clean fight fellows. No low blows. Come out boxing.*
SFX: *Ding ding. Sound of feet, jabbing.*
BARNEY: *I love you.*
DINOSAUR: *Dinosaur noise.*
BARNEY: *You love me.*
DINOSAUR: *Dinosaur getting madder and madder.*
ANNCR.: *Monday October 3rd it's Barney vs. the dinosaurs of Jurassic Park. The place: all 14 Title Wave locations. The time: midnight to 1:00 a.m. Be the first to pick up Jurassic Park just released and on sale for $14.99.*
BARNEY: *We're a happy fami...*
SFX: *Sound of pummeling.*
ANNCR.: *Monday October 3rd. Midnight to 1:00 a.m. Be there!*
ANNCR.: *Title Wave. Ding ding. Get into it.*

Merit/National

COMMERCIAL, OVER 30 SECONDS
Women's Health
CREATIVE DIRECTOR *Fred Bertino*
COPYWRITER *Al Lowe*
PRODUCER *Greg Roman*
AGENCY *Hill, Holliday, Connors, Cosmopulos*
STUDIO *Soundtrack*
CLIENT *Harvard Community Health Plan*

MAN 1: *You know, I went for my mammogram just last week.*
MAN 2: *How was it?*
MAN 1: *It was fine, fine...I'm so glad. It was such a relief...*
MAN 2: *Oh, I know what you mean. I just went for my Pap smear.*
MAN 1: *Oh?*
MAN 2: *I get one regularly, of course.*
MAN 1: *Of course, me too. Was there any problem?*
MAN 2: *It was a little abnormal, but they followed up on it, immediately. They've been truly wonderful...Well, they always have been...I like 'em.*
VO: *It's often been said that if men had the same health concerns as women, they'd have no trouble getting all the care they need.*
MAN 1: *Oh, and...I've got a little secret.*
MAN 2: *What? What? What? What?*
MAN 1: *(coyly) I think I'm uh...*
MAN 2: *You aren't...Get out of town...*
MAN 1: *Yeah.*
MAN 2: *When?!*
VO: *Well, at Harvard Community Health Plan, we make sure women get all the care they need—from regular mammograms and Pap smear tests to complete prenatal care.*
MAN 2: *Oh George, this is so exciting...I'm so happy for you...high five.*
VO: *Harvard Community Health Plan. We're what health care should be.*
MAN 2: *I assume Estelle is the mother...*
MAN 1: *Oh, come on, you nut...*

Merit/National

COMMERCIAL, OVER 30 SECONDS
Jump, Corporate Chicken, Radio Call-In Show
CREATIVE DIRECTOR *Donna Weinheim*
COPYWRITERS *Cliff Freeman, Michelle Roufa*
PRODUCER *Anne Kurtzman*
AGENCY *Cliff Freeman & Partners*
STUDIO *Clack Sound Studio*
CLIENT *Little Caesars*

TALK SHOW HOST: *Tonight live, the debate continues: who came up with the idea of pizza for a buck, the chicken...*
SFX: *Buck!*
HOST: *Or the owner of Little Caesars...*
MR. I: *Good evening, Barry.*
SFX: *Buck!*
HOST: *Now, people are starting to believe the chicken.*
MR. I: *I know, I'm amazed. I'm the guy who started Little Caesars, I came up...*
SFX: *Buck!*
MR. I: *Please, let me finish...*
SXF: *Buck!*
MR. I: *I didn't interrupt him, why does he interrupt me?*
SFX: *Buck, buck!*
HOST: *Alright now, gentlemen, let's take our first call—from Edwards, Mississippi.*
SFX: *Thousands of chickens bucking and clucking.*
HOST: *How many chickens are on there?*
MR. I: *Sounds like hundreds. Must be a conference call or something.*
ANNCR.: *Get a medium sized Little Caesars pizza for a buck, your pizza, pizza bonus when you buy two pizzas with two toppings for $8.98!*
LITTLE CAESAR: *Pizza, pizza!*
HOST: *Balsa, Kentucky—hello!*
CALLER: *I look at it two ways; one, no offense, chickens are stupid and they got no ideas, but two—if you think about it, pizza for a buck is chicken feed, and chicken feed is what you feed chickens...*
HOST: *(cutting off caller) Nashville, hello.*

Merit/National

COMMERCIAL, OVER 30 SECONDS
Truth: Sackman
ART DIRECTOR *Dave Gardiner*
CREATIVE DIRECTORS *Rich Herstek, Peter Favat*
COPYWRITERS *Ken Lewis, Stu Cooperrider*
PRODUCERS *Harry McCoy, Chris Palumbo*
AGENCY *Houston Effler Herstek Favat*
STUDIO *Soundtrack*
CLIENT *Massachusetts Department of Public Health*

SACKMAN: *You may get cancer or heart disease. But one thing I doubt you'll ever get from tobacco companies is the truth. They keep saying you can't get hooked on cigarettes. But the truth is, nicotine is very addictive. In fact, many smokers keep lighting up even after they lose their vocal cords to cancer. My name is Janet Sackman. I'm not here because I got hooked and I had cancer. I'm here because I was a model in cigarette ads and helped convince a lot of young people to smoke. I hope now I can convince you not to.*

Merit/National

COMMERCIAL, OVER 30 SECONDS
Tree
CREATIVE DIRECTORS *Larry Tolpin, Stephen Creet, Michael McLaughlin*
COPYWRITER *Stephen Creet*
PRODUCER *Marie Robertson*
MUSIC *Harris Cole Wilde, BBDO Canada*
STUDIO *Production House, Harris Cole Wilde*
CLIENT *Molson Breweries*

TOMMY LEE JONES: *Hey. Red Dog here. I got a bone to pick. Not with you in particular. Unless you're one of them dawgs I see barking up the wrong tree. Never mind for a moment whether you got the wrong tree or the right — why are you barking up a freakin' tree in the first place? See, makes no sense. If there's somethin' up there, it sure as hell ain't gonna come down with you barkin' your fool head off. Quit your yelping. Walk away. Sooner or later whatever's up there's gonna come down. Now I don't care if you spend all night howling up a tree but you're keeping me up all night. And believe me when I don't get my beauty sleep, I am not a pretty sight.*
ANNCR.: *Red Dog Beer. You are your own dog.*

GRAPHIC DESIGN

GOLD AND SILVER MEDALISTS

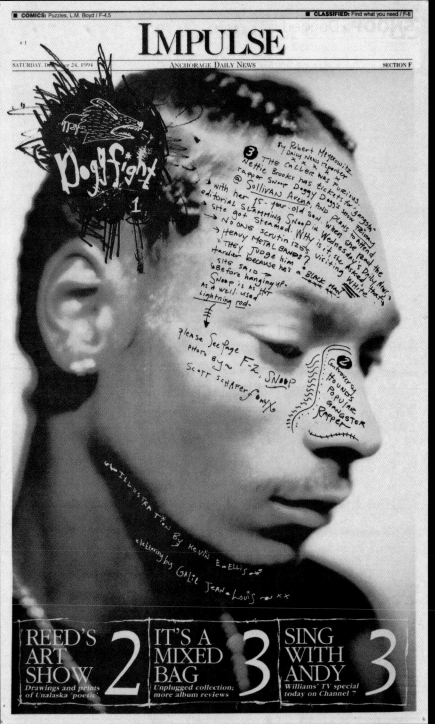

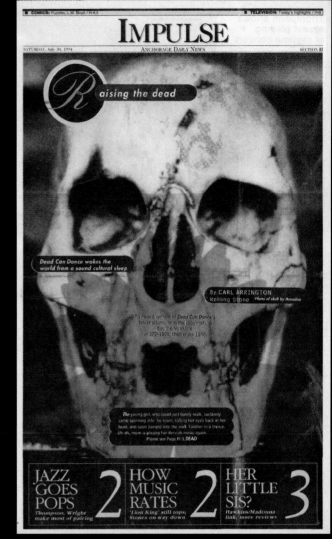

Silver Medalist/National

FULL PAGE OR SPREAD
Soul Music
ART DIRECTOR *Galie Jean-Louis*
CREATIVE DIRECTOR *Galie Jean-Louis*
DESIGNER *Galie Jean-Louis*
PHOTOGRAPHER *Amy Guip*
ILLUSTRATOR *Galie Jean-Louis*
STUDIO *Galie Jean-Louis*
CLIENT *Anchorage Daily News*

Silver Medalist/National

FULL PAGE OR SPREAD
Raising the Dead
ART DIRECTOR *Galie Jean-Louis*
CREATIVE DIRECTOR *Galie Jean-Louis*
DESIGNER *Galie Jean-Louis*
PHOTOGRAPHER *Annalisa*
STUDIO *Galie Jean-Louis*
CLIENT *Anchorage Daily News*

Silver Medalist/National

COVER
This Is a Hug in Cyberspace
ART DIRECTORS *Carl Lehmann-Haupt,*
Nancy Kruger Cohen
DESIGNERS *Carl Lehmann-Haupt,*
Nancy Kruger Cohen
EDITOR *Susan Szenasy*
COPYWRITER *Karrie Jacobs*
CLIENT *Metropolis*

Silver Medalist/National

FULL PAGE OR SPREAD
Man of the Year
CREATIVE DIRECTOR *Fred Woodward*
DESIGNER *Geraldine Hessler*
ILLUSTRATOR *David Cowles*
CLIENT *Rolling Stone*

ADDITIONAL AWARD

Distinctive Merit
ILLUSTRATION, EDITORIAL, FULL PAGE OR SPREAD

ILLUSTRATION BY DAVID COWLES

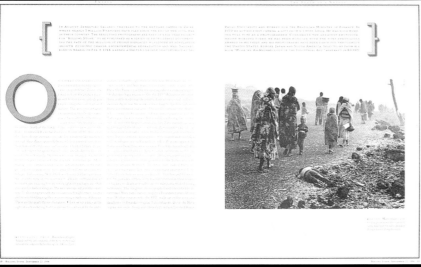

Gold Medalist/National

MULTIPAGE
Rwanda {The Death of a Nation}
CREATIVE DIRECTOR *Fred Woodward*
DESIGNERS *Fred Woodward, Gail Anderson*
PHOTO EDITOR *Jodi Peckman*
PHOTOGRAPHER *Sebastião Salgado*
CLIENT *Rolling Stone*

ADDITIONAL AWARD

Merit
PHOTOGRAPHY, EDITORIAL, SERIES

Gold Medalist/International

MULTIPAGE
Cut, May Issue
ART DIRECTOR *Hideki Nakajima*
DESIGNERS *Hideki Nakajima, Yuko Kasuga,*
Iwao Miura, Masashi Nakayama,
Kenichi Kawakami
EDITOR IN CHIEF *Ken Sato*
PHOTOGRAPHERS *Paolo Roversi,*
Marion de Beaupre, Roger-Viollet, Dalmas,
Ellen Von Unwerth, Steven Klein
CLIENT *Rockin'on Inc.*

ティム・ロス

Tim Roth

クエンティン・タランティーノ

Quentine Tarantino

ユマ・サーマン

Uma Thurman

クシシュトフ・キェシロフスキ

Krzysztof Kieślowski

人生ではなにかを超えて

Kate Moss in Tokyo!!

Photographs by Itaru Hirama

Silver Medalist/International

MULTIPAGE
Cut, December Issue
ART DIRECTOR *Hideki Nakajima*
DESIGNERS *Hideki Nakajima, Yuko Kasuga, Iwao Miura,*
Masashi Nakayama, Kenichi Kawakami
EDITOR IN CHIEF *Ken Sato*
PHOTOGRAPHERS *Michel Tigue, Jean Baptiste Mondino,*
Albert Watson, Takaya Endo, Itaru Hirama
CLIENT *Rockin'on Inc.*

MATT DILLON

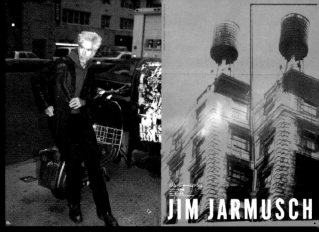

JIM JARMUSCH

Je ne ressens plus le besoin de délirer sur le personnage, avant, avec le metteur en scène. Je pense qu'un personnage, ça se comprend très vite, ou alors pas du tout.

J H
A

ジャン＝ユーグ・アングラド

JEAN-HUGUES ANGLADE

Je suis une Lolita capricieuse, une baby-doll Chanel, une jeune fille qui rêve du Prince charmant. Mais, en plus profond de moi, je suis quelqu'un de timide. J'ai toujours peur de décevoir, de ne pas être à la hauteur.

V P

ヴァネッサ・パラディ

VANESSA PARADIS

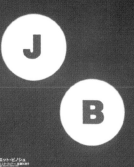

Je ne suis pas d'une nature nostalgique. Après "Les Amants du Pont-Neuf", je savais qu'il ne m'était plus possible de regarder en arrière, que je devais à tout prix survivre par et dans le présent.

J
B

ジュリエット・ビノシュ

JULIETTE BINOCHE

Silver Medalist/International

MULTIPAGE
Cut, July Issue
ART DIRECTOR *Hideki Nakajima*
DESIGNERS *Hideki Nakajima, Yuko Kasuga,*
Iwao Miura, Masashi Nakayama,
Kenichi Kawakami
EDITOR IN CHIEF *Ken Sato*
PHOTOGRAPHERS *Jeffrey Thurnher,*
Miyamoto Kei Bun, Gilles-Marie Zimmermann,
Michel Comte, Satoshi Saikusa
CLIENT *Rockin'on Inc.*

Gold Medalist/National

SINGLE
Cobain by the Editors of Rolling Stone
CREATIVE DIRECTOR *Fred Woodward*
DESIGNER *Fred Woodward*
PHOTO EDITOR *Denise Sfraga*
PHOTOGRAPHERS *Various*
CLIENT *Little Brown and Company*

ADDITIONAL AWARD

Distinctive Merit
BOOK JACKET, SINGLE

"I thought he was one of the more beautiful quiet people. I always sensed this really intense sense of fantasy around him, through his music and a really intense sense of atmosphere." —Curt Kirkwood lead singer, Meat Puppets

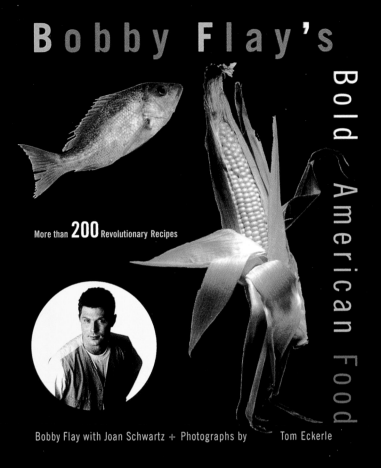

Bobby Flay's

Bold American Food

More than **200** Revolutionary Recipes

Bobby Flay with Joan Schwartz + Photographs by Tom Eckerle

Silver Medalist/National

SINGLE
Bobby Flay's Bold American Food
ART DIRECTOR *Adriane Stark*
DESIGNERS *Adriane Stark, Christine Licata*
AUTHOR *Bobby Flay*
PHOTOGRAPHER *Tom Eckerle*
STUDIO *Stark Design*
CLIENT *Warner Books*

Silver Medalist/National

SINGLE
Saving Wildlife Since 1895
ART DIRECTOR *Stephen Doyle*
CREATIVE DIRECTORS *William Drenttel,*
Stephen Doyle
DESIGNER *Mats Hakansson*
COPYWRITER *Don Goddard*
ILLUSTRATOR *Christopher Wormell*
STUDIO *Drenttel Doyle Partners*
CLIENT *The Wildlife Conservation Society*

Silver Medalist/National

SINGLE
e. e. cummings @ 100
ART DIRECTOR *Karen Salsgiver*
CREATIVE DIRECTOR *Karen Salsgiver*
DESIGNERS *Karen Salsgiver, Laura Howell,*
Angela Voulangas
AGENCY *Salsgiver Coveney Associates Inc.*
CLIENT *The New York Public Library*

Silver Medalist/International

SINGLE
Graphis Alternative Photography 95
ART DIRECTOR *B. Martin Pedersen*
CREATIVE DIRECTOR *B. Martin Pedersen*
DESIGNER *B. Martin Pedersen*
PHOTOGRAPHER *Joseph Pluchino*
STUDIO *Pedersen Design Inc.*
CLIENT *Graphis*

ADDITIONAL AWARD

Merit
BOOK JACKET, SINGLE

Gold Medalist/International

SINGLE
Ego no ki
ART DIRECTOR *Hiroaki Nagai*
CREATIVE DIRECTOR *Tatsuo Ishida*
DESIGNERS *Hiroaki Nagai, Kyoko Iida*
COPYWRITER *Tatsuo Ishida*
PHOTOGRAPHER *Katsuhiro Ichikawa*
CLIENT *Rikuyosha*

Silver Medalist/International

SINGLE
Astroboy Taroo
ART DIRECTOR *Ken Shinohara*
CREATIVE DIRECTOR *Atsushi Takeuchi*
DESIGNER *Ken Shinohara*
COPYWRITER *Shu Tokunari*
ILLUSTRATORS *Takanori Aiba, Ken Shinohara,*
Parms Takahashi
CLIENT *Nichinoken*

Silver Medalist/International

SINGLE
Sam Goes to the City
ART DIRECTOR *Ken Shinohara*
CREATIVE DIRECTOR *Atsushi Takeuchi*
DESIGNER *Ken Shinohara*
COPYWRITER *Shu Tokunari*
ILLUSTRATORS *Takanori Aiba,*
Parms Takahashi, Ken Shinohara
CLIENT *Nichinoken*

Silver Medalist/International

SINGLE
Kunst-Werk-Körper
ART DIRECTOR *Andréas Netthoevel*
PHOTOGRAPHER *Tiziana de Silvestro*
PUBLISHER *Edition Braus*
STUDIO *second floor south*

Silver Medalist/International

SINGLE
Hidden Japan
ART DIRECTOR *Kijuro Yahagi*
DESIGNER *Kijuro Yahagi*
PHOTOGRAPHER *Kijuro Yahagi*
CLIENT *Takenaka Corporation*

Silver Medalist/International

SINGLE
Creatures: Junko Mada Works
ART DIRECTOR *Hitomi Sago*
DESIGNERS *Hitomi Sago, Asako Kaneko*
PHOTOGRAPHERS *Naoko Hiroishi,*
Kazunari Koyama, Makoto Ohmori
ILLUSTRATOR *Junko Mada*
PRODUCER *Atsuhide Nakajima*
STUDIO *Hitomi Sago Design Office*
CLIENT *Korinsha Press & Co., Ltd.*

Silver Medalist/International

SINGLE
Graphis Typography 1
ART DIRECTOR *B. Martin Pedersen*
CREATIVE DIRECTOR *B. Martin Pedersen*
DESIGNER *B. Martin Pedersen*
STUDIO *Pedersen Design Inc.*
CLIENT *Graphis*

ADDITIONAL AWARD

Merit
BOOK JACKET, SINGLE

Silver Medalist/International

SINGLE
The Boy Who Ate Around
CREATIVE DIRECTOR *Henrik Drescher*
DESIGNER *Stephanie Power*
COPYWRITER *Henrik Drescher*
ILLUSTRATOR *Henrik Drescher*
STUDIO *Reactor Art + Design*
CLIENT *Hyperion Books*

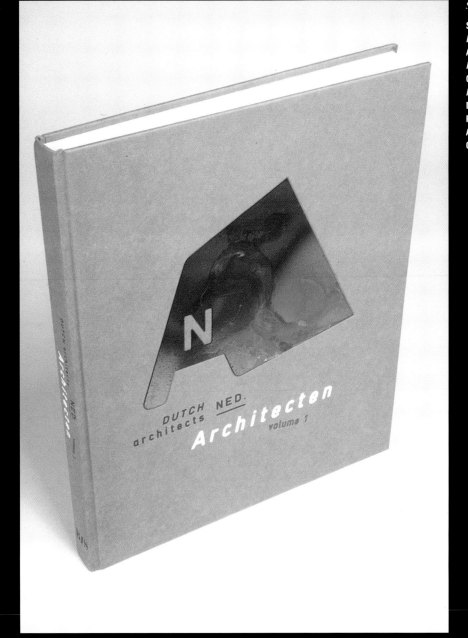

Silver Medalist/International

SINGLE
Dutch Architects, Vol. 1
ART DIRECTORS *Jacques Koeweiden,*
Paul Postma
CREATIVE DIRECTORS *Jacques Koeweiden,*
Paul Postma
DESIGNERS *Jacques Koeweiden, Paul Postm*
PHOTOGRAPHER *Marc van Praag*
AGENCY *Koeweiden Postma Associates*
CLIENT *Bis Publishers*

Silver Medalist/National

TITLE FOR PROMOTION, SINGLE
VH1 Sunday Open
ART DIRECTOR *Kevin Largent*
CREATIVE DIRECTOR *Lauren Zalaznick*
PRODUCER *Jason Harrington*
DIRECTOR *Jason Harrington*
CLIENT *VH1*

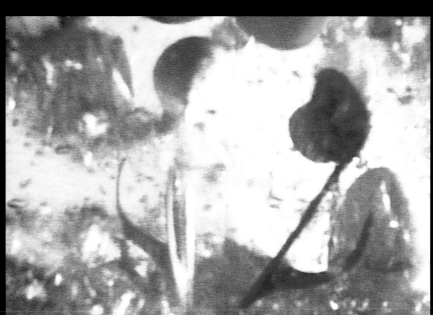

Gold Medalist/National

SPECIAL EFFECTS AND COMPUTER GRAPHICS, SINGLE
Frogs
ART DIRECTOR *Michael Smith*
CREATIVE DIRECTORS *Michael Hutchinson,*
Ric Anello
COPYWRITER *Dave Swaine*
ANIMATRONICS *Stan Winston Studio*
PRODUCER *Chan Hatcher*
DIRECTOR *Gore Verbinski*
MUSIC *Tom Woodard, Hummingbird*
AGENCY *D'Arcy Masius Benton & Bowles*
CLIENT *Anheuser-Busch/Budweiser*

ADDITIONAL AWARD

Silver Medalist
ADVERTISING, TELEVISION, COMMERCIAL,
30 SECONDS OR LESS

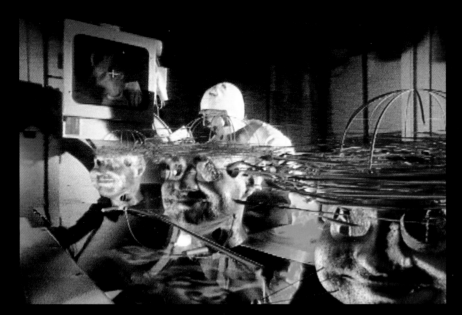

Silver Medalist/International

SPECIAL EFFECTS AND COMPUTER GRAPHICS, SINGLE
Yesterday When I Was Mad
ANIMATION DIRECTORS *Ian Bird, John Wake*
CREATIVE DIRECTOR *Howard Greenhalgh*
DESIGNERS *Ian Bird, John Wake, Rob Fellows*
COMPUTER ANIMATION *601 FX*
PRODUCER *Megan Hollister*
POST-PRODUCTION *Soho 601*
DIRECTOR *Howard Greenhalgh*
MUSIC *The Pet Shop Boys*
COMPOSITOR *James Bygrave*
CLIENT *The Pet Shop Boys*

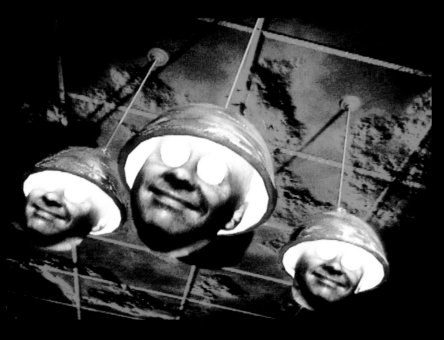

Gold Medalist/International

ANIMATION, SINGLE
Within/Without
ART DIRECTOR *Benita Raphan*
CREATIVE DIRECTOR *Benita Raphan*
DESIGNER *Benita Raphan*
COPYWRITERS *Jean François Delacampagne,*
Benita Raphan
PHOTOGRAPHER *Benita Raphan*
PRODUCER *Keith Griffiths,*
Koninck Projects Ltd.
DIRECTOR *Benita Raphan*
SOUND *Marshall Group Sound Design*
AGENCY *Benita Raphan Design*
CLIENT *Arts Council of England, Channel 4*
Television

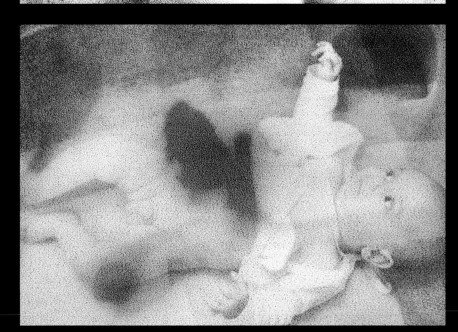

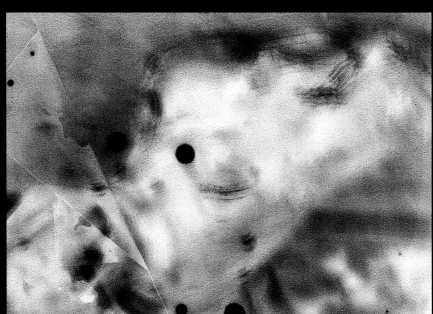

Silver Medalist/National

CAMPAIGN
The Limited 1994 Annual Shareholders' Meeting
CREATIVE DIRECTORS *Kent Hunter,*
Aubrey Balkind
DESIGNERS *Robert Wong, Arturo Aranda*
PHOTOGRAPHERS *Julie Powell, Brad Feinknopf*
AGENCY *Frankfurt Balkind Partners*
CLIENT *The Limited, Inc.*

"Sell it at **4**" "Sell it at **4**"

"Sell it at **4**"

Gold Medalist/National

ANNUAL REPORT
CBOT 1994 Annual Report
ART DIRECTOR *Dana Arnett*
CREATIVE DIRECTOR *Dana Arnett*
DESIGNER *Curt Schreiber*
COPYWRITERS *Anita Liskey, Michael Oakes*
PHOTOGRAPHER *François Robert*
STUDIO *VSA Partners, Inc.*
CLIENT *Chicago Board of Trade*

UNIFEM ANNUAL REPORT 1993

DEUTSCHE HANDELSBANK AG
GRUPPE CREDIT LYONNAIS

Bericht über das Geschäftsjahr 1993

MERCHANT BANK

VORWERK
ANNUAL
REPORT
1993

Gold Medalist/National

BOOKLET, FOLDER, OR BROCHURE, SINGLE
VH1 Honors Program
ART DIRECTORS *Cheri Dorr, Sharon Werner*
CREATIVE DIRECTOR *Cheri Dorr*
DESIGNER *Sharon Werner*
COPYWRITER *Dan Hedges*
PHOTOGRAPHERS *Various*
PRODUCER *Diversified Graphics Inc.*
STUDIO *Werner Design Werks Inc.*
CLIENT *VH1*

VH-1 HONORS
VH-1 HONORS
VH-1 HONORS
VH-1 HONORS
CONTENTS
SPONSORED BY:
Sprint
Dodge/Plymouth Neon
Lipton Original Iced Tea
Sebastian International
Diet Rite
Volkswagen Jetta
Clothestime
1994
VH-1 HONORS
Celebrating
music that matters
SHRINE AUDITORIUM
Los Angeles
JUNE TWENTY SIX 1994

Silver Medalist/National

BOOKLET, FOLDER, OR BROCHURE, SINGLE
Special Cases: Natural Anomalies and Historical
Monsters
DESIGNERS *Nicholas Lowie, Sheridan Lowrey*
PHOTOGRAPHERS *John Kiffe, Douglas Benjamin*
STUDIO *J. Paul Getty Trust, Publication Services*
CLIENT *The Getty Center for the History of Art and the*
Humanities

Silver Medalist/National

BOOKLET, FOLDER, OR BROCHURE, SINGLE
OK Soda Media
ART DIRECTOR *Steve Sandstrom*
CREATIVE DIRECTOR *Charlotte Moore*
DESIGNER *Steve Sandstrom*
COPYWRITER *Jean Rhode*
PHOTOGRAPHER *Doug Petty*
ILLUSTRATOR *Daniel Clowes*
AGENCY *Wieden & Kennedy*
STUDIO *Sandstrom Design*
CLIENT *Coca-Cola/OK Soda*

WAX MODEL OF MAN WITH TUMOR IN LEFT EYE

WARREN ANATOMICAL MUSEUM, HARVARD MEDICAL SCHOOL

PHOTOGRAPH 1985
BY ROSAMOND PURCELL

Special Cases:

NATURAL
ANOMALIES

September 24
– December 17,
1994

HISTORICAL
MONSTERS

ADDITIONAL PACKAGING OF "OK-NESS"

OTHER BOTTLES DESIGNED SPECIFICALLY FOR "OK" SODA

Silver Medalist/National

BOOKLET, FOLDER, OR BROCHURE, SERIES
Wieland Campaign
ART DIRECTOR *Neil Powell*
CREATIVE DIRECTOR *Joe Duffy*
DESIGNER *Neil Powell*
PHOTOGRAPHERS *Mark LaFavor,*
Hugh Kretschmer
STUDIO *Duffy Design*
CLIENT *Wieland Furniture Company*

Silver Medalist/National

BOOKLET, FOLDER, OR BROCHURE, SERIES
The Edison Project Booklets
ART DIRECTORS *Stephen Doyle, Tom Kluepfel*
DESIGNERS *Rosemarie Turk, Gary Tooth,*
Mats Hakansson, Katrin Schmitt-Tegge
ILLUSTRATORS *Brian Cairns, Jessie Hartland,*
Allan Drummond, Jon Agee
PHOTOGRAPHER *Gentl & Hyers*

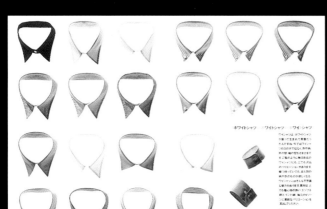

Silver Medalist/International

BOOKLET, FOLDER, OR BROCHURE, SERIES
Mujirushi-Ryohin Clothing Catalogue, Fall 1994
ART DIRECTOR *Masaaki Hiromura*
BRAND DIRECTORS *Ikko Tanaka, Kazuko Koike*
DESIGNERS *Masaaki Hiromura,*
Toshiyuki Kojima
COPYWRITER *Yoichi Umemoto*
PHOTOGRAPHER *Takashi Oyama*
CLIENT *Ryohin-Keikaku Co., Ltd.*

Gold Medalist/National

PACKAGING, SERIES
OK Can Series
ART DIRECTOR *Todd Waterbury*
CREATIVE DIRECTORS *Todd Waterbury,*
Peter Wegner, Charlotte Moore
DESIGNER *Todd Waterbury*
COPYWRITER *Peter Wegner*
ILLUSTRATORS *Charles Burns, Daniel Clowes,*
Calef Brown, David Cowles
AGENCY *Wieden & Kennedy*
CLIENT *The Coca-Cola Company*

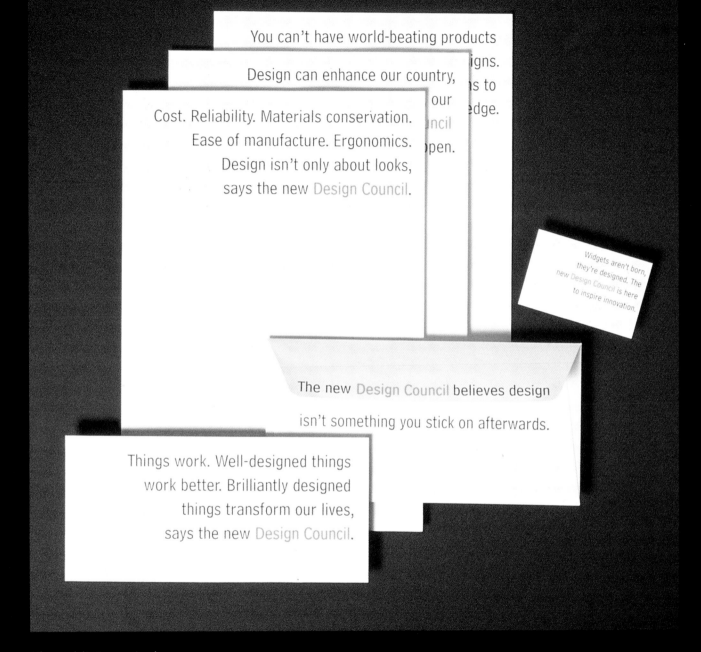

You can't have world-beating products
...igns.
Design can enhance our country,
...s to
...our
...edge.
Cost. Reliability. Materials conservation.
...ncil
Ease of manufacture. Ergonomics.
...pen.
Design isn't only about looks,
says the new Design Council.

Widgets aren't born,
they're designed. The
new Design Council is here
to inspire innovation.

The new Design Council believes design

isn't something you stick on afterwards.

Things work. Well-designed things
work better. Brilliantly designed
things transform our lives,
says the new Design Council.

Silver Medalist/International

LETTERHEAD, BUSINESS CARD, ENVELOPE
Design Council Stationery
ART DIRECTOR *David Stuart*
CREATIVE DIRECTOR *David Stuart*
DESIGNERS *Peter Carrow, Rosa Loeffel*
COPYWRITER *Peter Collingwood*
STUDIO *The Partners*
CLIENT *Design Council*

ON February 14, 1989, the religious leader of one country issued a death edict against a citizen of another country. Five years later Salman Rushdie is still a man with no fixed address.

The novel that provoked the death sentence, *The Satanic Verses*, continues to be available in bookstores and libraries throughout the United States and many other countries. But Rushdie is in hiding, still writing nearly every day, making public appearances on occasion—but effectively under threat, marked as with an incandescent X on his chest and back.

Gold Medalist/National

PUBLIC SERVICE, SINGLE
Salman Rushdie Flyer
ART DIRECTORS *Stephen Doyle,*
William Drenttel
DESIGNER *Stephen Doyle*
STUDIO *Drenttel Doyle Partners*

Named one of the top U.S. Companies to work for in *The 100 Best Companies to Work for in America*, Herman Miller has been a design leader for decades. (But is it fun to work there?) Under the leadership of creative director Stephen Frykholm (He's a real gas!), the team at Herman Miller has helped the company win awards like the AIGA Design Leadership and Fortune & American Center for Design Beacon Award. The NY Art Director's Club, CA, Graphis, ID, and AIGA Communication Graphics have also recognized Herman Miller's graphic design. (Some of these awards are really cool.) Herman Miller offers an attractive beginning designer's salary (not gr... but enough to pay the rent). Interested candidates ... a BFA or MFA degree (and a lively imaginati... ...ly by sending a maximum of twenty slides of re... and a resume by June, 1994. Please include educa... and work experience references, (Don't worry, young designers getting the job before you didn't have much either.) Send resumes to: Herman Miller Inc., Staffing department 0162, PO Box 302, Zeeland, Michigan 49464-0302. (Don't try to buck the system by sending your stuff directly to Steve. He'll lose it.) Include a self-addressed, stamped envelope for return of slides; please do not send actual portfolios. Selected candidates will be contacted by August, 1994 to arrange interviews. (We'll buy lunch and give you the real low-down.)

Silver Medalist/National

POSTER, OTHER THAN ADVERTISING, SINGLE
Herman Miller Design Position Poster
ART DIRECTOR *Yang Kim*
CREATIVE DIRECTOR *Yang Kim*
DESIGNER *Yang Kim*
COPYWRITER *Clark Malcolm*
ILLUSTRATOR *Yang Kim*
PRINTER *Etheridge Company*
CLIENT *Herman Miller Inc.*

Silver Medalist/National

POSTER, OTHER THAN ADVERTISING, SINGLE
Was/Saw
ART DIRECTOR *Stephen Doyle*
DESIGNER *Gary Tooth*
PHOTOGRAPHER *Davies & Starr*
STUDIO *Drenttel Doyle Partners*
CLIENT *American Center for Design*

Peace on Earth

Vertical Butt Stroke to groin.

Seasons Greetings

Smash to face.

Happy Holidays

Jab to throat.

Silver Medalist/National

POSTER, OTHER THAN ADVERTISING, SERIES
Holiday Posters
ART DIRECTOR *Todd Fedell*
CREATIVE DIRECTOR *Russ Haan*
DESIGNER *Todd Fedell*
COPYWRITER *Russ Haan*
ILLUSTRATOR *U.S. Marine Corps*
AGENCY *After Hours Creative*
CLIENT *Vent*

DISTINCTIVE MERIT AWARDS

Oh, horrors'

Tony Magistrale is upset. It's a woozily humid mid-August morning, the last day of summer classes, and the University of Vermont professor of English, midway through his final lecture, has just been thrown a curve.

"Do you know what my problem is with your class, Professor Magistrale?" asks a young student, as she nervously pulls on the brim of her baseball cap. "I'm getting no respect for taking it. When I go to the library for books, people ask me why I'm reading this, this . . . . trash."

Magistrale understands. In fact, during the six years he has taught this course, he has grown used to such rude questioning himself. Called in its present form "The Films and Novels of Stephen King," it compares the best-selling horror novelist to many of the masters of American literature. Most frustrating is the fact that many of his critics have never even read King's work. "I always want to reply, 'Get off your high horse. Don't pretend you're Mr. or Mrs. Eliot.'" Magistrale tells the student. "King is a contemporary Faulkner or Dickens. His work touches on great themes. He just happens to be a more accessible writer."

Dwight Garner is a free-lance writer who lives in New York City.

The young woman brightens, as do the other students in the class. Heads nod in agreement. Later, another student says, "Maybe I can get my dad to read *The Stand.* Then he'll understand."

AT AGE 42, TONY MAGISTRALE IS AMERIca's leading Stephen King scholar – a man who has spent the past decade trying (and usually failing) to get other academics to understand his passion for the man from Belfast, Maine. Nor is Magistrale alone in his ardor. He's at the forefront of a group of several dozen academics who teach and analyze King's books with the same rigor that previous generations of scholars brought to, say, *The Divine Comedy* or *The Iliad.*

Thanks to these enthusiasts, there are now more books about Stephen King's work (roughly 30) than there are books by King himself (34). And at schools like the University of Vermont, in Burlington, where Magistrale has taught a class on King since 1988, students are rushing to enroll. When more than 40 students signed up for his course this past summer, Magistrale was forced to add a second section.

The term "Stephen King scholar" may sound like an *Continued on Page 22*

Some argue that Stephen King is the Charles Dickens of our day. Others say his work has no place in a college curriculum.
By Dwight Garner

ILLUSTRATION BY RALPH GIGUERE **15**

Distinctive Merit/National

FULL PAGE OR SPREAD
Oh, Horrors
ART DIRECTOR *Lucy Bartholomay*
CREATIVE DIRECTOR *Lucy Bartholomay*
DESIGNER *Lucy Bartholomay*
ILLUSTRATOR *Ralph Giguere*
CLIENT *The Boston Globe*

Distinctive Merit/National

COVER
The Arab Paradox
ART DIRECTOR *Lucy Bartholomay*
CREATIVE DIRECTOR *Lucy Bartholomay*
DESIGNER *Lucy Bartholomay*
ILLUSTRATOR *Brian Cronin*
CLIENT *The Boston Globe*

Distinctive Merit/National

COVER
Here's Looking at You, Kids
ART DIRECTOR *Lucy Bartholomay*
CREATIVE DIRECTOR *Lucy Bartholomay*
DESIGNER *Lucy Bartholomay*
ILLUSTRATOR *Scott Menchin*
CLIENT *The Boston Globe*

plate has little bearing on what kind of canapes result from its eggs. Salmon caviar is a beautiful orange in color and can be quite delicious. Whitefish produces the small, crunchy, bitter eggs sold as "golden caviar," which makes a lovely garnish in quantities too small to have much effect on the taste of a finished dish. The caviar of the Icelandic lumpfish is an inky black mass of tiny eggs that makes an excellent lubricant for car door locks in winter.

Beluga caviar is the roe of the beluga sturgeon, an immense fish of the Caspian Sea, the great inland ocean whose bounty over the centuries has been one of the prime perquisites of ruling Russia. Beluga is prized for the size and color of its eggs and the delicacy of its flavor, but many connoisseurs consider size a luxury not worth paying for and delicacy a matter of personal preference. The two closest relatives to the beluga are the other Caspian Sea sturgeons, which are in descending order of size and cost the ossetra and the sevruga. (Any of these may be designated malossol, which means low in salt, although that is a relative term; the threshold is 1 percent.)

Many people with access to all three kinds prefer either the ossetra or sevruga to beluga. At a recent tasting, which included samples of each from two of New York's finest specialty stores, one can of beluga was definitely spoiled—oily, bitter, and fishy—and the other was delicate to the edge of blandness. But the small, gray-green eggs of sevruga were delicious—nicely salted, but sweet and almost fruity, creamy and mouth-filling; while the black ossetra won praise for velvety texture and a vivid, fresh taste of the sea.

This is an argument for tasting caviar, whenever possible, before buying it. Of course if you have to order by mail this will be difficult, and not

even all retail stores are so accommodating. But a mistake in buying caviar can be one you will regret for a long time. Beluga costs around $10 an ounce, and an ounce is barely a serving, especially if you allow guests to serve themselves. It makes three medium-size hors d'oeuvres, which is what a typical guest might consume—a figure arrived at by averaging one guest who will eat five of them and another who will taste one to be polite. Ossetra, in a recent catalog from Caviarteria, a leading New York importer that also ships by mail, was $40 for the smallest, ounce-and-a-half jar; sevruga was $30. There are also some cheaper alternatives. Caviar from the American paddlefish, a relative of the sturgeon, is very acceptable and costs only around $11 an ounce. "Pressed" caviar is the concentrated remains of sturgeon eggs that were broken in processing or too soft to pack; it has a very intense flavor and a jammy, almost chewy texture. It sells for about $22 an ounce. Mark Russ Federman of the specialty-foods store Russ & Daughters, which supplies many New York caterers, says his pressed caviar is preferred by many of his European customers. But it's not how you would choose to introduce someone to the pleasures of caviar.

Because, in truth, a lot of people don't like caviar at all when they first taste it. "Two million people a year eat caviar in this country," says Bruce Sobol of Caviarteria, "and all the others have an opinion about it." Caviar is not a food anyone can be indifferent to; it asserts its presence with every spoonful, with every egg that splits open and bathes the tongue in its delicate elixir of salt. It is the only food with no known threshold of excess. A spoonful may be enough, but a bowlful is not too much. No wonder we serve it on New Year's Eve.

roe by roe

AMERICAN GOLDEN WHITEFISH
The small, crunchy, slightly bitter roe of the whitefish makes an excellent topping for boiled or baked potatoes, with or without sour cream.

AMERICAN STURGEON (PADDLEFISH)
The paddlefish, a relative of the sturgeon, is harvested in the Tennessee River basin; quality is very variable, but at its best it can almost pass for beluga with most people, at less than a third the cost.

FLYING FISH (GREEN)
A variety of the orange flying-fish roe (see below) tinted green by wasabi, the pungent Japanese horseradish.

PRESSED CAVIAR
The thick, jammy residue of eggs that were broken in processing, it has a very intense flavor that is a bit of an acquired taste. It goes best diluted with something mild like sour cream and spread on something substantial and crunchy: a crisp potato pancake, say.

SALMON CAVIAR
These beautiful, large reddish orange eggs tend to be salter than those of the sturgeon, and the flavor is less complex, but at less than $40 a pound, they can be heaped high in a bowl for guests to spoon up with abandon, or spread on a toasted, thinly sliced bagel with cream cheese for a New Year's Day brunch.

SEVRUGA
The smallest (and least expensive) of the Caspian Sea sturgeon caviars, it is the choice of many connoisseurs for its sweet, almost fruity flavor and firm texture.

BELUGA
The queen of the caviars, with large, elegant, mild-tasting eggs that burst on the tongue with a fresh taste of the ocean; serve it with the smallest spoons you can find, preferably ram's horn or mother-of-pearl.

FLYING FISH (ORANGE)
Popular in sushi, these small, crunchy eggs have a mild flavor and are good for garnish or spread thinly on a buttered cracker.

OSSETRA
In size and price, intermediate between sevruga and beluga, these light-to-dark brown eggs typically have a more assertive flavor than either: wonderful with crème fraiche on a warm blini.

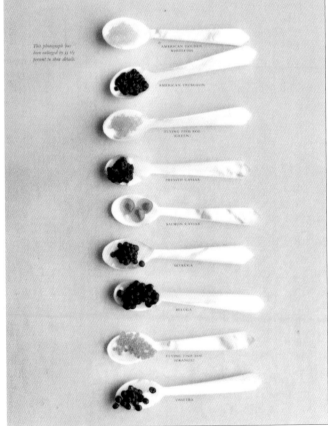

This photograph has been enlarged by 25% percent to show details.

AMERICAN GOLDEN WHITEFISH

AMERICAN STURGEON

FLYING FISH ROE (GREEN)

PRESSED CAVIAR

SALMON CAVIAR

SEVRUGA

BELUGA

FLYING FISH ROE (ORANGE)

OSSETRA

110

(facing page, top)
Distinctive Merit/National

FULL PAGE OR SPREAD
Plums
ART DIRECTOR *Gael Towey*
DESIGNER *Eric Pike*
PHOTOGRAPHERS *Victor Schrager, Thibault Jeanson*
CLIENT *Martha Stewart Living*

(facing page, bottom)
Distinctive Merit/National

FULL PAGE OR SPREAD
Caviar
ART DIRECTOR *Gael Towey*
DESIGNER *Eric Pike*
PHOTOGRAPHER *Carlton Davis*
CLIENT *Martha Stewart Living*

Distinctive Merit/National

MULTIPAGE
Confessions of Sir Psycho Sexy
CREATIVE DIRECTOR *Fred Woodward*
DESIGNERS *Fred Woodward, Geraldine Hessler*
PHOTO EDITOR *Jodi Peckman*
PHOTOGRAPHER *Matthew Rolston*
CLIENT *Rolling Stone*

ADDITIONAL AWARDS

Merit
FULL PAGE OR SPREAD

Merit
PHOTOGRAPHY, EDITORIAL, SERIES

Distinctive Merit/National

MULTIPAGE
Spices
ART DIRECTOR *Gael Towey*
DESIGNER *Eric Pike*
COPYWRITER *Bill Hamilton*
PHOTOGRAPHER *Victoria Pearson*
CLIENT *Martha Stewart Living*

spices

If I cried, "Open sesame!" you might not know that I was talking about spices. In fact, you might walk away from me at a party. But when Ali Baba opened the door to the robbers' den with those famous words, he was alluding to the fact that a ripe sesame pod will burst open at the gentlest touch, scattering its seeds—its "riches."

Or if I shouted, "Holy smoke!" you might leave the floor. But holy smoke, literally translated as such from an extant papyrus, was an incense composed of twenty-six spices known to the ancient Egyptians.

Spices, those two-dozen-or-so dried buds, barks, roots, seeds, berries and other fruits of tropical plants that we commonly call cinnamon or coriander or ginger, are among the oldest useful substances known to man. They are more important to the history of the world than gasoline, moon rocks, gunpowder, or the movies. And in the same potent way that a bit of saffron might stain your finger, spices have entered the language, with characteristic insinuation. A spicy story, after all, is a good one.

As every civilization at every century has known, spices speak magically to the senses. Though they sleep in a rack at the back of a cabinet, consider this: You might not be standing in your kitchen if someone hadn't wanted pepper on his food in the fifteenth century. The search for trade routes to spice sources put the world as we know it on the map, lacing the globe like the blades of mace on a nutmeg. Marco Polo went east for spices. Columbus went west. The places they discovered had been using the spices they found for thousands of years. To unstopper a bottle of clove and sniff is literally to capture a "sense" of history: the breath of Chinese courtiers, who kept cloves in their mouths to scent them when speaking to the emperor.

Spices, in fact, predate recorded history and figure in most that's been written. The Assyrians claimed that the gods themselves drank a wine made from sesame. Jesus Christ spoke of the inherent power of faith "even if no larger than a tiny mustard seed." Until the first century B.C., Arabs controlled the spice trade from the East, buying Indian, Chinese, and Indonesian spices on the coast of India, and carrying them west to Mediterranean markets.

It was the Romans who established the use of spices in the West as a way of flavoring food. They broke the Arab trade monopoly, employing monsoon winds to shorten the sea trip to India. It was not until the eleventh and twelfth centuries, though, that spices gained a wide hold on the tastes of Western Europe. Returning Crusaders brought back Eastern spices, mostly in Venetian ships. Spices revived the bland medieval diet, preserved food, and disguised food that was bad. They also made maritime Venice rich. Rarities like pepper were literally worth their weight in gold.

It was inevitable that Venice's spice wealth would provoke envy and enmity. The fifteenth century's "age of exploration," which included Columbus's four voyages and Magellan's circumnavigation of the globe, was not launched by restlessness, adventure, or curiosity, but by a race for routes to spices. The world was discovered as a result. The Portuguese rounded the Cape of Good Hope, crafting the African continent. By the seventeenth century, the Dutch knew and ruled Indonesia, and by the early nineteenth century, the British had colonized India.

History lingers in spices as it can't in books. Many of the world's oldest ways are alive and thriving in spice use, found in all the old places. In northern Italy, the Emilia-Romagnans still grate nutmeg like cheese on their Bolognese sauce. Superstitious Sicilian brides and grooms still carry cumin seeds through the ceremony to ensure a happy life. The berrie seeds that African slaves brought to the South—*benne* is Bantu for sesame—are baked into wafers and brittle. At their sources and at all the stops along the old routes, the long-traded spices still form the basic blends of food seasoning: Indian garam masala, North African ras el hanout, and Chinese five-spice.

The United States now leads the world in importing and using spices—more than 830 million pounds in 1994—in part because of their presence in processed and fast

OPPOSITE: Poussins (baby chickens) are rubbed with a cinnamon-brown five-spice blend, a red Hungarian-paprika mix, and an Indian turmeric-yellow curry blend. Spice flavors are infused as the meat roasts, while the skins crisp with beautiful color.

TEXT BY BILL HAMILTON PHOTOGRAPHS BY VICTORIA PEARSON

foods. Turmeric is what makes ballpark mustard yellow; coriander is what flavors the franks. And Americans are discovering spices at home because of a growing taste for ethnic foods: Chinese, Mexican, Thai, and Caribbean cooking.

"There's a definite change in our eating habits all across the country," says Camille Appel, manager of consumer communications for McCormick & Co., the world's largest spice company. "Different population groups are moving in, and they're bringing their native tastes with them. And we're also sharing them with the rest of us, in restaurants. And we're learning that we like these flavors."

If Americans are discovering what the rest of the world already knew, that spices make food more interesting, it couldn't be more timely. "We're also trying to be a little more health conscious," says Appel. "We're trying to lower our fats, we're trying to lower our sodium. People are finding out that when they do that, they have to put some flavor back in."

For that flavor to have full impact, storing spices properly is important. Often treated more as collectibles than condiments, spices do in fact deteriorate. "Spices degrade the moment they're taken off the plant," says Philip Teverow, spice buyer for Dean & DeLuca, a New York specialty-food store. "There's a continual process of perishing, losing their essential oils—their flavor—to evaporation. The more you expose them to air, the faster they will degrade."

The best rule of thumb is to buy and store spices whole and grind them yourself as needed (see "Customizing Classic Blends," right). "To preserve the spice's flavor, preserve the spice intact," says Teverow. Tightly stoppered glass jars will best protect spices from air and infestation. Certain spices, such as paprika and cayenne, invite bugs and are best kept refrigerated. All spices need to be kept away from light, which fades both color and flavor, and from heat. Choose a

drawer or closed cabinet shelf away from the stove. Stored properly, most whole and ground spices will last for at least one year.

If you decide to set up a stock of new spices, don't assume you need to buy them all at once. Buy the ones you like the smell and taste of and feel likely to use in the foods you're curious to cook. And experiment—the real beauty of spices is the brilliant way in which they blend.

Among the world's great tastes are spice blends, such as curry: the sharp, tooth-cleaning taste of green cardamom, the fiery sugar of ginger, coriander's woody orange, black pepper's teasy heat, cumin's gravelike freshness, and mustard's bitter bite. Spices bring together the foods they flavor hypnotically, like a warm voice telling a rich story: the sweet, smoky cinnamon that aromatizes the rice of a *tagine*, or the buttery-nutty vanilla in a custard.

Variety may be the spice of life, but spices are life's variety. Live a little.

CUSTOMIZING CLASSIC BLENDS

Spice blends are at their best when whole spices are mixed, roasted together, and ground freshly as needed. Cinnamon quills and nutmegs can be grated easily with a small, finely perforated hand grater, and berries such as allspice will grind in a pepper mill. But some spices, such as star anise, are hard and difficult to pound by hand, and seeds are small and stony mostly. A hand-held electric coffee mill is useful for grinding these types. (Buy an inexpensive one especially for this purpose, to avoid the accidental curried cup of java.) Roast whole spices briefly in a skillet over medium heat, then grind. Addition to a spice mixture lend a provocative note to a standard blend. Basic ingredients for four famous blends and their variations are as follows (see the recipe section for proportions):

Curry: An Indian spice blend of black pepper, fenugreek, cumin, whole or ground turmeric, mustard, dried whole or ground ginger, coriander, cinnamon, cloves, and dried red chiles. Additions can include crushed fresh curry leaves (which are unrelated to the spice) and green cardamoms (found in Sri Lankan curries).

Garam masala: A northern Indian mixture of cumin, coriander, cardamom, and cloves. Variations include nutmeg, caraway, cinnamon, bay leaves, black pepper, cloves, mace, black cumin, and nigella.

Ras el hanout: This Moroccan blend of up to twenty spices will always consist of cardamom, mace, allspice, cinnamon, cloves, dried or ground ginger, black pepper, cayenne, coriander, and cumin. Additions include galangal, grains of paradise (a cardamom relative), or cubeb (an Indonesian pepper relative).

Five-spice: The best-known Chinese spice blend contains star anise, Szechuan pepper, cinnamon, fennel seeds, and cloves. Additions of ginger, licorice root, and cardamom add depth.

OPPOSITE, CLOCKWISE FROM TOP LEFT: Whole spices roasted and ground as needed make the freshest blends (counterclockwise from top right): garam masala, curry, Chinese five-spice, and ras el hanout. Salmon marinated in Szechuan peppercorns and soy sauce is "smoked" over star anise, cinnamon, and tea. Custards capture the delicacy of spices such as saffron and ginger. Lamb tagine, browned with ras el hanout and simmered with prunes, is served with harissa sauce and flatbread. ABOVE: Papaya softens the garam masala in basmati-rice pilaf, wrapped in silver leaf.

SEE THE RECIPE SECTION

Distinctive Merit/National

MULTIPAGE
Pumpkins & Squash
ART DIRECTOR *Gael Towey*
DESIGNER *Eric Pike*
PHOTOGRAPHERS *Victor Schrager, Christopher Baker*
CLIENT *Martha Stewart Living*

Distinctive Merit/National

MULTIPAGE
Peonies
ART DIRECTOR *Gael Towey*
DESIGNER *Gael Towey*
PHOTOGRAPHER *Davies & Starr*
CLIENT *Martha Stewart Living*

Distinctive Merit/International

MULTIPAGE
Cut Covers
ART DIRECTOR *Hideki Nakajima*
DESIGNERS *Hideki Nakajima, Yuko Kasuga,*
Iwao Miura, Masashi Nakayama,
Kenichi Kawakami
EDITOR IN CHIEF *Ken Sato*
PHOTOGRAPHERS *Itaru Hirama, Ed Caraeff,*
Annie Leibovitz, Steven Meisel, Paolo Roversi,
Marion de Beaupre, Jeffrey Thurnher
CLIENT *Rockin'on Inc.*

Distinctive Merit/International

MULTIPAGE
Cut, September Issue
ART DIRECTOR *Hideki Nakajima*
DESIGNERS *Hideki Nakajima, Yuko Kasuga,*
Iwao Miura, Masashi Nakayama,
Kenichi Kawakami
EDITOR IN CHIEF *Ken Sato*
PHOTOGRAPHERS *Bruce Weber, Herb Ritts,*
Yoram Kahana, Douglas Kirkland
CLIENT *Rockin'on Inc.*

特集 タンゴ
愚かしくも愛しい、フランス式男と女の愛の狂騒劇

夢を信用したいと思ったことがある▶ フランス映画に一度も本場のタンゴのことを思い出して▶ ...

Distinctive Merit/International

MULTIPAGE
Cut, March Issue
ART DIRECTOR *Hideki Nakajima*
DESIGNERS *Hideki Nakajima, Yuko Kasuga,*
Iwao Miura, Masashi Nakayama,
Kenichi Kawakami
EDITOR IN CHIEF *Ken Sato*
PHOTOGRAPHERS *Luc Roux, Albert Watson,*
Kurt Markus
CLIENT *Rockin'on Inc.*

エマニュエル・ベアール

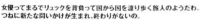

女優ってまるでリュックを背負って国から国を渡り歩く旅人のようだわ。
つねに新たな問いかけが生まれ、終わりがないの。

I had locked into what was pretty
much a hectic obsession,
which gave me enormous focus and energy
and fire to burn,
because it was coming out of pure fear
and self-loathing and self-hatred.
**I'd get on stage and
it was hard for me to stop.**
That's why my shows were so long.

**BRUCE
SPRINGSTEEN**

ブルース・スプリングスティーン

Distinctive Merit/National

FULL ISSUE
Generation Next
CREATIVE DIRECTOR *Fred Woodward*
DESIGNERS *Fred Woodward, Gail Anderson,
Geraldine Hessler, Lee Bearson*
PHOTO EDITORS *Jodi Peckman, Denise Sfraga*
PHOTOGRAPHERS *Various*
CLIENT *Rolling Stone*

ADDITIONAL AWARD

Merit
COVER

Distinctive Merit/International

FULL ISSUES
*Dogs Issue, Paper Game Issue, Swiss Cross and
Passport Issue*
ART DIRECTORS *Karin Bolliger, Barbara Erb,
Lukas Huggenberg, Urs Arnold*
CREATIVE DIRECTOR *Urs Arnold*
DESIGNERS *Karin Bolliger (Dogs), Lukas Huggenberg
(Paper Game), Barbara Erb (Swiss Cross and
Passport)*
PHOTOGRAPHER *Mathias Hofstetter*
AGENCY *Arnold Design Switzerland*
CLIENT *Canon/Walter Rentsh AG, Switzerland*

(facing page)
Distinctive Merit/National

HOUSE PUBLICATION, SINGLE ISSUE
Interact: American Center for Design Journal
ART DIRECTOR *Eric Wagner*
DESIGNERS *Grant Davis, Anthony Ma,
Lance Rutter, Eric Wagner*
ILLUSTRATOR *Eric Wagner*
STUDIO *Tanagram*
CLIENT *American Center for Design*

interact american center for design journal

TEXTS & DOCUMENTS

EMPATHY, FORM, AND SPACE

PROBLEMS IN GERMAN AESTHETICS,
1873–1893

Robert Vischer
1873

Conrad Fiedler
1878

Heinrich Wölfflin
1886

Adolf Göller
1887

Adolf Hildebrand
1893

August Schmarsow
1893

INTRODUCTION AND TRANSLATION
BY HARRY FRANCIS MALLGRAVE AND ELEFTHERIOS IKONOMOU

Distinctive Merit/National

SINGLE
Sarah McLachlan Book
ART DIRECTORS *Susan Mendola, Angela Skouras*
CREATIVE DIRECTOR *Susan Mendola*
DESIGNER *Angela Skouras*
COPYWRITER *Michael Schwartz*
PHOTOGRAPHERS *Dennis Keeley, Kharen Hill,
David Atlas*
ILLUSTRATOR *Sarah McLachlan*

Distinctive Merit/National

SINGLE
*Empathy, Form, and Space: Problems in German
Aesthetics, 1873–1893*
DESIGNER *Laurie Haycock Makela*
STUDIO *J. Paul Getty Trust, Publication Services*
CLIENT *The Getty Center for the History of Art
and the Humanities*

(facing page, top)
Distinctive Merit/National

SINGLE
*This Heritage Remembered VI: O. Henry:
One Dozen Stories*
ART DIRECTOR *Lana Rigsby*
SERIES DIRECTOR *Robert J. Downs, Jr.*
DESIGNERS *Lana Rigsby, Michael Thede,
Troy S. Ford*
PROLOGUE AUTHOR *JoAnn Stone*
PHOTOGRAPHER *Geof Kern*
ILLUSTRATOR *Michael Thede*
STUDIO *Rigsby Design, Inc.*
CLIENT *Heritage Press*

(facing page, bottom)
Distinctive Merit/National

SINGLE
Pat Hackett Christmas Card 1993
ART DIRECTOR *Janet Kruse*
CREATIVE DIRECTOR *Janet Kruse*
DESIGNER *Traci Daberko*
AGENCY *The Leonhardt Group*
STUDIO *The Leonhardt Group*
CLIENT *Pat Hackett, Artist Representative*

Distinctive Merit/National

SINGLE
Covenants and Contracts
ART DIRECTOR *Michael Barile*
CREATIVE DIRECTOR *Michael Barile*
DESIGNERS *Michael Barile, Glenn Hoffman*
COPYWRITER *Clark Malcolm*
PHOTOGRAPHER *Jim Powell*
PRINTER *Herman Miller Corporate Publishing Services*
CLIENT *Herman Miller Inc.*

Distinctive Merit/National

SINGLE
Reorientations: Looking East
ART DIRECTOR *Takaaki Matsumoto*
CREATIVE DIRECTOR *Takaaki Matsumoto*
DESIGNER *Takaaki Matsumoto*
AUTHORS *Lynn Gumpert, Miwon Kwon, Lynne Cooke*
PHOTOGRAPHERS *Ellen Page Wilson and others*
STUDIO *Matsumoto Incorporated*
CLIENT *The Gallery at Takashimaya*

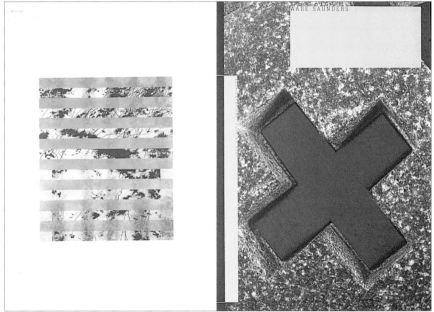

Distinctive Merit/International

SINGLE
Exercices de style
ART DIRECTORS *Angela Grauerholz, Judith Poirier*
CREATIVE DIRECTORS *Maxim Flores, Justine Fournier,*
Danielle Gingras, Judith Poirier
DESIGNERS *Frédérique Daubal, Maxim Flores,*
Justine Fournier, Patrick Giasson, Danielle Gingras,
Mario Guay, Francisco Sottolichio, Katja Wegener
AGENCY *Département de Design, Université de Québec*
à Montréal
STUDIO *Les Maîtres Typographes Zibra*
CLIENT *Typomondo*

PRODUCTS
BY DESIGN

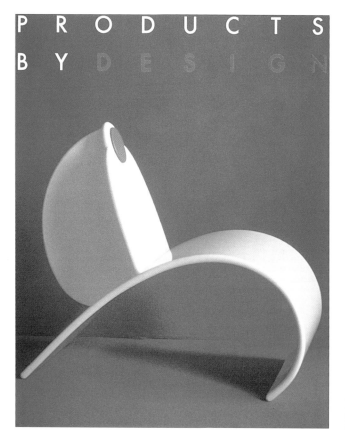

PACKAGING

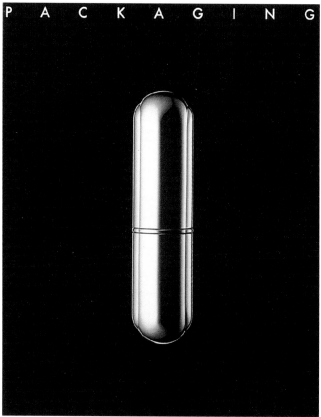

DESIGN

BROCHURES

(facing page, top left)
Distinctive Merit/International

SINGLE
Graphis Products by Design 1
ART DIRECTOR *B. Martin Pedersen*
CREATIVE DIRECTOR *B. Martin Pedersen*
DESIGNER *B. Martin Pedersen*
STUDIO *Pedersen Design Inc.*
CLIENT *Graphis*

(facing page, top right)
Distinctive Merit/International

SINGLE
Graphis Packaging 6
ART DIRECTOR *B. Martin Pedersen*
CREATIVE DIRECTOR *B. Martin Pedersen*
DESIGNER *B. Martin Pedersen*
STUDIO *Pedersen Design Inc.*
CLIENT *Graphis*

ADDITIONAL AWARD

Distinctive Merit
BOOK JACKET, SINGLE

(facing page, bottom left)
Distinctive Merit/International

SINGLE
Graphis Design 95
ART DIRECTOR *B. Martin Pedersen*
CREATIVE DIRECTOR *B. Martin Pedersen*
DESIGNER *B. Martin Pedersen*
PHOTOGRAPHER *Albert Zimmerman*
STUDIO *Pedersen Design Inc.*
CLIENT *Graphis*

ADDITIONAL AWARD

Distinctive Merit
BOOK JACKET, SINGLE

(facing page, bottom right)
Distinctive Merit/International

SINGLE
Graphis Brochures 1
ART DIRECTOR *B. Martin Pedersen*
CREATIVE DIRECTOR *B. Martin Pedersen*
DESIGNER *B. Martin Pedersen*
STUDIO *Pedersen Design Inc.*
CLIENT *Graphis*

ADDITIONAL AWARD

Distinctive Merit
BOOK JACKET, SINGLE

Distinctive Merit/National

SERIES
Do It! Guides
ART DIRECTOR *Michael Bierut*
DESIGNERS *Michael Bierut, Agnethe Glatved*
PHOTOGRAPHER *John Paul Endress*
ILLUSTRATOR *Nicholas Fasciano*
STUDIO *Pentagram Design*
CLIENT *Redefinition Books*

Distinctive Merit/National

TITLE FOR PROMOTION, SINGLE
News Weasels Show Open
ART DIRECTOR *Jill Taffet*
CREATIVE DIRECTOR *Jill Taffet*
DESIGNER *Mark Osborne*
PRODUCER *Karin Rainey*
DIRECTOR *Mark Osborne*
MUSIC *John Wiggins*
STUDIO *E! Entertainment Television*
CLIENT *E! Entertainment Television*

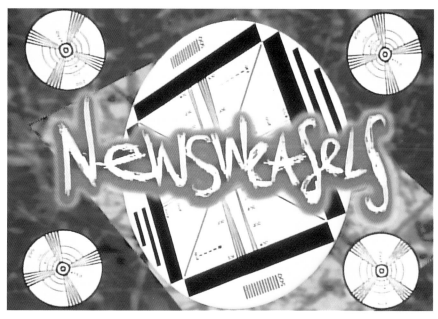

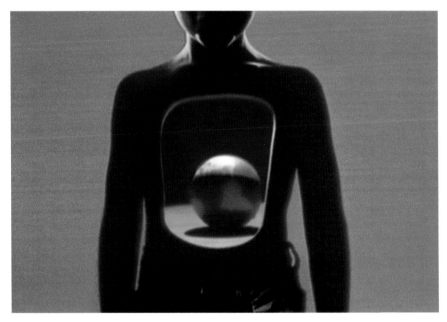

Distinctive Merit/National

TITLE FOR PROMOTION, CAMPAIGN
VH1 Honors Campaign
ART DIRECTOR *James Spindler*
CREATIVE DIRECTOR *Thomas Tercek*
PRODUCER *James Spindler*
DIRECTOR *Geoff Kern*
CLIENT *VH1*

Distinctive Merit/National

SPECIAL EFFECTS AND COMPUTER GRAPHICS, SINGLE
We're Ballplayers, and We're Okay
ART DIRECTOR *Darryl McDonald*
CREATIVE DIRECTORS *Dan Wieden, Susan Hoffman*
COPYWRITER *Jim Riswold*
VISUAL EFFECTS *R/Greenberg Associates*
POST-PRODUCTION *Red Car Editorial*
DIRECTOR *Terry Gilliam*
AGENCY *Wieden & Kennedy*
CLIENT *Nike*

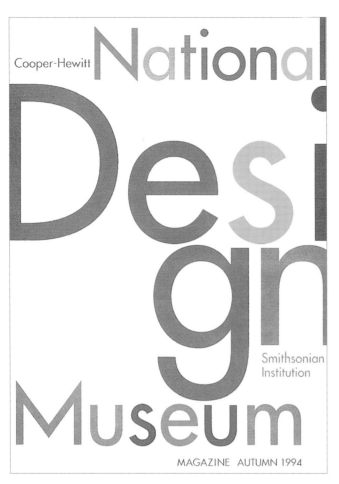

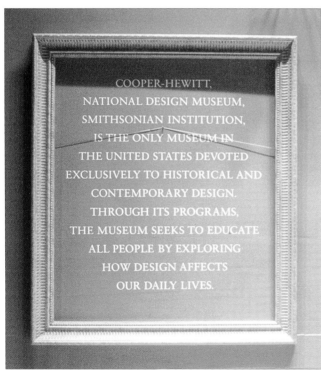

Distinctive Merit/National

CAMPAIGN
National Design Museum
ART DIRECTOR *Stephen Doyle*
CREATIVE DIRECTORS *Stephen Doyle,*
William Drenttel
DESIGNERS *Miguel Oks, Terry Mastin,*
Katrin Schmitt-Tegge
PHOTOGRAPHER *Scott Frances*
STUDIO *Drenttel Doyle Partners*
CLIENT *Cooper-Hewitt, National Design Museum,*
Smithsonian Institution

Distinctive Merit/National

ANNUAL REPORT
Musicland Stores Corporation Annual Report
ART DIRECTORS *Sharon Werner, Amy Quinlivan*
CREATIVE DIRECTOR *Kent Hensley*
DESIGNERS *Sharon Werner, Amy Quinlivan*
COPYWRITER *Marcia Appel*
PHOTOGRAPHERS *Bill Phelps, Lizzie Himmel,*
Brendon Baathrick
STUDIO *Quinlivan Werner Design*
CLIENT *Musicland Stores Corporation*

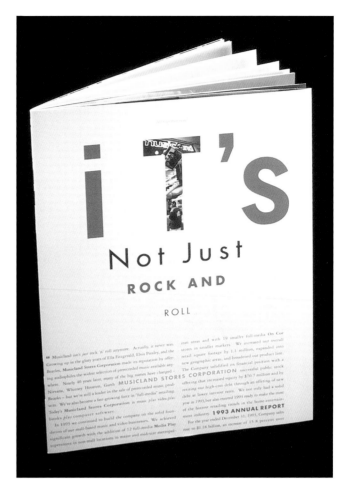

Distinctive Merit/National

ANNUAL REPORT
The Progressive Corporation 1993 Annual Report
ART DIRECTORS *Mark Schwartz, Joyce Nesnadny*
CREATIVE DIRECTORS *Mark Schwartz,*
Joyce Nesnadny
DESIGNERS *Mark Schwartz, Joyce Nesnadny,*
Michelle Moehler
COPYWRITER *Peter B. Lewis*
PHOTOGRAPHER *Zeke Berman*
ILLUSTRATIONS *Merriam Webster, Inc.*
AGENCY *Nesnadny + Schwartz*
CLIENT *The Progressive Corporation*

Distinctive Merit/National

ANNUAL REPORT
Mickelberry Communications Annual Report 1993
ART DIRECTOR *Peter Harrison*
DESIGNER *Susan Hochbaum*
COPYWRITER *Delphine Hirasuna*
PHOTOGRAPHER *John Paul Endress*
ILLUSTRATOR *Phillippe Lardy*
STUDIO *Pentagram Design*
CLIENT *Mickelberry Communications*

GARRY KNOX
BENNETT
JONATHAN BONNER
JAMES CARPENTER
WENDELL CASTLE
JOHN DUNNIGAN
MICHELLE HOLZAPFEL
THOMAS HUCKER
MICHAEL HURWITZ
TOM LOESER
WENDY MARUYAMA
ALPHONSE MATTIA
RICHARD SCOTT
NEWMAN
ALBERT PALEY
GAETANO PESCE
TIMOTHY PHILBRICK
JAMES SCHRIBER
ROSANNE SOMERISON
WENDY WAHL
ED ZUCCA

MASTER
WORKS
TWO

CONTEMPORARY ART SERIES

1

NOVEMBER 4 – JANUARY 8 . 1995 (2)

VERNON FISHER

3

4

ENVIRONMETAL DESIGN

PATRICIA BELTON OLIVER
CHAIR, ENVIRONMENTAL DESIGN DEPARTMENT

"In the Environmental Design Department, we endeavor to teach habits of mind—curiosity, wonder, open-mindedness, and the capacity to think critically and creatively—which enable an understanding of **process** and the **interconnectedness** of things, and an ability to suspend judgment, which becomes useful in designing in new situations. Ours is an educational structure that relies on interactions and interdependencies that are dynamic and consequently promote flexibility, which is essential to the process of learning. We believe in binding, not bounding."

(facing page, top)
Distinctive Merit/National

BOOKLET, FOLDER, OR BROCHURE, SINGLE
Masterworks Two
ART DIRECTOR *Michael Bierut*
DESIGNERS *Michael Bierut, Esther Bridavsky*
PHOTOGRAPHERS *Various*
STUDIO *Pentagram Design*
CLIENT *Peter Joseph Gallery*

(facing page, bottom)
Distinctive Merit/National

BOOKLET, FOLDER, OR BROCHURE, SINGLE
Vernon Fisher Exhibition Catalogue
ART DIRECTOR *Renate Gokl*
DESIGNER *Renate Gokl*
COPYWRITER *Buzz Spector*
PHOTOGRAPHER *Vernon Fisher*
CLIENT *Krannert Art Museum*

Distinctive Merit/National

BOOKLET, FOLDER, OR BROCHURE, SINGLE
Art Center College of Design Catalogue 1995–96
DESIGN DIRECTOR *Rebeca Méndez*
CREATIVE DIRECTOR *Stuart I. Frolick*
DESIGNER *Darin Beaman*
ASSOCIATE DESIGNER *Chris Haaga*
EDITOR *Julie Suhr*
PHOTOGRAPHER *Steven A. Heller*
STUDIO *Art Center Design Office*
CLIENT *Art Center College of Design*

Distinctive Merit/International

BOOKLET, FOLDER, OR BROCHURE, SINGLE
Directions Spring and Summer '94
ART DIRECTOR *Benny Lau*
CREATIVE DIRECTOR *Steve Meltzer*
DESIGNER *Benny Lau*
COPYWRITER *Fiona Upward*
ILLUSTRATORS *Michael McKeever, Dee Dee Choy*
AGENCY *J. Walter Thompson Direct, Hong Kong*
CLIENT *The Swank Shop*

Distinctive Merit/International

BOOKLET, FOLDER, OR BROCHURE, SINGLE
Advertising Law International Brochure
CREATIVE DIRECTORS *Lynn Trickett, Brian Webb*
DESIGNERS *Lynn Trickett, Brian Webb,*
Steve Edwards
COPYWRITER *Neil Mattingley*
CLIENT *The Simkins Partnership*

Distinctive Merit/International

BOOKLET, FOLDER, OR BROCHURE, SINGLE
James Yunker Spring and Summer 1994
ART DIRECTOR *Del Terrelonge*
PHOTOGRAPHER *Shin Sugino*
AGENCY *Terrelonge*
CLIENT *James Yunker*

Distinctive Merit/International

BOOKLET, FOLDER, OR BROCHURE, SINGLE
The Czech Technology Park, Brno
CREATIVE DIRECTOR *Michael Denny*
DESIGNERS *John Bateson, Rachael Dinnis,
Jonathan Simpson*
PHOTOGRAPHERS *Tim Flach, Damien Gillie*
CLIENT *The Czech Technology Park, Brno*

Distinctive Merit/International

BOOKLET, FOLDER, OR BROCHURE, SINGLE
Fliessender Verkehr
ART DIRECTOR *Franz Merlicek*
CREATIVE DIRECTOR *Franz Merlicek*
GRAPHICS *Tina Feiertag*
COPYWRITER *Stefan Pott*
PRODUCER *Werner Stupka*
AGENCY *Demner & Merlicek*
CLIENT *Rhenus AG*

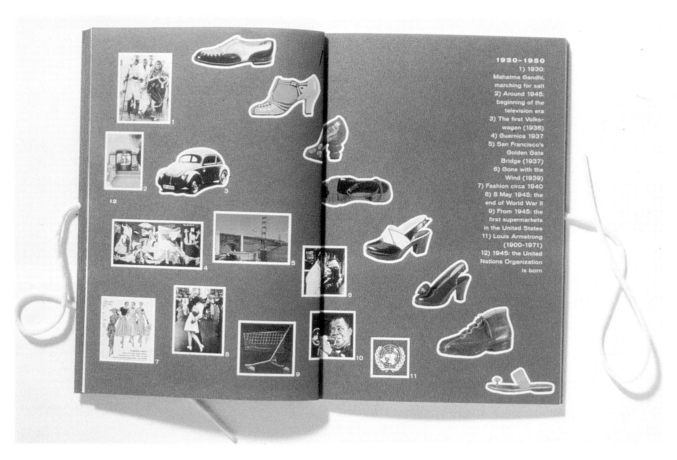

Distinctive Merit/International

BOOKLET, FOLDER, OR BROCHURE, SINGLE
Bally Corporate Identity Booklet
ART DIRECTOR *Antonie Reinhard*
CREATIVE DIRECTOR *Christian Jaquet*
DESIGNER *Antonie Reinhard*
COPYWRITER *Christian Jaquet*
PHOTOGRAPHERS *Various*
ILLUSTRATORS *Various*
AGENCY *Seiler DDB Needham AG Bern*
CLIENT *Bally International AG*

Distinctive Merit/International

BOOKLET, FOLDER, OR BROCHURE, SERIES
Bally Magalogues
ART DIRECTOR *Antonie Reinhard*
CREATIVE DIRECTOR *Antonie Reinhard*
DESIGNER *Martin Gaberthüel*
COPYWRITER *Margrit Brunswick*
PHOTOGRAPHER *Hanspeter Schneider*
AGENCY *Seiler DDB Needham AG Bern*
CLIENT *Bally International AG*

Distinctive Merit/National

PACKAGING, SINGLE
David Byrne "David Byrne" Limited-Edition
CD Package
ART DIRECTOR *Robert Bergman-Unger*
DESIGNER *Robert Bergman-Unger*
PHOTOGRAPHER *Jean Baptiste Mondino*
STUDIO *Art w/o Borders Co.*
CLIENT *Warner Bros. Records, Sire, Luaka Bop*

Distinctive Merit/National

PACKAGING, SINGLE
Belvédère
CREATIVE DIRECTOR *Joe Duffy*
DESIGNER *Alan Lensink*
STUDIO *Duffy Design*
CLIENT *Phillips Beverage Company*

Distinctive Merit/International

PACKAGING, SINGLE
Woods Bagot 125-Year Anniversary Muscat
ART DIRECTOR *Barrie Tucker*
CREATIVE DIRECTOR *Barrie Tucker*
DESIGNERS *Barrie Tucker, Hans Kohla*
PROJECT COORDINATORS *Inga Lidums,*
James Dimitri
STUDIO *Tucker Design, Designer Wines*
CLIENT *Woods Bagot*

(facing page, top)
Distinctive Merit/National

PACKAGING, SERIES
Steelcase Surface Materials
ART DIRECTOR *John Bricker*
CREATIVE DIRECTORS *John Bricker, Joyce Bromberg*
DESIGNER *Gensler Graphics*
COPYWRITER *Jan Schichtel*
PHOTOGRAPHERS *Dan Clark and others*
ARTWORK *Grant Wood*
CLIENT *Steelcase*

(facing page, bottom)
Distinctive Merit/International

PACKAGING, SERIES
TOTO Ltd.
ART DIRECTOR *Kan Akita*
DESIGNERS *Kan Akita, Masayoshi Kodaira*
CLIENT *TOTO Ltd.*

Distinctive Merit/International

PACKAGING, SERIES
Leisure Spanish Olives
CREATIVE DIRECTOR *Robin Hall*
DESIGNER *Barry Gillibrand*
ILLUSTRATOR *Bob Haberfield*
CLIENT *Leisure Fine Food & Drinks Ltd.*

Distinctive Merit/International

PACKAGING, SERIES
Studio NOB Envelope
ART DIRECTOR *Akio Okumura*
DESIGNER *Katsuji Minami*
STUDIO *Packaging Create Inc.*
CLIENT *Studio NOB*

Distinctive Merit/National

ANNOUNCEMENT, INVITATION, OR MENU, SINGLE
Subpoena
ART DIRECTOR *Tony Pucca*
CREATIVE DIRECTOR *Tim Fisher*
DESIGNER *John Cason*
COPYWRITER *Tony Pucca*
ILLUSTRATOR *Mariel Llenza*
AGENCY *Fry Hammond Barr*
CLIENT *The Creative Club of Orlando*

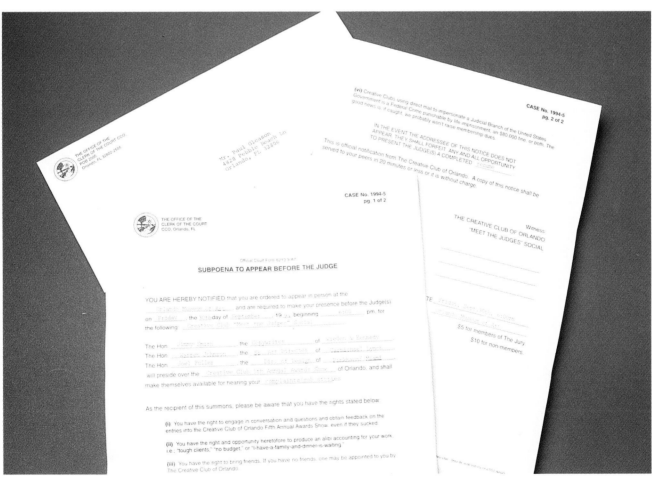

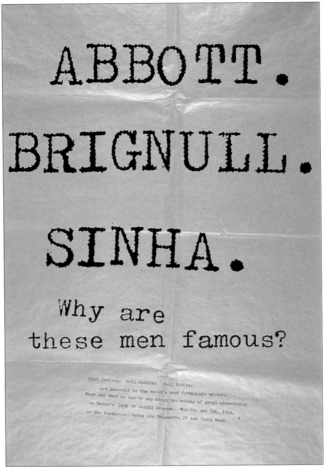

(facing page)
Distinctive Merit/International

ANNOUNCEMENT, INVITATION, OR MENU, SERIES
Batey Back to Basics Seminar
ART DIRECTOR *Eddie Wong*
CREATIVE DIRECTOR *Jim Aitchison*
DESIGNER *Eddie Wong*
COPYWRITERS *Sim Yang Seah, Jim Aitchison*
AGENCY *Batey Ads Singapore*
CLIENT *Batey Ads Singapore*

(above)
Distinctive Merit/National

CALENDAR OR APPOINTMENT BOOK
A Literary Book of Days
ART DIRECTOR *Louise Fili*
CREATIVE DIRECTOR *Louise Fili*
DESIGNERS *Louise Fili, Leah Lococo*
STUDIO *Louise Fili Ltd.*
CLIENT *Crown Publishing*

Distinctive Merit/National

CALENDAR OR APPOINTMENT BOOK
Elements of Time
ART DIRECTOR *Michael McGinn*
CREATIVE DIRECTOR *James A. Sebastian*
DESIGNERS *James A. Sebastian, Frank Nichols*
STUDIO *Designframe Inc.*
CLIENT *Strathmore Paper Co.*

Distinctive Merit/International

LOGO OR TRADEMARK
Dialog Logo
ART DIRECTOR *Peter Smith*
CREATIVE DIRECTOR *Peter Smith*
DESIGNER *Peter Smith*
STUDIO *Dialog Limited*

Distinctive Merit/International

LOGO OR TRADEMARK
London Radio Logo
ART DIRECTOR *John Rushworth*
CREATIVE DIRECTOR *John Rushworth*
DESIGNERS *John Rushworth, Nick Finney*
COPYWRITER *David Gibbs*
PHOTOGRAPHER *Phil Sayer*
STUDIO *Pentagram Design Ltd.*
CLIENT *London Radio Services Ltd.*

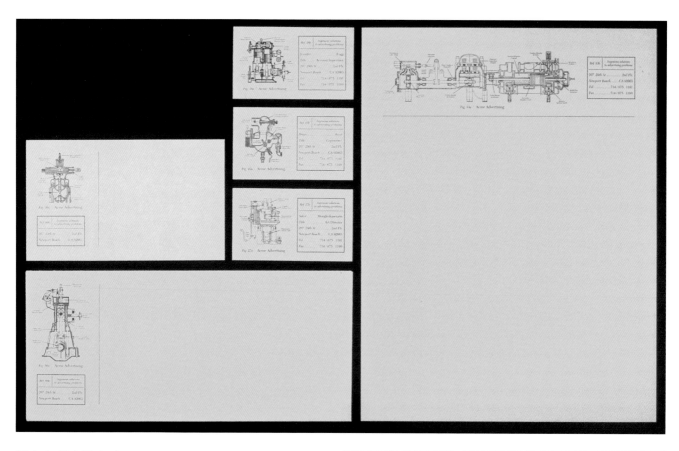

Distinctive Merit/National

LETTERHEAD, BUSINESS CARD, ENVELOPE
Acme Advertising Stationery
ART DIRECTOR *Sakol Mongkolkasetarin*
CREATIVE DIRECTOR *Sakol Mongkolkasetarin*
DESIGNER *Sakol Mongkolkasetarin*
COPYWRITER *Brian West*
ILLUSTRATOR *Sakol Mongkolkasetarin*
AGENCY *Acme Advertising*
CLIENT *Acme Advertising*

Distinctive Merit/National

LETTERHEAD, BUSINESS CARD, ENVELOPE
Donald M. Ward, C.P.A.
ART DIRECTOR *Patrick Short*
DESIGNER *Patrick Short*
PHOTOGRAPHER *Alex Bee*
STUDIO *BlackBird Creative*
CLIENT *Donald M. Ward, C.P.A.*

(facing page)
Distinctive Merit/National

CORPORATE IDENTITY PROGRAM
The Public Theater
ART DIRECTOR *Paula Scher*
DESIGNERS *Ron Louie, Lisa Mazur, Paula Scher*
STUDIO *Pentagram Design*
CLIENT *The Public Theater*

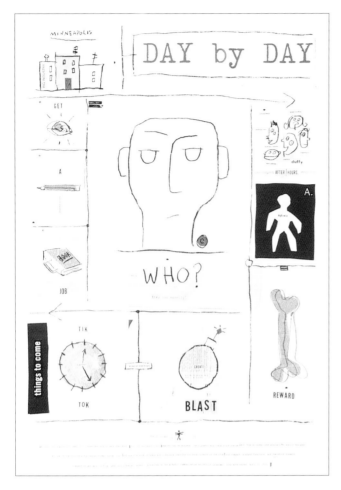

Distinctive Merit/National

POSTER, OTHER THAN ADVERTISING, SINGLE
Day by Day
ART DIRECTOR *Neil Powell*
CREATIVE DIRECTOR *Neil Powell*
DESIGNER *Neil Powell*
ILLUSTRATOR *Neil Powell*
STUDIO *Duffy Design*
CLIENT *Graphic Communication Society of Oklahoma*

Distinctive Merit/National

POSTER, OTHER THAN ADVERTISING, SINGLE
World Conservation
ART DIRECTORS *Team*
CREATIVE DIRECTOR *Joe Duffy*
DESIGNER *Neil Powell*
STUDIO *Duffy Design*
CLIENT *World Conservation*

Distinctive Merit/International

POSTER, OTHER THAN ADVERTISING, SINGLE
The 200th Anniversary of Sharaku
ART DIRECTOR *Koji Mizutani*
CREATIVE DIRECTOR *Koji Mizutani*
DESIGNER *Hiroshi Ohmizo*
PHOTOGRAPHER *Yoshihiko Ueda*
STUDIO *Mizutani Studio*
CLIENT *The Mainichi Newspapers*

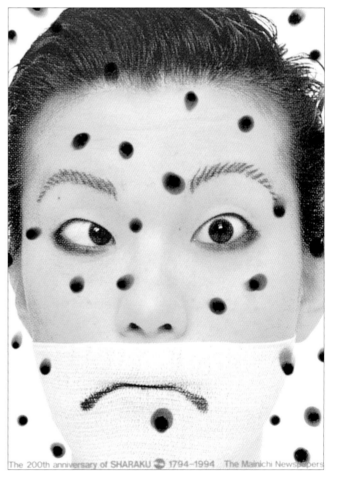

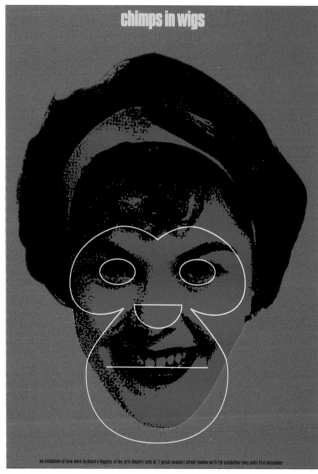

Distinctive Merit/National

POSTER, OTHER THAN ADVERTISING, SINGLE
King of the Hill
ART DIRECTOR *Randi Braun*
CREATIVE DIRECTOR *Peter Bemis*
DESIGNER *Kim Wexman*
COPYWRITER *David Lee*
AGENCY *Frankfurt Balkind Partners*
CLIENT *Gramercy Pictures*

Distinctive Merit/International

POSTER, OTHER THAN ADVERTISING, SINGLE
Thanks to the Sky of Toyama
ART DIRECTOR *Tatsuya Hatanaka*
CREATIVE DIRECTOR *Tatsuya Hatanaka*
DESIGNER *Tatsuya Hatanaka*
COPYWRITER *Tatsuya Hatanaka*
STUDIO *Sougo Kikaku Co. Ltd.*

Distinctive Merit/International

POSTER, OTHER THAN ADVERTISING, SINGLE
Chimps in Wigs
ART DIRECTOR *Michael Johnson*
DESIGNER *Michael Johnson*
STUDIO *Johnson Banks*
CLIENT *David O'Higgins*

Distinctive Merit/National

POSTER, OTHER THAN ADVERTISING, SERIES
Regan's Posters
ART DIRECTOR *Chris Hill*
CREATIVE DIRECTOR *Chris Hill*
DESIGNERS *Chris Hill, Jeff Davis, Laura Menegaz*
ILLUSTRATOR *Regan Dunnick*
STUDIO *The Hill Group*
CLIENT *Regan Dunnick*

Distinctive Merit/National

POSTER, OTHER THAN ADVERTISING, SERIES
Holiday Posters
ART DIRECTOR *Howard Brown*
DESIGNERS *Howard Brown, Mike Calkins*
COPYWRITER *Howard Brown*
ILLUSTRATOR *Mike Calkins*
STUDIO *Urban Outfitters, in-house*
CLIENT *Urban Outfitters Retail*

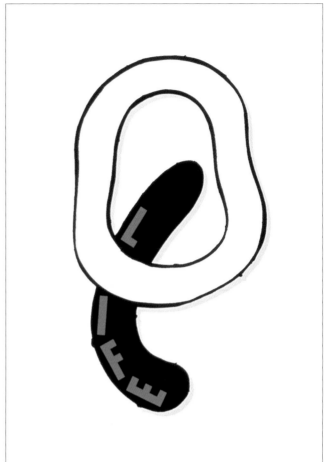

(facing page)
Distinctive Merit/International

POSTER, OTHER THAN ADVERTISING, SERIES
LIFE
ART DIRECTOR *Shin Matsunaga*
DESIGNER *Shin Matsunaga*
ILLUSTRATOR *Shin Matsunaga*
STUDIO *Shin Matsunaga Design Inc.*
CLIENT *Japan Design Committee*

(above)
Distinctive Merit/National

SELF-PROMOTION, SINGLE
Louise Fili Ltd. Promotion
ART DIRECTOR *Louise Fili*
CREATIVE DIRECTOR *Louise Fili*
DESIGNER *Louise Fili*
COPYWRITER *Steven Heller*
PHOTOGRAPHERS *Ed Spiro, David Barry*
STUDIO *Louise Fili Ltd.*
CLIENT *Louise Fili Ltd.*

(facing page, top)
Distinctive Merit/National

SELF-PROMOTION, SINGLE
One Thousand Words
ART DIRECTOR *Carlos Segura*
CREATIVE DIRECTOR *Carlos Segura*
DESIGNER *Carlos Segura*
COPYWRITER *John Cleland*
PHOTOGRAPHER *Geof Kern*
STUDIO *Segura Inc.*
CLIENT *John Cleland*

(facing page, bottom)
Distinctive Merit/National

SELF-PROMOTION, SINGLE
Brick
DESIGNER *Mark Wieland*
PHOTOGRAPHER *Mark Wieland*
STUDIO *Wieland Photography*

Distinctive Merit/National

SELF-PROMOTION, SERIES
Benefit Bluebird Paper Promotion
ART DIRECTOR *Stephen Doyle*
DESIGNER *Terry Mastin*
COPYWRITER *Stephen Doyle*
PRODUCER *Cameron Manning*
STUDIO *Drenttel Doyle Partners*
CLIENT *Champion International Corporation*

MERIT AWARDS

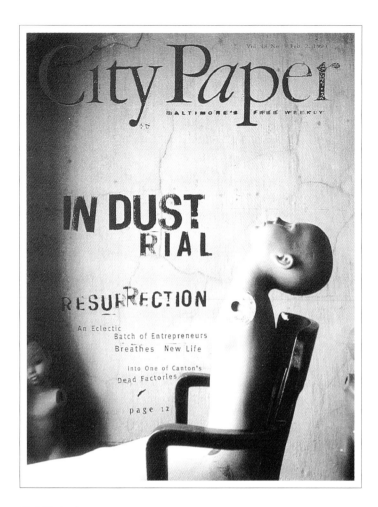

Merit/National

FULL PAGE OR SPREAD
Industrial Resurrection
ART DIRECTOR *George Mimnaugh*
CREATIVE DIRECTOR *George Mimnaugh*
DESIGNER *George Mimnaugh*
PHOTOGRAPHER *Rex Fly*
CLIENT *Baltimore City Paper*

Merit/National

FULL PAGE OR SPREAD
Opening Up
ART DIRECTOR *Galie Jean-Louis*
CREATIVE DIRECTOR *Galie Jean-Louis*
DESIGNER *Galie Jean-Louis*
ILLUSTRATOR *Galie Jean-Louis*
STUDIO *Galie Jean-Louis*
CLIENT *Anchorage Daily News*

Merit/National

FULL PAGE OR SPREAD
Primal Screen
ART DIRECTOR *Galie Jean-Louis*
CREATIVE DIRECTOR *Galie Jean-Louis*
DESIGNER *Galie Jean-Louis*
PHOTOGRAPHER *Amy Guip*
ILLUSTRATOR *Amy Guip*
STUDIO *Galie Jean-Louis*
CLIENT *Anchorage Daily News*

Merit/National

FULL PAGE OR SPREAD
A Portrait of Crime
ART DIRECTOR *Scott Minister*
CREATIVE DIRECTOR *Scott Minister*
DESIGNER *Scott Minister*
AGENCY *The Columbus Dispatch*
CLIENT *The Columbus Dispatch*

Merit/National

FULL PAGE OR SPREAD
Fear of Music
ART DIRECTOR *George Mimnaugh*
CREATIVE DIRECTOR *George Mimnaugh*
DESIGNERS *Joyce Hesselberth, George Mimnaugh*
COPYWRITER *David Dudley*
PHOTOGRAPHERS *Rex Fly, Michael Northrup,*
Geoff Graham
ILLUSTRATOR *Joyce Hesselberth*
CLIENT *Baltimore City Paper*

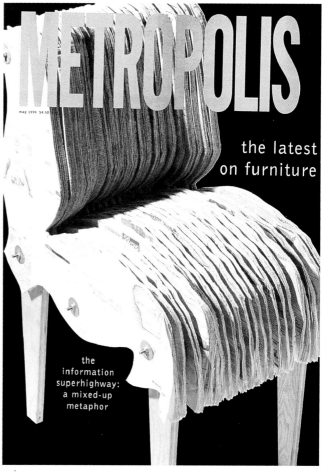

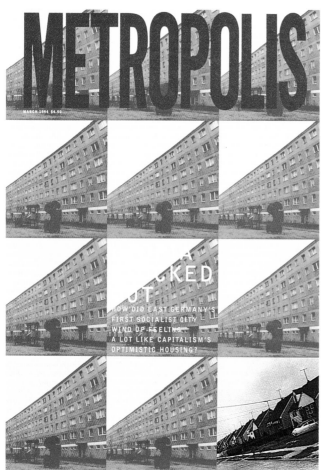

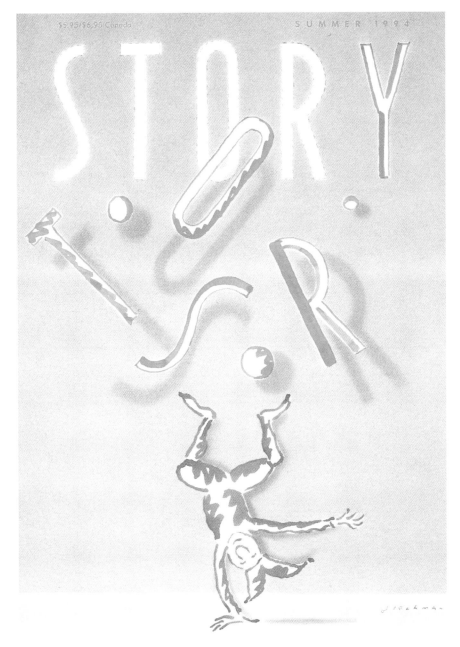

(facing page, top left)
Merit/National

COVER
A Toilet Brush with Greatness
ART DIRECTORS *Carl Lehmann-Haupt,*
Nancy Kruger Cohen
DESIGNERS *Carl Lehmann-Haupt,*
Nancy Kruger Cohen
EDITOR *Susan Szenasy*
CLIENT *Metropolis*

(facing page, top right)
Merit/National

COVER
The Latest on Furniture
ART DIRECTORS *Carl Lehmann-Haupt,*
Nancy Kruger Cohen
DESIGNERS *Carl Lehmann-Haupt,*
Nancy Kruger Cohen
EDITOR *Susan Szenasy*
PHOTOGRAPHER *Andrew Williamson*
CLIENT *Metropolis*

(facing page, bottom left)
Merit/National

COVER
Utopia Blocked Out
ART DIRECTORS *Carl Lehmann-Haupt,*
Nancy Kruger Cohen
DESIGNERS *Carl Lehmann-Haupt,*
Nancy Kruger Cohen
EDITOR *Susan Szenasy*
PHOTOGRAPHER *Phillipp Meyser*
CLIENT *Metropolis*

(facing page, bottom right)
Merit/National

COVER
The Marketing of Fear
ART DIRECTORS *Carl Lehmann-Haupt,*
Nancy Kruger Cohen
DESIGNERS *Carl Lehmann-Haupt,*
Nancy Kruger Cohen
EDITOR *Susan Szenasy*
PHOTOGRAPHER *Rick Albert*
CLIENT *Metropolis*

Merit/National

COVER
Story Magazine, Summer 1994
ART DIRECTOR *R. O. Blechman*
CREATIVE DIRECTOR *Clare Finney*
DESIGNER *R. O. Blechman*
ILLUSTRATOR *R. O. Blechman*

Merit/National

COVER
The Beastie Boys
CREATIVE DIRECTOR *Fred Woodward*
DESIGNER *Fred Woodward*
PHOTO EDITOR *Jodi Peckman*
PHOTOGRAPHER *Matthew Rolston*
CLIENT *Rolling Stone*

ADDITIONAL AWARD

Merit
PHOTOGRAPHY, EDITORIAL, FULL PAGE OR SPREAD

Merit/National

COVER
Melrose Place: The Hot Issue
CREATIVE DIRECTOR *Fred Woodward*
DESIGNER *Fred Woodward*
PHOTO EDITOR *Jodi Peckman*
PHOTOGRAPHER *Mark Seliger*
CLIENT *Rolling Stone*

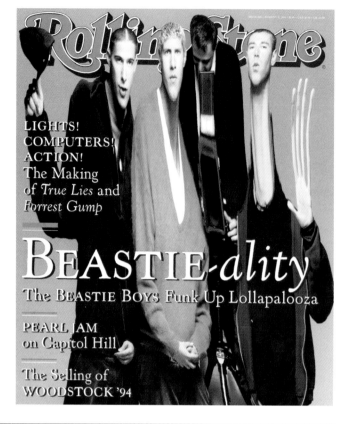

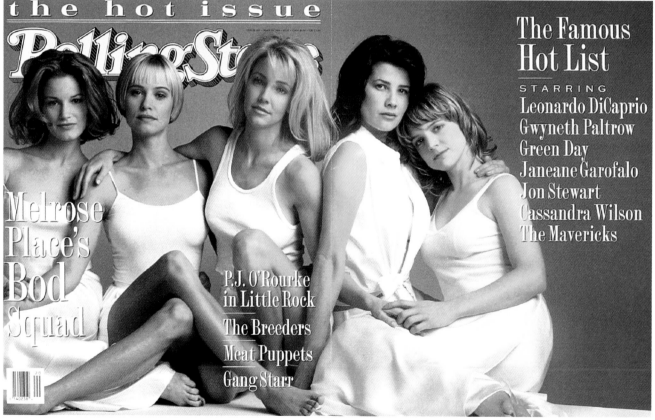

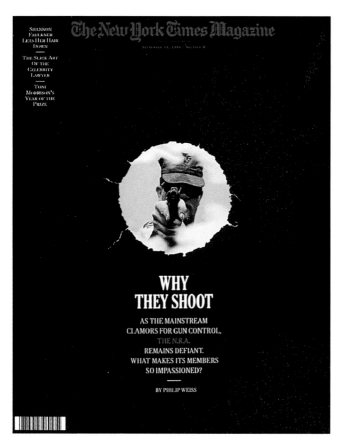

Merit/National

COVER
Why They Shoot
ART DIRECTOR *Janet Froelich*
DESIGNER *Lisa Naftolin*
PHOTO EDITOR *Kathy Ryan*
PHOTOGRAPHER *Mark Peterson*
CLIENT *The New York Times Magazine*

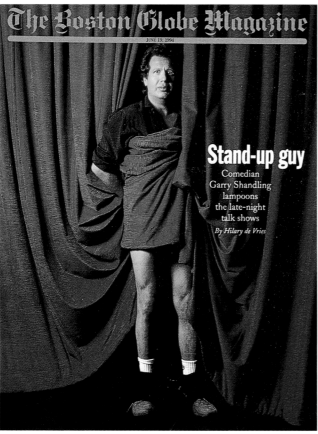

Merit/National

COVER
Gary Shandling
ART DIRECTOR *Lucy Bartholomay*
CREATIVE DIRECTOR *Lucy Bartholomay*
DESIGNER *Lucy Bartholomay*
PHOTOGRAPHER *Bill Greene*
CLIENT *The Boston Globe*

Merit/International

COVER
AdD Advertising and Design Magazine
ART DIRECTOR *Oswaldo Miranda*
CREATIVE DIRECTOR *Oswaldo Miranda*
DESIGNER *Oswaldo Miranda*
PHOTOGRAPHER *Steven Klein*
STUDIO *Miran Design Inc.*

Merit/International

COVER
Grafica
ART DIRECTOR *Oswaldo Miranda*
CREATIVE DIRECTOR *Oswaldo Miranda*
DESIGNER *Oswaldo Miranda*
COPYWRITERS *Various*
PHOTOGRAPHER *Jean-Paul Goude*
STUDIO *Miran Design Inc., Casa de Idgias*

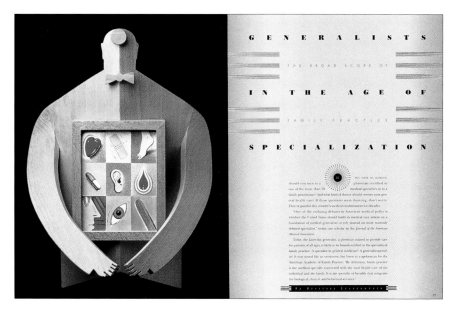

Merit/National

FULL PAGE OR SPREAD
Generalists in the Age of Specialization
ART DIRECTOR *Mark Geer*
DESIGNER *Mark Geer*
COPYWRITER *Geoffrey Leavenworth*
ILLUSTRATOR *Dave Calver*
STUDIO *Geer Design, Inc.*
CLIENT *Memorial Healthcare System*

Merit/National

FULL PAGE OR SPREAD
Roots
ART DIRECTOR *Gael Towey*
DESIGNER *Agnethe Glatved*
PHOTOGRAPHER *William Abranowicz*
STUDIO *Martha Stewart Living*
CLIENT *Martha Stewart Living*

Merit/National

FULL PAGE OR SPREAD
Winona
CREATIVE DIRECTOR *Fred Woodward*
DESIGNERS *Debra Bishop, Fred Woodward*
PHOTO EDITOR *Laurie Kratochvil*
PHOTOGRAPHER *Herb Ritts*
CLIENT *Rolling Stone*

Merit/National

FULL PAGE OR SPREAD
Brad Pitt
CREATIVE DIRECTOR *Fred Woodward*
DESIGNERS *Fred Woodward, Geraldine Hessler*
PHOTO EDITOR *Jodi Peckman*
PHOTOGRAPHER *Mark Seliger*
CLIENT *Rolling Stone*

Merit/National

FULL PAGE OR SPREAD
The Call of the Wild
CREATIVE DIRECTOR *Fred Woodward*
DESIGNERS *Fred Woodward, Lee Bearson*
PHOTOGRAPHER *James Balog*
CLIENT *Rolling Stone*

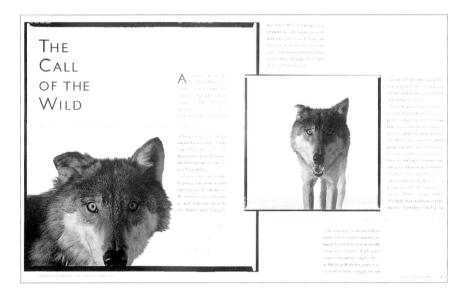

Merit/National

FULL PAGE OR SPREAD
Barry Diller
CREATIVE DIRECTOR *Fred Woodward*
DESIGNERS *Fred Woodward, Gail Anderson*
CLIENT *Rolling Stone*

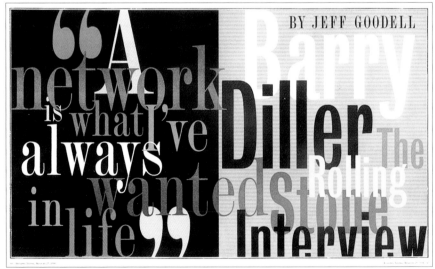

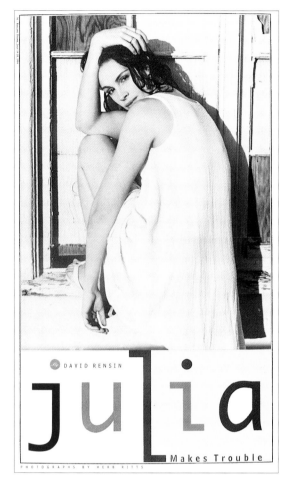

Merit/National

FULL PAGE OR SPREAD
Julia Makes Trouble
CREATIVE DIRECTOR *Fred Woodward*
DESIGNER *Fred Woodward*
PHOTO EDITOR *Jodi Peckman*
PHOTOGRAPHER *Herb Ritts*
CLIENT *Rolling Stone*

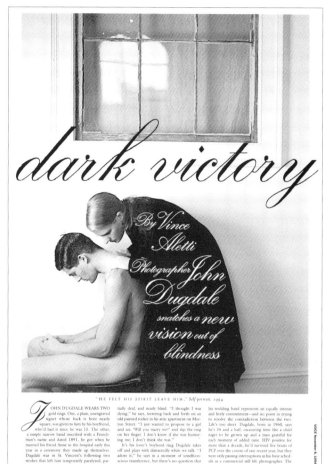

Merit/National

FULL PAGE OR SPREAD
Dark Victory
ART DIRECTOR *Audrey Shachnow*
DESIGNER *Ted Keller*
PHOTOGRAPHER *John Dugdale*
CLIENT *The Village Voice*

Merit/National

FULL PAGE OR SPREAD
Robert Redford
CREATIVE DIRECTOR *Fred Woodward*
DESIGNER *Fred Woodward*
PHOTO EDITOR *Jodi Peckman*
PHOTOGRAPHER *Albert Watson*
CLIENT *Rolling Stone*

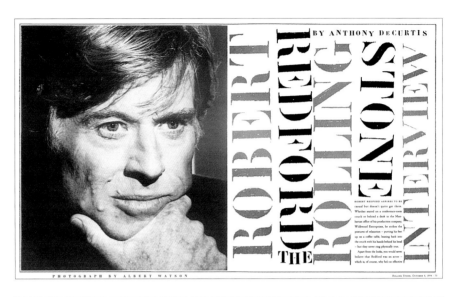

Merit/National

FULL PAGE OR SPREAD
The Sheriff Who Went to Pot
ART DIRECTOR *D. J. Stout*
DESIGNERS *D. J. Stout, Nancy McMillan*
COPYWRITER *Robert Draper*
PHOTOGRAPHERS *Rick Patrick, Annalisa*
CLIENT *Texas Monthly*

Merit/National

FULL PAGE OR SPREAD
A Hoplophobe among the Gunnies
ART DIRECTOR *Janet Froelich*
DESIGNER *Cathy Gilmore-Barnes*
PHOTO EDITOR *Kathy Ryan*
PHOTOGRAPHER *Mark Peterson*
CLIENT *The New York Times Magazine*

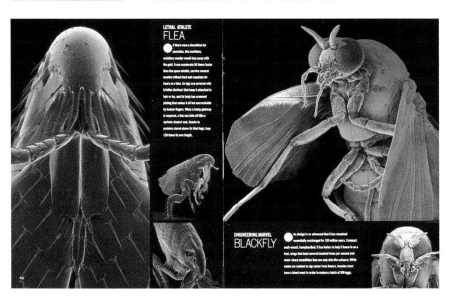

Merit/National

MULTIPAGE
Yikes!
ART DIRECTOR *Tom Bentkowski*
DIRECTOR OF PHOTOGRAPHY *David Friend*
DESIGNER *Mimi Park*
PHOTO EDITOR *Barbara Baker Burrows*
PHOTOGRAPHER *David Scharf*
CLIENT *Life Magazine*

ADDITIONAL AWARD

Merit
PHOTOGRAPHY, EDITORIAL, SERIES

MULTIPAGE
Yikes!
ART DIRECTOR *Tom Bentkowski*

Merit/National

MULTIPAGE
Generation X
ART DIRECTOR *Janet Froelich*
DESIGNER *Joel Cuyler*
PHOTO EDITOR *Kathy Ryan*
PHOTOGRAPHER *Leon A. Borensztein*
CLIENT *The New York Times Magazine*

(facing page)
Merit/National

MULTIPAGE
REM Monster Madness
CREATIVE DIRECTOR *Fred Woodward*
DESIGNER *Fred Woodward*
TYPOGRAPHER *Eric Siry*
PHOTO EDITOR *Jodi Peckman*
PHOTOGRAPHER *Mark Seliger*
CLIENT *Rolling Stone*

ADDITIONAL AWARD

Merit
PHOTOGRAPHY, EDITORIAL, SERIES

GENERATION 未知

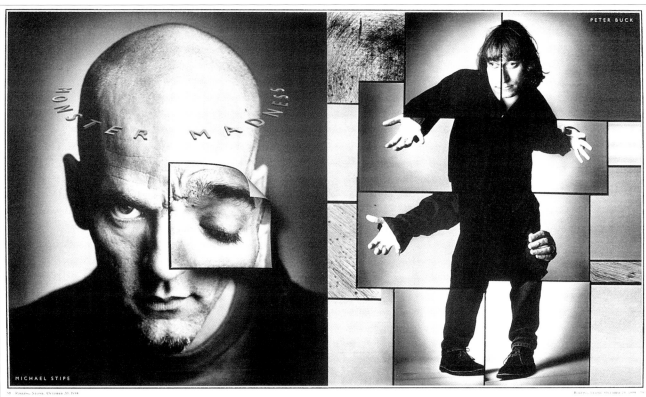

Merit/International

MULTIPAGE
Composite
ART DIRECTOR *Hideki Nakajima*
CREATIVE DIRECTORS *Masanobu Sugatsuke,*
Mika Mizutani
DESIGNER *Hideki Nakajima*
PHOTOGRAPHER *Satoshi Saikusa*
STUDIO *Rockin'on Inc.*
CLIENT *Asahi Press*

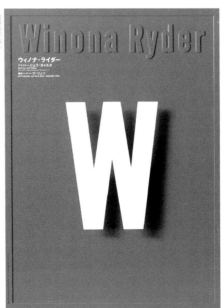

Merit/International

MULTIPAGE
Cut
ART DIRECTOR *Hideki Nakajima*
DESIGNERS *Hideki Nakajima, Yuko Kasuga,*
Iwao Miura, Masashi Nakayama, Kenichi Kawakami
EDITOR IN CHIEF *Ken Sato*
PHOTOGRAPHERS *Michel Haddi, Tim Richmond,*
Greg Gorman, Malucci, Herb Ritts
CLIENT *Rockin'on Inc.*

Merit/National

FULL ISSUE
Rough, September
ART DIRECTORS *Bryan L. Peterson, Jan Wilson*
DESIGNERS *Jan Wilson, Dave Eliason,*
Bryan L. Peterson, Nhan T. Pham
PHOTOGRAPHERS *Phil Hollenbeck, Pete Lacker,*
Holly Kuper
ILLUSTRATOR *Jan Wilson*
AGENCY *Peterson & Company*
STUDIO *Peterson & Company*
CLIENT *Dallas Society of Visual Communication*

Merit/National

FULL ISSUE
Metropolis: Entertainment
ART DIRECTORS *Carl Lehmann-Haupt,*
Nancy Kruger Cohen
DESIGNERS *Carl Lehmann-Haupt,*
Nancy Kruger Cohen
EDITOR *Susan Szenasy*

Merit/National

FULL ISSUE
Chicago Tribune Magazine: Good News
ART DIRECTOR *Dan Jursa*
CREATIVE DIRECTOR *Nancy J. Canfield*
DESIGNERS *Nancy J. Canfield, Tony Majeri*
EDITOR *Denis J. Gosselin*
COPYWRITERS *Various*
PHOTOGRAPHER *Peter Rosenbaum*

Merit/National

FULL ISSUE
Big Magazine
ART DIRECTOR *Vince Frost*
CREATIVE DIRECTOR *Vince Frost*
DESIGNER *Vince Frost*

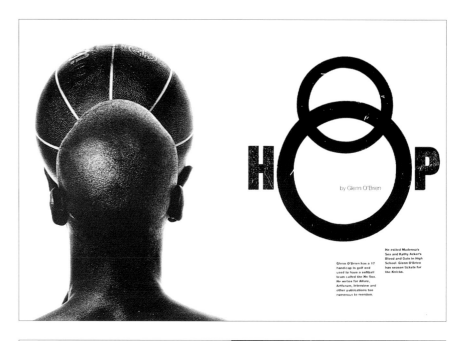

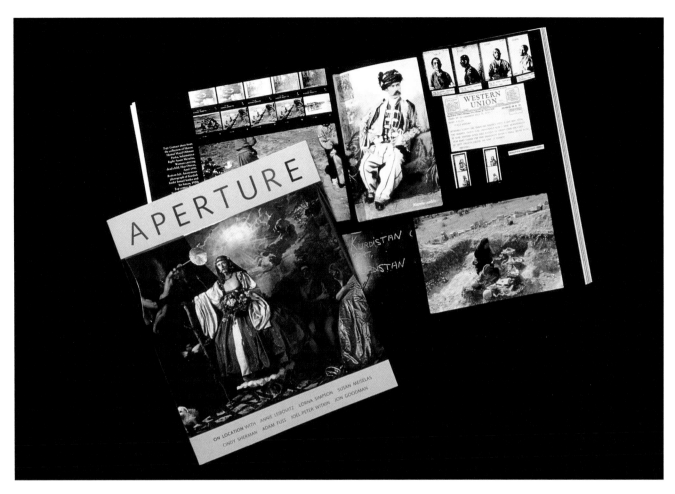

Merit/National

FULL ISSUE
Aperture: On Location
ART DIRECTOR *Yolanda Cuomo*
DESIGNERS *Yolanda Cuomo, Wendy Byrne,*
Francesca Richer
EDITOR *Melissa Harris*
PHOTOGRAPHERS *Various*
STUDIO *Yolanda Cuomo Design*

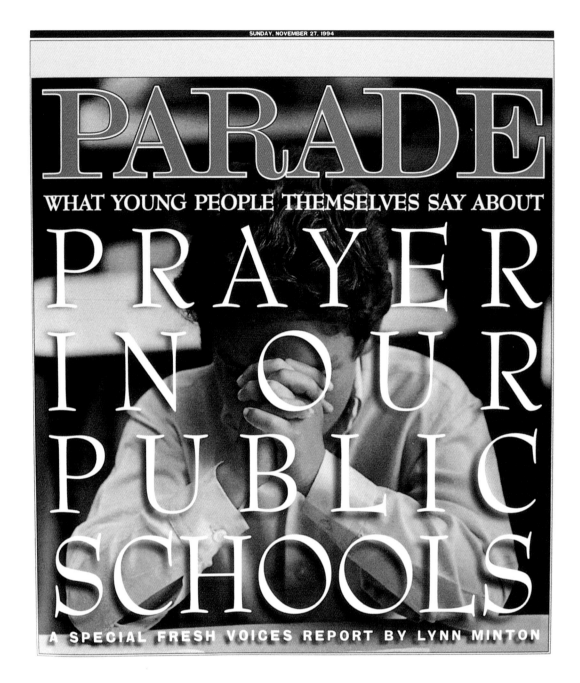

SUNDAY, NOVEMBER 27, 1994

PARADE

WHAT YOUNG PEOPLE THEMSELVES SAY ABOUT

PRAYER IN OUR PUBLIC SCHOOLS

A SPECIAL FRESH VOICES REPORT BY LYNN MINTON

Merit/National

COVER
Prayer in Our Public Schools
CREATIVE DIRECTOR *Ira Yoffe*
DESIGNERS *Ira Yoffe, Christopher Austopchuk,*
Jeffrey Brown
COPYWRITER *David Currier*
PHOTOGRAPHER *Bryce Flynn*
CLIENT *Parade Magazine*

Crimes and
Misdemeanors

Skin abuse is rampant. Sun exposure, dry heat, and pollution are accessories to the crime. The punishment: Wrinkles, lines, and scaly skin.

By Christian Wright

INDECENT EXPOSURE Exposure to UVA and UVB rays—whether on the beach or in a tanning bed—is the most heinous skin-care crime. Bikini by Frances Colin. These pages: Hair, John Sahag for John Sahag Workshop; makeup, Romão for Aridos Salon Inb; manicure, Lorino. Details, see Credits page.

Merit/National

MULTIPAGE
Crimes and Misdemeanors
DESIGN DIRECTOR *Shawn Young*
DESIGNER *Shawn Young*
PHOTOGRAPHER *Michael Thompson*
CLIENT *Allure*

Sun Exposure

Constantly rubbing **or touching the** face constitutes assault **in the second degree.**

Assault and Battery

Reckless Boozing

Possession of Nicotine

Sleep Deprivation

Negligence

LETHAL WEAPONS Hands carry around enough bacteria to make your skin a battleground. The evidence for poking and picking is more acne, scars, and red bumps poetically termed Picker's Nodules.

CEMENTED FOUNDATION Not removing makeup wasn't mentioned in Clinton's recent crime bill, but it's wrong just the same. The punishment: You may feel when you wake up and still have it on. Top by Ralph Lauren Collection. Short skirt by DKNY.

IN HOT WATER Too much of a good thing—in this case, hot water—is a misdemeanor in some circles. In small doses, water cleanses and refreshes. A downpour can strip skin of its natural moisture. Shirt by Mark Eisen. Hot pants by DKNY. Satin shoes by Bella Freud. Details, see Credits page.

Merit/National

FULL ISSUE
Upper and Lower Case, Vol. 21.1, Summer 1994
ART DIRECTORS *Woody Pirtle, John Klotnia*
DESIGNERS *Woody Pirtle, John Klotnia,*
Ivette Montes de Oca
STUDIO *Pentagram Design*
CLIENT *International Typeface Corporation*

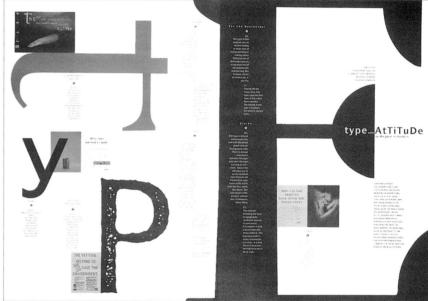

ADVERTISING CAMPAIGNS PROMOTING GOOD CAUSES HAVE LONG BEEN REGARDED BY THE AD COMMUNITY AS AN EASY SELL TO CLIENTS AND A SHOO-IN AT AWARDS SHOWS. BUT HOW DO AGENCIES CREATE PRO BONO CAMPAIGNS WHICH ARE ALSO EFFECTIVE? JADED CONSUMERS NO LONGER RESPOND TO ADS WHICH RESORT TO

USING SHOCKING, GRAPHIC IMAGES AND NEGATIVE COPY. THE BEST PRO BONO CAMPAIGNS THESE DAYS TAKE A POSITIVE APPROACH TO PERSUADING PEOPLE TO ACTION. MANY, LIKE THOSE SHOWN HERE, COMBINE A GOOD IDEA WITH ATTRACTIVE VISUALS TO MOTIVATE, RAISE AWARENESS, INSPIRE AND OFFER A GLIMMER OF HOPE.

Merit/National

FULL ISSUE
Upper and Lower Case, Vol. 21.3, Winter 1994
ART DIRECTORS *Woody Pirtle, John Klotnia*
DESIGNERS *Ivette Montes de Oca, Robert Spica*
STUDIO *Pentagram Design*
CLIENT *International Typeface Corporation*

(facing page, top)
Merit/International

FULL ISSUE
Baseline 17
ART DIRECTOR *Hans Dieter Reichert*
CREATIVE DIRECTOR *Hans Dieter Reichert*
DESIGNER *Hans Dieter Reichert*
DESIGN ASSISTANT *Brian Cunningham*
EDITOR *Mike Daines*
PHOTOGRAPHERS *Everald Williams,*
Hans Dieter Reichert
STUDIO *HDR Design*
CLIENT *Letraset Esselte*

(facing page, bottom)
Merit/International

FULL ISSUE
P Magazine, Issue 9
ART DIRECTOR *John Rushworth*
CREATIVE DIRECTOR *John Rushworth*
DESIGNERS *John Rushworth, Chiew Yong*
COPYWRITER *Renato Broglia*
PHOTOGRAPHERS *Various*
STUDIO *Pentagram Design Ltd.*
CLIENT *Polaroid Corporation*

Merit/National

MULTIPLE ISSUES
ZiNj Number 2, ZiNj Number 3
ART DIRECTOR *David Volsic*
CREATIVE DIRECTORS *David Volsic, Debra Harris*
DESIGNERS *David Volsic, Sheryl Lundgreen,*
Heidi Shelley
COPYWRITERS *Kevin Jones, Debra Harris*
PHOTOGRAPHERS *Murray Close, Chip Clark,*
Kevin Jones
ILLUSTRATORS *David Volsic,*
Carl P. Brest Van Kampen, Mark Hallet
AGENCY *Harris.Volsic Creative*
CLIENT *Interagency Task Force*

Merit/National

FULL ISSUE
Rough, March
ART DIRECTORS *Chuck Johnson, Ken Koester*
CREATIVE DIRECTOR *Chuck Johnson*
DESIGNERS *Chuck Johnson, Ken Koester, Rob Smith*
EDITORS *Margie Bowles, Phil Hollenbeck*
COPYWRITERS *Margie Bowles, Phil Hollenbeck,*
George Toomer, Max Wright
PHOTOGRAPHER *Phil Hollenbeck*
ILLUSTRATORS *Chuck Johnson, Ken Koester*
STUDIO *Brainstorm, Inc.*
CLIENT *Dallas Society of Visual Communication*

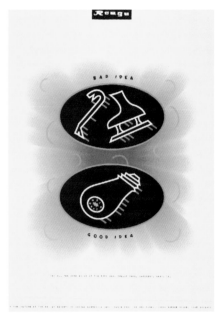

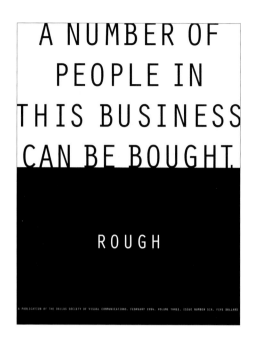

A NUMBER OF PEOPLE IN THIS BUSINESS CAN BE BOUGHT.

ROUGH

A PUBLICATION OF THE DALLAS SOCIETY OF VISUAL COMMUNICATIONS, FEBRUARY 1994, VOLUME THREE, ISSUE NUMBER SIX, FIVE DOLLARS

Merit/National

FULL ISSUE
Rough, February
ART DIRECTORS *Chuck Johnson, Ken Koester*
CREATIVE DIRECTOR *Chuck Johnson*
DESIGNERS *Chuck Johnson, Ken Koester, Rob Smith*
EDITORS *Margie Bowles, Phil Hollenbeck*
COPYWRITERS *Margie Bowles, Phil Hollenbeck, Ken Koester*
PHOTOGRAPHERS *Greg Watermann, Kent Kirkley*
STUDIO *Brainstorm, Inc.*
CLIENT *Dallas Society of Visual Communication*

Merit/National

SINGLE
A History of Women Photographers
ART DIRECTOR *Monika Keano*
DESIGNER *Joyce Rothschild*
AUTHOR *Naomi Rosenblum*
CLIENT *Abbeville Press*

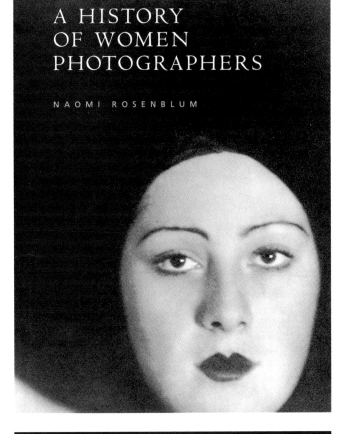

Merit/National

SINGLE
ABC
ART DIRECTOR *Stephen Doyle*
DESIGNER *Gary Tooth*
AUTHOR *William Wegman*
PHOTOGRAPHER *William Wegman*
STUDIO *Drenttel Doyle Partners*
CLIENT *Hyperion Books for Children*

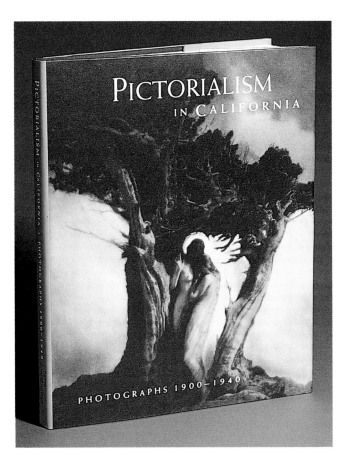

Merit/National

SINGLE
Pictorialism in California
DESIGNER *Kurt Hauser*
STUDIO *J. Paul Getty Trust, Publication Services*
CLIENT *J. Paul Getty Museum*

Merit/National

SINGLE
Style-Architecture and Building-Art: Transformations of Architecture in the Nineteenth Century and Its Present Condition
DESIGNER *Lorraine Wild*
AUTHOR *Hermann Muthesius*
STUDIO *J. Paul Getty Trust, Publication Services*
CLIENT *The Getty Center for the History of Art and the Humanities*

Merit/National

SINGLE
This Heritage Remembered V: Shakespeare
ART DIRECTOR *Woody Pirtle*
CREATIVE DIRECTOR *Woody Pirtle*
DESIGNERS *Woody Pirtle, John Klotnia, Ivette Montes de Oca*
COPYWRITER *Lee Herrick*
ILLUSTRATOR *Anthony Russo*
PRODUCER *Bob Downs*
STUDIO *Pentagram Design*
CLIENT *Heritage Press*

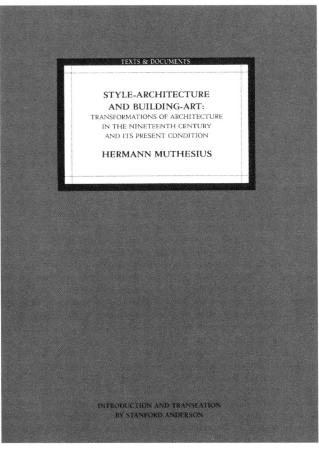

Merit/National

SINGLE

Bra Fashions by Stephanie
ART DIRECTOR *Seymour Chwast*
CREATIVE DIRECTOR *Seymour Chwast*
DESIGNER *Seymour Chwast*
COPYWRITER *Seymour Chwast*
ILLUSTRATOR *Seymour Chwast*
STUDIO *The Pushpin Group, Inc.*
CLIENT *Warner Books*

(facing page, top)
Merit/National

SINGLE

Roy Lichtenstein
ART DIRECTOR *Takaaki Matsumoto*
CREATIVE DIRECTOR *Takaaki Matsumoto*
DESIGNER *Takaaki Matsumoto*
MANAGING EDITOR *Anthony Calnek*
AUTHOR *Diane Waldman*
PHOTOGRAPHERS *Various*
STUDIO *Matsumoto Incorporated*
CLIENT *Solomon R. Guggenheim Museum*

(facing page, bottom)
Merit/National

SINGLE

Wildlife
ART DIRECTOR *John Ball*
CREATIVE DIRECTOR *John Ball*
DESIGNERS *John Ball, Gale Spitzley*
COPYWRITER *Reesey Shaw*
AGENCY *Mires Design, Inc.*
STUDIO *Mires Design, Inc.*
CLIENT *California Center for the Arts Museum*

Merit/National

SINGLE
Sessions! Norman Seeff
ART DIRECTOR *Norman Seeff*
CREATIVE DIRECTOR *Norman Seeff*
DESIGNER *Norman Seeff*
COPYWRITER *Norman Seeff*
PHOTOGRAPHER *Norman Seeff*
PRODUCER *WhaleSong, Inc.*
DIRECTORS *Robert and Lorie Goodman*
CLIENT *WhaleSong, Inc. Publisher*

Merit/National

SINGLE
After Art: Rethinking 150 Years of Photography
ART DIRECTOR *Douglas Wadden*
DESIGNER *Douglas Wadden*
PHOTOGRAPHERS *Various*
STUDIO *Design Collaborative/Seattle*
CLIENT *Henry Art Gallery*

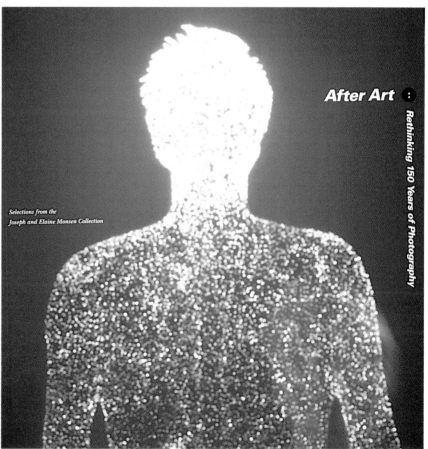

Merit/National

SINGLE
Jinnai Sakata Exhibition Catalogue
ART DIRECTOR *Takaaki Matsumoto*
CREATIVE DIRECTOR *Takaaki Matsumoto*
DESIGNER *Takaaki Matsumoto*
AUTHOR *John Perreault*
PHOTOGRAPHERS *Shigenori Hayashi, Kouki Suzuki*
STUDIO *Matsumoto Incorporated*
CLIENT *The Gallery at Takashimaya*

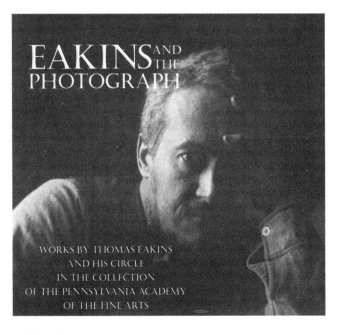

Merit/National

SINGLE
Eakins and the Photograph
ART DIRECTOR *Janice Wheeler*
CREATIVE DIRECTOR *Janice Wheeler*
DESIGNER *Janice Wheeler*
COPYWRITERS *Susan Danly, Cheryl Leibold*
PHOTOGRAPHERS *Rick Echelmeyer, Thomas Palmer*
ARTWORK *Eakins and his circle*
PRODUCER *Ken Sabol*
CLIENTS *Smithsonian Institution Press,
The Pennsylvania Academy of the Fine Arts*

Merit/National

SINGLE
Seeing the Unseen
ART DIRECTORS *Dona Bagley, Joan Hantz*
CREATIVE DIRECTOR *Rick Hock*
DESIGNER *Dona Bagley*
PHOTOGRAPHER *Harold E. Edgerton*
STUDIO *Windsor Street Design Association*
CLIENT *George Eastman House*

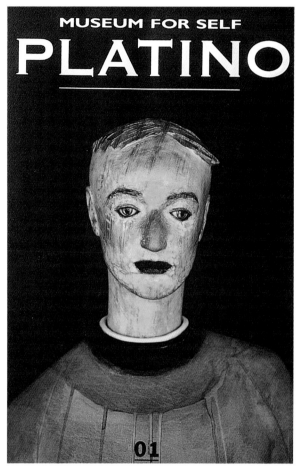

Merit/National

SINGLE
*Graphic Artists Guild Handbook: Pricing and Ethical
Guidelines, 8th Edition*
ART DIRECTOR *Simms Taback*
DESIGNER *Sheri G. Lee*
ILLUSTRATOR *John Hersey*
CLIENT *The Graphic Artists Guild*

ADDITIONAL AWARD

Merit
BOOK JACKET, SINGLE

Merit/International

SINGLE
Quarterly Magazine "Platino," No. 1
ART DIRECTOR *Kenzo Izutani*
CREATIVE DIRECTORS *Iruka Bando,
Yoshiyuki Tsuchiya*
DESIGNERS *Kenzo Izutani, Aki Hirai*
PHOTOGRAPHERS *Zigen, Miyako Ishiuchi,
Yasuyuki Amazutsumi, Ichigo Sugawara*
SCULPTOR *Katsura Funakoshi*
CLIENT *Platinum Guild International*

Merit/International

SINGLE
Shapes and Shades of Kanazawa: Keiichi Tahara
ART DIRECTOR *Toshio Yamagata*
DESIGNER *Toshio Yamagata*
EDITOR *Jiro Dejima*
PHOTOGRAPHER *Keiichi Tahara*
STUDIO *Shiseido Co. Ltd.*
CLIENT *Takakuwa Art Printing Co., Ltd.*

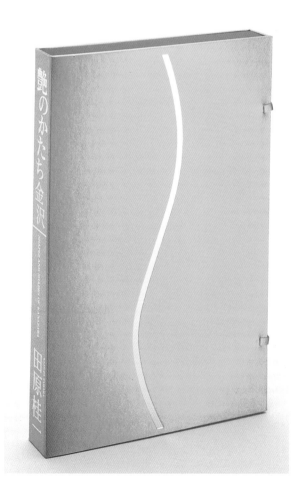

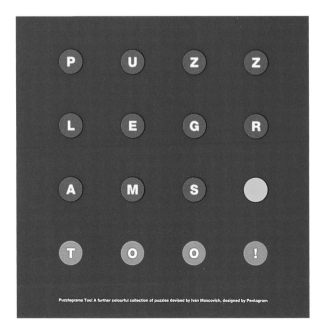

Merit/International

SINGLE
Namba Story
ART DIRECTOR *Takashi Matsuura*
CREATIVE DIRECTOR *Takashi Matsuura*
DESIGNER *Takashi Matsuura*
COPYWRITER *Hajime Morita*
ILLUSTRATOR *Koichi Yokoi*
PRODUCER *Koichi Yokoi*
DIRECTOR *Hajime Morita*
AGENCY *ATA Co., Ltd.*
CLIENT *Namba Festival Association*

Merit/International

SINGLE
Lucian Freud: Recent Work
DESIGNER *Derek Birdsall RDI*
COPYWRITER *Catherine Lampert*
PRODUCER *Martin Lee, Omnific*
CLIENT *Whitechapel Art Gallery, London*

Merit/International

SINGLE
Puzzlegrams Too!
ART DIRECTOR *David Hillman*
CREATIVE DIRECTOR *David Hillman*
DESIGNERS *David Hillman, Emily Chow*
COPYWRITER *David Gibbs*
CLIENT *Pentagram Design Ltd.*

Merit/International

SINGLE
Anyone Can Swim
DESIGNER *Madeleine Bennett*
COPYWRITER *Martin Firrell*
ILLUSTRATOR *Madeleine Bennett*
STUDIO *Madeleine Bennett Design*
CLIENT *Martin Firrell, Providence Press*

(facing page, top)
Merit/International

SINGLE
Farewell to Bosnia
ART DIRECTOR *Yolanda Cuomo*
DESIGNERS *Yolanda Cuomo, Gilles Peress*
PHOTOGRAPHER *Gilles Peress*
STUDIO *Yolanda Cuomo Design*
CLIENT *Scalo Editions*

(facing page, bottom)
Merit/International

SERIES
Picador Travel Classics
ART DIRECTOR *Fiona Carpenter*
ILLUSTRATOR *Jane Poulton*
DIRECTORS *Peter Straus, Jon Riley*
CLIENT *Picador*

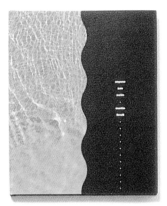

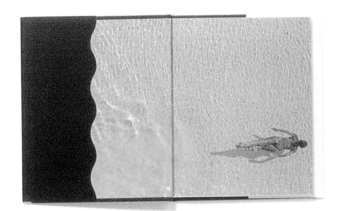

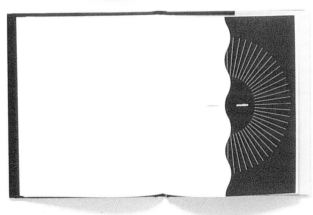

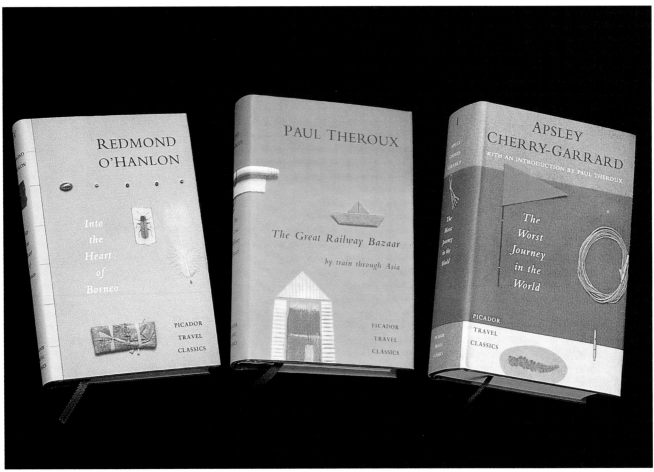

Merit/National

SINGLE
Subtraction
ART DIRECTOR *Carol Carson*
CREATIVE DIRECTOR *Carol Carson*
DESIGNER *Benita Raphan*
AUTHOR *Mary Robison*
PHOTOGRAPHER *Geoff Spear*
ILLUSTRATOR *Benita Raphan*
STUDIO *Benita Raphan Design*
CLIENT *Knopf/Random House*

Merit/National

SINGLE
The Book of Guys
ART DIRECTOR *Paul Buckley*
DESIGNER *Paul Buckley*
ILLUSTRATOR *Paul Buckley*
STUDIO *Penguin Design*
CLIENT *Penguin Books*

(facing page, top left)
Merit/National

SINGLE
The Three Stooges Scrapbook
ART DIRECTOR *Steven Brower*
DESIGNER *Steven Brower*
ILLUSTRATOR *Steven Brower*
CLIENT *Carol Publishing Group*

(facing page, top right)
Merit/National

SINGLE
Next
ART DIRECTOR *Adriane Stark*
CREATIVE DIRECTOR *Deborah Morton Hoyt*
DESIGNER *Adriane Stark*
PHOTOGRAPHER *Alicia Exum*
STUDIO *Stark Design*
CLIENT *W. W. Norton*

(facing page, bottom left)
Merit/National

SINGLE
Bebop
ART DIRECTOR *David Tran*
DESIGNER *Francine Kass*
PHOTOGRAPHY *Frank Driggs Collection,
Archive Photos*
CLIENT *Oxford University Press*

(facing page, bottom right)
Merit/National

SINGLE
City Signs
ART DIRECTOR *Sheri G. Lee*
DESIGNER *Sheri G. Lee*
COPYWRITER *Gail Deibler Finke*
ILLUSTRATOR *Sheri G. Lee*
STUDIO *joyfunstudio*
CLIENT *Madison Square Press*

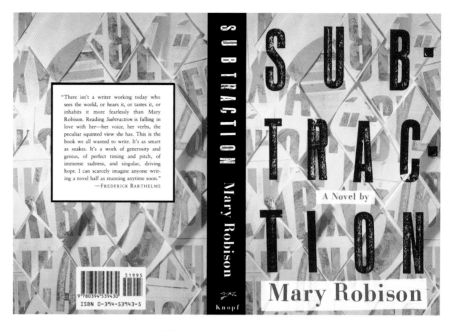

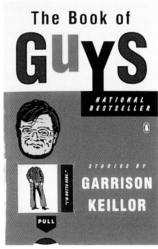

"There isn't a writer working today who sees the world, or hears it, or tastes it, or inhabits it more fearlessly than Mary Robison. Reading *Subtraction* is falling in love with her—her voice, her verbs, the peculiar squinted view she has. This is the book we all wanted to write. It's as smart as snakes. It's a work of generosity and genius, of perfect timing and pitch, of immense sadness, and singular, driving hope. I can scarcely imagine anyone writing a novel half as stunning anytime soon."
—FREDERICK BARTHELME

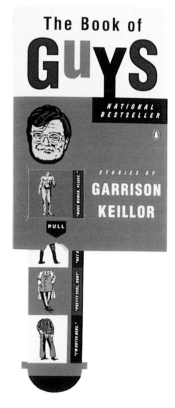

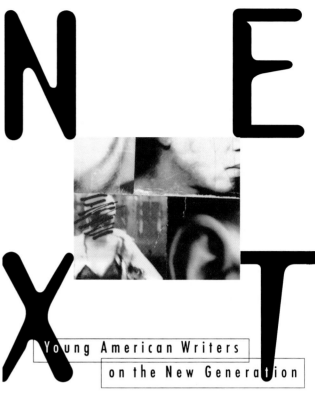

N E X T

Young American Writers
on the New Generation

edited by ERIC LIU

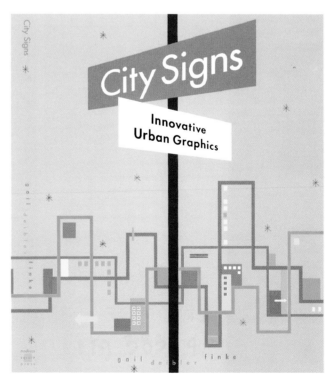

Merit/International

SINGLE
In the Language of Love
ART DIRECTORS *John Pylypczak, Diti Katona*
DESIGNERS *John Pylypczak, Renata Chubb*
PHOTOGRAPHER *Karen Levy*
STUDIO *Concrete Design Communications Inc.*
CLIENT *Harper Collins*

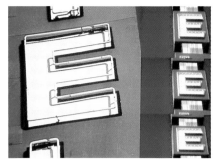

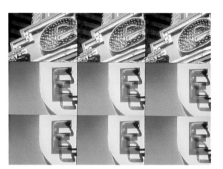

Merit/National

TITLE FOR PROMOTION, SINGLE
Q & E! Show Open
ART DIRECTOR *Jill Taffet*
CREATIVE DIRECTOR *Jill Taffet*
DESIGNER *Alice Song*
PHOTOGRAPHER *Stokes/Kohne*
PRODUCER *Karin Rainey*
MUSIC *Elyse Schiller, Jim Watson*
STUDIO *E! Entertainment Television*
CLIENT *E! Entertainment Television*

Merit/National

TITLE FOR PROMOTION, SINGLE
E! Sign ID: 10
ART DIRECTOR *Jill Taffet*
CREATIVE DIRECTOR *Jill Taffet*
DESIGNER *Laura Paresky*
PHOTOGRAPHER *Laura Paresky*
PRODUCER *Karin Rainey*
MUSIC *Elyse Schiller, Jim Watson*
STUDIO *E! Entertainment Television*
CLIENT *E! Entertainment Television*

Merit/National

TITLE FOR PROMOTION, SINGLE
Howard Stern Show Open
ART DIRECTOR *Jill Taffet*
CREATIVE DIRECTOR *Jill Taffet*
DESIGNER *Jill Taffet*
PRODUCERS *Karin Rainey, Ira Brooks*
PRODUCTION COMPANY *Travisano Digiacomo*
DIRECTOR *Jill Taffet*
MUSIC *John Wiggins*
CLIENT *E! Entertainment Television*

Merit/National

TITLE FOR PROMOTION, SINGLE
Wolf Promo
CREATIVE DIRECTORS *Marc Shmuger, Kyle Cooper*
DESIGNER *Garson Yu*
COPYWRITER *Steve Hull*
PRODUCER *J & G Productions with*
R/Greenberg Associates, West
DIRECTOR *Richard Greenberg*
STUDIO *Columbia Pictures*

Merit/National

TITLE FOR PROMOTION, SINGLE
E! Remembers Show Open
ART DIRECTOR *Jill Taffet*
CREATIVE DIRECTOR *Jill Taffet*
DESIGNER *Jill Taffet*
PRODUCER *Karin Rainey*
DIRECTOR *Fred Macdonald*
MUSIC *Elyse Schiller*
STUDIO *Olive Jar Animation*
CLIENT *E! Entertainment Television*

Merit/National

TITLE FOR PROMOTION, SINGLE
Nick at Nite Programming Tape
ART DIRECTOR *Alex Weil*
CREATIVE DIRECTOR *Lisa Judson*
DESIGNER *Alex Weil*
COPYWRITER *Alex Weil*
PRODUCER *Kim Rosenblum*
DIRECTOR *Alex Weil*
MUSIC *Tom Pomposello*
STUDIO *Charlex*
CLIENT *Nick at Nite Marketing*

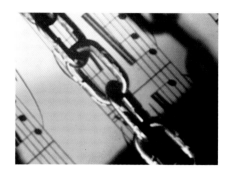

Merit/National

TITLE FOR PROMOTION, SINGLE
Saturday Night Live 20th-Anniversary Opening
DESIGNERS *John Dire, Michael Riley*
SPECIAL-EFFECTS EDITOR *Burtis Scott*
PHOTOGRAPHERS *Sheila Metzner (still photography),*
Toby Phillips (live-action photography)
PRODUCERS *R/Greenberg Associates,*
Savoy Commercials, NBC Productions
DIRECTORS *Toby Phillips, Jim Signorelli*
CLIENT *NBC/Saturday Night Live*

Merit/International

TITLE FOR PROMOTION, SINGLE
Super Saturday
ART DIRECTOR *Yasutaka Taga*
PHOTOGRAPHER *Yutaka Nozaki*
ILLUSTRATOR *Yasutaka Taga*
DIRECTOR *Shingo Kiritani*
AGENCY *Yasutaka Taga*
CLIENT *Kitanihon Broadcasting*

Merit/National

TITLE FOR PROMOTION, CAMPAIGN
VH1 Darcy's Music Packaging
ART DIRECTOR *Rob Grobengieser*
CREATIVE DIRECTOR *Lauren Zalaznick*
DESIGNERS *Anne Marie Gilligan, Thomas Gallagher*
PRODUCER *Rob Grobengieser*
DIRECTOR *Rob Grobengieser*
CLIENT *VH1*

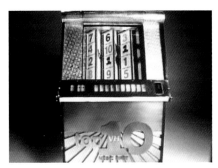

Merit/National

TITLE FOR PROMOTION, CAMPAIGN
VH1 Top-Ten Packaging
CREATIVE DIRECTOR *Lauren Zalaznick*
PRODUCER *Jon Klein*
DIRECTORS *Bill Price, Chris Weinstein*
AGENCY *Optic Nerve*
CLIENT *VH1*

Merit/International

TITLE FOR PROMOTION, CAMPAIGN
TV Addicts (Channel 4 Presentations,
Attention Grabbers)
ART DIRECTOR *Steve White*
CREATIVE DIRECTOR *Glenn Carwithen*
DESIGNER *Glenn Carwithen*
COPYWRITER *Glenn Carwithen*
PRODUCER *Charlie Druce*
DIRECTOR *Glenn Carwithen*
MUSIC *Nick Berry, Moulinaire SFX*
STUDIO *Brewers Production and Post-Production*
CLIENT *Channel 4*

Merit/National

SPECIAL EFFECTS AND COMPUTER GRAPHICS, SINGLE
Delivery
ART DIRECTORS *Rick Hansen, Russell Sinclair*
CREATIVE DIRECTOR *Charlie Miesmer*
COPYWRITERS *Ted Cohn, Peter Smith, Jimmy Segal*
COMPUTER GRAPHICS *R/Greenberg Associates*
PRODUCERS *Steve and Linda Horn Productions,
R/Greenberg Associates*
POST-PRODUCTION *R/Greenberg Associates*
DIRECTOR *Steve Horn*
MUSIC *Maverick Music*
AGENCY *BBDO New York*
CLIENT *Pizza Hut*

Merit/National

ANIMATION, SINGLE
Buy Low, Buy Lower
ART DIRECTOR *Bob Hoffman*
CREATIVE DIRECTOR *Bob Hoffman*
DESIGNER *David Levine*
COPYWRITER *Jay Courtney*
ILLUSTRATOR *David Levine*
PRODUCER *J. J. Sedelmaier*
DIRECTOR *J. J. Sedelmaier*
MUSIC *Shapiro*
AGENCY *Gearon/Hoffman*
STUDIO *J. J. Sedelmaier Productions, Inc.*
CLIENT *Brown & Company*

Merit/National

SINGLE
Scissors
ART DIRECTOR *Bernard Urban*
CREATIVE DIRECTOR *Joe Anson*
PHOTOGRAPHER *Bernard Urban*
AGENCY *Anson-Stoner Inc.*
CLIENT *Gary Lambert Salon*

Merit/International

SINGLE
Public Library St. Kilda Signage
ART DIRECTOR *Garry Emery*
CREATIVE DIRECTOR *Emery Vincent Design*
DESIGNER *Emery Vincent Design*
CLIENT *Ashton Raggett McDougall Architects*

Merit/National

CAMPAIGN
Red Tab Point-of-Sale Program
ART DIRECTOR *Steve Sandstrom*
CREATIVE DIRECTOR *Mike Koelker*
DESIGNER *Steve Sandstrom*
COPYWRITER *Mike Koelker*
AGENCY *Foote, Cone & Belding, San Francisco*
STUDIO *Sandstrom Design*
CLIENT *Levi Strauss & Co.*

Merit/National

CAMPAIGN
JBL OnBoard
ART DIRECTOR *Jane Brady*
CREATIVE DIRECTOR *Christian Uhl*
DESIGNER *Ben Segal*
COPYWRITER *Mike Mooney*
PHOTOGRAPHER *Mark Steele*
STUDIO *Fitch Inc.*
CLIENT *JBL Consumer Products*

(facing page)
Merit/International

CAMPAIGN
Shin-Yokohama Raumen Museum
ART DIRECTOR *Takanori Aiba*
DESIGNER *G & D*
PRODUCER *Takanori Aiba*
DIRECTOR *Takanori Aiba*
CLIENT *Shin-Yokohama Raumen Museum*

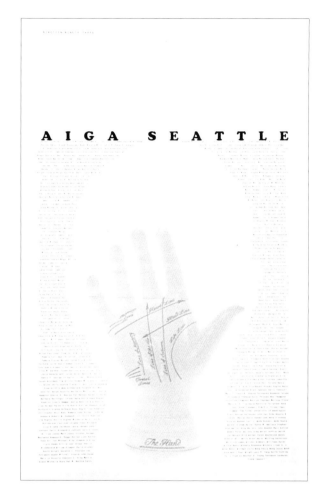

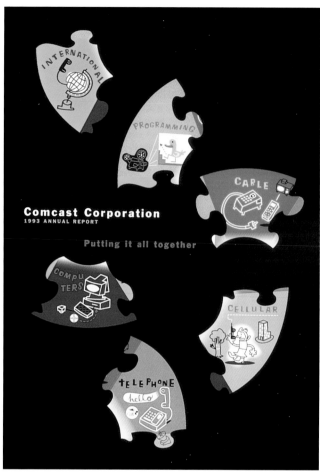

Merit/National

ANNUAL REPORT
AIGA, Seattle 1993 Annual Report
ART DIRECTOR *John Van Dyke*
CREATIVE DIRECTOR *John Van Dyke*
DESIGNER *John Van Dyke*
COPYWRITER *Karen Wilson*
PHOTOGRAPHER *Abrams/Lacagnina*
STUDIO *Van Dyke Company*
CLIENT *AIGA, Seattle*

Merit/National

ANNUAL REPORT
Comcast Corporation 1993 Annual Report
CREATIVE DIRECTORS *Aubrey Balkind, Kent Hunter*
DESIGNER *Kin Yuen*
COPYWRITERS *Michael Clive, Comcast Corporation*
PHOTOGRAPHERS *Various*
ILLUSTRATOR *J. Otto Siebold*
AGENCY *Frankfurt Balkind Partners*
CLIENT *Comcast Corporation*

Merit/National

ANNUAL REPORT
Sigma Circuits Annual Report 1994
ART DIRECTORS *George Mimnaugh, Joan Libera*
CREATIVE DIRECTOR *Joan Libera*
DESIGNER *George Mimnaugh*
ILLUSTRATOR *Marvin Mattelson*
STUDIO *Libera and Associates*
CLIENT *Sigma Circuits, Inc.*

Merit/National

ANNUAL REPORT
ICOS Corporation 1993 Annual Report
ART DIRECTOR *John Van Dyke*
CREATIVE DIRECTOR *John Van Dyke*
DESIGNERS *John Van Dyke, Ann Kumasaka*
COPYWRITERS *Tom McCarthy, ICOS Corporation*
PHOTOGRAPHER *Jeff Corwin*
ILLUSTRATOR *Stephanie Schilling*
STUDIO *Van Dyke Company*
CLIENT *ICOS Corporation*

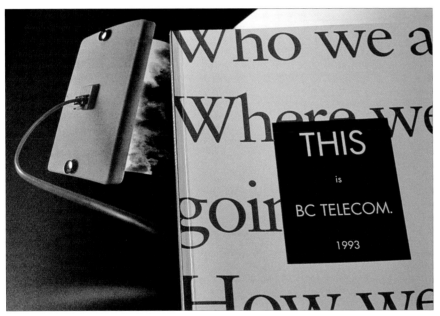

Merit/National

ANNUAL REPORT
BC Telecom 1993 Annual Report
ART DIRECTORS *John Van Dyke, Dave Mason*
CREATIVE DIRECTORS *John Van Dyke, Dave Mason*
DESIGNERS *John Van Dyke, Dave Mason*
COPYWRITER *Tom McCarthy*
PHOTOGRAPHER *Jim LaBounty*
STUDIO *A Design Collaborative*
CLIENT *BC Telecom*

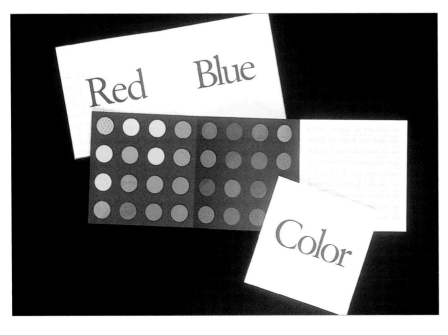

Merit/National

ANNUAL REPORT
Pallas Textiles In the Name of Color
ART DIRECTOR *Michael Gericke*
DESIGNERS *Donna Ching, Sharon Harel*
COPYWRITER *Maeve Slavin*
PHOTOGRAPHER *Luca Vignelli*
STUDIO *Pentagram Design*
CLIENT *Pallas Textiles*

Merit/National

ANNUAL REPORT
Success Is the One Thing No Woman Can Fake
ART DIRECTOR *Lara Gilmore*
CREATIVE DIRECTORS *Jane Talcott, Mike Rogers,*
John Staffen
COPYWRITER *Rachel Howald*
AGENCY *DDB Needham Worldwide/New York*
CLIENT *DDB Needham Worldwide/New York*

SUCCESS IS THE ONE THING NO WOMAN CAN FAKE.

DDB NEEDHAM APPLAUDS THE 1994 CLASS OF WOMEN ACHIEVERS.
OUR RESPECT AND ADMIRATION TO YOU ALL, ESPECIALLY OUR OWN DAWN HUDSON.

Merit/National

ANNUAL REPORT
Natural Resources Defense Council 1993
Annual Report
ART DIRECTOR *Jurek Wajdowicz*
DESIGNERS *Lisa LaRochelle, Jurek Wajdowicz*
COPYWRITERS *Emilie Trautmann,*
Kathrin Day Lassila
PHOTOGRAPHERS *Richard Elkins and others*
STUDIO *Emerson, Wajdowicz Studios, Inc.*
CLIENT *Natural Resources Defense Council*

NATURAL RESOURCES DEFENSE COUNCIL 1993 Annual Report

Merit/National

ANNUAL REPORT
Molecular Dynamics 1993 Annual Report
ART DIRECTOR *Bill Cahan*
CREATIVE DIRECTOR *Bill Cahan*
DESIGNER *Bob Dinetz*
COPYWRITER *Carole Melis*
PHOTOGRAPHER *Mark Hanauer*
STUDIO *Cahan & Associates*
CLIENT *Molecular Dynamics*

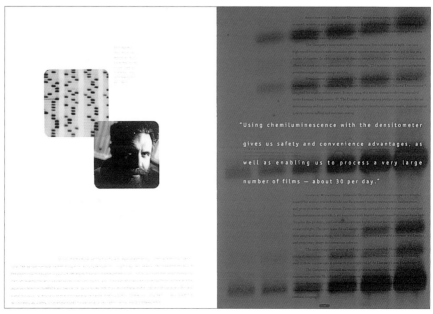

"Using chemiluminescence with the densitometer gives us safety and convenience advantages, as well as enabling us to process a very large number of films — about 30 per day."

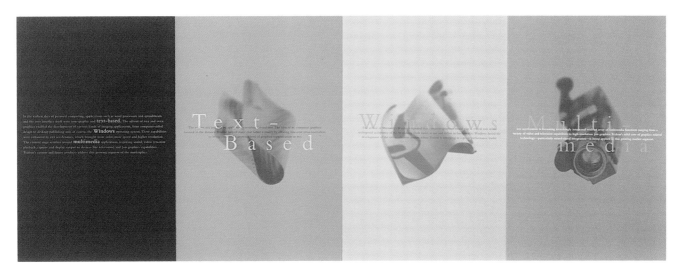

Merit/National

ANNUAL REPORT
Trident Microsystems 1994 Annual Report
ART DIRECTOR *Bill Cahan*
CREATIVE DIRECTOR *Bill Cahan*
DESIGNER *Bob Dinetz*
COPYWRITER *Tim Peters*
PHOTOGRAPHER *Holly Stewart*
STUDIO *Cahan & Associates*
CLIENT *Trident Microsystems, Inc.*

Merit/National

ANNUAL REPORT
The Limited 1993 Annual Report
CREATIVE DIRECTORS *Kent Hunter, Aubrey Balkind*
DESIGNERS *Robert Wong, Arturo Aranda*
COPYWRITER *Robert Minkoff*
PHOTOGRAPHERS *Julie Powell and others*
AGENCY *Frankfurt Balkind Partners*
CLIENT *The Limited, Inc.*

Merit/National

ANNUAL REPORT
Landmark Annual Report
ART DIRECTOR *Amy Elizabeth Farr*
CREATIVE DIRECTOR *Eric Haggman*
DESIGNER *Amy Elizabeth Farr*
COPYWRITERS *Eric Haggman, Peter Caroline*
AGENCY *Haggman Advertising*
CLIENT *Massachusetts Government Land Bank*

Merit/National

ANNUAL REPORT
1993 Houston Public Television Annual Report
ART DIRECTOR *Mark Geer*
DESIGNER *Mark Geer*
COPYWRITERS *Joe Militello, Karen Kephart*
PHOTOGRAPHY *Station Archives*
STUDIO *Geer Design, Inc.*
CLIENT *Houston Public Television*

Merit/National

ANNUAL REPORT
The Rockefeller Foundation Annual Report
ART DIRECTORS *Susan Evans, Brian Sisco*
DESIGN FIRM *Sisco & Evans Ltd.*
DESIGNERS *Susan Evans, Brian Sisco*
PHOTOGRAPHERS *Jonathan Becker and others*
CLIENT *The Rockefeller Foundation*

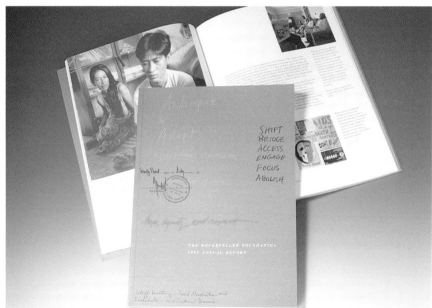

Merit/National

ANNUAL REPORT
One Company Divided
ART DIRECTOR *Steve Wedeen*
CREATIVE DIRECTOR *Steve Wedeen*
DESIGNER *Steve Wedeen*
COPYWRITER *Steve Wedeen*
PHOTOGRAPHER *Michael Barley*
STUDIO *Vaughn Wedeen Creative*
CLIENT *Lasertechnics, Inc.*

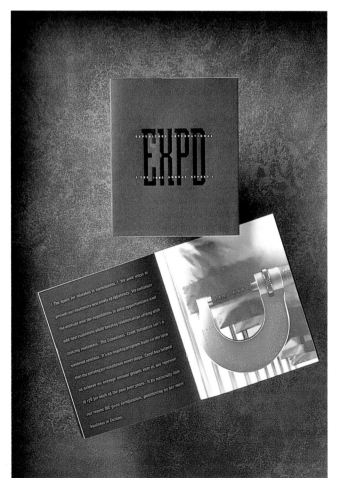

Merit/National

ANNUAL REPORT
Horizon Bank, a Savings Bank: The Fiscal 1994
Annual Report
ART DIRECTOR *Kerry Leimer*
CREATIVE DIRECTOR *Kerry Leimer*
DESIGNER *Kerry Leimer*
COPYWRITER *David Eldred*
PHOTOGRAPHER *Tyler Boley*
STUDIO *Leimer Cross Design*
CLIENT *Horizon Bank*

Merit/National

ANNUAL REPORT
Aldus Corporation 1993 Annual Report
ART DIRECTOR *Kerry Leimer*
CREATIVE DIRECTOR *Kerry Leimer*
DESIGNERS *Kerry Leimer, Craig Terrones*
COPYWRITER *Kerry Leimer*
PHOTOGRAPHER *Tyler Boley*
ILLUSTRATOR *Mark Fox*
STUDIO *Leimer Cross Design*
CLIENT *Aldus Corporation*

Merit/National

ANNUAL REPORT
Expeditors International 1993 Annual Report
ART DIRECTOR *Kerry Leimer*
CREATIVE DIRECTOR *Kerry Leimer*
DESIGNER *Kerry Leimer*
COPYWRITER *Kerry Leimer*
PHOTOGRAPHER *Tyler Boley*
STUDIO *Leimer Cross Design*
CLIENT *Expeditors International*

Merit/National

ANNUAL REPORT
ARIAD Pharmaceuticals 1993 Annual Report
ART DIRECTOR *Woody Pirtle*
DESIGNERS *John Klotnia, Ivette Montes de Oca*
PHOTOGRAPHER *Ivette Montes de Oca*
STUDIO *Pentagram Design*
CLIENT *ARIAD Pharmaceuticals*

Merit/National

ANNUAL REPORT
Portland Brewing Annual Report
ART DIRECTOR *Sally Morrow*
DESIGNER *Sally Morrow*
COPYWRITER *Portland Brewing*
PHOTOGRAPHY *Stock*
ILLUSTRATIONS *Stock*
AGENCY *Sandstrom Design*
CLIENT *Portland Brewing*

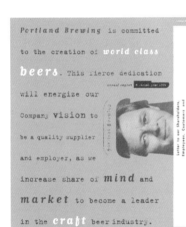

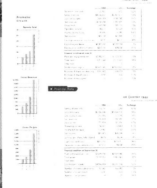

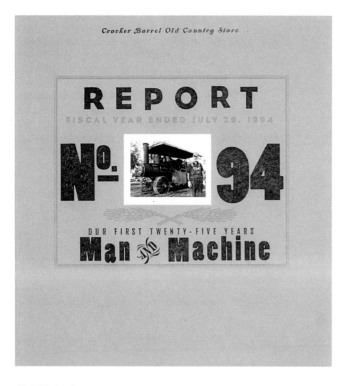

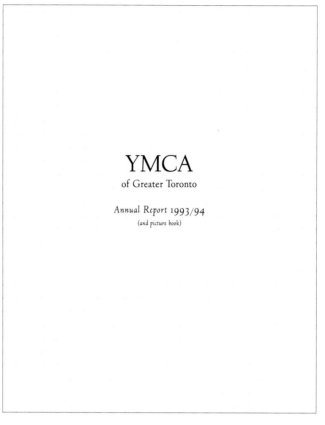

Merit/National

ANNUAL REPORT
Cracker Barrel Old Country Store
1994 Annual Report
ART DIRECTOR *Thomas Ryan*
CREATIVE DIRECTOR *Thomas Ryan*
DESIGNER *Thomas Ryan*
COPYWRITER *John Baeder*
PHOTOGRAPHER *McGuire*
ILLUSTRATOR *Paul Ritscher*
AGENCY *Corporate Communications, Inc.*
STUDIO *Thomas Ryan Design*
CLIENT *Cracker Barrel Old Country Store, Inc.*

Merit/International

ANNUAL REPORT
YMCA Annual Report
ART DIRECTORS *John Pylypczak, Diti Katona*
DESIGNERS *John Pylypczak, Renata Chubb*
PHOTOGRAPHERS *John Pylypczak, Diti Katona,*
Roman Pylypczak
STUDIO *Concrete Design Communications Inc.*
CLIENT *YMCA*

Merit/International

ANNUAL REPORT
Superior Metal Printing 1993 Annual Report
ART DIRECTOR *Craig Hutton*
CREATIVE DIRECTOR *Craig Hutton*
DESIGNER *Craig Hutton*
COPYWRITER *John Lim*
PHOTOGRAPHER *Hatty Gottschalk*
STUDIO *Su Yeang Design*
CLIENT *Superior Metal Printing*

Merit/International

ANNUAL REPORT
Annual Report 1993/1994
ART DIRECTOR *Silvio Galbucci*
CREATIVE DIRECTOR *Silvio Galbucci*
PHOTOGRAPHER *Patrick Rohner*
ILLUSTRATOR *Schnitzler Schule*
AGENCY *Matter Galbucci Leo Burnett*
CLIENT *Association of Foreign Banks in Switzerland*

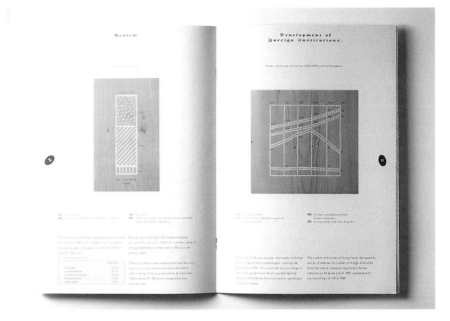

Merit/International

ANNUAL REPORT
19th Brazilian Creative Annual
ART DIRECTOR *Javier Talavera*
CREATIVE DIRECTOR *Javier Talavera*
DESIGNER *Claudia Issa*
PHOTOGRAPHERS *Arnaldo Pappalardo,*
Reinaldo Coser
PRODUCER *Fabio B. Cardoso*
AGENCY *Foote, Cone & Belding, São Paulo*
CLIENT *Clube de Criação de São Paulo*

Merit/National

BOOKLET, FOLDER, OR BROCHURE, SINGLE
SYZYGY
ART DIRECTOR *Matthew L. Doty*
DESIGNER *Matthew L. Doty*
COPYWRITER *Matthew L. Doty*
PHOTOGRAPHER *Barbara Strong Doty*
ILLUSTRATOR *Matthew L. Doty*
PRODUCERS *Matthew L. Doty, Barbara Strong Doty*
ILLUSTRATOR *Lili Hertzler*
AGENCY *Strong Productions, Inc.*
CLIENT *Strong Productions, Inc.*

Merit/National

BOOKLET, FOLDER, OR BROCHURE, SINGLE
Advancing the Science of Investing
ART DIRECTOR *John Bielenberg*
CREATIVE DIRECTOR *Greg Galle*
DESIGNERS *John Bielenberg, Allen Ashton*
COPYWRITER *Maureen Oddone*
PHOTOGRAPHER *Doug Menuez*
AGENCY *Mathew Krieger & Associates*
STUDIO *Bielenberg Design*
CLIENT *Wells Fargo Nikko Investment Advisors*

Merit/National

BOOKLET, FOLDER, OR BROCHURE, SINGLE
Albert Paley: Organic Logic
DESIGNERS *Michael Bierut, Esther Bridavsky*
PHOTOGRAPHER *Bruce Miller*
STUDIO *Pentagram Design*
CLIENT *Peter Joseph Gallery*

Merit/National

BOOKLET, FOLDER, OR BROCHURE, SINGLE
MTV Video Music Awards Program Guide
ART DIRECTORS *Stacy Drummond, Jeffrey Keyton, Tracy Boychuk, David Felton, Johan Vipper*
ILLUSTRATORS *Various*
AGENCY *MTV Off Air Creative*
CLIENT *MTV Music Television*

Merit/National

ANNUAL REPORT
Woodland Park Zoological Society 1993
Annual Report
ART DIRECTOR *Dennis Clouse*
DESIGNERS *Dennis Clouse, Traci Daberko*
COPYWRITERS *Dennis Clouse, J. Pasquarelli*
PHOTOGRAPHERS *Dennis Clouse, Traci Daberko*
ILLUSTRATOR *Dennis Clouse*
STUDIO *The Leonhardt Group*
CLIENT *Woodland Park Zoological Society, Seattle*

Merit/National

BOOKLET, FOLDER, OR BROCHURE, SINGLE
Redefining the Instant Image
ART DIRECTOR *Jon Craine*
CREATIVE DIRECTOR *Jon Craine*
DESIGNERS *John Rushworth, Jon Craine*
ILLUSTRATOR *Pentagram, United Kingdom*
PRODUCER *Polaroid Corporation, United Kingdom*
CLIENT *Polaroid Corporation*

Merit/National

BOOKLET, FOLDER, OR BROCHURE, SINGLE
Art Catalogue for Armory Show, November 1994
ART DIRECTOR *Kimberly Baer*
CREATIVE DIRECTOR *Kimberly Baer*
DESIGNER *Margaret van Oppen*
COPYWRITERS *Karen Moss, Carolyn Wendt*
PHOTOGRAPHER *David Familian*
STUDIO *Kimberly Baer Design Associates*
CLIENT *Pasadena Art Alliance*

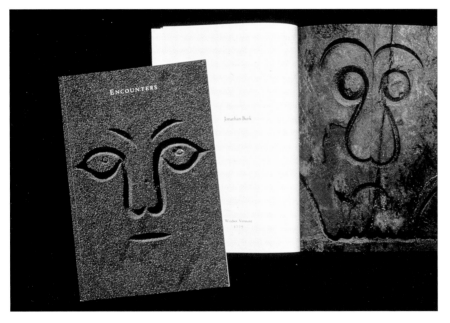

Merit/National

BOOKLET, FOLDER, OR BROCHURE, SINGLE
Encounters
DESIGNER *Catt Lyon Design*
PHOTOGRAPHER *Gregory Thorpe*
CLIENT *The Hennegan Company*

Merit/National

BOOKLET, FOLDER, OR BROCHURE, SINGLE
Champion Explained Corporate Booklet
ART DIRECTORS *Stephen Doyle, Tom Kluepfel*
DESIGNERS *Chuck Robertson, Mats Hakansson,*
Vanessa Eckstein, Gary Tooth
STUDIO *Drenttel Doyle Partners*
CLIENT *Champion International Corporation*

Merit/National

BOOKLET, FOLDER, OR BROCHURE, SINGLE
The Aeron Chair by Herman Miller
ART DIRECTOR *Michael Barile*
CREATIVE DIRECTOR *Michael Barile*
DESIGNERS *Michael Barile, Yang Kim*
COPYWRITER *Debra Wierenga*
PHOTOGRAPHERS *Nick Merrick, Jim Hedrich*
ILLUSTRATOR *Gould Design*
PRINTER *Etheridge Company*
CLIENT *Herman Miller Inc.*

Merit/National

BOOKLET, FOLDER, OR BROCHURE, SINGLE
Country Music Memories
ART DIRECTOR *Marti Golon*
DIRECTOR OF DESIGN *Tom Bentkowski*
PHOTO EDITOR *Adrienne Aurichio*
PHOTOGRAPHER *Hans Neleman*
CLIENT *Life Magazine*

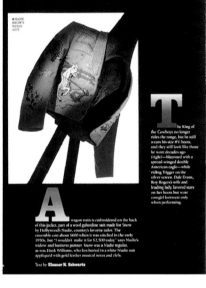

Merit/National

BOOKLET, FOLDER, OR BROCHURE, SINGLE
Ethical Culture Fieldston Schools Viewbook
ART DIRECTOR *Anthony Rutka*
DESIGNER *Priscilla Henderer*
COPYWRITER *Joan Weadock*
PHOTOGRAPHER *Mark Jenkinson*
STUDIO *Rutka Weadock Design*
CLIENT *Ethical Culture Fieldston Schools*

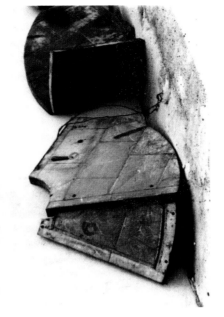

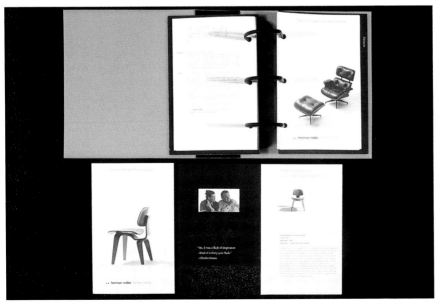

Merit/National

BOOKLET, FOLDER, OR BROCHURE, SINGLE
Objects: Sixteen L.A. Sculptors
ART DIRECTOR *Rebeca Méndez*
DESIGNER *Darin Beaman*
COPYWRITERS *The featured artists*
PHOTOGRAPHERS *Art Center photography students*
STUDIO *Art Center Design Office*
CLIENT *Art Center College of Design*

Merit/National

BOOKLET, FOLDER, OR BROCHURE, SINGLE
Grayhawk
ART DIRECTOR *Steve Ditko*
CREATIVE DIRECTOR *Steve Ditko*
DESIGNERS *Steve Ditko, Stacy Johansen*
COPYWRITER *Jerry Rose*
ILLUSTRATOR *John Kleber*
STUDIO *CFD Design*
CLIENT *Grayhawk Development*

Merit/National

BOOKLET, FOLDER, OR BROCHURE, SINGLE
Herman Miller for the Home Binder
ART DIRECTOR *Michael Barile*
CREATIVE DIRECTOR *Michael Barile*
DESIGNERS *Michael Barile, Yang Kim, Adam Smith,
Glenn Hoffman*
COPYWRITER *Dick Holm*
PHOTOGRAPHY *Phil Schaafsma,
Herman Miller Archives*
PRINTER *Burch Inc.*
CLIENT *Herman Miller Inc.*

Merit/National

BOOKLET, FOLDER, OR BROCHURE, SINGLE
Motorola It Doesn't Take a Genius Kit
ART DIRECTOR *James Carlton*
CREATIVE DIRECTOR *James Carlton*
DESIGNERS *Krista Ferdinand, Victoria Huang*
COPYWRITER *Brian Agne*
ILLUSTRATOR *Richard Goldberg*
STUDIO *Design Horizons International*
CLIENT *Motorola*

Merit/National

BOOKLET, FOLDER, OR BROCHURE, SINGLE
Brochure
ART DIRECTOR *Nora Vaivads*
CREATIVE DIRECTOR *Gary Goldsmith*
DESIGNER *Nora Vaivads*
COPYWRITER *Justin Rohrlich*
PHOTOGRAPHY *Stock*
STUDIO *Goldsmith/Jeffrey*
CLIENT *CondoExchange*

Merit/National

BOOKLET, FOLDER, OR BROCHURE, SINGLE
1995 Consumer Catalogue
ART DIRECTOR *David Covell*
CREATIVE DIRECTOR *Michael Jager*
DESIGNERS *David Covell, Ian Factor, Dan Sharp,*
Jim Anfuso, Mark Sylvester, John Phemister
COPYWRITER *David Shriber*
STUDIO *Jager Di Paola Kemp Design*
CLIENT *Burton Snowboards*

Merit/National

BOOKLET, FOLDER, OR BROCHURE, SINGLE
Hush Puppies Riverbuck Brochure
ART DIRECTOR *Jaimie Alexander*
DESIGNER *Paul Westrick*
COPYWRITER *Sarah Spatt*
PHOTOGRAPHER *Mark Steele*
STUDIO *Fitch Inc.*
CLIENT *Hush Puppies Company*

Merit/National

BOOKLET, FOLDER, OR BROCHURE, SINGLE
Buttered Side Up Brochure
ART DIRECTOR *David Lerch*
DESIGNER *David Lerch*
COPYWRITERS *Bernard Brunon, Edward Albee,*
Mary Ross Taylor
PHOTOGRAPHER *Thomas A. DuBrock*
STUDIO *Geer Design, Inc.*
CLIENT *Lawndale Art and Performance Center*

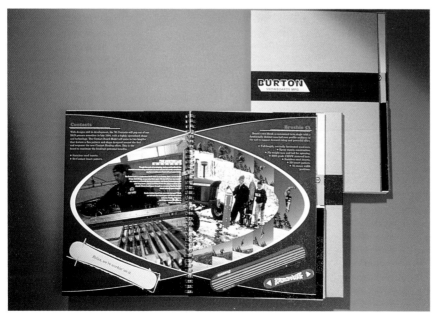

Merit/National

BOOKLET, FOLDER, OR BROCHURE, SINGLE
1995 Dealer Catalogue
ART DIRECTOR *David Covell*
CREATIVE DIRECTOR *Michael Jager*
DESIGNERS *David Covell, Ian Factor, Dan Sharp,*
Keith Brown
COPYWRITER *David Shriber*
STUDIO *Jager Di Paola Kemp Design*
CLIENT *Burton Snowboards*

Merit/National

BOOKLET, FOLDER, OR BROCHURE, SINGLE
Connections 2: Explorations in the Getty Center
Collections Brochure
DESIGNER *Mike Fink*
STUDIO *J. Paul Getty Trust, Publication Services*
CLIENT *The Getty Center for the History of Art and*
the Humanities

Merit/National

BOOKLET, FOLDER, OR BROCHURE, SINGLE
Kivar Performa for DSI
ART DIRECTOR *Mickey Boisvert*
DESIGNER *Mickey Boisvert*
COPYWRITER *Susan G. Mattei*
PHOTOGRAPHER *Adam Laipson*
CLIENT *Decorative Specialties International Inc.*

Merit/National

BOOKLET, FOLDER, OR BROCHURE, SINGLE
Separating Black and White Photography
ART DIRECTOR *Tom Geismar*
DESIGNER *Cathy Schaefer*
PHOTOGRAPHER *David Arky*
STUDIO *Chermayeff & Geismar*
CLIENT *Monadnock Paper Mills, Inc.*

Merit/National

BOOKLET, FOLDER, OR BROCHURE, SINGLE
Stochastic Screening: Pre-Press Issues
ART DIRECTOR *Tom Geismar*
DESIGNER *Cathy Schaefer*
PHOTOGRAPHER *David Arky*
STUDIO *Chermayeff & Geismar*
CLIENT *Monadnock Paper Mills, Inc.*

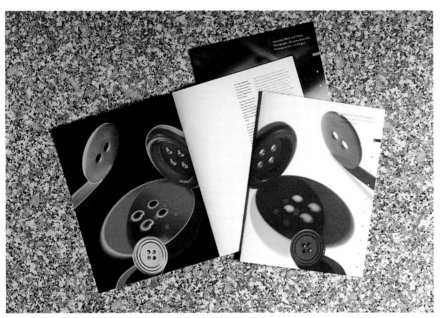

Merit/National

BOOKLET, FOLDER, OR BROCHURE, SINGLE
Separating Color Photography: Pre-Press Issues
ART DIRECTOR *Tom Geismar*
DESIGNER *Cathy Schaefer*
PHOTOGRAPHER *David Arky*
STUDIO *Chermayeff & Geismar*
CLIENT *Monadnock Paper Mills, Inc.*

Merit/National

BOOKLET, FOLDER, OR BROCHURE, SINGLE
Alfred Now: Contemporary American Ceramics
ART DIRECTOR *Renate Gokl*
DESIGNER *Renate Gokl*
COPYWRITERS *Donald Kuspit, Nancy Weekly*
PHOTOGRAPHER *Brian Oglesbee*
CLIENT *Krannert Art Museum*

Merit/National

BOOKLET, FOLDER, OR BROCHURE, SINGLE
Hartwick Recruitment Publications
ART DIRECTOR *Anthony Rutka*
DESIGNER *Priscilla Henderer*
COPYWRITER *Joan Weadock*
PHOTOGRAPHERS *David Zickl, Bob Krist,*
Daniel Husted
ILLUSTRATORS *Reagan Dunnick, Scott Morgan,*
Michael Halbert, Joel Peter Johnson, Brian Cairns,
Robert Neubecker, Gary Kelley, Dan Yaccarino,
Anthony Chiappin, Tom Garrett, Lisa Adams,
Sandra Hendler, Susan Blubaugh
STUDIO *Rutka Weadock Design*
CLIENT *Hartwick College*

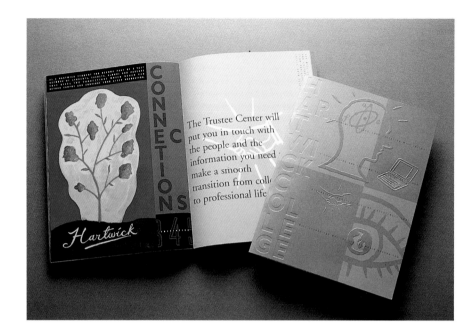

Merit/National

BOOKLET, FOLDER, OR BROCHURE, SINGLE
Remembering the WPA
ART DIRECTOR *Don Sibley*
DESIGNERS *Don Sibley, Donna Aldridge*
COPYWRITER *Kevin Johnson*
PHOTOGRAPHERS *Various*
ILLUSTRATORS *Various*
STUDIO *Sibley/Peteet Design*
CLIENT *Weyerhauser Paper Company*

Merit/National

BOOKLET, FOLDER, OR BROCHURE, SINGLE
Captured Spirits: John Geldersma Sculpture 1964–1994
ART DIRECTOR *Megan Barra*
CREATIVE DIRECTOR *Herman Mhire*
DESIGNER *Megan Barra*
COPYWRITER *William Moreland*
PHOTOGRAPHERS *Robley Dupleix, John Chaisson*
ARTWORK *John Geldersma*
STUDIO *Trinity Design & Advertising for the*
Creative Spirit
CLIENT *University Art Museum*

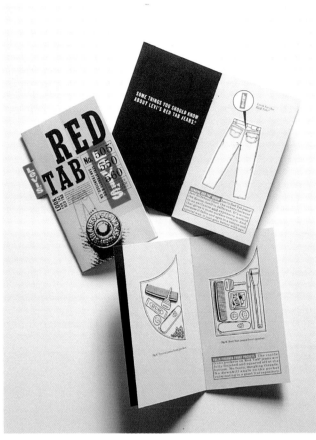

A photographic gallery **1** Three

M E T E R

Merit/National

BOOKLET, FOLDER, OR BROCHURE, SINGLE
*Surface Level 1994: Laminate Surfaces from
Formica Corporation*
ART DIRECTOR *Kevin B. Kuester*
CREATIVE DIRECTOR *Kevin B. Kuester*
DESIGNER *Bob Goebel*
COPYWRITER *David Forney*
PHOTOGRAPHERS *Don Freeman, New York,
Dayton's Photo Studio, Minneapolis*
AGENCY *The Kuester Group*
CLIENT *Formica Corporation*

Merit/National

BOOKLET, FOLDER, OR BROCHURE, SINGLE
Red Tab Pocket Brochure
ART DIRECTOR *Steve Sandstrom*
CREATIVE DIRECTOR *Mike Koelker*
DESIGNER *Steve Sandstrom*
COPYWRITER *Mike Koelker*
AGENCY *Foote, Cone & Belding, San Francisco*
STUDIO *Sandstrom Design*
CLIENT *Levi Strauss & Co.*

Merit/National

BOOKLET, FOLDER, OR BROCHURE, SINGLE
Meter Catalogue
ART DIRECTOR *Danielle Flagg*
CREATIVE DIRECTORS *Marty Weiss, Nat Whitten*
COPYWRITER *Marty Weiss*
AGENCY *Weiss, Whitten, Stagliano, Inc.*
CLIENT *Weiss, Whitten, Stagliano, Inc.*

Merit/International

BOOKLET, FOLDER, OR BROCHURE, SINGLE
This Is Me
ART DIRECTOR *Robin Hunnam*
CREATIVE DIRECTOR *Robin Hunnam*
DESIGNER *Robin Hunnam*
COPYWRITER *Conrad Bird*
ILLUSTRATORS *14 twentieth-century artists*
CLIENT *ID Kort AB*

Merit/International

BOOKLET, FOLDER, OR BROCHURE, SINGLE
Habsburg Brochure Spring/Summer 1995:
Fine Hunting and Society Fashion
ART DIRECTOR *Franz Merlicek*
CREATIVE DIRECTOR *Franz Merlicek*
DESIGNER *Harald Stroebel*
COPYWRITER *Andreas Putz*
PHOTOGRAPHY *Bernhard Angerer and stock*
ILLUSTRATOR *Juergen Mick*
PRODUCER *Werner Stupka*
AGENCY *Demner & Merlicek*
CLIENT *Kleidermanufaktur Habsburg*

Merit/International

BOOKLET, FOLDER, OR BROCHURE, SINGLE
The Blue Book
ART DIRECTOR *Feico Derschow*
CREATIVE DIRECTOR *Manfred Riemel*
DESIGNER *Feico Derschow*
COPYWRITER *Manfred Riemel*
PHOTOGRAPHER *Horst Stasny*
PRODUCER *Sabine Huelss*
CLIENT *Eiler & Riemel*

Merit/National

BOOKLET, FOLDER, OR BROCHURE, SERIES
Knoll Parachute
ART DIRECTOR *Tom Geismar*
DESIGNERS *Emanuela Frigerio, Weston Bingham*
COPYWRITER *David Boorstin*
PHOTOGRAPHERS *Bill White, Laurance Aiuppy,*
Paul Harris
STUDIO *Chermayeff & Geismar*
CLIENT *The Knoll Group*

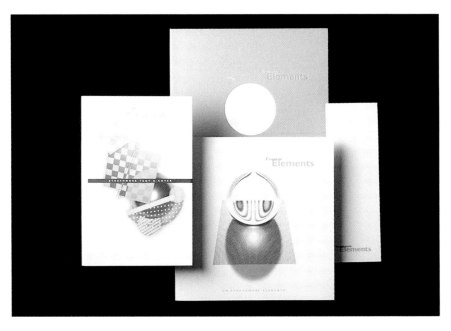

Merit/National

BOOKLET, FOLDER, OR BROCHURE, SERIES
Elements Introductory Package
ART DIRECTORS *Margaret Biedel, James A. Sebastian*
CREATIVE DIRECTOR *James A. Sebastian*
DESIGNERS *James A. Sebastian, Margaret Biedel,*
Brian Fingeret, Sarah Kloman, Frank Nichols
COPYWRITERS *Brian Fingeret, Margaret Biedel,*
Sarah Kloman
PHOTOGRAPHERS *Various*
ILLUSTRATORS *Various*
STUDIO *Designframe Inc.*
CLIENT *Strathmore Paper Co.*

Merit/National

BOOKLET, FOLDER, OR BROCHURE, SERIES
T. J. Martell
ART DIRECTOR *Scott Wadler*
DESIGNERS *Scott Wadler, Tim Morse,*
Todd Barthelman, Karl Cantarella
COPYWRITERS *Cheryl Family, David Shane*
ILLUSTRATORS *Tim Morse, Karl Cantarella*
AGENCY *MTV Networks Creative Services*
CLIENT *T. J. Martell*

(facing page)
Merit/National

BOOKLET, FOLDER, OR BROCHURE, SERIES
SVRA Covers
ART DIRECTOR *John Muller*
CREATIVE DIRECTOR *John Muller*
DESIGNERS *Shana Eck, John Muller*
COPYWRITER *David Marks*
PHOTOGRAPHER *Klemantaski*
AGENCY *Muller & Company*
CLIENT *Sportscar Vintage Racing Association*

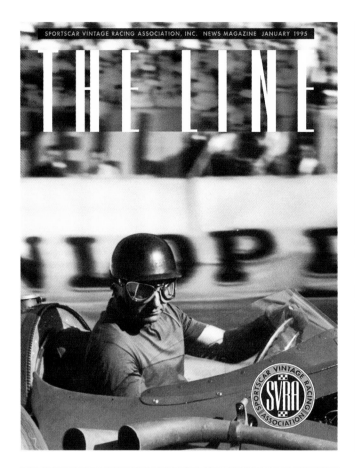

SPORTSCAR VINTAGE RACING ASSOCIATION, INC. NEWS MAGAZINE JANUARY 1995

THE LINE

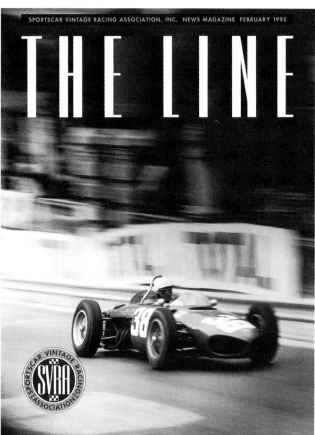

SPORTSCAR VINTAGE RACING ASSOCIATION, INC. NEWS MAGAZINE FEBRUARY 1995

THE LINE

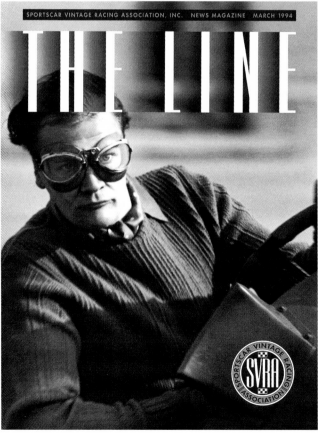

SPORTSCAR VINTAGE RACING ASSOCIATION, INC. NEWS MAGAZINE MARCH 1994

THE LINE

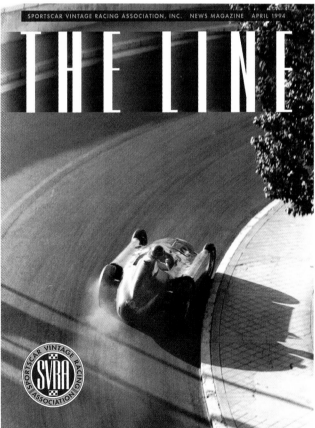

SPORTSCAR VINTAGE RACING ASSOCIATION, INC. NEWS MAGAZINE APRIL 1994

THE LINE

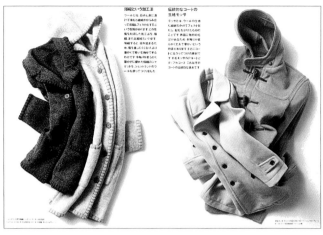

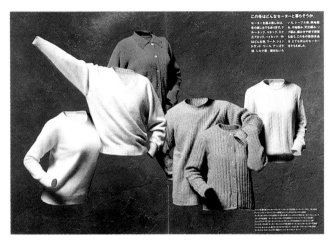

Merit/International

BOOKLET, FOLDER, OR BROCHURE, SERIES
Mujirushi-Ryohin Clothing Catalogue, Winter 1994
ART DIRECTOR *Masaaki Hiromura*
BRAND DIRECTORS *Ikko Tanaka, Kazuko Koike*
DESIGNERS *Masaaki Hiromura, Toshiyuki Kojima*
COPYWRITER *Yoichi Umemoto*
PHOTOGRAPHER *Takashi Oyama*
ILLUSTRATOR *Kazuya Takeuchi*
CLIENT *Ryohin-Keikaku Co., Ltd.*

Merit/International

BOOKLET, FOLDER, OR BROCHURE, SERIES
Bally Magalogues
ART DIRECTOR *Antonie Reinhard*
CREATIVE DIRECTOR *Antonie Reinhard*
DESIGNER *Martin Gaberthüel*
COPYWRITER *Margrit Brunswick*
PHOTOGRAPHER *Hanspeter Schneider*
AGENCY *Seiler DDB Needham AG Bern*
CLIENT *Bally International AG*

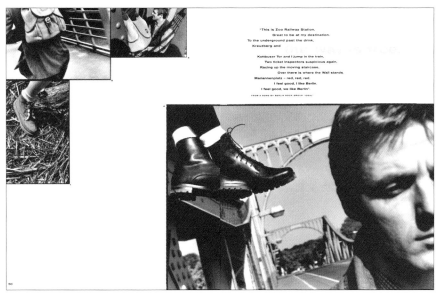

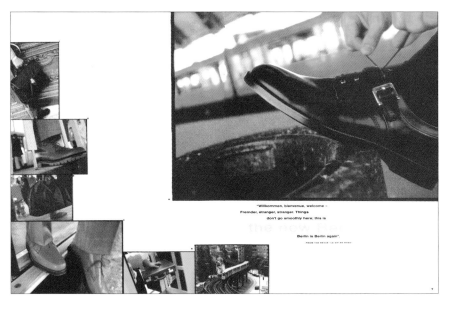

Merit/International

BOOKLET, FOLDER, OR BROCHURE, SERIES
Butterfield & Robinson Winter Trips
ART DIRECTOR *Frank Viva*
CREATIVE DIRECTORS *Frank Viva, Doug Dolan*
DESIGNER *Frank Viva*
COPYWRITER *Doug Dolan*
ILLUSTRATORS *Frank Viva, Karen Satok*
STUDIO *Viva Dolan Communications & Design*
CLIENT *Butterfield & Robinson*

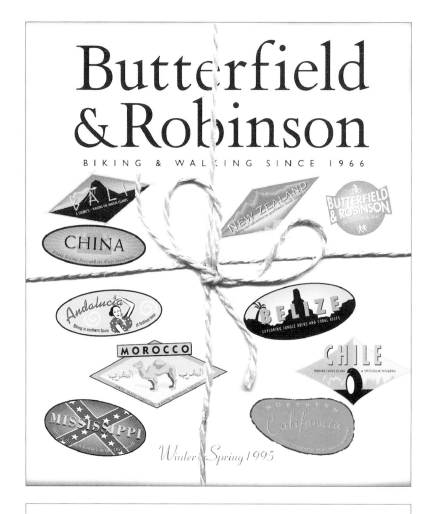

Merit/International

BOOKLET, FOLDER, OR BROCHURE, SERIES
Butterfield & Robinson Homes Away
ART DIRECTOR *Frank Viva*
CREATIVE DIRECTORS *Frank Viva, Doug Dolan*
DESIGNER *Karen Satok*
COPYWRITER *Doug Dolan*
STUDIO *Viva Dolan Communications & Design*
CLIENT *Butterfield & Robinson*

Merit/National

PACKAGING, SINGLE
Carta Italiana
ART DIRECTOR *Louise Fili*
CREATIVE DIRECTOR *Louise Fili*
DESIGNER *Louise Fili*
ILLUSTRATOR *Melanie Parks*
STUDIO *Louise Fili Ltd.*
CLIENT *Chronicle Books*

Merit/National

PACKAGING, SINGLE
Nick at Nite Upfront Folder
ART DIRECTOR *Kenna Kay*
CREATIVE DIRECTOR *Lisa Judson*
DESIGNER *Sharon Werner*
COPYWRITERS *Evan Baily, Alan Katz*
ILLUSTRATOR *Sharon Werner*
CLIENT *Nickelodeon*

Merit/National

PACKAGING, SINGLE
Moonshine Shoe Creme
ART DIRECTOR *Marion English*
CREATIVE DIRECTOR *Terry Slaughter*
DESIGNER *Marion English*
PHOTOGRAPHER *David Webb*
AGENCY *Slaughter-Hanson*
CLIENT *Plainclothes—Private Label Shoe Polish*

Merit/National

PACKAGING, SINGLE
Afterburn CD
ART DIRECTOR *Carlos Segura*
CREATIVE DIRECTOR *Carlos Segura*
DESIGNER *Carlos Segura*
PHOTOGRAPHER *Eric Dinyer*
ILLUSTRATOR *Carlos Segura*
STUDIO *Segura Inc.*
CLIENT *TVT Records, Waxtrax Records*

Merit/National

PACKAGING, SINGLE
Audubon Coffee Label
ART DIRECTOR *Miriam Lisco*
CREATIVE DIRECTOR *Miriam Lisco*
DESIGNERS *Miriam Lisco, Michael Stearns*
COPYWRITERS *Lynn Parker, Parker LePla*
ARTWORK *John James Audubon, Stark Museum of Art,*
Orange, Texas
CLIENT *Park Bench, Inc., dba Audubon Coffee™*

Merit/National

PACKAGING, SINGLE
Madonna "Bedtime Stories" Special Package
ART DIRECTORS *Fabien Baron, Patrick Li*
DESIGNERS *Fabien Baron, Patrick Li*
PHOTOGRAPHER *Patrick Demarchelier*
STUDIO *Baron & Baron Advertising*
CLIENT *Warner Bros. Records, Maverick, Sire Records*

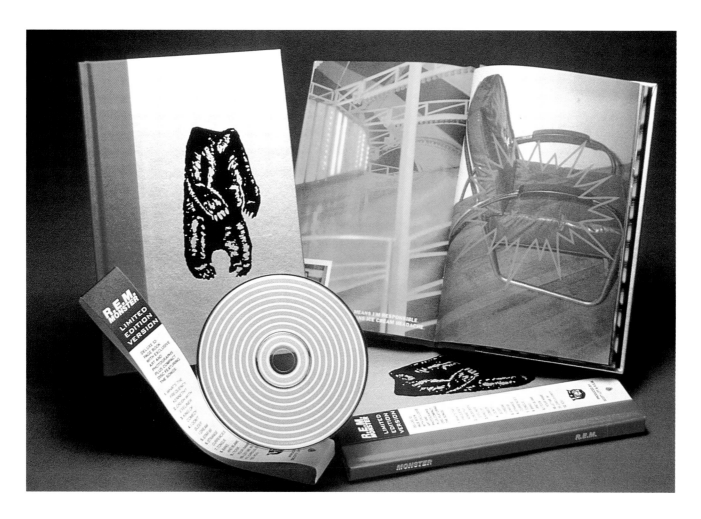

Merit/National

PACKAGING, SINGLE
REM "Monster" Limited Edition
ART DIRECTORS *Tom Recchion, Chris Bilheimer,*
Michael Stipe
DESIGNERS *Tom Recchion, Chris Bilheimer,*
Michael Stipe
PHOTOGRAPHERS *Chris Bilheimer, Christy Bush,*
Jem Cohen, Brooke Dillon
STUDIO *Warner Bros. Records, in-house art department*
CLIENT *Warner Bros. Records*

Merit/National

PACKAGING, SINGLE
Hear Box Sets
ART DIRECTOR *Lisa Laarman*
DESIGNER *Lisa Laarman*
PHOTOGRAPHER *John Soares*
CLIENT *Hear Music*

Merit/National

PACKAGING, SINGLE
Mattei's Tavern
ART DIRECTOR *Mark Oliver*
DESIGNER *Mark Oliver*
COPYWRITER *Mark Oliver*
ILLUSTRATIONS *Stock*
AGENCY *Mark Oliver, Inc.*
CLIENT *Firestone Vineyard*

Merit/National

PACKAGING, SINGLE
Barrel No. 112
ART DIRECTOR *Neil Powell*
CREATIVE DIRECTOR *Joe Duffy*
DESIGNERS *Neil Powell, Alan Leusink*
COPYWRITER *John Jarvis*
STUDIO *Duffy Design*
CLIENT *The Stroh Brewery*

Merit/International

PACKAGING, SINGLE
VOX
CREATIVE DIRECTOR *Don Williams*
DESIGNER *Eddie Turley*
COPYWRITER *Don Williams*
STUDIO *P. I. Design Consultants*
CLIENT *The Gaymer Group*

Merit/International

PACKAGING, SINGLE
Anton's Chocolate Chip Biscuits
ART DIRECTOR *Aziz Cami*
CREATIVE DIRECTOR *Aziz Cami*
DESIGNER *Marita Lashko*
ILLUSTRATOR *Roy Knipe*
STUDIO *The Partners*
CLIENT *Gourmet Direct Ltd.*

Merit/International

PACKAGING, SINGLE
Edition
ART DIRECTOR *Sibylle Haase*
CREATIVE DIRECTORS *Sibylle Haase, Harald Schweers*
DESIGNERS *Katja Hirshfelder, Regina Spiekermann*
AGENCY *Atelier Haase & Knels*
CLIENT *Stanwell Tobacco*

Merit/International

PACKAGING, SINGLE
Chalkham Hill Press
ART DIRECTOR *Mike Frampton*
CREATIVE DIRECTOR *Tony Pods*
DESIGNER *Mike Frampton*
COPYWRITER *Tony Pods*
ILLUSTRATOR *Mike Frampton*
PRODUCER *Mike Frampton*
DIRECTOR *Mike Frampton*
AGENCY *Framptons International*
STUDIO *Framptons International*
CLIENT *Chalkham Hill Press*

Merit/International

PACKAGING, SINGLE
Duchy Originals
ART DIRECTOR *Mary Lewis*
DESIGNER *Mary Lewis*
COPYWRITER *Mary Lewis*
PHOTOGRAPHER *Laurie Evans*
STUDIO *Lewis Moberly*
CLIENT *Duchy of Cornwall*

(facing page, top)
Merit/National

PACKAGING, SERIES
Kool Wraps, CD Gift Packaging
ART DIRECTOR *Jay Sylvester*
CREATIVE DIRECTOR *Jay Sylvester*
DESIGNER *Jay Sylvester*
ILLUSTRATORS *Michael Bartalos, James Yang,*
Zita Asbaghi, Paul Bowman
AGENCY *Artistes of Fortune*
CLIENT *Kool Wraps*

(facing page, bottom)
Merit/National

PACKAGING, SERIES
Planet Kids
ART DIRECTOR *Amy Knapp*
CREATIVE DIRECTOR *Peter T. Allen*
DESIGNER *Amy Knapp*
ILLUSTRATOR *Gary Baseman*
PRODUCER *Marianne Rice*
PROJECT ADMINISTRATOR *Kathy Riani*
STUDIO *DFS Design Group*
CLIENT *DFS Merchandising*

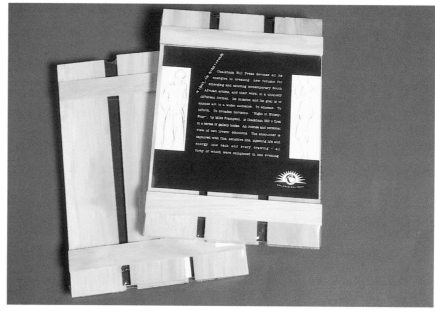

Merit/National

PACKAGING, SERIES
Keds Shoe Packaging
ART DIRECTOR *Jeff Pacione*
DESIGNERS *Beth Novitsky, Carolina Senior*
PHOTOGRAPHER *Peter Medilik*
ILLUSTRATOR *Jeff Pacione*
STUDIO *Fitch Inc.*
CLIENT *Keds Company*

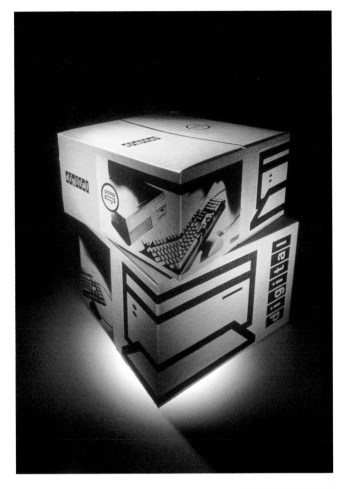

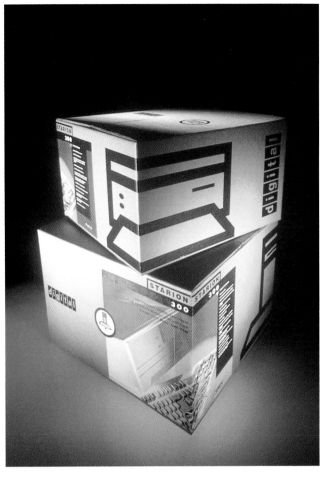

Merit/National

PACKAGING, SERIES
DEC PC Packaging System
ART DIRECTORS *Robert Wood, Tammie Hunt*
CREATIVE DIRECTOR *Robert Wood*
PHOTOGRAPHER *Peter Medilik*
STUDIO *Fitch Inc.*
CLIENT *Digital Equipment Corporation*

Merit/International

PACKAGING, SERIES
Boots Laundry
ART DIRECTOR *Mary Lewis*
DESIGNERS *Kasia Rust, Mary Lewis*
STUDIO *Lewis Moberly*
CLIENT *The Boots Company Plc*

Merit/International

PACKAGING, SERIES
Circus Sugar
ART DIRECTOR *Frauke Dirksen*
CREATIVE DIRECTOR *Ralph Taubenberger*
COPYWRITER *Axel Simon*
ILLUSTRATOR *Frauke Dirksen*
AGENCY *Heye + Partner*
CLIENT *Südzucker AG*

Merit/International

PACKAGING, SERIES
Hats of the World Sugar
ART DIRECTOR *Frauke Dirksen*
CREATIVE DIRECTOR *Ralph Taubenberger*
COPYWRITER *Axel Simon*
ILLUSTRATOR *Frauke Dirksen*
AGENCY *Heye + Partner*
CLIENT *Südzucker AG*

Merit/International

PACKAGING, SERIES
UCC Black Coffee 900 ml
ART DIRECTOR *Takaaki Goto*
CREATIVE DIRECTOR *Jyushiro Miura*
DESIGNER *Takaaki Goto*
CLIENT *UCC Ueshima Coffee Co., Ltd.*

Merit/National

ANNOUNCEMENT, INVITATION, OR MENU, SINGLE
Maisel Birth Announcement
CREATIVE DIRECTOR *Richard Anwyl*
DESIGNER *Karen Betz*
COPYWRITER *Richard Anwyl*
PHOTOGRAPHER *Jay Maisel*
CLIENT *Jay and L. A. Maisel*

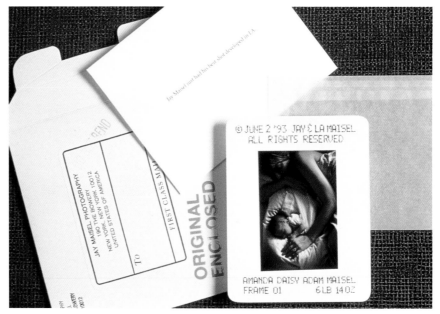

Merit/National

ANNOUNCEMENT, INVITATION, OR MENU, SINGLE
Matthew Spitzley's Birth Announcement
ART DIRECTOR *John Ball*
PHOTO ART DIRECTOR *Jose Serrano*
DESIGNER *John Ball*
PHOTOGRAPHER *Carl VanderSchuit*
AGENCY *Mires Design, Inc.*
STUDIO *Mires Design, Inc.*
CLIENT *Gale and John Spitzley*

Merit/National

ANNOUNCEMENT, INVITATION, OR MENU, SINGLE
MTV Video Music Awards Invitation
ART DIRECTOR *Christopher Davis*
CREATIVE DIRECTOR *Jeffrey Keyton*
DESIGNER *Christopher Davis*
COPYWRITER *David Lanfair*
PHOTOGRAPHER *Christopher Davis*
AGENCY *MTV Off Air Creative*
CLIENT *MTV Music Television*

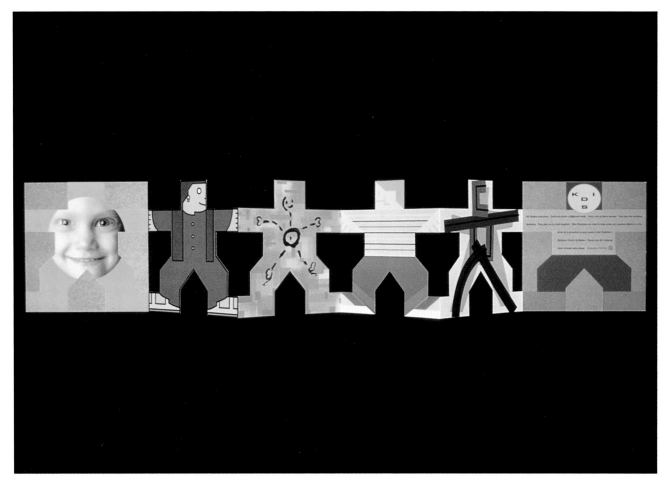

Merit/National

ANNOUNCEMENT, INVITATION, OR MENU, SINGLE
Holiday Shapes Christmas Card
ART DIRECTOR *Chuck Johnson*
CREATIVE DIRECTOR *Chuck Johnson*
DESIGNER *Chuck Johnson*
COPYWRITER *Chuck Johnson*
PHOTOGRAPHER *Will Crocker*
ILLUSTRATORS *Bryan Flynn, Rob Smith,*
Chuck Johnson, Ken Koester
STUDIO *Brainstorm, Inc.*
CLIENT *Yaquinto Printing*

Merit/National

ANNOUNCEMENT, INVITATION, OR MENU, SINGLE
Cine City: Film and Perceptions of Urban
Space 1895–1995 Brochure
DESIGNER *David Mellen*
STUDIO *J. Paul Getty Trust, Publication Services*
CLIENT *The Getty Center for the History of Art and*
the Humanities

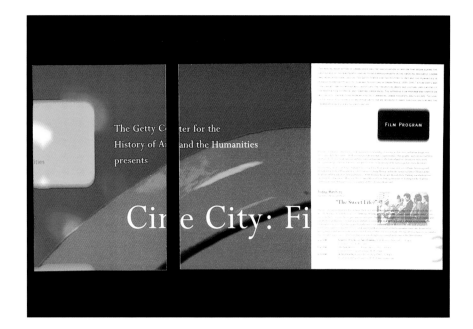

Merit/National

ANNOUNCEMENT, INVITATION, OR MENU, SINGLE
Connections 2: Explorations in the Getty Center
Collections Announcement
DESIGNER *Mike Fink*
STUDIO *J. Paul Getty Trust, Publication Services*
CLIENT *The Getty Center for the History of Art and*
the Humanities

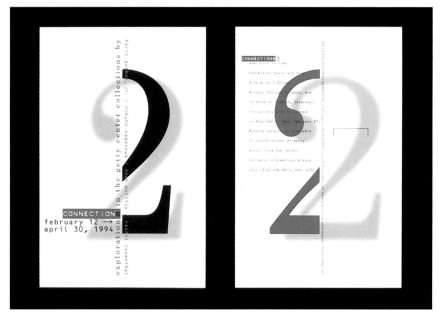

Merit/National

ANNOUNCEMENT, INVITATION, OR MENU, SINGLE
SHR Perceptual Management Christmas Card
ART DIRECTOR *Barry Shepard*
DESIGNER *Nathan Joseph*
COPYWRITER *Nathan Joseph*
AGENCY *SHR Perceptual Management*
CLIENT *SHR Perceptual Management*

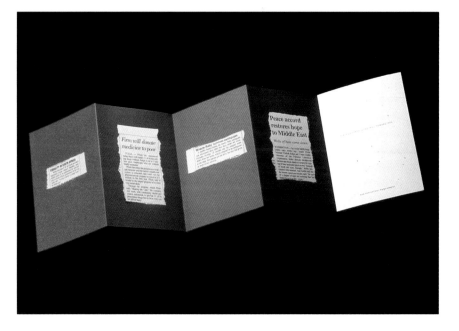

Merit/National

ANNOUNCEMENT, INVITATION, OR MENU, SINGLE
Peace Xmas 1994
ART DIRECTOR *Jeff Labbe*
DESIGNER *Jeff Labbe*
COPYWRITER *Jeff Labbe*
PHOTOGRAPHER *Kimball Hall*
PAPER *French Paper Co.*
STUDIO *Jeff Labbe Design*

Merit/National

ANNOUNCEMENT, INVITATION, OR MENU, SINGLE
Highlands Wine Menu
ART DIRECTORS *Marion English, Rebecca Fulmer*
CREATIVE DIRECTOR *Terry Slaughter*
STUDIO *Slaughter-Hanson*
CLIENT *Highlands Bar and Grill*

Merit/National

ANNOUNCEMENT, INVITATION, OR MENU, SINGLE
Billboard Music Video Conference Invitation
ART DIRECTOR *Cheri Dorr*
CREATIVE DIRECTOR *Cheri Dorr*
DESIGNER *Greenberg Kingsley, New York*
ILLUSTRATOR *Karen Greenberg*
CLIENT *VH1/MTV Networks*

Merit/National

ANNOUNCEMENT, INVITATION, OR MENU, SERIES
Shaw Contract Mailer
ART DIRECTOR *Rory Myers*
CREATIVE DIRECTORS *Bob Wages, Ted Fabella*
DESIGNER *Rory Myers*
PHOTOGRAPHER *Rob Cushman*
AGENCY *Axcess Marketing Group, Inc.*
STUDIO *Wages Design*
CLIENT *Shaw Contract Group*

Merit/International

CALENDAR OR APPOINTMENT BOOK
The Calendar "Scratch-A-Day"
ART DIRECTOR *Takashi Fukui*
CREATIVE DIRECTOR *Takashi Fukui*
DESIGNER *Takashi Fukui*
PHOTOGRAPHER *Kazuhiro Takahashi*
STUDIO *Dentsu, Inc.*
CLIENT *Nissho Co., Ltd.*

Merit/International

CALENDAR OR APPOINTMENT BOOK
Skylights, Lufthansa
ART DIRECTOR *Jürg Andermatt*
DESIGNER *Rolf Querengässer*
PHOTOGRAPHER *Jürg Andermatt*
CLIENT *Lufthansa German Airlines*

Merit/National

LOGO OR TRADEMARK
Ott Photography Logo
ART DIRECTOR *Bob Dennard*
CREATIVE DIRECTOR *Bob Dennard*
DESIGNER *Chris Wood*
STUDIO *Dennard Creative, Inc.*
CLIENT *Jeff Ott Photography*

Merit/National

LOGO OR TRADEMARK
Artwalk Logo
ART DIRECTOR *Kaoru Sato*
CREATIVE DIRECTOR *Jeffrey Morris*
DESIGNER *Kaoru Sato*
CLIENT *Coalition for the Homeless*

Merit/National

LOGO OR TRADEMARK
Gambling Logo
ART DIRECTOR *Ralph Watson*
CREATIVE DIRECTOR *Kurt Tausche*
DESIGNER *Ralph Watson*
AGENCY *Tausche Martin Lonsdorf*
CLIENT *Georgia Council on Compulsive Gambling*

Merit/National

LOGO OR TRADEMARK
Jack's Roasted Nuts Logo
ART DIRECTORS *Matt Finnigan, Joan Matteucci*
DESIGNER *Matt Finnigan*
PHOTOGRAPHER *Matt Finnigan*
STUDIO *Sol Design Team*
CLIENT *Jack Thompson, Jack's Roasted Nuts, Co.*

Merit/International

LOGO OR TRADEMARK
Torneos Y Competencias Logo
ART DIRECTOR *Steff Geissbuhler*
DESIGNER *Robert Matza*
STUDIO *Chermayeff & Geismar*
CLIENT *Torneos Y Competencias*

Merit/National

LETTERHEAD, BUSINESS CARD, ENVELOPE
Creative Search
ART DIRECTOR *Patrick Short*
DESIGNER *Patrick Short*
COPYWRITER *Nomad Short Subjects*
ILLUSTRATOR *Patrick Short*
STUDIO *BlackBird Creative*
CLIENT *Creative Search*

Merit/National

LETTERHEAD, BUSINESS CARD, ENVELOPE
Ott Photography Stationery
ART DIRECTOR *Bob Dennard*
CREATIVE DIRECTOR *Bob Dennard*
DESIGNER *Chris Wood*
STUDIO *Dennard Creative, Inc.*
CLIENT *Jeff Ott Photography*

Merit/National

LETTERHEAD, BUSINESS CARD, ENVELOPE
The Stone Kitchen Stationery
ART DIRECTOR *Mark Geer*
DESIGNER *Mark Geer*
PHOTOGRAPHER *Key Sanders*
ILLUSTRATOR *Mark Geer*
STUDIO *Geer Design, Inc.*
CLIENT *The Stone Kitchen*

Merit/National

LETTERHEAD, BUSINESS CARD, ENVELOPE
ACME Stationery Package
ART DIRECTOR *Dave Eliason*
CREATIVE DIRECTOR *Bryan L. Peterson*
DESIGNER *Dave Eliason*
AGENCY *Peterson & Company*
STUDIO *Peterson & Company*
CLIENT *ACME Rubber Stamp Co.*

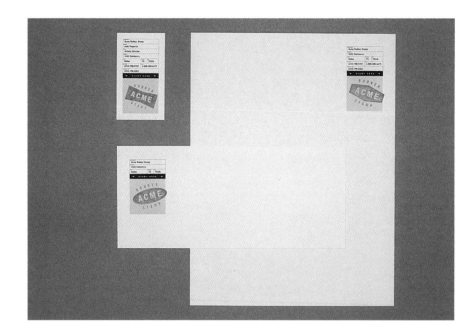

Merit/National

LETTERHEAD, BUSINESS CARD, ENVELOPE
Linda J. Holland Stationery
ART DIRECTOR *Rick Baptist*
DESIGNER *Rick Baptist*
ILLUSTRATOR *Rick Baptist*
AGENCY *FGI*
CLIENT *Linda J. Holland*

Merit/International

LETTERHEAD, BUSINESS CARD, ENVELOPE
Dialog Letterhead, Comp Slip, Business Card,
Report Cover
ART DIRECTOR *Peter Smith*
CREATIVE DIRECTOR *Peter Smith*
DESIGNER *André Soukias*
CLIENT *Dialog Limited*

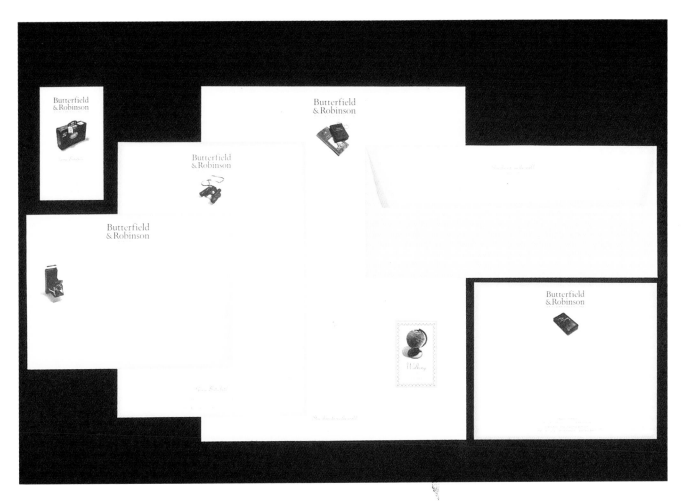

Merit/International

CORPORATE IDENTITY PROGRAM
Butterfield & Robinson Stationery
ART DIRECTOR *Frank Viva*
DESIGNER *Frank Viva*
PHOTOGRAPHER *Hill Peppard*
STUDIO *Viva Dolan Communications & Design*
CLIENT *Butterfield & Robinson*

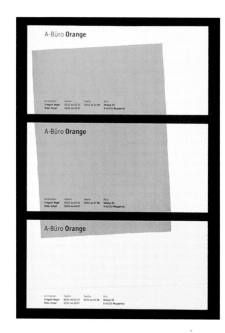

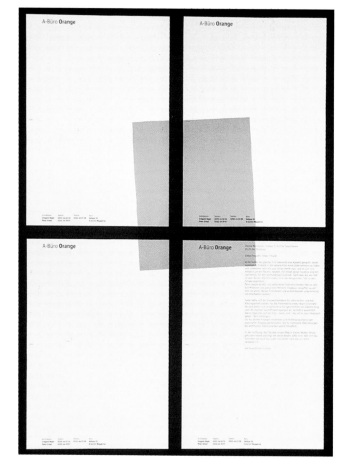

Merit/International

LETTERHEAD, BUSINESS CARD, ENVELOPE
A-Büro Orange
ART DIRECTOR *Klaus Hesse*
CREATIVE DIRECTOR *Christine Hesse*
DESIGNER *Monika Irmer*
CLIENT *A-Büro Orange*

Merit/National

CORPORATE IDENTITY PROGRAM
Edge Reps
DESIGNER *Todd Waterbury*
STUDIO *Wieden & Kennedy*
CLIENT *Edge Reps*

Grade AA. Nature designed the egg as a complete food. Close to perfect, yet precariously fragile in its raw state. Much like the creative process. Because an idea carefully conceived and incubated can still get scrambled in the end. Unless, of course, you let J.W. Fry crack the problem. With Fry, your ideas really cook.

Watchmaking. A stranger approaches you and asks, "Got a light?" Your clients want the same thing. A solution to their problem. Illumination. A spark. You, of course, have all kinds of ideas just waiting to catch fire. And J.W. Fry is a photographer that could strike the perfect match between your creative vision and his own.

Stick With It. Creative solutions have all kinds of ingredients. Some unseen, but important all the same. J.W. Fry is just such an invisible hero. He makes things sizzle, persevering until the problem's solved. He'll not only take a photograph. He'll flavor it to your taste. Butter. Bacon drippings. Bear grease, if need be.

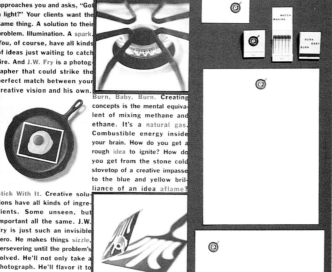

Burn, Baby, Burn. Creating concepts is the mental equivalent of mixing methane and ethane. It's a natural gas. Combustible energy inside your brain. How do you get a rough idea to ignite? How do you get from the stone cold stovetop of a creative impasse to the blue and yellow brilliance of an idea aflame?

Merit/National

CORPORATE IDENTITY PROGRAM
Business Card and Envelope
ART DIRECTORS *Chris Cortilet, Jeff Schwigert*
DESIGNER *Y-M Design Team*
COPYWRITER *Amie Valentine*
PHOTOGRAPHER *J. W. Fry*
STUDIO *Yamamoto/Moss*
CLIENT *J. W. Fry Photography*

Merit/National

CORPORATE IDENTITY PROGRAM
VH1 Honors Business Paper Series
ART DIRECTOR *Cheri Dorr*
CREATIVE DIRECTOR *Cheri Dorr*
DESIGNERS *Cheri Dorr, Susanna Ko*
PHOTOGRAPHER/STYLIST *Lee Friedman*
MODEL MAKER *Clockwork Apple, New York*
CLIENT *VH1*

Merit/International

CORPORATE IDENTITY PROGRAM
Vereinsbank
ART DIRECTOR *Gottschalk + Ash International*
DESIGNERS *Fritz Gottschalk, Andreas Gossweiler,
Erich Gross, Peter Jaray, Heather LaFleur,
Barbara Muller, Fabian Schmidt, Manuel Suess*
CLIENT *Vereinsbank*

We stimulate aspiring artists to confront their individual creative powers. For our world of intense competition and rapid change, we prepare individuals with confidence, self reliance, integrity, and responsibility. Julian Stanczak

pAi Nt iN g

Painting students learn the theory and practice of painting from a widely experienced faculty of committed painters whose works have been exhibited and collected throughout the US and abroad. Painting students also learn from one another. Their individual studios are well designed for them to observe the growth of each other's work, to exchange attitudes, and to learn how to respond to diverse ideas and forms through one-on-one teaching and group critiques. We encourage students to define and express their own ideas, rather than be limited by any dogma or trend. CIA's proximity to a world-class art museum and a large contemporary art center allows students to continually update their knowledge of the history and current climate of painting. It also challenges their aesthetic sense and generates a feeling of belonging to an ancient and ongoing community of painters. Other catalysts for students' growth are visits by distinguished artists and a new program to exchange painting students with British art schools. Our thorough attention to each student leads to the self-discipline and depth of perception that are needed in pragmatic fields. Painting graduates have succeeded in graduate school, teaching, art administration, operation of galleries and museums, and as practicing, exhibiting artists.

Merit/National

PUBLIC SERVICE, SINGLE
Cleveland Institute of Art Catalogue 1994–95
ART DIRECTORS *Joyce Nesnadny, Mark Schwartz*
CREATIVE DIRECTORS *Joyce Nesnadny, Mark Schwartz*
DESIGNERS *Joyce Nesnadny, Brian Lavy*
COPYWRITER *Anne Brooks Ranallo*
PHOTOGRAPHERS *Robert Muller, Mark Schwartz*
AGENCY *Nesnadny + Schwartz*
STUDIO *Nesnadny + Schwartz*
CLIENT *Cleveland Institute of Art*

To Hundreds Of Families In St. Paul It's A Home.

Merit/National

PUBLIC SERVICE, SINGLE
Box
ART DIRECTOR *Wendy Hansen*
CREATIVE DIRECTOR *Lyle Wedemeyer*
DESIGNER *Wendy Hansen*
COPYWRITER *Chris Preston*
PRODUCER *Renee Kirsch*
AGENCY *Martin/Williams*
CLIENT *Salvation Army*

STAY IN SCHOOL

William Wegman TDI

Merit/National

PUBLIC SERVICE, SINGLE
Stay in School Bus Poster
ART DIRECTOR *Stephen Doyle*
DESIGNER *Gary Tooth*
PHOTOGRAPHER *William Wegman*
STUDIO *Drenttel Doyle Partners*
CLIENT *TDI*

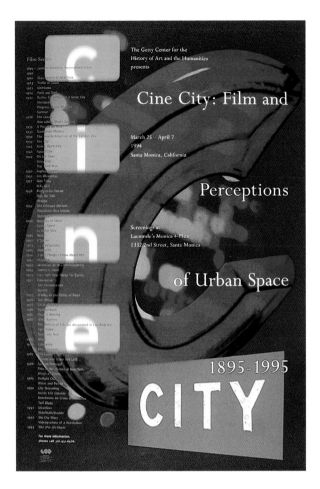

Merit/National

POSTER, OTHER THAN ADVERTISING, SINGLE
Cine City: Film and Perceptions of Urban Space
1895–1995
DESIGNER *David Mellen*
STUDIO *J. Paul Getty Trust, Publication Services*
CLIENT *The Getty Center for the History of Art and the Humanities*

Merit/National

POSTER, OTHER THAN ADVERTISING, SINGLE
Bay Street Bird
ART DIRECTOR *Paul Davis*
DESIGNER *Paul Davis*
ILLUSTRATOR *Paul Davis*
STUDIO *Paul Davis Studio*
CLIENT *Bay Street Theatre Festival 1994*

Merit/National

POSTER, OTHER THAN ADVERTISING, SINGLE
Human Rights Watch 1994
ART DIRECTOR *Paul Davis*
DESIGNER *Paul Davis*
ILLUSTRATOR *Paul Davis*
STUDIO *Paul Davis Studio*
CLIENT *Human Rights Watch Film Festival*

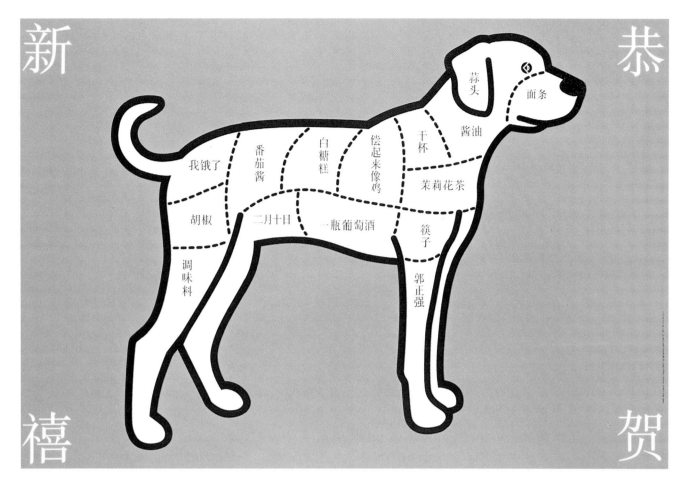

Merit/National

POSTER, OTHER THAN ADVERTISING, SINGLE
Happy New Year
ART DIRECTOR *Sam Kuo*
DESIGNER *Sam Kuo*
COPYWRITER *Sam Kuo*
ILLUSTRATOR *Sam Kuo*
STUDIO *Kuo Design Group*
CLIENT *Kuo Design Group*

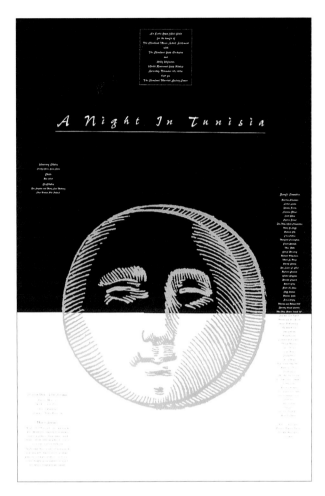

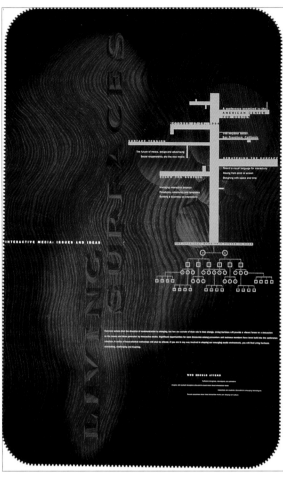

Merit/National

POSTER, OTHER THAN ADVERTISING, SINGLE
A Night in Tunisia
ART DIRECTOR *Gregory Oznowich*
DESIGNER *Gregory Oznowich*
COPYWRITER *Beatrice Kay Wyse*
ILLUSTRATIONS *Clip art*
AGENCY *Watt, Roop & Co.*
CLIENT *The Cleveland Music School Settlement*

Merit/National

POSTER, OTHER THAN ADVERTISING, SINGLE
Living Surfaces
ART DIRECTOR *Anthony Ma*
DESIGNER *Anthony Ma*
COPYWRITERS *Paul Souza, Rob Dewey*
ILLUSTRATOR *Grant Davis*
STUDIO *Tanagram*
CLIENT *American Center for Design*

Merit/National

POSTER, OTHER THAN ADVERTISING, SINGLE
Risk
ART DIRECTOR *Stephen Doyle*
DESIGNERS *Gary Tooth, Stephen Doyle*
STUDIO *Drenttel Doyle Partners*
CLIENT *Type Directors Club*

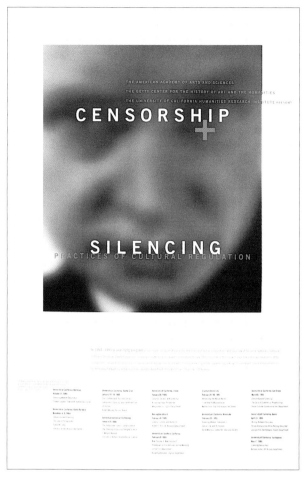

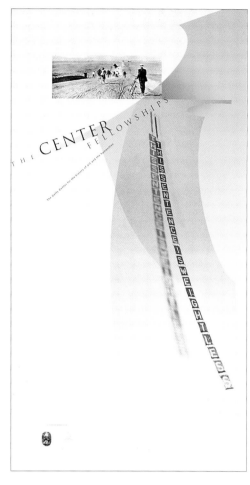

Merit/National

POSTER, OTHER THAN ADVERTISING, SINGLE
Censorship and Silencing: Practices of Cultural Regulation
DESIGNERS *Sean Adams, Noreen Morioka*
STUDIO *J. Paul Getty Trust, Publication Services*
CLIENT *The Getty Center for the History of Art and the Humanities*

Merit/National

POSTER, OTHER THAN ADVERTISING, SINGLE
The Getty Center for the History of Art and the Humanities
ART DIRECTOR *Rebeca Méndez*
CREATIVE DIRECTOR *Rebeca Méndez*
DESIGNER *Rebeca Méndez*
PHOTOGRAPHERS *John Kiffe, Jobe Benjan*
ARTWORK *George Brotch*
CLIENT *The Getty Center for the History of Art and the Humanities*

Merit/National

POSTER, OTHER THAN ADVERTISING, SINGLE
Wolf Teaser
ART DIRECTOR *Kim Wexman*
CREATIVE DIRECTOR *Peter Bemis*
COPYWRITER *Ari Sherman*
PHOTOGRAPHER *Michael O'Neil*
AGENCY *Frankfurt Balkind Partners*
CLIENT *Columbia Pictures*

Merit/National

POSTER, OTHER THAN ADVERTISING, SINGLE
AIGA Communication Graphics Call for Entries
ART DIRECTOR *Woody Pirtle*
DESIGNERS *Woody Pirtle, Ivette Montes de Oca*
ILLUSTRATOR *Woody Pirtle*
STUDIO *Pentagram Design*
CLIENT *AIGA*

Merit/National

POSTER, OTHER THAN ADVERTISING, SINGLE
Richard III
ART DIRECTOR *James Victore*
DESIGNER *James Victore*
PRODUCER *Julie Sheehan*
DIRECTOR *Scott Cargle*
STUDIO *Victore Design Works*
CLIENT *The Shakespeare Project*

Merit/National

POSTER, OTHER THAN ADVERTISING, SINGLE
Twelfth Night
ART DIRECTOR *James Victore*
DESIGNER *James Victore*
PRODUCER *Julie Sheehan*
DIRECTOR *Scott Cargle*
STUDIO *Victore Design Works*
CLIENT *The Shakespeare Project*

Then and now: 35 years of graphic, exhibit and environmental design. Ivan Chermayeff, Tom Geismar, John Grady and Steff Geissbuhler present the work of Chermayeff & Geismar Inc. at F.I.T. on Thursday November 10th at 7pm

Merit/National

POSTER, OTHER THAN ADVERTISING, SINGLE
Chermayeff & Geismar AIGA Lecture,
Then and Now
ART DIRECTOR *Ivan Chermayeff*
DESIGNER *Ivan Chermayeff*
STUDIO *Chermayeff & Geismar*
CLIENT *AIGA, New York chapter*

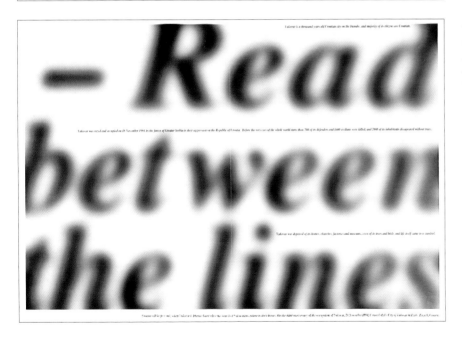

Merit/International

POSTER, OTHER THAN ADVERTISING, SINGLE
Read Between the Lines
ART DIRECTOR *Boris Ljubicic*
CREATIVE DIRECTOR *Boris Ljubicic*
DESIGNER *Boris Ljubicic*
COPYWRITER *Boris Ljubicic*
ILLUSTRATOR *Boris Ljubicic*
STUDIO *Studio International*
PRODUCER *Studio International*
DIRECTOR *Boris Ljubicic*
CLIENT *Council of the City of Vukovar in Exile*

Merit/International

POSTER, OTHER THAN ADVERTISING, SINGLE
No Draw in Life
ART DIRECTOR *Toshiyuki Kojima*
DESIGNER *Toshiyuki Kojima*
COPYWRITER *Toshiyuki Kojima*
STUDIO *Hiromura Design Office Inc.*

Merit/International

POSTER, OTHER THAN ADVERTISING, SINGLE
The Protective Vehicles
ART DIRECTOR *Yuji Tokuda*
CREATIVE DIRECTOR *Yuji Tokuda*
DESIGNER *Yuji Tokuda*
PHOTOGRAPHER *Hatsuhiko Okada*
AGENCY *Dentsu, Inc.*
CLIENT *Dentsu Cotec Inc.*

Merit/International

POSTER, OTHER THAN ADVERTISING, SINGLE
*Diary in Paris, Reiko Saito Photography
Exhibition II*
ART DIRECTORS *Reiko Saito, Hisashi Katsumura*
CREATIVE DIRECTOR *Reiko Saito*
DESIGNER *Hisashi Katsumura*
PHOTOGRAPHER *Reiko Saito*
STUDIO *Dentsu, Inc.*

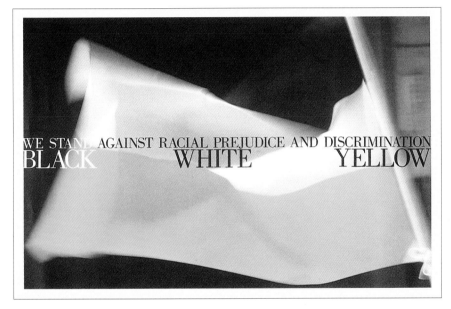

Merit/International

POSTER, OTHER THAN ADVERTISING, SINGLE
*We Stand Against Racial Prejudice and
Discrimination*
ART DIRECTOR *Junichi Morimoto*
CREATIVE DIRECTOR *Junichi Morimoto*
DESIGNERS *Yoshinari Hisazumi, Yuichi Hara*
COPYWRITER *Mie Ikeda*
PHOTOGRAPHER *Noato Kimura*
PRODUCER *Mie Ikeda*
CLIENT *Documenta Company*

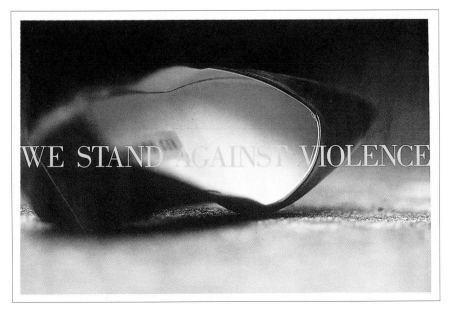

Merit/International

POSTER, OTHER THAN ADVERTISING, SINGLE
We Stand Against Violence
ART DIRECTOR *Junichi Morimoto*
CREATIVE DIRECTOR *Junichi Morimoto*
DESIGNERS *Yoshinari Hisazumi, Yuichi Hara*
COPYWRITER *Mie Ikeda*
PHOTOGRAPHER *Naoto Kimura*
PRODUCER *Mie Ikeda*
CLIENT *Documenta Company*

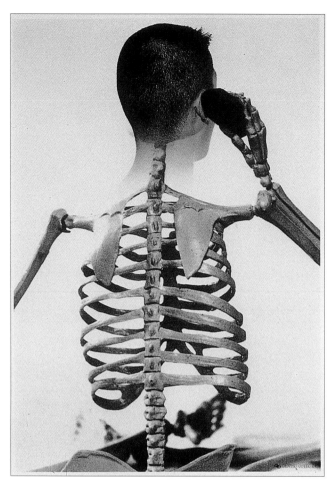

Merit/International

POSTER, OTHER THAN ADVERTISING, SINGLE
A Man
ART DIRECTOR *Takashi Fukui*
DESIGNER *Takashi Fukui*
PHOTOGRAPHER *Kazuhiro Takahashi*
AGENCY *Dentsu, Inc.*
STUDIO *Dentsu Cotec Inc.*
CLIENT *Dentsu Cotec Inc.*

Merit/International

POSTER, OTHER THAN ADVERTISING, SINGLE
A Woman
ART DIRECTOR *Takashi Fukui*
DESIGNER *Takashi Fukui*
PHOTOGRAPHER *Kazuhiro Takahashi*
AGENCY *Dentsu, Inc.*
STUDIO *Dentsu Cotec Inc.*
CLIENT *Dentsu Cotec Inc.*

Merit/International

POSTER, OTHER THAN ADVERTISING, SINGLE
*Diary in Paris, Reiko Saito Photography
Exhibition I*
ART DIRECTORS *Reiko Saito, Hisashi Katsumura*
CREATIVE DIRECTOR *Reiko Saito*
DESIGNER *Hisashi Katsumura*
PHOTOGRAPHER *Reiko Saito*
STUDIO *Dentsu, Inc.*

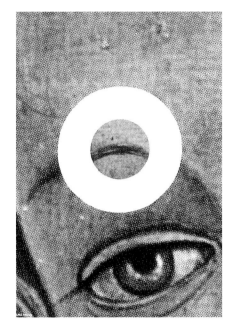

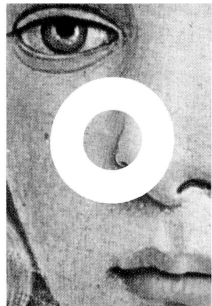

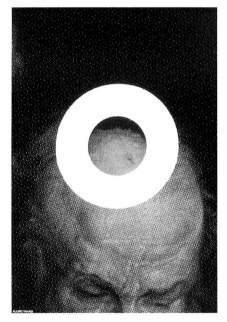

Merit/International

POSTER, OTHER THAN ADVERTISING, SERIES
One's Point of View
ART DIRECTOR *Kijuro Yahagi*
DESIGNER *Kijuro Yahagi*

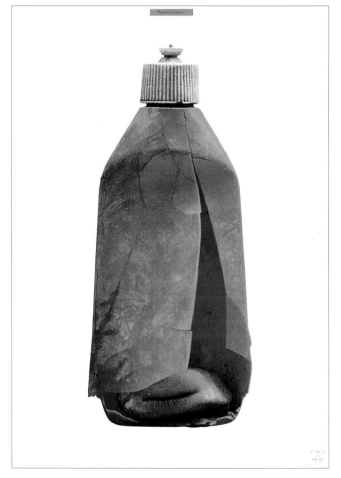

(facing page)
Merit/International

POSTER, OTHER THAN ADVERTISING, SERIES
Memento Mori
ART DIRECTOR *Shotaro Sakaguchi*
DESIGNER *Shotaro Sakaguchi*
PHOTOGRAPHER *Shotaro Sakaguchi*
AGENCY *Dentsu, Inc.*
STUDIO *Dentsu Cotec Inc.*
CLIENT *Dentsu Cotec Inc.*

(above)
Merit/National

SELF-PROMOTION, SINGLE
Parallel T-Shirts
ART DIRECTORS *Neil Powell, Alan Leusink*
CREATIVE DIRECTOR *Joe Duffy*
DESIGNERS *Neil Powell, Alan Leusink*
ILLUSTRATORS *Neil Powell, Alan Leusink*
STUDIO *Duffy Design*
CLIENT *Parallel Productions*

This is what happens when a client fires an agency.

Coming from an advertising agency, what we are about to suggest may surprise you.

It has been our experience that the single best way for a client to build his business is to fire his agency.

We are referring not to the firings that wash in on the morning tide of the daily ad columns. The kind of firing we are talking about is far more difficult.

But potentially more rewarding.

Namely, the ability to breathe life and spirit into an advertising idea; the talent to ignite, inflame, inspire; to fill an agency with passion, excitement and enthusiasm.

We've been very lucky. We have clients that fire us on a daily basis. Clients who question. Clients who push. Clients who challenge preconceived notions of how advertising should look, feel and sound. Clients who are comfortable with the fact that good ideas will make them uncomfortable.

Fire your agency and you will find its people will work harder for you; will play over their heads; will do groundbreaking work. When this happens, the result is advertising that not only wins sales for a client. But critical acclaim.

Take the recent International Advertising Festival at Cannes, the industry's most prestigious competition. Better yet, take the past three years of Cannes.

For an unprecedented three years in a row, DDB Needham won more Lions than any other agency in the world.

This year we took home 21 Lions. For 15 clients from 7 countries.

For clients with big budgets. Clients with small budgets. And clients with no budgets.

Clients from all corners of the world with marketing challenges as different as the languages they speak. Yet with one thing in common. They view advertising not as art. Not as science. But as business.

They are totally committed to inspiring creativity because they understand and value its power. And have seen firsthand just how big a contribution it can make to their business.

They've come to the realization that in a world of product parity, great advertising is very often the marketing difference.

Don't get us wrong. We aren't shifting the onus of doing great work onto our clients. But they do share the responsibility. The simple fact is that great clients make great agencies. It doesn't work the other way around.

Or put another way, even the best ideas an agency has are only dry kindling without the spark that comes from the client.

So, now you know what happens when a client fires an agency. But that's only half the story. You should hear what happens when an agency fires a client.

Call me, Keith Reinhard, at 212-415-3028.

Merit/National

SELF-PROMOTION, SINGLE
This Is What Happens When a Client Fires an Agency
ART DIRECTOR *John Staffen*
CREATIVE DIRECTORS *Mike Rogers, John Staffen*
COPYWRITER *Mike Rogers*
AGENCY *DDB Needham Worldwide/New York*
CLIENT *DDB Needham Worldwide/New York*

Merit/National

SELF-PROMOTION, SINGLE
Louise Fili Ltd. Promotion
ART DIRECTOR *Louise Fili*
CREATIVE DIRECTOR *Louise Fili*
DESIGNERS *Louise Fili, Leah Lococo*
COPYWRITER *Steven Heller*
PHOTOGRAPHERS *Ed Spiro, David Barry*
STUDIO *Louise Fili Ltd.*
CLIENT *Louise Fili Ltd.*

Merit/National

SELF-PROMOTION, SINGLE
Pleasure Place Mailer
ART DIRECTOR *Morton Jackson*
CREATIVE DIRECTOR *Morton Jackson*
DESIGNER *Morton Jackson*
PHOTOGRAPHER *Martin Schulman*
STUDIO *Graffito*
CLIENT *Pleasure Place*

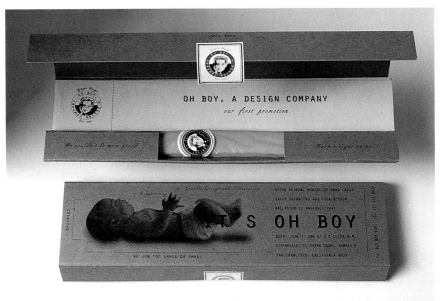

Merit/National

SELF-PROMOTION, SINGLE
Birth Announcement
ART DIRECTOR *David Salanitro*
DESIGNER *David Salanitro*
COPYWRITER *David Salanitro*
STUDIO *Oh Boy, A Design Company*
CLIENT *Oh Boy, A Design Company*

Merit/National

SELF-PROMOTION, SINGLE
Identities by O & J Design, Inc.
ART DIRECTOR *Andrzej J. Olejniczak*
DESIGNERS *Andrzej J. Olejniczak,*
Andrew Jablonski, Inhi Clara Kim,
Lia Camara-Mariscal
COPYWRITER *Nancy L. Baxter*
CLIENT *O & J Design, Inc.*

Merit/National

SELF-PROMOTION, SINGLE
No. IX, Toy Box
ART DIRECTOR *Janet Kruse*
DESIGNERS *Janet Kruse, Traci Daberko*
PHOTOGRAPHERS *Bill Cannon, Marco Prozzo*
ILLUSTRATORS *Various*
PRODUCER *Dan Snyder*
CLIENT *Pat Hackett, Artist Representative*

Merit/National

SELF-PROMOTION, SINGLE
How Good Is Your Taste?
ART DIRECTOR *Michael Gericke*
DESIGNERS *Michael Gericke, Ed Chiquitucto*
COPYWRITER *Frederick Shamlian*
ILLUSTRATOR *Pentagram Design*
STUDIO *Pentagram Design*
CLIENT *Pentagram Design*

Merit/National

SELF-PROMOTION, SINGLE
Pushpin Jr.
ART DIRECTOR *Seymour Chwast*
CREATIVE DIRECTOR *Seymour Chwast*
DESIGNER *Roxanne Slimak*
COPYWRITER *Seymour Chwast*
STUDIO *The Pushpin Group, Inc.*
CLIENT *The Pushpin Group, Inc.*

Merit/National

SELF-PROMOTION, SINGLE
Agency Print Piece
ART DIRECTOR *Grant Richards*
CREATIVE DIRECTORS *Todd Tilford, Grant Richards*
COPYWRITER *Todd Tilford*
PRODUCER *Gail Beckman*
AGENCY *The Richards Group*
CLIENT *The Richards Group*

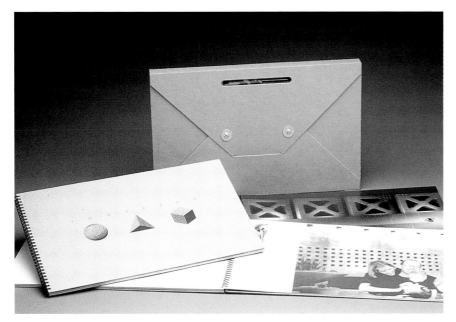

Merit/National

SELF-PROMOTION, SINGLE
Set Design Promotion
ART DIRECTORS *Gary M. Hill, Bill Tonnesen*
CREATIVE DIRECTOR *Bill Tonnesen*
DESIGNER *Gary M. Hill*
COPYWRITER *Bill Tonnesen*
AGENCY *Dunn & Hill*
CLIENT *Tonnesen Sets*

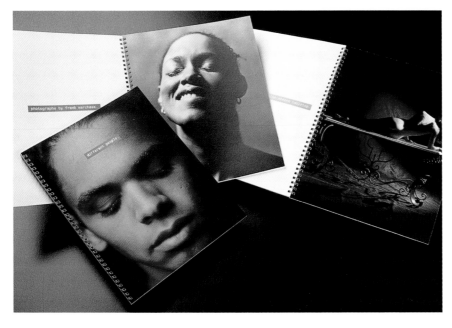

Merit/National

SELF-PROMOTION, SINGLE
Marchese Brochure
ART DIRECTOR *Don Carter*
DESIGNER *Don Carter*
COPYWRITER *Don Carter*
PHOTOGRAPHER *Frank Marchese*
PRODUCER *Susan Bunn*
AGENCY *Mintz & Hoke*
CLIENT *Frank Marchese*

Merit/National

SELF-PROMOTION, SINGLE
TV Dinner
ART DIRECTOR *Douglass Grimmett*
DESIGNER *Douglass Grimmett*
COPYWRITER *Douglass Grimmett*
ILLUSTRATOR *Douglass Grimmett*
CLIENT *Douglass Grimmett*

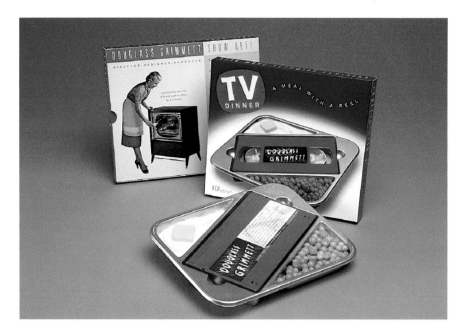

Merit/International

SELF-PROMOTION, SINGLE
A Bag of Batey Culture
ART DIRECTOR *Eddie Wong*
CREATIVE DIRECTOR *Jim Aitchison*
DESIGNER *Eddie Wong*
COPYWRITERS *Ian Batey, Sim Yang Seah,*
Jim Aitchison
ILLUSTRATIONS *Eddie Wong and stock*
AGENCY *Batey Ads Singapore*
CLIENT *Batey Ads Singapore*

Merit/National

SELF-PROMOTION, SERIES
Champion Carnival Text and Cover Sourcebooks
ART DIRECTOR *Bart Crosby*
CREATIVE DIRECTOR *Bart Crosby*
DESIGNER *Angela Norwood*
PHOTOGRAPHER *Laurie Rubin*
STUDIO *Crosby Associates Inc.*
CLIENT *Champion International Corporation*

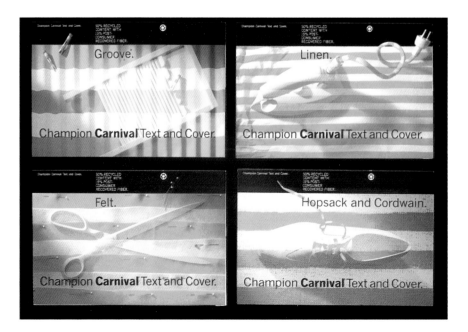

PHOTOGRAPHY

GOLD AND SILVER MEDALISTS

GOLD AND SILVER MEDALISTS

Gold Medalist/National

FULL PAGE OR SPREAD
Henry Rollins
CREATIVE DIRECTOR *Fred Woodward*
PHOTO EDITOR *Jodi Peckman*
PHOTOGRAPHER *Matt Mahurin*
CLIENT *Rolling Stone*

Henry Rollins

Trent Reznor of *Nine Inch Nails*

Silver Medalist/National

FULL PAGE OR SPREAD
The Color of Hunger
ART DIRECTOR *Tom Bentkowski*
DESIGNER *Marti Golon*
DIRECTOR OF PHOTOGRAPHY *David Friend*
PHOTO EDITOR *Barbara Baker Burrows*
PHOTOGRAPHER *Odd R. Andersen*
CLIENT *Life Magazine*

Silver Medalist/National

FULL PAGE OR SPREAD
Quentin Tarantino
CREATIVE DIRECTOR *Fred Woodward*
DESIGNERS *Fred Woodward, Gail Anderson,*
Dan Winters
PHOTO EDITOR *Laurie Kratochvil*
PHOTOGRAPHER *Dan Winters*
CLIENT *Rolling Stone*

ADDITIONAL AWARD

Distinctive Merit
**GRAPHIC DESIGN, EDITORIAL DESIGN, MAGAZINE,
CONSUMER OR BUSINESS, FULL PAGE OR SPREAD**

The BIG Picture

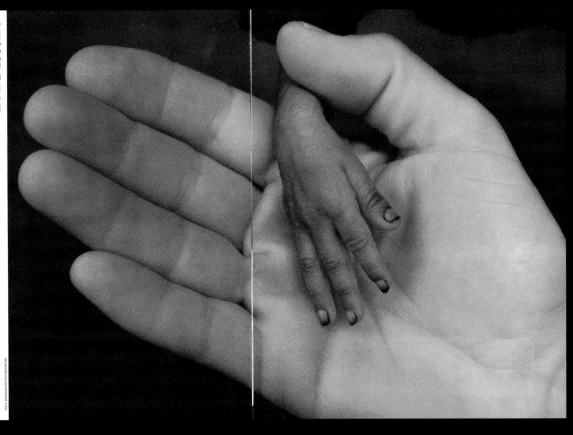

The Color of Hunger

Purple is said to be the color of passion. How then do we account for the purple fingers of this child—one of 20 million people in Ethiopia and other parts of eastern Africa currently threatened by famine? Perhaps it's because at the age of six months she weighs less than four and a half pounds and can barely open her mouth to drink the milk offered by relief workers. Perhaps, experts say, it's because of an iron deficiency, which is the most common cause of this beautiful, horrible discoloration in malnourished children. Or perhaps it's because suffering is, in its way, a kind of grotesque passion.

16

Quentin Tarantino

QUENTIN TARANTINO

madman of movie mayhem, has a mother. How's that for a shocker? She has seen *Reservoir Dogs*, the 1992 heist film, that made a cult sensation of her writer-director-actor son and raised the stakes on movie gore with a 30-minute torture scene featuring the severing of an ear. "That happens to be my mother's favorite scene," says Tarantino, 31, a high-school dropout who has gone from video-store clerk to genius auteur du jour in just a few feverishly busy years. Mom has just checked out *Pulp Fiction*, a wildly ambitious and darkly comic crime anthology about Los Angeles lowlife that won the Palme d'Or at Cannes, opened the prestigious New York Film Festival and put her son in the hot contender line at next year's Oscars. Although the film includes shootings, stabbings, S&M, homosexual rape and a drug-overdose sequence that leaves audiences reeling, Mom doesn't flinch. Tarantino's West Hollywood, Calif., bachelor apartment is another matter. "That's not particularly my decorating style," she says with a laugh.

Our Tarantino is hardly the sort of glitzy home in the Hills one might imagine to house a hillbilly Generation-X-rated triple threat on the verge of becoming his own one-man genre. Rather the homes — OK, messy — pad looks like a kitschy pop-culture Valhalla. Movie posters, videos, laser discs, albums, fanzines, books and assorted film artifacts fill every available inch. Along with memorabilia from his own movies — including that razor used in the infamous ear-slicing scene — there's a frighteningly lifelike bust of B-movie diva Barbara Steele, a pack of genuine *Texas Chainsaw* chili, a *Zorro* knife given to him by Jennifer Beals, a Robert Vaughn doll, cases by the dozen, or bottles: Pepsi and what is undoubtedly one of the world's most impressive collections of film- and TV-related board games.

"I've been collecting all this shit for years," says Tarantino, who is wearing a Racer X T-shirt today. "Then I finally decided I wanted to start collecting something new. At first

The director of PULP FICTION *and* RESERVOIR DOGS *guns* *the engine on screen violence and twisted wit* By David Wild

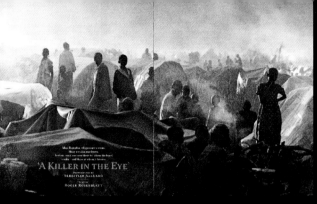

'A KILLER IN THE EYE'

PHOTOGRAPHS BY
SEBASTIÃO SALGADO

TEXT BY
ROGER ROSENBLATT

'Bodies appear in an explosion of spray at the top of a steep falls, and then spin and tumble down like logs on the way to a mill.'

'It is a marketplace, perhaps the largest in the world. One mass sells radios parts, another booth trades thousands...'

'The killers sleep and eat with the others, and brush alongside them as they walk, and, possibly, wait for another opportunity to strike.'

'A new pump is being installed in the brown lake, but it's too late. An epidemic awaits.'

HIDDEN IN THE FOLDS

THE LANGUOR OF DRAPERY IN THE CLASSICAL MODE

Velvet-and-metal collar, above, by Anat Grossowsky, about $350.
At Anat Grossowsky, 24 rue Sedaine, Paris. Bronze chiffon coat, Bill Blass, $1,330.
At Saks Fifth Avenue. Right: Rayon dress, about $703, and peplum, about $715,
both by Comme des Garçons. At Barneys New York.

PHOTOGRAPHS BY SARAH MOON

SERIES
Hidden in the Folds
ART DIRECTOR *Janet Froelich*
DESIGNER *Cathy Gilmore-Ba*
PHOTOGRAPHER *Sarah Moon*
CLIENT *The New York Times*

Chiffon dress with draped back, above, by Donna Karan. To order, through Bergdorf Goodman.
Left: Strapless mousseline dress, Bill Blass, $4,690. At Saks Fifth Avenue.

PHOTOGRAPHS BY SARAH MOON FOR THE NEW YORK TIMES

Rayon-and-cotton bolero, above, by Comme des Garçons, about $2,275. At Barneys New York.
Right: Layered silk-chiffon bias dress, Robert Danes, $3,890. At Bergdorf Goodman.

PHOTOGRAPHS BY SARAH MOON FOR THE NEW YORK TIMES

The Twilight of the Texas Rangers

For 170 years, the legendary lawmen have faced down cattle rustlers, serial killers, and every threat imaginable. Now they must grapple with their most dangerous foe: the modern world.

BY ROBERT DRAPER

The end of a long ride: Retired Ranger Joaquin Jackson of Alpine.

Silver Medalist/National

SERIES
The Twilight of the Texas Rangers
ART DIRECTOR *D. J. Stout*
DESIGNERS *D. J. Stout, Nancy McMillan*
COPYWRITER *Robert Draper*
PHOTOGRAPHER *Dan Winters*
CLIENT *Texas Monthly*

IN THE SUMMER OF 1993, JOAQUIN JACKSON, THE senior member of the Texas Rangers, drove from his outpost in Alpine to the Austin headquarters, where he informed his superiors that he was hanging up his spurs. Assistant commander Bruce Casteel was visibly upset by the news. "Joaquin, you're not ready to quit," he protested. "You need to stay."

Jackson shook his head. "I just can't do it," he said.

Everyone present knew what Jackson meant. Though he had been a Ranger for the past 27 years, the strapping six-foot-five lawman was only 57 and had several good years left. The murderers and drug smugglers, he could handle just as capably as always. What Joaquin Jackson could not handle were the changes taking place within his beloved Texas Rangers. "Well," said one of the secretaries after a long silence, "I guess this is the end of one era and the start of another."

In fact, the new era had already begun, and it had made Jackson sick to his stomach. Forty Department of Public Safety employees had recently been made finalists for nine new Ranger positions. Five of the forty applicants were women. Friends within the DPS had told Jackson that two of the nine jobs were going to be filled by women, no matter what. Since no woman had ever been named a Ranger before, this information came as a shock to Jackson. As veteran lawmen went, Jackson had a reputation for open-mindedness. He had vocally encouraged the 1973 hiring of the Rangers' first Hispanic officer in more than fifty years. He believed that any good law enforcement agency had to adapt with the times and was hopeful that by the year

Glenn Elliott of Longview (opposite) quit the Rangers in 1987. Below: A Ranger's boots may display his distinctive badge.

2000, Rangers would be computer experts who primarily tangled with white-collar criminals. Now, women Rangers—that was something else again. Jackson knew a few excellent female FBI agents and always thought that a woman's intuitive powers were useful investigative tools. But a Ranger had to be more than an investigator. A Ranger had to live off the land, had to withstand days of sleepless pursuit, had to fight back mobs and overpower psychopathic murderers. That was what a Ranger did. That was what Joaquin Jackson had done for the past 27 years. Could a woman do all that? Jackson was skeptical, but he wanted to see who the DPS would come up with.

When Jackson found out, he was infuriated. Cheryl Steadman was promoted from a clerical job that involved processing warrants. The other newly appointed female Ranger, Marrie Garcia, had spent the past several years in San Antonio's driver's license service. Like Steadman, Garcia had never worked a criminal case in her life. Neither Jackson nor any of the other Rangers he talked to could remember a Ranger being plucked from the ranks of the driver's license service.

This was hardly a trivial matter. After all, the elite force of 87 Texas officers has a hand in the state's biggest criminal cases, from the crime-scene investigation of the Branch Davidian compound to the pursuit of mass murderers, serial rapists, and drug lords. Arguably, Steadman and Garcia were two of the least qualified recruits in the Rangers' 170-year history. And, Jackson thought bitterly, that was obviously beside the point. DPS director Jim Wilson and Ranger chief Maurice Cook had turned their backs on tradition and responded to the political lash. So a new era was dawning, all right, and the men of Jackson's era wanted no part of it. "When they hired those

two women, that clinched it for me," Jackson says today. Another Ranger, with 18 years on the force, turned in his badge as well, citing the women as his reason. A third veteran, after putting an end to his 23 years of service, was heard to say, "Well, I'm the last rat getting off the sinking ship."

Even so, the veterans left quietly, their disenchantment with the brotherhood surmounted only by their aversion to airing dirty Ranger laundry. The hiring of the women Rangers was seen as a quirky sign of progress by the media, which did not bother to investigate whether these particular women possessed even the most rudimentary qualifications for the job. When reporters asked Marrie Garcia's father if she was up to the challenge, he declared, "Watch her shoot," as if Rangers were ever known for their marksmanship. For her part, Cheryl Steadman told the media how she placated the DPS interviewers by saying, "A good female Ranger will wear whatever she's told," as if Rangers were ever known for conformity. But then again, this was the new era.

To Joaquin Jackson and his peers, the quota-hiring of women Rangers suggests a kind of political emasculation, one that makes a mockery of the legendary law enforcement corps. To critics of the Rangers, the event was twenty years behind schedule, further proof that the state's most sanctimonious good old boys could not be trusted to march in step with the modern world.

Certainly it is true that the recent history of the Texas Rangers is the history of an organization at odds with the changing times. In a sense, however, the Rangers have always been in sync with Texas—or rather, with the part of Texas that, for better and for worse, distinguishes Texans from the rest

Despite an exemplary record, Hispanic Ranger Ray Martinez of New Braunfels (above and opposite) was never promoted.

of the world. No other state boasts an equivalent to the Rangers, and in no other state would the Rangers survive its many controversies. The question, Are the Rangers necessary? involves matters so deeply embedded in the Texas psyche that it is almost never addressed. For that matter, America as a whole is entranced by this indigenous lawman; hence the recently released movie *A Perfect World* (starring Clint Eastwood as a Ranger), the television series *Walker, Texas Ranger*, and the innumerable movies and books preceding them. As such, the movement to overhaul the Texas Rangers, and the Rangers' cynical and defensive reaction to that movement, are knotted together in our state's tangled web of romance and realpolitik, honor and progress, myth and mortality. The knot is what binds us, and what forms the noose we cannot slip.

A RETIRED RANGER STARED DREAMILY AT THE plaque he kept on his wall, bearing the name of his most famous predecessors. "Leander McNelly," he murmured at last, and his voice almost caved in with emotion as he quoted one of McNelly's men, "Lord, how I would have charged hell with a handbucket behind the leadership of that man!"

Rangers are faithful keepers of Ranger mythology, and it all begins with McNelly, the youthful captain under whose command a pintsize brigade slaughtered countless criminals and Mexicans from 1874 until 1877. To the Rangers and their admiring historians, McNelly is an appealing composite of warlord and Christ figure: courageous and gentlemanly, utterly

DISTINCTIVE MERIT AWARDS

Distinctive Merit/National

FULL PAGE OR SPREAD
Another Day at the Border
ART DIRECTOR *Janet Froelich*
DESIGNER *Nancy Harris*
PHOTO EDITOR *Kathy Ryan*
PHOTOGRAPHER *James Nachtwey*
CLIENT *The New York Times Magazine*

(facing page, top)
Distinctive Merit/National

FULL PAGE OR SPREAD
A Domestic Moment
ART DIRECTOR *Tom Bentkowski*
DESIGNER *Jean Andreuzzi*
DIRECTOR OF PHOTOGRAPHY *David Friend*
PHOTOGRAPHER *Joseph Rodriguez*
CLIENT *Life Magazine*

(facing page, bottom)
Distinctive Merit/National

FULL PAGE OR SPREAD
Worse than Death
ART DIRECTOR *Tom Bentkowski*
DESIGNER *Jean Andreuzzi*
DIRECTOR OF PHOTOGRAPHY *David Friend*
PHOTO EDITOR *Barbara Baker Burrows*
PHOTOGRAPHER *Glenn Hartung*
CLIENT *Life Magazine*

The BIG Picture

A tender domestic moment: One-year-old Jacqueline sits on a gun-littered carpet while Daddy shows her how to hold a pistol and Mommy smiles with fond approval. Such is life in East Los Angeles, a violent barrio where sidearms are as common as boom boxes and inspire almost as casual a reaction. In any reasonable world a mother would gasp, *Get that gun out of my baby's hand!* But Yvonne, whose man belongs to a powerful street gang, does not live in a reasonable world. And let's face it, neither do the rest of us.

America today is an armed camp, with 67 million handguns in circulation. Every year some 640,000 of us are confronted by a criminal with a handgun, and violence begets violence as fear of guns sells more guns in an endless feedback loop. All too often the casualties are children. Each day 13 youngsters are killed by guns and 30 others are wounded; in 1991 alone, 5,356 died. We are murdering the future, and the trigger is often pulled by a child. Our schools, where tens of thousands of guns are carried to class every day, have become a killing ground.

We have a choice: Give up guns or give up lives. And after years of dithering, we're showing symptoms of resolve: the Brady bill, Jesse Jackson's Save the Children campaign, a few programs that offer cash and amnesty for unlicensed firearms—and there's that ingenious toys-for-guns exchange that recently harvested almost 1,000 firearms in a single New York City police precinct. The idea has caught on in other cities, and that's good news. It won't rip out the social, economic and emotional roots of violence, but it will save some lives, and it may give children like Jacqueline a bunny instead of a trigger to squeeze.

—CLAUDIA GLENN DOWLING

12

The BIG Picture

Worse than Death

It began on a quiet Sunday morning when sparks from a faulty wire turned a Cincinnati home into an inferno. Dennis Rogers, 22, rushed out of the house but then plunged back into the flames to save his children, Shawn, three, and Sadie, six months. Overcome by smoke and critically burned, he was pulled from the pyre more dead than alive. When Rogers finally regained consciousness, he learned the full extent of the disaster. Firefighters had managed to save Shawn, but Sadie had not survived.

OPEN HERE

Distinctive Merit/National

FULL PAGE OR SPREAD
What's New York the Capital of Now?
ART DIRECTOR *Janet Froelich*
DESIGNER *Cathy Gilmore-Barnes*
PHOTO EDITOR *Kathy Ryan*
PHOTOGRAPHER *Michael O'Neill*
CLIENT *The New York Times Magazine*

ADDITIONAL AWARD

Merit
**GRAPHIC DESIGN, EDITORIAL DESIGN,
MAGAZINE, CONSUMER OR BUSINESS, FULL ISSUE**

Distinctive Merit/National

FULL PAGE OR SPREAD
DJ Red Alert
CREATIVE DIRECTOR *Fred Woodward*
PHOTO EDITOR *Denise Sfraga*
PHOTOGRAPHER *Alicia Exum*
CLIENT *Rolling Stone*

(facing page, top)
Distinctive Merit/National

FULL PAGE OR SPREAD
Skate Till You Die
CREATIVE DIRECTOR *Fred Woodward*
DESIGNER *Lee Bearson*
PHOTO EDITOR *Denise Sfraga*
PHOTO ILLUSTRATION *Alicia Exum*
CLIENT *Rolling Stone*

(facing page, bottom)
Distinctive Merit/National

FULL PAGE OR SPREAD
Carrot Top
CREATIVE DIRECTOR *Fred Woodward*
DESIGNER *Fred Woodward*
PHOTO EDITOR *Jodi Peckman*
PHOTOGRAPHER *Mark Seliger*
CLIENT *Rolling Stone*

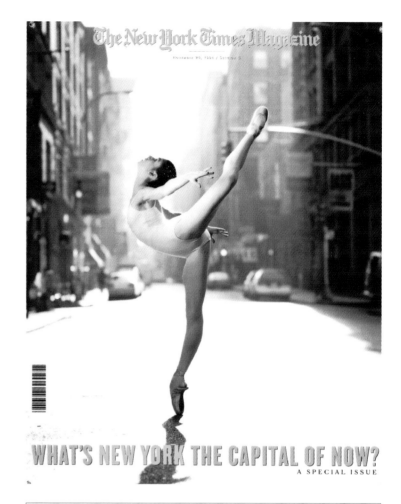

The New York Times Magazine

WHAT'S NEW YORK THE CAPITAL OF NOW?
A SPECIAL ISSUE

DJ Red Alert

ROLLING STONE 3] GENERATION NEXT

PHOTO ILLUSTRATION BY EKUM

‹BY PETER WILKINSON›

SKATE TILL YOU DIE ››THE FAST TIMES AND TRAGIC

DEATH OF JEFF PHILLIPS, THE KING OF TEXAS SKATEBOARDING ››

THE FRIENDS OF JEFF PHILlips gathered around a VCR to pay tribute. It was the night of Dec. 29, 1993, at Craig Johnson's house, in Dallas. Someone put a video from 1988 in the machine. Most of the mourners, Johnson included, were professional skateboarders, and since they'd been drinking beer and Cuervo for hours, they hooted when they saw their images on the TV. From the mantel, a blown-up color photograph of Jeff looked down: Jeff with the unruly mop of brown hair, the high cheekbones and meager stubble, the wide-set, weary eyes.

The room fell silent. There he was on the screen: tall, square-shouldered, graceful Jeff at 6 feet 2 inches, looking huge on the ramp, muscling himself back and forth in the half-pipe, gathering speed. He rode backward up to the lip, planted his hand, swung himself completely upside down, then shifted his weight, twisted around and dropped back onto the ramp. A perfect Phillips 66: his signature maneuver, the one few other skaters could ever do.

In the dim light of Craig Johnson's living room, Jeff skated again. Then, with the push of a button, he was gone.

As they grieved in the days following his death, Jeff's friends talked about how adulthood always mystified him and seemed blissfully out of his reach. Jeff thought maturity confined you like a necktie. "Why grow up?" he would ask. "Just because somebody says?"

Even at 30, Jeff, winner of three national skateboarding competitions, still lived a boy's life. He skated all the time, wildly, powerfully, balls out, as they say in Texas. In his little house atop a wooded hill in northeast Dallas, Jeff pulled frequent all-nighters, building models of spaceships and Japanese cartoon heroes, painting and gluing alongside glass tanks filled with snakes, chameleons, spiders, lizards and turtles. If Jeff needed to think, he climbed 60 feet up a nearby sycamore to a plywood treehouse – his favorite sanctuary.

Jeff spent a lot of time in the treehouse in 1993. The indoor skateboard park he owned was losing money. Alison Young, the ethereal blonde who had been his girlfriend for 10 years, had moved out of their house to a place of her own. He was depressed for good reasons. But none of his friends could have predicted that Jeff would take a .357 Magnum and shoot himself in the head early Christmas Day.

A few days after the funeral, Alison was packing up Jeff's belongings. She dragged his mattress out to the street for a Salvation Army pickup. Skaters from all over the country and Mexico kept calling, asking the same difficult question: "What was up with the dude?" Alison searched for an answer. "It's like

ROLLING STONE, SEPTEMBER 8, 1994 · 57

Carrot Top's jokes deal with college concerns like getting drunk and laid.

"Eventually I'm going to outgrow this," he says. "But I connect with them pretty well."

It's Show Time!

By RICH COHEN

The ROLLING STONES are taking
their rock & roll circus back on the road.

But is it still the greatest show on earth?

"I got news
for you,"
says Richards.
"We're still
a bunch of
tough bastards.
String us up
and we still
won't die."

These days,
when Jagger
sings about
satisfaction,
he may be
thinking less
of willing
teen-age girls
than of the
neat aesthetics
of a well-
turned deal.

(facing page)
Distinctive Merit/National

SERIES
The Rolling Stones
CREATIVE DIRECTOR *Fred Woodward*
DESIGNERS *Fred Woodward, Lee Bearson*
PHOTO EDITOR *Jodi Peckman*
PHOTOGRAPHER *Anton Corbijn*
CLIENT *Rolling Stone*

(right)
Distinctive Merit/National

SERIES
Mennonites: Endless Exodus
ART DIRECTOR *Tom Bentkowski*
DESIGNER *Tom Bentkowski*
DIRECTOR OF PHOTOGRAPHY *David Friend*
PHOTOGRAPHER *Larry Towell*
CLIENT *Life Magazine*

JOURNEY

EXODUS

Distinctive Merit/National

SERIES
Scotland by the Yard
ART DIRECTOR *Janet Froelich*
DESIGNER *Lisa Naftolin*
PHOTOGRAPHER *Sarah Moon*
CLIENT *The New York Times Magazine*

(facing page)
Distinctive Merit/National

GRAPHIC DESIGN, SERIES
Erickson's Self-Promotion Mailer
ART DIRECTOR *Jeff Griffith*
DESIGNER *Jeff Griffith*
COPYWRITER *Larry Bennett*
PHOTOGRAPHER *Jim Erickson*
PRODUCER *Suzanne Moore*
AGENCY *Griffith Advertising Design*
CLIENT *Erickson Production*

MERIT AWARDS

Merit/International

FULL PAGE OR SPREAD
Gravity
ART DIRECTOR *Tiger Savage*
CREATIVE DIRECTOR *Andy McKay*
COPYWRITER *Paul Silburn*
PHOTOGRAPHER *Nadav Kander*
AGENCY *Simons Palmer Denton Clemmow
and Johnson*
CLIENT *Nike UK, Sportswear*

Merit/International

FULL PAGE OR SPREAD
Gain
ART DIRECTOR *Tiger Savage*
CREATIVE DIRECTOR *Andy McKay*
COPYWRITER *Paul Silburn*
PHOTOGRAPHER *Nadav Kander*
AGENCY *Simons Palmer Denton Clemmow
and Johnson*
CLIENT *Nike UK, Sportswear*

Merit/International

FULL PAGE OR SPREAD
Nude No. 6
ART DIRECTOR *Nadav Kander*
PHOTOGRAPHER *Nadav Kander*

(facing page)
Merit/International

SERIES
Loch, Trees, Beach
ART DIRECTOR *Nigel Rose*
CREATIVE DIRECTOR *Trevor Beattie*
COPYWRITER *Murray Partridge*
PHOTOGRAPHER *Nadav Kander*
AGENCY *TBWA, Holmes Knight Ritchie*
CLIENT *Macdonald and Muir, Glenmorangie Whisky*

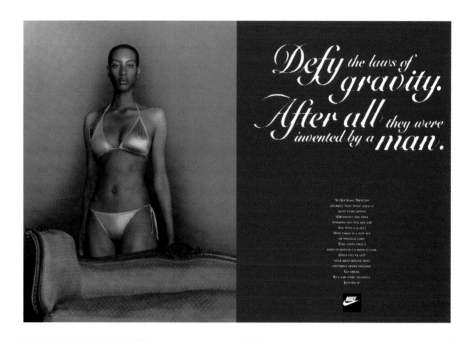

Merit/International

SERIES
Skin, Boys, Swimmer
ART DIRECTOR *Warren Eakins*
COPYWRITER *Evelyn Monroe*
PHOTOGRAPHER *Nadav Kander*
AGENCY *Wieden & Kennedy, Amsterdam*
CLIENT *Nike*

Merit/National

FULL PAGE OR SPREAD
Brassica
ART DIRECTOR *Gael Towey*
DESIGNER *Claudia Bruno*
PHOTOGRAPHER *Maria Robledo*
CLIENT *Martha Stewart Living*

Merit/National

FULL PAGE OR SPREAD
Chickens
ART DIRECTOR *Gael Towey*
DESIGNER *Gael Towey*
PHOTOGRAPHER *Victor Schrager*
CLIENT *Martha Stewart Living*

Merit/National

FULL PAGE OR SPREAD
The Cranberries
CREATIVE DIRECTOR *Fred Woodward*
PHOTO EDITORS *Jodi Peckman, Fiona McDonagh*
PHOTOGRAPHER *Raymond Meeks*
CLIENT *Rolling Stone*

Merit/National

FULL PAGE OR SPREAD
Perry Farrell
CREATIVE DIRECTOR *Fred Woodward*
PHOTO EDITOR *Jodi Peckman*
PHOTOGRAPHER *Mark Seliger*
CLIENT *Rolling Stone*

(facing page, top)
Merit/National

FULL PAGE OR SPREAD
Seinfeld
CREATIVE DIRECTOR *Fred Woodward*
DESIGNERS *Fred Woodward, Gail Anderson*
PHOTO EDITOR *Jodi Peckman*
PHOTOGRAPHER *Mark Seliger*
CLIENT *Rolling Stone*

(facing page, bottom)
Merit/National

FULL PAGE OR SPREAD
Anaconda
ART DIRECTOR *Tom Bentkowski*
DESIGNER *Mimi Park*
DIRECTOR OF PHOTOGRAPHY *David Friend*
PHOTOGRAPHER *James Balog*
CLIENT *Life Magazine*

The **KING** of Prime-Time **COMEDY** by Fred Schruers

Photographs by MARK SELIGER

ROLLING STONE, SEPTEMBER 22, 1994 · 47

IMAGINE A 30-FOOT, 300-POUND CORSET THAT TIGHTENS EACH TIME YOU EXHALE. THAT'S HOW AN ANACONDA SLOWLY SUFFOCATES A VICTIM, BE IT A SIX-FOOT ALLIGATOR OR A SIX-FOOT SWIMMER. AT LEAST AN ANACONDA WAITS UNTIL IT NO LONGER FEELS LIFE BEFORE SWALLOWING ITS MEAL—WHOLE. ALTHOUGH IT CANNOT SWALLOW ANYTHING AS BULKY AS AN ADULT HUMAN, THAT IS NO CONSOLATION TO THE PERSON THE ANACONDA HAS SUFFOCATED.

SERIES
Woodstock
ART DIRECTOR *Tom Bentkowski*
DESIGNER *Marti Golon*
DIRECTOR OF PHOTOGRAPHY *David Friend*
PHOTOGRAPHER *Gregory Heisler*
CLIENT *Life Magazine*

Merit/National

SERIES
Cindy Crawford
CREATIVE DIRECTOR *Fred Woodward*
DESIGNER *Fred Woodward*
PHOTO EDITOR *Laurie Kratochvil*
PHOTOGRAPHER *Herb Ritts*
CLIENT *Rolling Stone*

Merit/National

SERIES
Gang Wars
ART DIRECTOR *D. J. Stout*
DESIGNERS *D. J. Stout, Nancy McMillan*
COPYWRITER *Audrey Duff*
PHOTOGRAPHER *Dan Winters*
CLIENT *Texas Monthly*

"WE GET ALL HYPED UP—WE DO A DRIVE-BY" A REPORT FROM THE FRONT LINES OF THE SAN ANTONIO GANG WARS. BY AUDREY DUFF PHOTOGRAPHS BY DAN WINTERS

I'S ONE-FIFTEEN IN THE MORNING ON A Sunday in May. At the Alazan Apache Courts, one of San Antonio's toughest housing projects, seven teenage boys wearing designer jeans and polo shirts huddle behind the fence and garbage dumpster that separate the rear courtyard from the street. The boys crack jokes and suck down forty-ounce bottles of malt liquor.

The cover is decent here. They can see the street through the fence, and they have memorized every car at the neighborhood and its owner. Anyone cruising by looking to shoot somebody would have difficulty aiming into the shadows of the Courts. The boys, ranging in age from sixteen to eighteen, are members of three different gangs that get along—usually. They

LAST YEAR, THERE WERE 3.5 DRIVE-BY SHOOTINGS A DAY IN SAN ANTONIO. SAYS A POLICEMAN: "PEOPLE ARE AFRAID TO GO OUTSIDE."

lean against the dumpster or sit with their backs against a concrete wall. Just blocks away live their "enemies," members of rival gangs from neighboring housing projects: the Cassiano Homes, the San Juan Homes, the Villa Veramendi, and the Victoria Courts, all warring fiefdoms clustered on San Antonio's West Side.

"You always got to watch your back," says one of the boys, a sixteen-year-old who joined his first gang when he was eleven. He chats amiably about what he and his friends do for fun. "We get really drunk," he says. "We get all hyped up, and we do a drive-by or something like that."

At that moment, five shots rip through the air, and he and the others fall silent. The shots were loud and close. All seven boys start running through the rear courtyard—toward the gunfire. If the shooters make another pass, the boys can see who it is.

The boys backtrack through the soggy yard, where laundry hangs from clotheslines and the grass needs cutting, and they are a little edgier than they were before. Behind a sagging sheet, a dark figure approaches the boys with a gleaming gun in his hand. He yells something in Spanish as he points the gun at them and slides back the chamber. Is this it?

The moment is tense, but the boy turns out to be a friend. The others laugh at his performance and return to their spots against the wall and the dumpster, but something has changed. The air is electric. They chuckle and say they are not afraid. "Things like that happen here all the time," says one. Mean-

while, the teenager with the gun paces around the periphery of the group, watching their backs.

No one got hurt that night, but the incident brings into relief the two San Antonios: one a thriving city of beauty, history, and culture that draws tourists from around the country, and the other a city of warring youths, where small children are killed in their beds by stray gunfire. In 1993 there were 1,262 drive-by shootings reported in San Antonio, which has a population of 935,933. (The police department estimates that for every drive-by that is reported, ten are not.) In contrast, Dallas, with a population of 1,007,618, reported 221 drive-by shootings last year. Fort Worth's police department recorded 186 drive-bys, and in Austin there were an estimated 50. (Houston and El Paso don't keep figures on drive-by shootings but group them with homicides or assaults.)

"People are afraid to go outside. Children are afraid to play outside," says San Antonio police officer George Sexton. Until recently, Sexton patrolled Military Drive, a favorite Sunday-night cruising strip on the South Side where gang members go to meet girls. Gun-toting teens routinely turn the strip into a war zone. Says Sexton: "Drive-bys are the biggest fear we have in this town."

M ARKY SITS AT THE KITCHEN table of his family's three-bedroom apartment at the Alazan Apache Courts, where he lives with his mother, elder brother, younger sister, and sister-in-law. His brown eyes are still droopy at eleven-fifteen on a weekday morning because, he says, he heard shots outside his home late last night and got up to investigate. Marky lives on the West Side, where the Hispanic gangs predominate.

Marky's sister-in-law, who is 21 years old and seven months' pregnant, sits on the couch in the living room watching soap operas on TV. A mirror and a print of flowers on the wall behind her hide only a few of the dozen or so holes in the wall.

"The first time we got shot up, it was my mom and her boyfriend sitting in here," Marky says, yawning and rubbing his beefy neck. "The guys who did it were looking for me and my older brother because we were LA Boys and these guys were Kings. They were 'forks down' and we were 'forks up.'"

The sign of a pitchfork—made with the thumb, index finger, and middle finger—pointing either up or down indicates which of the two broad alliances of San Antonio's Hispanic gangs a particular gang belongs to. Gangs that use forks down are in the Black Circle; those that use forks up are in the Blue Circle. Wearing "colors," such as black or blue bandannas (called rags), can also tip off gang members as to who their friends are. And each individual gang has its own set of hand signs, usually the first letter of the gang's name.

Marky joined the LA Boys, named by Lanier High School football players who used the Lanier Athletics logo for their name, when he was in the seventh grade. "Me and my best friend wanted to get in because they had a lot of parties and a

GUNS AND POSES: AFTER GANG MEMBERS PICK OUT THEIR WEAPONS IN PAWNSHOPS OR GUN SHOWS, A FRIEND WHO IS OVER 21 BUYS THEM. GANG MEMBERS AREN'T ALWAYS YOUTHFUL—THE MAN ABOVE IS IN HIS THIRTIES—BUT THE YOUNGEST CAN BE THE MOST DANGEROUS, ACCORDING TO THE POLICE. "I REMEMBER THE FIRST TIME I SHOT A REAL GUN," SAYS MARKY, SIXTEEN (TOP LEFT—WITH AN ASSAULT RIFLE—AND RIGHT). "IT'S LIKE A HIGH . . ." EVERY GANG HAS ITS SYMBOLS: MARKY'S TATTOOS, TWEETY AND "D INC," PROCLAIM PAST AFFILIATIONS; AT LEFT, A MEMBER OF THE NO POSSE WEARING A NOTRE DAME CAP SHOWS OFF A STAB WOUND.

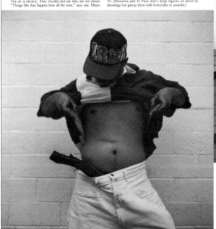

OPPOSITE: A TEENAGER SHOWS OFF HIS PIECE TO A FORMER GANG MEMBER (LEFT). THE HISPANIC GANGS ARE DIVIDED INTO TWO BROAD ALLIANCES; THE SIGN OF A PITCHFORK POINTING EITHER UP OR DOWN INDICATES WHICH ONE A GANG BELONGS TO. "FORKS DOWN"—SHOWN AS A GRAFFITO (ABOVE LEFT) AND A HAND SIGN "THROWN" BY A GANG MEMBER (ABOVE)—MEANS ALLEGIANCE TO THE BLACK CIRCLE. THROWING HAND SIGNS AT A RIVAL GANG CAN TRIGGER A DRIVE-BY SHOOTING. GANG MEMBERS ALSO ANNOUNCE THEIR LOYALTIES BY WEARING THEIR GANG'S "COLORS"—A BANDANNA, OR "RAG." LEFT: A MEMBER OF THE NO POSSE SHOWS HIS COLORS.

lot of chicks," he says. "We had to get rolled in [beaten up] by about fifteen guys in the plaza right here at the Courts for initiation, but my dad had always kicked my ass, so I didn't give a shit. That one huge guy looked at my friend Juan, so I thought he was going to let him, but he went *pow* and I hit the wall and bounced off it, and he kept hitting me, and I don't know how, but I got up, and they all beat me into a corner. Afterward they said, 'You made it. You can cry now.' But I didn't want to cry."

When Marky was thirteen, he quit the LA Boys and joined Damage, Inc. He strips off his shirt to display his tattoos—proof of his allegiance. On his left shoulder is a yellow Tweety bird clutching a handgun, left over from the days when he belonged to the LA Boys. Beneath the heavily armed bird is another tattoo: D Inc.

By the time Marky was fourteen, he had taken part in several drive-by shootings. Drive-bys are almost always committed by organized street gangs. Anything can trigger a drive-by—a turf battle, a squabble over a girlfriend, a "throwing" hand signs at rival gangs, an invitation, or the sheer thrill of it. "Drive-bys start when people from another gang act big shit and be, like, 'You're nobody,'" Marky explains, "and some people get serious and get out the guns."

Gang members get their guns from pawnshops or gun shows; after they pick out their weapons, a companion who is over 21 buys them. "I remember the first time I shot a real gun," Marky murmurs with a faraway look in his eyes. "It's like a high, and you like it, and you want to do it again and again and again. I don't remember doing my first drive-by—that was a long time ago. But I remember using my first Tec-9

[a semi-automatic pistol]. We were driving around and we said, 'Let's hit up some houses.' I was on the passenger side and they said, 'Go, Mark! Go!' I just shot like that—*pow-pow-pow*!" Marky points his right hand out to the side and jerks it high in the air. "It was kicking, and I didn't know it would do that. My friends thought that was cool, but they were all scared too."

Marky says no regrets one drive-by that killed innocent people. "We went to the wrong house. It was like the house was all shady and shit. I saw it on the news. They didn't like. I felt bad about it. I didn't want to think about it." He looks away and frowns. "I don't think about it."

Explaining why he participates in "gangbanging"—a word that in his milieu describes not gang rape but a long list of activities that includes beating people up, stealing cars, throw-

ing hand signs to incite rival gangs, and doing drive-bys—Marky says, "It's fun. It's exciting. We get crazy. Everybody thinks I come from a messed-up family and my mom don't love me and shit like that, but that's not it."

Still, Marky describes a childhood filled with physical abuse. "My dad used to hit me, and my mother would just watch or go to her room and shut the door. I stole money from my grandmother when I was little to buy soda and candy—twenty bucks. She told my dad, and he beat the shit out of me. He always wore boots, so he used to kick me with them. I once told him, 'Hit me when you're sober, why don't you?'" Marky has not seen his father in four years.

O FFICER RICK RIOJAS IS A LARGE MAN who is quick to laugh at any joke, but after three years in the trenches of gang warfare in San Antonio, his good humor is wearing thin. "They're all a bunch of dumb kids," Riojas says with a sigh. "They may do some horrible crimes, but it's easy to catch them because they think like kids."

The 35-year-old Riojas is a member of the San Antonio Police Department's gang unit, which was formed in June 1991. The gang unit saturates trouble spots with patrolling officers and mobile police stations. Its sixteen members pho-

The Black Garden

Elderly Abkhazians wait in line to
convert their money from the
useless Georgian currency into
Russian rubles

A gardener working by a
statue of Stalin and a headless
Lenin in the front yard of a
hospital in Sukhumi

A moment of prayer for those killed in an attempted coup two days before in
Freedom Square, Grozny, capital of the Chechen Republic

Photographs by Jason Eskenazi

Merit/National

SERIES
The Black Garden
ART DIRECTOR *Jill Korostoff*
DIRECTOR OF PHOTOGRAPHY *Peter Howe*
PHOTOGRAPHER *Jason Eskenazi*
CLIENT *Outtakes*

A young girl's image reflected
in a mirror on the wall that
separates her family from
a Baku Oilfield

Going to the Sukhumi morgue to
reclaim the bodies of sons killed in
a Georgian ambush

ABOVE RIGHT

Men in Gadauta try to telephone
from a street box during the
Russian blockade

ABOVE

A semblance of normalcy returns
to Sukhumi's Prospect Mira two weeks
after the Georgian pullout

Laundry hangs in front of the abandoned synagogue
in the town of Krasnayasloboda, Azerbaijan

LEFT

A young mother and
three children flee
the bombing in
Stepanakert on a
helicopter to Yerevan

BELOW

The bodies of 126 soldiers were
discovered in a mass grave behind the
hospital in Sukhumi six months
after a Georgian ambush

BELOW

The Freedom Oil Field,
where Stalin organized
his first strikes

A woman mourns the death of her brother in Tbilisi

An orphan lies sedated in Kharbert near Yerevan

A soldier searches for the body of his brother in Sukhumi

A mourning ceremony in Krasnayasloboda

Merit/National

SERIES
From Russia, with Hope and Fear
ART DIRECTOR *Janet Froelich*
DESIGNER *Nancy Harris*
PHOTO EDITOR *Kathy Ryan*
PHOTOGRAPHER *Sebastião Salgado*
CLIENT *The New York Times Magazine*

Merit/National

SERIES
Pentimento
ART DIRECTOR *Janet Froelich*
DESIGNER *Jamie Olivieri*
PHOTOGRAPHER *David Seidner*
CLIENT *The New York Times Magazine*

Merit/National

SERIES
Beauty on the Edge
DESIGN DIRECTOR *Shawn Young*
DESIGNER *Shawn Young*
PHOTOGRAPHER *Herb Ritts*
CLIENT *Allure*

The asymmetrical Aphrodite: Anjelica Huston wears a men's shirt by Giorgio Armani and drawstring pants by Calvin Klein. These pages: Hair, Kevin Mancuso; makeup, Carol Shaw for Lorac. Details, see Credits page.

Beauty
On the Edge

Anjelica Huston on love, marriage, and
wanting to be blond. And, oh yes—Jack too.

PHOTOGRAPHED BY HERB RITTS

By Betsy Sharkey

njelica Huston is never completely at ease with life, a skittishness born, she says, of not quite knowing when the ax will fall next. She traces that feeling back to the year she was 17 and the phone call that came in the night, bringing her word that her mother, former New York City Ballet dancer Enrica Soma, had been killed in a car crash in the South of France. It taught her early on that nothing is permanent.

Long and lean, cut like a Thoroughbred, Huston has an aristocratic grace with which she weathers the disappointments and the indignities of a life lived in public. "Loss is always at its worst when it's new," she says. "That's not to say it ever goes away or that you ever get over it, really—and of course there are new losses around every dubious corner." When the ax does fall, though, Huston is single-minded in trying to patch up the damage.

Now the 43-year-old actress is doing a bit of delicate reconstructive surgery on the tatters of her relationship with Jack Nicholson. Their often turbulent 16-year love affair ended in 1989 when she, and the rest of the world, read in the press that Nicholson was expecting a child with former waitress Rebecca Broussard.

The forum for the current Huston-Nicholson rapprochement is *The Crossing Guard*, a new movie written and directed by Sean Penn and co-starring the former lovers. "For me, the idea of working with Jack is always interesting," she says. "I've always felt we have a connection when we work, and a connection too when we don't work." Huston is a master of understatement and abstract speech, or—put more precisely—of polite evasion.

In *The Crossing Guard*, Huston plays Mary Manning to Nicholson's Freddy Gale. The story is about the death of their daughter, killed by a drunk driver. While Freddy can't let go of the past, Mary has learned to forgive, and move on.

Though the connection with Nicholson, and Huston's willingness to forgive him for breaking it, have become a theme in the interviews she is doing for the film, one can't help but wonder if things are really so tidy. As content as she says she is these days, Huston seems to display an almost obsessive need to put a different face on the public debacle

Reluctant icon. Above: Turtleneck by Calvin Klein. Right: Cashmere sweater by Calvin Klein. Following page: Coat by Jil Sander. Details, see Credits page.

> "I desperately wanted to
> be a sort of blond
> Audrey Hepburn when
> I was little."

that was the end of their love affair. Nicholson, meanwhile, has never seemed like someone in search of absolution. The actor has since had a second child with Broussard, is enmeshed in another claim of paternity by yet another waitress, and still argues that he was never meant to be monogamous.

Huston's confident, forgiving stance is a measure of how far she has come in her life. "I think if I could change something about my early years, I could have spent more time feeling less sorry for myself," she says. "I think I would like to have forgiven myself more—I was pretty hard on myself."

When she was just 16, her father, the legendary filmmaker John Huston, cast her in a leading role in *A Walk With Love and Death*. Savaged by critics for her portrayal of a medieval maiden, she dropped out of sight for a decade. "I truly felt hideous," she has said of that time. "I felt ugly. I felt off-center.... I hadn't believed in the movie in the first place. Still, I wasn't prepared for how bad the response would be." Eventually, Huston began to take tiny offbeat parts in everything from obscure one-act plays to the TV show *Laverne & Shirley*. She would triumphantly redeem herself in 1986, taking home an Oscar for her performance as Maerose, the tough-funny 'Mafia princess, in *Prizzi's Honor*, another film directed by her father.

Since that early time, few critics have taken issue with her talent. Most of the difficulties have come in trying to define her, at least in the terms Hollywood usually bestows upon its leading ladies.

Early on, Nicholson identified Huston's essential quality as "class, deep class." Penn, who believes there are not many actresses who can hold their own opposite Nicholson, says, "She has a certain weight and dignity about her."

Huston says she has always invested the characters she plays with all the drama of her own experience. The characters, in turn, let her express what she's feeling at the moment, giving this guarded woman a series of safe, public catharses.

Though she has spent a lifetime in front of it, Huston does not have a natural affection for the camera. Visually, her style is one of confrontation, not love. She is still haunted by overhearing her parents suggest at age 15 that she would never be pretty. Although she brokered her exotic looks into top modeling jobs in London and New York (continued on page 222)

THE HAUNTING CITY
LIFE AND DEATH IN BENARAS

Photographs by Mary Ellen Mark

India has been dominant in my work since my first trip there in the late sixties. It has been the source for three of my books, *Falkland Road* (1980), *Mother Theresa's Missions of Charity* (1985), and *Indian Circus* (1993). Last year I produced a documentary film photographed and directed by my husband, Martin Bell, *The Amazing Plastic Lady*, about a traveling circus in South India.

India is the country that fascinates me most—the country that draws me back to complete projects started many years ago. Benaras is one of them. For me it is the most haunting city in India, full of mystery and passion. It is a city of life. It is a city of death.

The demands of my professional life in New York are difficult and stressful. At such times I imagine myself in Benaras, pretending I am on a boat floating down the Ganges. It is late afternoon. As my boat travels past the ghats, the stairways leading to the river, I imagine songs, chants, ringing bells, prayers and lowing cows. Twilight fades into the darkness and slowly lights appear from the ancient buildings along the river's edge. The glimmering candles bobbing on the water give the early evening atmosphere a ghostly and eerie quality. I'm suffused by the smell of jasmine garlands. All is peace. There is no place I would rather be.

The photographs in this portfolio were taken over a quarter of a century. Benaras is visually rich and yields images of wide-ranging subject matter. There are photographs of hippies of the 'sixties' who visited the city in their search for spirituality and drugs. I photographed real sadhus and fake sadhus, body builders, blind children and even a maharajah. I see these not merely as reflections of an exotic country, but photographs that cross cultural boundaries and reflect the universality of human experience. As in all my work, I aim for design, atmosphere and spontaneity, but most important to me is developing personal photographic intimacy with my subjects.

Benaras is most famous for the daily bathing and cremation rituals along the river ghats. I not only photographed that lively activity, but the more private workings of the people and the city. I made pictures at the Mani Karam Burning Ghat which is an essential aspect of life in Benaras. I also tried to show these people performing the rituals that accompany the death ceremony. In some cases, I photographed people just before death in their hospice-like dwellings in the city.

This is an incomplete body of work. I dream of returning to Benaras for an extended time to finish it and eventually produce a book. Five years ago, on my final day of photographing in Benaras, I said goodbye to one of the woodcutters at the Mani Karam Burning Ghat. "Nice to meet you," he said. "Be sure and come back here when you die."

MARY ELLEN MARK

Merit/National

SERIES
The Haunting City
ART DIRECTOR *Jill Korostoff*
DIRECTOR OF PHOTOGRAPHY *Peter Howe*
PHOTOGRAPHER *Mary Ellen Mark*
CLIENT *Outtakes*

ADDITIONAL AWARD

Merit
FULL PAGE OR SPREAD

"I see these not merely as reflections of an exotic country, but photographs which cross cultural boundaries and reflect the universality of human experience."

"I said goodbye to one of the woodcutters at the Mani Karam Burning Ghat. 'Nice to meet you' he said, 'Be sure and come back here when you die'."

(left)
Merit/National

SERIES
The Capital Call Girls
ART DIRECTOR *D. J. Stout*
DESIGNERS *D. J. Stout, Nancy McMillan*
COPYWRITER *Robert Draper*
PHOTOGRAPHER *Dan Winters*
CLIENT *Texas Monthly*

(facing page, top)
Merit/National

SERIES
Redwoods Forever
ART DIRECTOR *Lou DiLorenzo*
DESIGNER *Diane Bertolo*
PHOTO EDITOR *Bill Black*
PHOTOGRAPHER *Karen Kuehn*
CLIENT *Travel Holiday*

(facing page, bottom)
Merit/International

SERIES
Der Weg nach oben
ART DIRECTOR *Sigi Mayer*
COPYWRITER *Sigi Mayer*
PHOTOGRAPHER *Horst Stasny*
STUDIO *Sigi Mayer*
CLIENT *Modern Times*

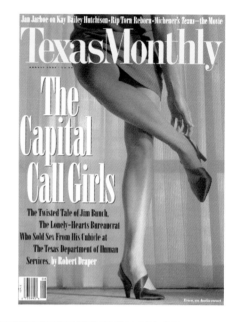

Redwoods Forever

In most travel guides, "northern California" means the San Francisco Bay area, the cultural counterweight to Los Angeles. But these longtime rivals have far more in common with each other than either has with the real northern California—a vast backcountry where you can drive for 200 miles in the nation's most populous state without

encountering a town with as many as 30,000 people. Cross the Golden Gate, leave the suburbs and the wineries behind, and you will enter a California that has never quite shared in the golden dream that is the state's formative myth. It is gorgeous terrain, rugged and rural, but its climax forests and swift rivers have always been regarded more benignly by visitors than by home folks, to whom the forests represent the main source of livelihood and the rivers represent a threat of killer floods. So remote is this

In Lady Bird Johnson Grove, at Redwood National Park (left), the life cycles of an infant child and a centuries-old tree converge. A wall in Fern Canyon (above).

by **PAUL BURKA** · photographed by **KAREN KUEHN**

der weg nach oben

eine lyrische modestory,
erzählt von sigi mayer (concept) & horst stasny (foto)

fashion by setball

4780 m seehöhe

Merit/National

FULL PAGE OR SPREAD
Dinner Invitation Announcement Poster
ART DIRECTOR *Bob Gill*
PHOTOGRAPHER *Carl Fischer*
CLIENT *The Art Directors Club*

ILLUSTRATION

GOLD AND SILVER MEDALISTS

GOLD AND SILVER MEDALISTS

Silver Medalist/National

SERIES
Open to Suggestion
ART DIRECTOR *Janet Froelich*
DESIGNER *Lisa Naftolin*
ILLUSTRATOR *Françoise Berthoud*
CLIENT *The New York Times Magazine*

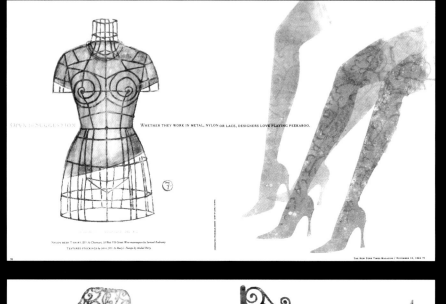

OPEN to SUGGESTION

WHETHER THEY WORK IN METAL, NYLON OR LACE, DESIGNERS LOVE PLAYING PEEKABOO.

NYLON MESH T-SHIRT, $35 At Charivari, 18 West 57th Street. Wire mannequin by Samuel Rushanny.
TEXTURED STOCKINGS by DKNY, $15. At Macy's. Pumps by Michel Perry.

THE NEW YORK TIMES MAGAZINE / NOVEMBER 13, 1994 73

CHENILLE SWIRL DRESS, $680 by Kalinka. At Shen, 1001 Madison Avenue.

CHATEAU-STYLE IRON GATE, custom-made by Randolph Marshall for Les Métalliers Champenois.

ILLUSTRATIONS BY FRANÇOISE BERTHOUD

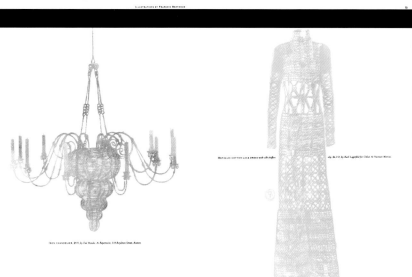

IRON CHANDELIER, $975, by Dal Mondo. At Repertoire, 114 Boylston Street, Boston.

METALLIC COTTON LACE DRESS with silk chiffon slip, $6,150, by Karl Lagerfeld for Chloé. At Neiman Marcus.

ILLUSTRATIONS BY FRANÇOISE BERTHOUD

Silver Medalist/National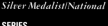

SERIES
Piccolo Mondo
ART DIRECTOR *Janet Froelich*
ILLUSTRATOR *Maira Kalman*
CLIENT *The New York Times*

piccolo mondo

Spring
children's wear
takes a
Roman holiday.

Story and Illustrations
by Maira Kalman

On Via di Pasico,
up the street from
Caffè Bella Roma, the
ancient Gelsomina
scraggles to the
window, lowers her
basket and pulls
up the daily
delivery of milk.

In the pomeriggio,
Vincenzo D'Amore, of
Vicolo del Divino Amore,
promenades his
turtle Pipo around the
Piazza del Popolo.

Surrounded by
the hot winds of
the baking
focaccia, the
poet Giovanni
stands on
long, skinny
legs making
sandwiches and
poems, poems
and sandwiches.

Signora Scamorza's
class went to the
Vatican to see a
painting of a man
holding a fire in his
palm. She said he
was a saint, and the
children were not.

In the park behind
the Castel St. Angelo, where
shy Emperor Hadrian
was buried, kissing couples
make good soccer goals.

When Count Piccolomini
takes caffè near the
Piazza di Spagna, his
dachshund Dora
will get a better seat
than you will.

Silver Medalist/National

FULL PAGE OR SPREAD
Sam Cooke's SAR Records Story
ART DIRECTOR *Iris Keitel*
CREATIVE DIRECTOR *Alisa Ritz*
DESIGNERS *Diana Graham, Cody Rasmussen*
COPYWRITER *Peter Guralnick*
ILLUSTRATOR *Angelo Tillery*
CLIENT *ABKCO Records*

ADDITIONAL AWARD

Merit
GRAPHIC DESIGN, EDITORIAL DESIGN, BOOK, SINGLE

DISTINCTIVE MERIT AWARDS

83 STEVEN BRILL

FOUNDER, CEO, COURT TV

◆ **LAST YEAR:** — ◆ **AGE:** 44 ◆ **CREDITS:** O.J. Simpson, the Bobbitts, the Menendez brothers, and the charm of highbrow scandalmongering have made this three-year-old cable station big business. ◆ **DEBITS:** Though Brill cashes in on the tabloid TV boom while savoring hard-news cachet, the rest of the media ape him like crazy, diluting his franchise.

84 RICHARD MOSK

CHAIRMAN, MPAA RATINGS BOARD

◆ **LAST YEAR:** — ◆ **AGE:** 54 ◆ **CREDITS:** Because an NC-17 rating can mean financial death, Hollywood's most powerful directors scramble to appease Mosk and his 10-member ratings board—giving them more power over final cut than any studio head. ◆ **DEBITS:** The MPAA continually gets dissed for being softer on violence than on sex.

85 HOWARD STERN

RADIO AND TV PERSONALITY

◆
PORTRAIT
BY HANOCH
PIVEN

◆ **LAST YEAR:** — ◆ **AGE:** 40 ◆ **CREDITS:** Made over $40 million from his No. 1 book (soon to be a movie) *Private Parts*; has the clout to not get axed despite nearly $2 million in FCC obscenity fines. ◆ **DEBITS:** A late-night show for Fox was reportedly nixed after Murdoch saw his raunchy New Year's Eve special. Stern blames creative differences.

86 MEG RYAN

ACTRESS

◆ **LAST YEAR:** — ◆ **AGE:** 33 ◆ **CREDITS:** *When a Man Loves a Woman* not only confirmed her status as Hollywood's favorite romantic ingenue but expanded her range and could win her an Oscar nomination; will earn $8 million for her role in *The Women*. ◆ **DEBITS:** She's known for passing on high-profile films—*Maverick* being the most recent.

59

(*facing page*)
Distinctive Merit/National

FULL PAGE OR SPREAD
Howard Stern
ART DIRECTOR *Jill Armus*
CREATIVE DIRECTOR *Bob Newman*
DESIGNER *Jill Armus*
PHOTOGRAPHER *Monica Stevenson*
ILLUSTRATOR *Hanoch Piven*
CLIENT *Entertainment Weekly*

(*above*)
Distinctive Merit/International

FULL PAGE OR SPREAD
Strippers Hermengildo Sabat
ILLUSTRATOR *Seymour Chwast*
AGENCY *The Pushpin Group, Inc.*
CLIENT *Sección Aurea, Fundación Artes Visuales*

MERIT AWARDS

MERIT AWARDS

Merit/National

FULL PAGE OR SPREAD
Some Risk Doesn't Look Like Risk
ART DIRECTOR *Guy Marino*
DESIGNER *Guy Marino*
ILLUSTRATOR *Brad Holland*
CLIENT *Bankers Trust*

Merit/National

FULL PAGE OR SPREAD
Art Directors Club of Cincinnati Poster
ILLUSTRATOR *Brad Holland*
CLIENT *Art Directors Club of Cincinnati*

Merit/National

FULL PAGE OR SPREAD
Lucia di Lammer Moor
ART DIRECTOR *Jan Obye*
CREATIVE DIRECTOR *Ann Murphy*
DESIGNER *Rafal Olbinski*
ILLUSTRATOR *Rafal Olbinski*
AGENCY *Nappi-Eliran-Murphy*
CLIENT *New York City Opera*

Merit/National

FULL PAGE OR SPREAD
Garry Shandling
CREATIVE DIRECTOR *Fred Woodward*
DESIGNERS *Fred Woodward, Gail Anderson*
ILLUSTRATOR *Robert Risko*
CLIENT *Rolling Stone*

Merit/National

FULL PAGE OR SPREAD
How to Give Orders Like a Man
ART DIRECTOR *Janet Froelich*
DESIGNER *Nancy Harris*
ILLUSTRATOR *Gary Baseman*
CLIENT *The New York Times Magazine*

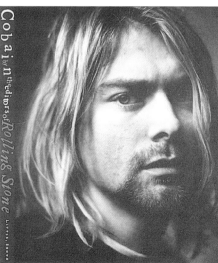

Merit/National

FULL PAGE OR SPREAD
Kurt Cobain
CREATIVE DIRECTOR *Fred Woodward*
DESIGNER *Fred Woodward*
ILLUSTRATOR *Philip Burke*
CLIENT *Rolling Stone*

KEEPING TIME BY JOHN SAYLES

A FICTION

THE OWNER ISN'T AROUND, so there is only an old man to help Mike with his kit. Each time Mike hands him another case from the van, he examines it, then nods and goes "Uh-huh" as if he's taking inventory. The old man is lanky, with maple-colored skin and eyes huge and soft behind thick lenses.

"Got to deal with the mess," he says when it's all inside and leaves Mike to set up alone.

The kit is pretty simple these days. Only two rack toms, floor tom, couple cymbals, the kick he just bought and the snare he's had forever. Mike looks to the back of the room where the old man is cleaning. The distance throws his time off, a gap between the push of the broom and the sweeping sound. Mike tightens the head on the snare. Need the firepower.

It is a club he hasn't played before, though *club* is an exaggeration. A former Grange hall with a makeshift bar, plywood sheet laid on shipping pallets for a stage. The stage is against the wall, which is better acoustics and always makes Mike feel more secure. The time outdoors in the storm with Blood Source, tumbling back into the ooze below the bandstand, neither the players in front nor the rain-soaked headbangers in the field noticed he was gone till his solo came up.

He's played worse.

If the janitor doesn't stick around for the first set, he'll be the oldest person in the club. Bet on it. The last show, keeping time under the new girl's vocal and looking out at the children in their torn clothes, washed in the red light, it sat on him hard.

The time he was keeping brought a picture to him, like it always did. This time he was breaking rocks on a chain gang, not a soulful, swinging, Sam Cooke kind of scene but something nasty and tired where each heavy-armed chop was another day off his life. It sat on him hard and heavy, and he looked out at the kids in the red light and thought, "Am I boring them, or are they boring me?"

"Man, you were buried in that groove tonight!" said Joey at the motel later. "Thought we'd have to call 911."

And later still, the phone call to his kid on the coast, the long stretches of dead air between them that Mike wanted to fill with drumming, screaming, something. "If it's too loud, you're too old," said the kid at the mixer board who'd kept creeping the volume up all night.

There was a time he'd be wired already, adrenaline pumping, just setting the kit up. Attack mode. Show time. Standing on the edge, waiting for the music to give him a nudge.

Mike's hands lay palm down on his thighs, dead meat.

The janitor comes up with a full dustpan to dump in a cardboard box next to the stage. He smiles at Mike.

"Mr. Time," he says, eyes flicking over the pieces of the drum kit. "Mr. Rhythm."

The old man chuckles to himself as he turns back

Though JOHN SAYLES is best known as an independent filmmaker ("Return of the Secaucus 7," "Eight Men Out," "Passion Fish"), he is also the author of three novels ("Union Dues," "Pride of the Bimbos," "Los Gusanos") and a collection of short stories ("The Anarchists' Convention").

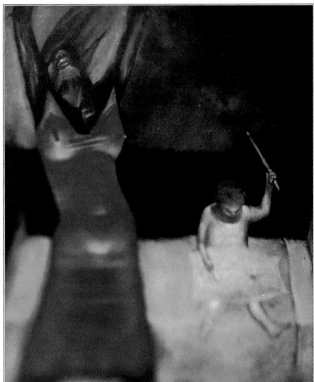

ILLUSTRATION BY MATT MAHURIN

Merit/National

FULL PAGE OR SPREAD
Keeping Time
CREATIVE DIRECTOR *Fred Woodward*
DESIGNER *Fred Woodward*
ILLUSTRATOR *Matt Mahurin*
CLIENT *Rolling Stone*

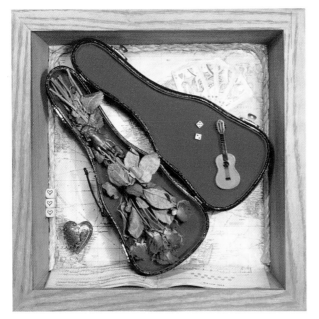

Merit/National

SERIES
VH1 Honors Awards
ART DIRECTOR *Cheri Dorr*
CREATIVE DIRECTOR *Cheri Dorr*
PHOTOGRAPHER *Lee Friedman*
ILLUSTRATOR *Melissa Meier*
PRODUCTION STUDIO *Robert Du Grenier Associates,*
New York
CLIENT *VH1*

Honey, They Shrunk the Planet. As communication and travel increasingly shorten the cultural distance from here to there, we find less and less reason to separate the National and International judgings. Instead, this year's Advertising and Graphic Design juries were drawn from both the United States and abroad, and each jury judged both the national and international work in its own discipline.

It is no small achievement to have one's work in this Art Directors Annual. The 74th National/9th International Annual Exhibition has been much praised as the strongest and best-looking show in years, and every winner in this book earned its place.

On the editorial side, we have taken great pains to present the winning work with elegance, clarity, and as much accuracy as humanly possible. The work deserves it.

—Myrna Davis
Executive Director, The Art Directors Club

1995 Recipients

Cooper Union
Robert Rindler, Dean

Michael Essl
Kaming Liu

F.I.T.
Jerry McDaniel, Chairperson

Erez Bahar
John Lamacchia
Chau Nguyen
Lisa Schofield

New York City Technical College
Joel Mason, Dept. Chairperson

Guy Champagne
Densford Jones
Tarunashwari Singh

Parsons School of Design
William Bevington, Dept. Chairperson

Parolio Matos
David Noboa
Liza Pagano
Gladys Yue

Pratt Institute
Joseph Roberts, Dept. Chairperson

Michael Kelly
Seungyun Je
Erik Ringerud
James Allan Spahr

Pratt Manhattan
Elliott Gordon, Dept. Chairperson

Bimo Pamungkas
Rie Shibayama

School of Visual Arts
Richard Wilde, Dept. Chairperson

Songju Hong
Robert Johnston
Terje Vist

1995 Donors

Roz Goldfarb
Walter Kaprielian
Ruth Lubell
The Art Directors Club, Inc.

The Visual Communicators Education Fund, Inc. (VCEF) was founded by the members of the Art Directors Club to aid and encourage the development of talented students entering the profession of art direction. It awards scholarship funds annually to advertising and design schools, who then designate the students who are to share them. Seven schools in the metropolitan area, listed opposite, were invited to participate this year. Department heads from each school selected the most deserving students entering their senior year of studies.

It was heartwarming to see the twenty-two student recipients gather at the Club for the award presentation, anticipating their names being called as their families and friends stood proudly by their sides. The evening served as an opportunity for the students to interact and for the department chairs to get to know each other or reminisce.

In recent years, one dollar from every entry into the Annual Exhibition has gone to the VCEF, and art auctions have been organized to which members and friends have contributed. All contributions to the VCEF are tax-deductible. The VCEF is planning new fund-raising activities for 1996. Our goal is to collaborate with more ADC members, to develop ideas and implement the ones we can to help aspiring art students fulfill their dreams.

—Richard MacFarlane
President, Visual Communicators Education Fund

Board of Directors

Carl Fischer,
Carl Fischer Photography, Inc.
President

Ruth Lubell,
Lubell Brodsky, Inc.
First Vice-President

Theodore Pettus,
Lockhart & Pettus
Second Vice-President

Leslie Singer,
Singer Design
Secretary

Bill Oberlander,
Kirshenbaum, Bond & Partners
Assistant Secretary/Treasurer

Executive Committee

Bob Cox,
The Cox Group, Inc.

Jack Mariucci

Minoru Morita

Martin Solomon,
Martin Solomon, Co.

Richard Wilde,
School of Visual Arts

74th National/9th International Annual Committee

Woody Pirtle,
Pentagram
Designer of Call for Entries

B. Martin Pedersen
Exhibition Chairperson

Parry Merkley
Judging Chairperson, Advertising

Dana Arnett
Judging Chairperson, Graphic Design

Awards Presentation Evening

Leslie Singer
Chairperson

Jean Govoni
Co-Chairperson

Woody Pirtle,
Pentagram
Invitation Design

Robert Spica,
Pentagram
Program/Winners Book Design

ADC Publications, Inc.

Seymour Chwast
Vice-President

Steven Brower
Secretary

Sara Giovanitti
Treasurer

Paul Davis
Maureen Gleason
Andrew Kner
Jackie Merri Meyer
B. Martin Pedersen
Advisors

The Art Directors Club Newsletter

Seymour Chwast
Sara Giovanitti
Editorial/Design Committee

Pat Riedman
Editor

Mary Fichter
Associate Editor

Re:Design, Inc.
Layout

Hall of Fame Committee

Richard Wilde
Selection Chairperson

Allan Beaver
William H. Buckley
Carl Fischer
Central Committee

Ed Brodsky
Lou Dorfsman
Steven Heller
Walter Kaprielian
Andrew Kner
Martin Solomon
Selection Committee

Visual Communicators Education Fund

Richard MacFarlane
President

Jessica Weber
First Vice-President

Lee Goodman
Second Vice-President

David MacInnes
Treasurer

William Brockmeier
Assistant Treasurer

Dorothy Wachtenheim
Secretary

Peter Adler
Assistant Secretary

Meg Crane
David Davidian
Walter Kaprielian
Directors

The Art Directors Club Committee Chairpersons

Robert S. Smith
Constitution

Shinichiro Tora
Japan Traveling Exhibition

Martin Solomon
Portfolio Review

Ruby Miye Friedland
Speaker Events

Ruth Lubell (acting chair)
Membership

The Art Directors Club
Advisory Board of Past Presidents

Allan Beaver
Robert Blattner
William Brockmeier
Ed Brodsky
William H. Buckley
David Davidian
Lou Dorfsman
Kurt Haiman
Walter Kaprielian
Andrew Kner
George Lois
John Peter
Eileen Hedy Schultz
Robert S. Smith
Karl Steinbrenner
William Taubin
Henry Wolf

The Art Directors Club Staff

Myrna Davis
Executive Director

Olga Grisaitis
Club Manager

Verice Weatherspoon
Membership Director

Eileen McClash
Development Associate

Mary Fichter
Public Relations

Angela Alvarez
Controller

Luis de Jesus
Director of Exhibitions

Antje Lenthe Arcia
Competition Coordinator

Glenn Kubota
Exhibition Associate

Ann Schirripa
Receptionist

Romy Maldonado
House Assistant

Margaret Busweiler
Raymond Hill
Waitstaff

Phillips Gold & Co., Inc.
Accountants

Chemical Bank N.A.
Bank

Cowan Gold,
Gubman, Sitomer, Goldstein & Edlitz
Legal Counsel

United States

Aarons, Lawrence
Adamec, Donald
Adamek, Tina
Adams, Gaylord
Adams, Steven
Addiss, Patricia
Adelman, Jim
Adler, Peter
Adorney, Charles S.
Ahlgrim, Dennis
Allen, Heidi Flynn
Anderson, Jack
Anderson, Joseph
Andreasen, Susan
Andreozzi, Gennaro
Angeloni, Rick
Aragaki, Phyllis
Armario, David
Armour, Lawrence
Arnold, Stephanie A.
Aronson, Herman
Arthur, Rochelle L.
Babitz, Jeff
Bach, Robert O.
Badrinath, Arati S.
Baer, Charles H.
Baer, Priscilla
Baker, Eric
Ballister, Ronald
Barber, Ray
Barker, Floyd
Baron, Richard M.
Barrett, Christine
Barrett, Elizabeth A.
Barrios, Juan Jose Tejeda
Barron, Don
Barthelmes, Robert
Barton, Gladys
Bauch, Nancy
Baumann, Mary K.
Beaven, Clifford J.
Beaver, Allan
Beckman, Arthur
Bender, Lois
Bennett, Edward J.
Bennett, George
Benson, Laurence Key
Berenter, Bill
Berg, John
Berger, Danielle
Berman, Matt
Bernard, Walter L.
Bertolami, Peter
Bertulis, Frank
Best, Robert
Bevington, William
Beylerian, George
Binzen, Barbara
Blank, Janet
Blank, Peter J.
Blattner, Robert
Blechman, R. O.
Blend, Robert H.
Bloch, Bruce
Block, David S.
Bloom, Karen M.
Blumberg, Arnold
Bluming, Joel
Boches, Edward

Bode, Robert
Bodenschatz, Sharon
Bonavita, Donna
Booth, George Warren
Bourges, Jean
Bowman, Harold A.
Boyd, Doug
Brady, Evelyn M.
Braguin, Simeon
Brauer, Fred J.
Braverman, Al
Brent, Michael
Breslin, Lynn Dreese
Brockmeier, Bill
Brodsky, Ed
Brody, Ruth
Brody, Sam
Brooks, Adrienne
Brower, Steven
Brown, Beverly
Brown, George
Brown, Mark Delane
Bruce, Robert
Brugnatelli, Bruno E.
Brumberg, Gary
Buckley, William H.
Burkhardt, Ron
Butler, Bonnie
Bynum, Peter
Cadge, Bill
Canniff, Bryan G.
Caporimo, James
Cardillo, James
Carew, Bob
Carnase, Michael
Carnase, Thomas
Carruthers, Roy
Casado, Ralph
Cason, Merrill
Cassell, Emmett
Castelli, Angelo
Catherines, Diana
Ceradini, David
Cernero, Tina
Chambers, Jean
Chang, Andrew
Chaplinsky, Anthony, Jr.
Chen, Jack C.
Chermayeff, Ivan
Cherry, John
Chester, Laurie
Chetter, Shirley E.
Christie, Alan
Church, Stanley
Chwast, Seymour
Clapps, John
Clark, Alice
Clark, Herbert H.
Clarke, Bud
Clarke, James V.
Clemente, Thomas F.
Cline, Mahlon
Cohen, Joel
Cohen, Peter
Coll, Michael
Conner, Elaine
Connors, Catherine
Cook, M. Deidre
Cooper, David A.
Corey, Lee

Costabel, Eva
Cotler, Sheldon
Cotler-Block, Susan
Coverdale, Jac
Cox, Phyllis Richmond
Cox, Robert
Craig, James Edward
Crane, Meg
Crane, Susan J.
Cronan, Michael
Crossley, Gregory
Crozier, Bob
Cullen, Leslie
Cumbie, James Ty
Curry, Allison Davis
Curry, Christine
Cutler, Ethel R.
Cutshaw, Gregory F.
Davidian, David
Davidson, Steven
Davis, Barbara Vaughn
Davis, David R.
Davis, Paul B.
Davis, Philip
Davis, Randi B.
Davis, Theodore M.
Defrin, Bob
DeGregorio, Tony
Del Sorbo, Joe
DeMartino, Erick
Demoney, Jerry
Derderan, Thomas
Deutsch, David
DeVito, Frank
Dignam, John
DiVincenzo, Dennis
Doppelt, Shelley
Dorfsman, Louis
Dorian, Marc
Douglas, Kay Elizabeth
Drace, Matthew
Drenttel, William
Drucker, Rina
Dubiel, Ann
Duffy, Donald H.
Dunn, Faith
Eckstein, Bernard
Edgar, Peter
Edwards, Geoffrey T.
Eidel, Zeneth
Eisenman, Nina
Eisenman, Stanley
Eisner, Robert
Ellis, Judith
Endewelt, Jack
Epstein, David
Epstein, Lee
Ericson, Shirley
Ermoyan, Suren
Fable, Kathleen Quinn
Factor, Ellen
Fama, Joseph
Fanno, George
Fedele, Gene
Federico, Gene
Fenga, Michael
Ferrell, John
Filson, Kristin
Finelli, Douglas
Fink, Len

Fiorentino, Lou
Fiorenza, Blanche
Fischer, Carl
Fletcher, Patricia
Flock, Donald P.
Fraioli, John
Frankfurt, Stephen O.
Franklin, Richard
Freeland, Bill
Freyss, Christina
Friedland, Ruby Miye
Friedman, Beverly
Frith, Michael K.
Frost, Oren
Fuchs, Aaron
Fujita, Neil
Fury, Leonard W.
Gable, Mark A.
Gabrich, Michelle
Gaeta, Raymond
Gage, Robert
Galioto, Rosemarie
Gallo, Danielle
Gardner, Bert
Gardner, Hope
Garlanda, Gino
Gavasci, Alberto Paolo
Geissbuhler, Steff
Gennarelli, Charles
Genova, Gerald J.
George, Jeffrey E.
George, Robert J.
Geranmayeh, Vida
Germakian, Michael
Geryak, John
Gessman, Carl
Gialleonardo, Victor
Gibson, Kurt
Ginsberg, Frank C.
Giovanitti, Sara
Giraldi, Bob
Glaser, Milton
Gleason, Maureen R.
Gluckman, Eric
Gobe, Marc
Goen, Tama Alexandrine
Goettel, Manfred
Gold, Bill
Goldberg, Irwin
Goldfarb, Roz
Goldsmith, Gary
Goodfellow, Joanne
Goodman, Lee
Goss, Jeff
Govoni, Jean
Grace, Roy
Greiss, Abe S.
Greiss, Adam
Gribben, Chip
Griffin, Jack
Griffith, Jeffrey
Groglio, Glen P.
Growick, Phillip
Grube, Susan
Grubshteyn, Raisa
Grunther, Ira Alan
Gruppo, Nelson
Guerre, Kimberly
Guild, S. Rollins
Guzman, George

Hack, Robert
Hagel, Bob
Haiman, Kurt
Halvorsen, Everett
Hama, Sho
Hamilton, Edward
Hamilton, Frances M.
Hammond, Francis
Haney, David
Harris, Cabell
Hartwell, Alan
Hassel, Barry
Hayes, Connie
Heit, Amy
Heller, Steven
Hendricks, William
Hensley, Randall
Herche, Maureen
Hess, Jannike
Hill, Chris
Hillsman, William G.
Hirsch, Peter
Hively, Charles
Hoashi, Jitsuo
Hochhalter, Gordon
Hoffenberg, Harvey
Hoffmann, Nancy
Hoffner, Marilyn
Holland, Barry K.
Holtz, Jennifer
Horn, Steve
Horowitz, Julia L.
Houser, William David
Howard, Paul
Hoyt, Debra Morton
Huang, David
Hurd, Jud
Hutter, Brian
Incorvaia, Vito
Ishii, Skip K.
Jablonski, Andrew
Jacobs, Harry
Jaffe, Holly
Jaffee, Lee Ann
Jalbert, Ted
Jamison, John E.
Janerka, Andrzej
Jerina, Patricia
Jervis, Paul
Johnston, Shaun
Jones, Karen C.
Jubert, Joanne
Kalayjian, Vasken
Kalish, Nicki
Kanai, Kiyoshi
Kaprielian, Walter
Kaufman, Paul
Kay, Norman S.
Keane, Ronan J.
Keens, Elizabeth A.
Kelly, Brian M.
Kenny, Alice
Kent, Nancy
Kenzer, Myron W.
Keyton, Jeffrey
Khalifa, Jana
Kiel, Ronald
Kier, Ellen Sue
Kim, Bok-Young
Kim, Hyeson

Klein, Hedy
Klein, Judith
Klyde, Hilda Stanger
Kner, Andrew
Knier, Maria
Knoepfler, Henry O.
Koepke, Gary
Kohler, Denis
Komai, Ray
Korpijaakko, Kati
Krauss, Oscar
Kurz, Anna
La Barge, Robert
Lafferty-Dimmick, Christine
La Marca, Howard
Lamarque, Abril
Landi, Joseph O.
Lanotte, Michael
La Petri, Anthony
La Rochelle, Lisa A.
Larstanna, Lawrence
Lassi, Mark
Lau, Pearl
Lavey, Kenneth H.
Lawrence, Marie Christine
Lazzarotti, Sal
Lebeck, Steven W.
Lebron, Michael A.
Lee, Ching
Lee, David
Lee, Edwin
Le Van, Donna Lee
LeVesque, Shawn
Levine, Peter
Levine, Rick
Liberman, Alexander
Lloyd, Douglas
Lois, George
Lopez, Antonio
Lott, George
Lowry, Alfred
Lubell, Ruth
Lucci, John
Luger, Diane
Luna, Dennis Lopez
Luria, Robert
Lurin, Larry
Lyon, Robert W., Jr.
Lyons, Michael J.
MacFarlane, Richard
MacInnes, David H.
Magdoff, Samuel
Magnani, Lou
Mancino, Anthony
Mann, Edward Marc
Manser, Pamela G.
Marcellino, Jean
Marcus, Eric
Margolis, David R.
Mariucci, Jack
Marquez, Andrea
Mason, Joel
Mayer, Susan
Mayhew, Marce
Mazzeo, Joan
Mazzeo, Michael
McCaffery, William
McErlain, Stephen J.
McGreevy, Nick
Mednick, Scott A.

Meher, Karen L.
Meher, Nancy A.
Merkley, Parry
Metzdorf, Lyle
Metzner, Jeffrey
Meyer, Jackie Merri
Meyers, Kimberly
Meyn, Robbie
Miano, Thomas A.
Milbauer, Eugene
Miller, Larry
Milligan, John
Minor, Wendell
Miranda, Michael
Mitsch, Steven
Mizerek, Leonard
Mizrahi, Marise
Modenstein, Sam
Mok, Clement
Montebello, Joseph
Montone, Ken
Moore, Diane
Moore, Richard
Moore, Robert
Moran, Paul
Morita, Minoru
Morooka, Mami
Morris, Ann
Morris, Leonard
Morrison, William R.
Morton, Amy
Morton, Thomas
Moses, Louie
Moss, Tobias
Moyer, Dale
Mueller, Robert
Murphy-Hamill, Virginia
Nelson, Daniel
Nessim, Barbara
Newman, Robert
Newman, Susan
Nichols, Mary Ann
Nichols, Raymond
Nicolas, Serres Cousine
Nissen, Joseph
Nix, Michael
Noether, Evelyn C.
Norman, Barbara J.
Noszagh, George
November, David
Oberlander, Bill
Occipinti, Sharon
O'Donnell, Lisa
Okladek, John
O'Neill, Hugh
Ortiz, Jose Luis
Oswald, Mindy
Ovryn, Nina
Owett, Bernard S.
Paccione, Onofrio
Paganucci, Robert
Palancio, John A.
Palecek, Jane
Paley, Valerie Ritter
Pallas, Brad
Panetta, Susan
Pappalardo, Jeff
Park, James
Parker, Jacques
Pascoe, Kathleen

Paul, Art
Pedersen, B. Martin
Peduto, Patrick
Peeri, Ariel
Perone, Christopher C.
Perrotti, Tony
Perry, Harold A.
Perry, Roberta
Peslak, Victoria I.
Peter, John
Peterson, Christos
Petrocelli, Robert
Petrone, Chris
Petrucelli, Daniel
Pettus, Theodore D.
Phelps, Steward
Philiba, Allan
Phillips, James
Phipps, Alma
Pilla, Michael
Pioppo, Ernest
Pliskin, Robert
Portner, Richard
Posen, Frances
Pozsonyi, Anthony
Procida, Robert
Quackenbush, Michael
Queener, Charles W.
Querze, Elissa
Raboy, Dick
Rand, Paul
Reed, Samuel
Reeks, Deck P.
Reid, Kendrick
Reinke, Herbert
Reitman, Harris
Reitzfeld, Robert
Renaud, Joseph Leslie
Reshen, Amber
Reshen, Patricia J.
Rhodes, David
Richards, Stan
Richert, Ruthann
Rietschel, Barbara
Riley, Elizabeth T.
Ritter, Arthur
Ritter-Mayer, Karen
Roberts, Barbara B.
Roberts, Kenneth
Robinson, Bennett
Rockwell, Harlow
Rodney, Drew Ann
Rohall, Susan
Romano, Andy
Rosenthal, Bobbi
Rosner, Charlie
Rosner, Eric
Ross, Andrew
Ross, Mark
Ross, Peter
Ross, Richard J.
Rossiello, Suzanna M.
Roston, Arnold
Roth, Tom
Rothrock, Salleigh
Rothstein, Bette
Rottenberg, Eta
Rousseau, Ann Marie
Rowe, Alan
Rubenstein, Mort

Rubin, Randee
Rubinsky, Shelley
Ruis, Thomas P.
Russell, Henry N.
Russo, Albert
Russo, Deborah
Ruther, Don
Ruzicka, Thomas
Sachs, Joseph
Sacklow, Stewart
Saido, Tatsuhiro
Saito, Moriyoshi
Saks, Robert
Sala, Loretta M.
Saladino, Peter
Salcer, Richard M.
Salpeter, Robert
Salser, James
Saltz, Ina
Samerjan, George
Sauer, Hans
Sayles, John
Saylor, David J.
Scali, Sam
Scarfone, Ernest
Schaefer, Peter J.
Schenk, Roland
Scher, Paula
Schermer, Susan
Scheuer, Glenn
Schmalz, Paul
Schmidt, Klaus F.
Schnaufer, Joyce
Schrager-Laise, Beverly
Schrijver, Robert W.
Schultz, Eileen Hedy
Schultz, Kate
Schwartz, Adriane
Schwartzman, Julie
Scocozza, Victor
Scott, Robert A.
Sculco, Georgina
Seabrook, Alexis
Seabrook, William, III
Sears, Amy
Segal, Leslie
Segerstrom-Sato, Rebecca
Seidler, Sheldon
Seisser, Tod
Sellers, John L.
Shachnow, Audrey
Shafer, Franci
Silverstein, Heidi K. Eckman
Silverstein, Louis
Simmons, Robert
Simpson, Milt
Singer, Leslie
Sirowitz, Leonard
Sisman, Lucy
Skolnik, Jack
Smith, Carol Lynn
Smith, Robert S.
Smith, Sheila
Smith, Virginia
Sobel, Edward
Sokol, Andrew
Solomon, Martin
Solsburg, Mark
Sosnow, Harold
Spangler, Lee

Spears, Harvey
Spegman, Jim
Stackell, Isaac
Stamatopoulos, Nancy
Stansfield, Shelly Laroche
Stanton, Mindy Phelps
Stapelfeldt, Karsten
Stefanides, Dean
Steigelman, Robert
Steinbrenner, Karl
Steiner, Vera
Stern, Barrie
Stewart, Gerald
Stone, Bernard
Storch, Otto
Storrs, Lizabeth
Strizver, Ilene
Strosahl, William
Sugiura, Shunsaku
Sullivan, Pamela
Sullivan, Sharon
Suth, Pat
Sutton, David
Sweeny, Ken
Sweet, Leslie A.
Tansman, Jo Ann
Tartaglia, Frank
Tasch, Alex
Taschetti, Vincent
Tashian, Melcon
Taubin, William
Tauss, Jack G.
Tekushan, Mark
Tenne, George
Thalasinos, Nell
Thomas, Steve
Thompson, Bradbury
Todd, Robert
Toland, Toni
Tora, Shinichiro
Torzecua, Marlena
Towners, John C.
Trasoff, Victor
Trowbridge, Susan B.
Tsiavos, Anastasios
Tully, Joseph P.
Twomey, John D.
Udell, Rochelle
Ultimo, Clare
Urrutia, Frank
Vasquez, George
Verdia, Haydee N.
Viggiano, Jeanne
Vischo-Gallagher, Amy
Vitale, Frank A.
Vogler, David L.
Volpe, Maria Laurenzi
Von Schreiber, Barbara
Vornberger, Cal
Vuong, Thuy
Wachtenheim, Dorothy
Wajdowicz, Jurek
Wallace, Joseph O.
Walsh, Linda
Warren, Allison
Wasserman, Kenneth
Waxberg, Larry
Weber, Denise A.
Weber, Jessica
Weber, Peter

Weinheim, Donna
Weisel, Mimi
Weithas, Art
West, Robert Shaw
Wiedling, Daphne
Wilde, Richard
Williams, Rodney C.
Witalis, Rupert
Wittenburg, Ross
Wolf, Henry
Wolf, Jay Michael
Wollner, Michael Kjell
Wong, Nelson
Wong, Robert H.
Woods, Laura
Woodward, Fred
Yoffe, Ira
Yonkovig, Zen
Young, Frank
Young, Shawn
Zabowski, Bill
Zaino, Carmile S.
Zanis, Leo
Zator, Lynette Marie
Zeitsoff, Elaine
Zhukov, Maxim
Zielinski, Mikael T.
Zlotnick, Bernie
Zollinger, Lisa A.
Zuzzolo, Richard J.
Zwiebel, Alan

Australia
Dilanchian,
   Katheryn Davidian
Kambourian, Ron
Lee, Lisa

Austria
Demner, Mariusz Jan
Klein, Helmut
Lammerhuber, Lois
Merlicek, Franz

Belgium
Behaeghel, Julien
Lemaitre, Pascal

Bermuda
Smith, Paul

Brazil
Lima, Beto
Miranda, Oswaldo
Petit, Fransesc
Rampazzo, Adeir

Canada
Davidson, Rob
Pepin, Pierre
Tolpin, Larry

Czech Republic
Jasanska, Lenka

Denmark
Simonsson, Dres Simon

Germany
Arke, Rainer
Baier, Mario
Gross, Frank
Hebe, Reiner
Koch, Claus
Kuge, Claus
Leu, Olaf
Mojen, Friederike
Mojen, Ingo
Nebl, Lothar
Platt, Stephan
Pospischill, Hans-Georg
Prommer, Helga
Todd, Samy J.
Weber, Njoschi

Greece
Konstantinidis, Vangelis

Hong Kong
Chan, Elman
Cheung, Eddy
Chuen, Tommy Li Wing
Jacobs, Byron
McCudden, Colleen

India
Pereira, Brendan

Iran
Alikhani, Iraj Mirza
Rezaei, Ladan

Israel
Reisinger, Dan

Italy
Guidone, Silvano
Pavone, Gerardo
Stoppini, Luca

Japan
Akiyama, Takashi
Aoba, Masuteru
Aotani, Hiroyuki
Asaba, Katsumi
Baba, Yuji
Brenoe, Peter
Fukushima, Takenobu
Furumura, Osamu
Hirai, Akio
Ichihashi, Ken
Ito, Yasuyuki
Iwaki, Michio
Iwata, Toshio
Izumiya, Masaaki
Kamijyo, Takahisa
Kaneko, Hideyuki
Kashimoto, Satoji
Katsui, Mitsuo
Kawamoto, Fumio
Kitazawa, Takashi
Kojima, Ryohei
Kotani, Mitsuhiko
Maeda, Kazuki
Matsui, Keizo
Matsumoto, Arata
Matsumoto, Takaharu
Matsumoto, Takao

Matsunaga, Shin
Matsuura, Iwao
Miyasaka, Kuniaki
Mizutani, Koji
Morimoto, Junichi
Nagatomo, Keisuke
Nakahara, Michio
Nakahara, Yasuharu
Nakamura, Makoto
Oba, Yoshimi
Ohama, Yoshitomo
Ohashi, Toshiyuki
Ohtaka, Takeshi
Okada, Syuji
Okamoto, Shigeo
Okuizumi, Motoaki
Okumura, Akio
Okura, Kyoji
Omori, Shigeshi
Oseko, Nobumitsu
Saito, Toshiki
Sakamoto, Hiroki
Sakamoto, Ken
Suzuki, Yasuo
Suzuki, Zempaku
Takahama, Yutaka
Takanokura, Yoshinori
Tanabe, Masakazu
Tanaka, Ikko
Tanaka, Soji George
Tomita, Ben
Tomoeda, Yusaku
Uejo, Norio
Usami, Michihiro
Watanabe, Masato
Watanabe, Yosiko
Yamamoto, Akihiro H.
Yamamoto, Yoji

Korea
Ahn, Dan
Chae, Ki Young
Chang, Don Ryun
Chung, Joon
Chung, Joy
Han, Kwang Soo
Hwang, Jung Suk
Jang, Jung Hak
Kang, Yeong-Joon
Kim, Chul Han
Kim, Doo Hwang
Kim, Duk Kyu
Kim, Een Seok
Kim, Hae Kyung
Kim, Hyun
Kim, Kwang Kyu
Kwon, Hyun Chang
Lee, Jae Chul
Paik, Nack Mi
Park, Dong Hee
Park, Seung Soon
Park, Woo Duk
Rhee, Sang-Chol
Seo, Woon Suk
Sohn, Hye-Won
Yoon, Woong Jin

Malaysia
Ho, Veronica
Hoi, Tatsun
Lee, Yee Ser Angie
Wong, Peter

Mexico
Beltran, Felix
Flores, Luis Efren Ramirez

Monaco
Turello, Amedeo M.

The Netherlands
Brattinga, Pieter
Dovianus, Joep
Van Lotringen, Walter

Philippines
Abrera, Emily A.

Portugal
Aires, Eduardo

Singapore
Aitchison, Jim
Eng, Chiet-Hsuen

Spain
Folch, Jose M. Trias

Switzerland
Dallenbach, Bilal
Bundi, Stephan
Jaggi, Moritz
Kueste, Helmut
Schuetz, Dominique
Syz, Hans G.
Welti, Philipp

United Kingdom
Baker, Jim
Stothard, Celia

FLATIRON
news

It
All
Starts
Here.

RM

Flatiron News · Flatiron Building, 175 Fifth Avenue—Suite 2327 New York, NY 10010 Tel · 212.627.5400 Fax · 212.691.0508

Illustration by Ruth Marten

YOUR BRUSH. OUR PALETTE.

STEVENS PRESS, NYC 212·581·7470

CQ406ARER01 CM B 16-MAR-94 13:14 ROCH EMPIRE GRAPHICS CON. 133L

In Heaven, the Art Directors live on iced cappuccino and

bon-bons in astounding oceanfront villas. Copywriters

have wide, flat heads on which to set beverages.

And everybody else has to jump through

hoops all day long.

How

to arrive

K　O　D　A　K

at the

proof.

Okay, snap out of it. It's still the nineties

and you've still got too much work, too little

time. ● Kodak knows what you're dealing

with these days. They've

been inside photography

and the graphic arts longer than anybody.

So they know what you go through to get

an idea from the shoot to the printed

page. And they know how to get you

there with products from films to plates,

digital cameras to proofing systems. Kodak

products at every point of the imaging

chain, connected by Kodak's color science.

Seamlessly. Beautifully. ● There are those

of us who would probably change places

with Fifi the circus poodle. And, in fact, do

much better with their 401K.

Cara Galowitz *is the Manager of Graphic Design Services at the Guggenheim Museum, where she designs exhibition catalogues, retail posters, ephemera, interior and exterior signage, and graphics for exhibitions. Galowitz recently received a first prize award from the American Association of Museums for designing the publication* Art of This Century: The Guggenheim Museum and Its Collection.

After graduating from Cooper Union and prior to working at the Guggenheim Museum, Galowitz designed the logo, signage, stationery, publications, and ephemera for the Museum of the City of New York and The Brooklyn Public Library.

Woody Pirtle *ran his own graphic-design practice in Dallas for ten years before joining Pentagram in New York as a partner in 1988. Earlier, he worked at The Richards Group and studied architecture and fine art at the University of Arkansas. His logotypes, posters, environmental graphics, and corporate communications are often published as examples of the best of their kind.*

Pirtle's work is in the permanent collections of the Museum of Modern Art and Cooper-Hewitt National Design Museum in New York, the Neue Sammlung Museum in Munich, and the Zurich Poster Museum. He has taught at the School of Visual Arts, is a member of the Alliance Graphique Internationale, and has served on the boards of the magazine HOW *and the American Institute of Graphic Arts.*